Educational
Psychology
Cases

Educational Psychology Cases

Second Edition

Gordon E. Greenwood
University of Florida—Gainesville

H. Thompson Fillmer
University of Florida—Gainesville

Forrest W. Parkay
Washington State University—Pullman

Merrill
Prentice Hall

Upper Saddle River, New Jersey
Columbus, Ohio

Library of Congress Cataloging in Publication Data

Greenwood, Gordon E., 1935–
    Educational psychology cases / Gordon E. Greenwood, H. Thompson Fillmer,
Forrest W. Parkay.—2nd ed.
      p. cm
    Rev. ed. of: Educational psychology cases for teacher decision-making. ©1999.
    "Contains the best cases from three previous casebooks: Case studies for teacher
decision-making. Professional core cases for teacher decision-making, and Educational
psychology cases for teacher decision-making"—Pref.
    Includes bibliographical references.
    ISBN 0-13-091846-6
    1. Educational psychology—Case studies.   2. Teaching—United States—Decision
making—Case studies.   3. Teachers—Training of—United States—Case studies.   I. Fillmer,
H. Thompson, 1932– II. Parkay, Forrest W. III. Greenwood, Gordon E., 1935–
Educational psychology cases for teacher decision-making.   IV. Title.

LB1051.G745 2002
370.15–dc21

                                          2001034039

Vice President and Publisher: Jeffery W. Johnston
Executive Editor: Kevin M. Davis
Production Editor: Mary Harlan
Production Coordination: Holly Henjum, Clarinda Publication Services
Design Coordinator: Diane C. Lorenzo
Cover Design: Linda Apple
Cover Art: International Stock
Production Manager: Laura Messerly
Director of Marketing: Kevin Flanagan
Marketing Manager: Amy June
Marketing Coordinator: Barbara Koontz

This book was set in Garamond Light by The Clarinda Company. It was printed and bound by Courier Kendallvill, Inc.
The cover was printed by The Lehigh Press, Inc.

Previous edition entitled *Educational Psychology Cases for Teacher Decision-Making.*

Prentice-Hall International (UK) Limited, *London*
Prentice-Hall of Australia Pty. Limited, *Sydney*
Prentice-Hall Canada, Inc., *Toronto*
Prentice-Hall Hispanoamericana, S.A., *Mexico*
Prentice-Hall of India Private Limited, *New Delhi*
Prentice-Hall of Japan, Inc., *Japan*
Prentice-Hall Singapore Pte. Ltd.
Editora Prentice-Hall do Brasil, Ltda., *Rio de Janeiro*

Merrill
Prentice Hall

10 9 8 7 6 5 4 3 2 1
ISBN 0-13-091846-6

DEDICATION

We wish to dedicate this book to our wives: Patti, Dorothy, and Arlene. They are the wind under our sails, the love that lights up our lives.

Preface

This book is a result of conversations between the senior author and Kevin Davis, Executive Editor at Prentice Hall/Merrill. Both felt the need for an educational psychology casebook that placed a heavy emphasis on learning and instruction and that contained the best cases from three previous casebooks: *Case Studies for Teacher Decision-Making, Professional Core Cases for Teacher Decision-Making,* and *Educational Psychology Cases for Teacher Decision-Making.* The current volume is the result and is presented as a second edition of *Educational Psychology Cases,* although it contains only 11 of the cases originally presented in the first edition. Ten cases were taken from *Professional Core Cases,* and nine from *Case Studies.* Since Dr. Tom Fillmer, Professor Emeritus at University of Florida, and Dr. Forrest Parkay, Professor at Washington State University, had served as coauthors of the previous volumes, they also served in the same capacity for this book.

The 30 cases presented in this book are based on actual teaching situations contributed by many teachers from several states as either the "most difficult" or "most frequently recurring" case they had faced. All names of people and places have been changed, and all cases have deliberately been left open-ended, problem-centered, and unresolved in order to provoke stimulating discussion, analysis, and decision making. The intention is that the cases be used as application vehicles that serve as a middle step between regular coursework and actual teaching experience.

■ Key Features

This book contains a number of features that will make it useful to the educational psychology instructor.

1. The table of contents contains a brief overview of each case. This feature may be of value to the instructor and to students when selecting cases.

2. Each case begins with a listing of the psychological theories and sets of principles that may be especially useful for analyzing and resolving the case. This may help the instructor select which cases are most relevant to the content being taught.

3. At the end of most cases is some additional material relevant to the case. This may take the form of a student cumulative record, sample test items, or background data on students, such as grades and parents' occupations. Such information will add further information for case analysis and promote realism.

4. At the end of each case is a series of 10 questions, each of which focuses on the case from the perspective of a different psychological theory or set of principles. These questions will help to stimulate discussion and analysis of the case.

5. Appendix A presents a theory guide that indicates which psychological content areas, theories, and sets of principles are especially useful in analyzing and resolving the cases.

6. Appendix B contains information on how to use cases in the college classroom. It is our experience that many college instructors have had little experience using cases and are not sure where to obtain such information.

▪ Acknowledgments

The authors wish to thank the many people who made this book possible, especially Patti Greenwood and Mary Remer for their excellent work in preparing the manuscript. We also wish to thank the professionals at Prentice Hall/Merrill for their quality editing and proofreading work. Needless to say, this book would not have been possible if numerous teachers hadn't taken the time to write up their cases for us. Finally, we wish to thank the reviewers of this manuscript for their helpful work: Mary Ann McLaughlin, Clarion University of Pennsylvania; Betty M. Davenport, Campbell University; Carroll Tyminski, Elizabethtown College; and Gary Daytner, Ball State University.

Contents

Part 1

INTRODUCTION TO EDUCATIONAL PSYCHOLOGY

An educational psychologist has been awarded a contract by the school district to develop, implement, and train school personnel in the procedures for evaluating teachers for merit pay purposes. When he meets with the school district development committee, he finds the committee divided on such issues as the nature and measurement of effective teaching, the value of process-product research methodology, the use of classroom observation procedures, and the strengths and weaknesses of using standardized achievement tests on a pretest-posttest basis as a measure of student learning.

Part 2

HUMAN DEVELOPMENT

A first-grade elementary teacher and the building principal meet to make a promotion-retention decision about Juan Rodriguez, a physically small, somewhat emotionally immature boy from a large Hispanic family in which English is a second language. Juan has difficulty reading and

Part 4

LEARNING AND INSTRUCTION

Part 5

MOTIVATION AND CLASSROOM MANAGEMENT

Part 6

ASSESSMENT AND EVALUATION

her second-period U.S. history class especially object when they don't get the grades they expect to receive on a unit exam. When the teacher eases up on her grading procedures, she gets accused of being an easy grader by other teachers.

Educational
Psychology
Cases

Introduction

■ Educational Psychology and Teaching

What is the science of educational psychology, and how does it relate to the art of teaching? The first chapter of most educational psychology textbooks usually explores the parameters of the field of educational psychology, its history of development, its research methodology, and how its theories, models, and principles are relevant to the educational practitioner. Although a few experts, such as B. F. Skinner, have argued that teaching can be reduced to a technology, the majority seem to agree that teaching fits Gage's (1985) definition of an art as "any process or procedure whose tremendous complexity . . . makes the process in principle one that cannot be reduced to systematic formulas" (p. 4).

One very common explanation of the relationship between educational psychology and teaching is that effective decision making is the basic skill underlying good teaching and that the research, theories, models, principles, and techniques derived from educational psychology allow teachers to become better decision makers. Ormrod (1995) points out, "But above all, we are *decision-makers*: we must continually choose among many possible strategies for helping students learn, develop, and achieve. In fact, two researchers (Clark & Peterson, 1986) have estimated that teachers must make a nontrivial instructional decision approximately once every two minutes!" (p. 4). Gage and Berliner (1992) add that educational psychology has especially contributed to teacher decision making in five areas: (1) instructional objectives, (2) student differences, (3) learning and motivation, (4) teaching methods, and (5) evaluation.

How do teachers use such empirically derived knowledge from the field of educational psychology as they make decisions? Eggen and Kauchak (1997) cite an example. "Should teachers wait longer to give students time to think through a question fully, or will long pauses result in choppy lessons that drag? Research

1

doesn't provide a precise answer, so teachers must use their professional judgment and decide how much wait-time to give and how quickly the lesson should be moved along" (p. 13).

As this questioning strategy example illustrates, teaching is a complex activity that requires the teacher to constantly make decisions before, during, and after interacting with students in the classroom. The authors of this book believe the following:

1. That the decision making of teachers is primarily based on teachers' personal belief systems.
2. That education courses should help teachers examine and identify their personal beliefs, especially about teaching, and integrate them with the research-based theories and principles they are learning in their courses.
3. That case materials like the ones presented in this book provide vehicles that can be used to help teachers clarify their personal beliefs and learn to apply the theories and principles they are studying in their coursework.

Case Studies and Teacher Education

Many programs and techniques have been developed over the years to prepare preservice and in-service teachers for the real world of teaching. Systematic observation instruments, microteaching, competency-based programs, parent involvement techniques, and protocol materials in various forms, to name a few, have all been used. In recent years, case studies have become increasingly popular as application and discussion vehicles in training teachers, and many, if not most, educational psychology textbooks now contain brief cases as a regular feature in each chapter. Additionally, a number of casebooks, such as this one, have been written, and some college instructors build an entire course around the use of cases rather than the usual lecture/discussion approach.

What is a case, and what is its role in teacher education? Eggen and Kauchak (1997) define cases as "segments or samples of students' and teachers' experiences in the teaching-learning process and other professional events" (p. 11). Cases may take a variety of forms. Most are based on actual events. Cases can vary considerably in length, format, and the degree to which they are strictly objective reports as opposed to more fictional representations of reality. They may also differ considerably in focus. Some can focus on an individual student's problem, for example, whereas others might concentrate on a teacher working with an entire class. Although most cases are written, some can be in other forms, such as audiovisual, computer software, and demonstrations and roleplaying.

The case format we have used in this book is the written dialogue format similar to that used in movie scripts or screenplays. We prefer this format for a number of reasons. First, such a format is familiar through the influence of such media as TV and movies. Second, it offers the kind of "reality" that students experience when they observe in schools or even see themselves teaching through videotaping such as is done in techniques like microteaching. Third, the dialogue format more naturally lends itself to activities designed to follow up case studies, such as role playing, sociodrama, and the videotaping of students "acting out" the courses of action they recommend to the teacher in the case. Fourth, a number of state teacher certification programs involve the direct observation of teaching behavior using observation instruments during the first year of teaching. The dialogue format more closely portrays the kind of behavior observed. Fifth, the behavior in the dialogue can be used as "behavioral evidence" by the students to support the interpretations made when they analyze a case. What people say and do is more a directly observed behavior than a summary of facts or incidents or a paraphrasing of events. Finally, since we see the use of case studies as a middle step between coursework and actual teaching experience, the more closely the case format resembles events actually unfolding in schools, the better. In short, we view cases as more realistic vehicles for the analysis of behavior and the generation of courses of action in the real world of teaching.

Whatever form cases take, they may be viewed as application tools that have the potential for helping preservice and in-service teachers develop and shape their metacognitive decision-making abilities. Case studies may be viewed as mediators between traditional courses and workshops and actual teaching experience. Broudy (1990) has argued that the use of cases in teacher education may even help teaching truly become a profession. Noting that "a profession professes a body of concepts that structure its field of practice" (p. 450), he observes that "teacher education has not developed a set of problems that can legitimately claim to be so general and important that all who are qualified to teach and to teach teachers should be familiar with them and their standard interpretations and solutions" (p. 452). He further contends that such a professional core of problems in education should be identified and presented to preservice and in-service teachers in the form of case studies, as has been done in such professions as medicine and law.

The 30 cases presented in this book are drawn from three previous casebooks and were selected because they are especially suited to the typical content covered in an introductory educational psychology course. Six areas of content are covered by the cases: (1) introduction to educational psychology (its nature, history, and methods, as well as its relationship to teaching), (2) child and adolescent development, (3) cultural diversity, (4) learning and instruction, (5) motivation and classroom management, and (6) assessment and evaluation.

Sample Case

The following case is entitled "Learning the Lines" and was published in the first edition of this book. It will be presented in its entirety, after which decision-making strategies for analyzing and resolving the case will be considered.

Learning the Lines

Amy Pace and Tracy Kirk are English teachers at Smithfield Consolidated High School, located in Smithfield, a Midwestern city with a population of 20,000. Situated in the center of hundreds of acres of farms and villages, Smithfield is both the supply center for the farmers and the cultural center for all the residents in the surrounding countryside. Area pupils are bused to the high school, which has an enrollment of approximately 2,500 pupils made up of approximately 89% white, 10% African-American, and 1% other.

Amy is 22 years old and graduated with a B.Ed. from the local state teachers college at the end of the spring semester. In the summer she married her college boyfriend, Carl. The couple moved to a farmhouse on 70 acres owned by Carl's family which they gave to the newlyweds as a wedding present. Immediately upon their move to Smithfield, Amy was offered and accepted a position as teacher of English at Smithfield High School.

Tracy was born and reared in Smithfield and graduated from the same college as Amy 15 years ago. Like Amy, she returned to Smithfield after her graduation. When the consolidated high school was built, Tracy obtained a position as English teacher, and she has taught there continuously ever since. Because Tracy and her husband, a local merchant, knew Carl and Carl's family, they worked hard to make Amy and Carl feel welcome in both the school and the community.

The week prior to the beginning of classes, the faculty and staff held a three-day workshop, during which Amy and Tracy sat together. Tracy took every opportunity to introduce Amy to the other teachers. On the last day of the workshop, Frank Carr, the principal, asked Amy and Tracy to meet with him in his office after the workshop ended. They agreed to do so and had reached the office just as Frank arrived.

FRANK: Thank you both for meeting with me on such short notice, but there's a matter I need to discuss with you as early in the school year as possible.

TRACY: (smiling) And I bet I can guess what it is.

FRANK: OK. Guess.

TRACY: I'll bet you want to talk with us about producing the first senior play that Smithfield Consolidated High School has ever had.

FRANK: Bingo! I guess the same parents who talked with me have been talking with you also. (Looking to Amy) Not only is our school an educational center for the entire area, it's also a cultural center.

TRACY: That's true. Even our friends who have no children look forward to attending all the school events.

FRANK: Which leads me to the reason I asked you to meet with me this afternoon. Since we've been able to employ Amy, we're now in a position to produce a senior play this year. And I'd like you two to be in charge of it.

TRACY: What play would you like us to produce?

FRANK: Since you're both English teachers, I'll leave that up to you. I'm sure there are plays that are typically selected by English teachers to be produced by high school students.

AMY: Yes, there are. I saved my college textbook from my "Teaching English in the High School" course. It has a list of such plays for students to produce.

TRACY: Good, we can go through them and select one. (Turning to Frank) I have a question about practicing. Since most of our students are bused to school, we won't be able to practice after school. Will it be OK to practice in our classes?

FRANK: It seems to me that the production of a play is certainly an appropriate topic to study in an English class. And I know that both of you have a senior class during both the second and third periods. I don't know why you couldn't combine classes for play practice. In fact, one of you could take a group to the auditorium when it's free while the other works with groups making scenes, costumes, and so on. You can work those things out as you see fit. But be assured that I consider the play an appropriate assignment for students in an English class.

AMY: I like that idea. It'll certainly encourage more students to participate.

FRANK: I'd really prefer to have all the students participate. There are certainly enough jobs in play production to involve lots of students. You have scenery, costumes, stagehands, prompters, and gofers, as well as actors.

TRACY: Do you know yet when the play will be presented?

FRANK: I've checked the school calendar and talked with parent groups in the various communities whose pupils attend SCHS about preferable times. We want to present the play late in the school year for many reasons. It would give you more time to prepare for the presentation. The play will be our biggest project of the year, so it will help us end the academic year on a high note. And it will leave school personnel, parents, and students with a good feeling about SCHS. The dates that seem to be the best for all the groups I talked with are Wednesday through Saturday, May 14 to 17. The consensus was that it should begin at 7:00 each evening. Parents liked the idea of having a Saturday matinee at 2:00.

TRACY: That sounds great! It'll give us plenty of time to teach a comprehensive unit on drama as well as prepare for the presentation of a play.

AMY: Yes, and as you say, it'll be a great culminating academic experience for our seniors.

FRANK: (adding) And it will also be an effective public relations effort for our high school. (Pauses and smiles) That is, of course, if the play is well done. So, at this point, I'll end our meeting and let you two begin whatever you need to do to get this project under way.

After leaving Frank's office, Tracy and Amy go to Amy's classroom to talk more about their new assignment.

TRACY: Obviously, one of the first things we should do is to decide what play we'll present.

AMY: During the meeting I mentioned that I have a book that lists plays suitable for high school pupils to perform. I just remembered that I enrolled in a drama class, and the theater professor was really interested in drama productions in high school. I think I'll call him and see if he'd recommend some plays.

TRACY: (enthusiastically) Oh, that's really a good idea. I'd feel more comfortable choosing a play that someone with experience in high school productions recommended.

AMY: OK. I'll call him this week. I'm sure he'd still remember me. I was in his class my senior year.

TRACY: We have a lot of decisions to make very soon, such as how do we recruit students to be in the play? How many do we need? How will we match students with parts that are appropriate for them?

AMY: That's right! And we'll have to talk about how we can select students who are able to learn long parts and act well. And also how often we'll rehearse.

TRACY: Well, let's do what we can do now. You call your professor and read your book on plays. Then after we clear everything with Frank, we'll meet again and get down to serious business.

The following Monday, Amy and Tracy arrive in the parking lot at the same time. They talk as they walk together to the school building.

AMY: I talked with Professor Arnold Saturday afternoon. He told me that in the 15 years he'd been working with interns in high school, he's found that *Macbeth* is definitely the classical play most commonly performed in high schools.

TRACY: That's good news. If other high schools can do it, so can we. But I wish we had information on how to go about preparing the students.

AMY: Me, too. I had a college class on teaching English in high school, but I don't recall that we even discussed anything about how to teach pupils to present a play.

TRACY: I'm sure I didn't study anything like that in college either. Now I'm sorry I didn't try out for a play somewhere along the line. Then I would've learned at least one approach to directing a play.

AMY: (with concern) I'm not even sure how to select the main characters. Students in these roles have a lot of memorizing to do and a lot of stage directions to remember.

TRACY: That's right. I'm also concerned about how we should assign roles. I know pupils who would be terrific as lead actors, and I know others who would be awful. Is it appropriate for us just to assign major roles to pupils we know can handle them? It seems to me that *Macbeth* has only seven major characters: Macbeth, Lady Macbeth, King Duncan, Banquo Macduff, Malcolm, Ross, and Lennox. The rest are gentlemen, officers, soldiers, murderers, attendants, messengers, witches, and ghosts. I think it would be OK to encourage some of our best students to sign up for the major roles. If we have several people sign up for one role, we can have an audition and select the one we think would do the best job.

AMY: That sounds good to me. Then we could list each of the minor acting roles along with support roles like stagehands, ushers, costumers, set designers, makeup specialists, light operators, prompters, and so forth. I'll bet we can find a job in the play for every senior.

TRACY: (enthusiastically) I really like that idea! That would make it truly a class play! Do you have time to meet after the last class today and organize these lists?

AMY: Yes. I think we're on a roll now! I want to keep it moving. We can probably decide which students we should encourage to sign up for the major roles, as well as list all the support jobs and how many students we need for each of them. Then we could prepare the sign-up sheets for each of our classes, post them tomorrow, and have our actors and crew identified by the middle of the week.

TRACY: That's fine with me—the sooner the better. I'll see you in my room after the last class.

By midweek all the pupils in the four senior English classes had signed up for at least one job connected to the play. Tracy and Amy had invited students they thought would be able to play the leading roles to sign up for particular parts. By Thursday afternoon they had auditioned all the students who had applied for major roles and interviewed or auditioned those who had applied for supporting or minor roles in the play.

On Monday morning at 9:00 both Tracy and Amy were in their classrooms distributing a paper to each student that explained that student's role in the senior play.

TRACY: Congratulations. Each of you will have an important role in the first senior class play ever to be presented by SCHS. Of course, I'm sure that you all want it to be a first-class production so you can set an example for all successive classes to strive to match. The papers I'm distributing to you indicate what role you have in our play. You could have signed up for either an acting or a support role. All of you were given the type of role you requested. All students in senior English classes will have some role to play in producing the play. Ms. Pace also is handing out the parts and jobs to her students.

MARK: When we practice the play, will we all be able to practice together?

TRACY: This class and Ms. Pace's second-period class and both of the third-period classes will be able to practice together whenever Ms. Pace and I think we should. It will be more difficult for the second- and third-period classes to practice at the same time because there are other classes involved. But we'll make arrangements for all the cast and support workers to rehearse at the same time when we get closer to showtime. But for now, you actors, especially the leads, need to begin memorizing your lines immediately because many of you have large parts to learn.

BETH: I've never had to memorize long parts before. What's the best way to memorize lines?

JAY: I was just about to ask the same thing. There must be a best way to do that.

TRACY: Probably the most efficient way is to copy all your speaking parts in the order that they appear in the play. Then start with the first few lines of the first part. Read them over and over again until you can say them from memory. Then go on to the next few lines. Keep that up until you've memorized the whole thing. You should also identify cues that will help you know when to come in.

JAY: (speaking out) Wow! That sounds like it'll take a long time!

TRACY: Well, it might if you have a really long part. But it's the most logical and direct way to learn your parts. Start at the very beginning and move right through until you come to the end. Practice makes perfect!

Amy has also assigned acting and support roles to her students, who begin to ask questions about how to learn their lines.

PAM: (after raising her hand and being recognized) Ms. Pace, I really have a long part. I don't know how to memorize such a long part. Can you give me some suggestions on how to do it?

AMY: That's really an important question, Pam. And I'm sure that there are other students here who have the same concern (Many other pupils nod their heads.) I think the best method is to actually try to become the character. Read through the entire play and see what your character does and says. Get a feeling for the type of person your character is. How does your character interact with other characters? How does your character respond to certain things? What is your character's role in the story? Where does your part fit into the plot of the story? (Tim raises his hand.) Tim?

TIM: How does doing that stuff help us remember our lines?

AMY: Well, when you know all about the character you're playing and how he fits into the overall play, you have a good idea of his thoughts and ideas and generally how he'd respond to different situations. So even though you may not be able to recite the part exactly, you'll be able to respond generally the way your character would respond. (To the class) So your assignment for tomorrow is to read the entire play and become acquainted with all the characters in the play. Begin to practice thinking and acting like your character. Then return to the beginning of the play and reread the seven scenes of Act I very carefully. We'll discuss that act in class.

After school, Amy goes to Tracy's room to see how her class responded to their assignments of roles for the play. Tracy was still in her room.

AMY: (walking into the room) Hi. I'm glad you're still here.

TRACY: (startled) Oh! (Pauses) Amy, I'm glad you came over. How'd your assignments go?

AMY: Well, the students with large parts seemed to be overwhelmed at the prospect of memorizing so much material.

TRACY: (smiling) That's exactly what happened in my class.

AMY: My kids were so excited when we were talking about the play last week that I was really excited, too. But now that they're worried about learning their parts, I'm worried too.

TRACY: Me too. One of the students asked me if I could tell him a way to memorize his part.

AMY: (excited) That happened in my class, too! What *did* you tell him?

TRACY: Well, I told him to copy all his character's speaking parts. Then begin to read the first few lines over and over until he had them memorized. Then go on to the next few, and so on. And to pay attention to cues on where to come in.

AMY: (upset) Oh, gosh! I told them just the opposite. I told them to read the whole thing and see how their part fits in. I also told them to learn how the character thinks and responds to things and to essentially try to become the character.

TRACY: Isn't that called the holistic approach, or something like that?

AMY: Yes. I think so. I remember one of my professors talking about it in an educational psychology class. He said it was a good approach to remembering material. In fact, here's an old handout he gave us in the class. It gives some reasons why children forget things and what to do about it. I thought it might be useful sometime, so I saved it. (Hands Tracy a paper entitled "Why People Forget")

TRACY: (studies the paper) Well, these suggestions look pretty straightforward. And it doesn't make sense at all to have half of our actors using one approach and the other half using a different one. I'd like to have them use the approach you described, but I don't think I know it well enough to teach them how to use it.

AMY: Well, I have two suggestions. I could teach you the approach and you could teach your class. Or I could teach it to your class. But I'd rather teach it to you because you need to know it to be sure that your students are using it appropriately. Do you have to be home before 5:30?

TRACY: No. David doesn't get home until almost 6:00, and we're going out to dinner at 7:00.

AMY: Good. (Pointing to a chair at a table) Sit right down here. We're going to plan how we'll teach these pupils to remember their lines.

Two weeks later, all four senior English classes are in the auditorium having their first all-cast practice. They plan to start at the beginning and go through the entire play. Amy and Tracy have asked them to try to speak their parts from memory as much as possible. The stage crew will learn what needs to be done in the various acts of the play. The first scene is over. The sound crew did well with the lightning and thunder. The three witches knew their parts.

TRACY: (loudly) That's a good Scene One, people! Now let's get ready for Scene Two. Duncan, Malcolm, Donalbain, Lennox, Sergeant, Ross, and Attendants. Enter stage left. Sergeant, crawl in from stage left. OK. Begin. (Silence) Duncan, speak up.

DUNCAN: "What bloody man is that? He can report, as seemeth by his pliget, of the revolt of the newest state."

TRACY: Duncan, that word is "plight," not "pliget." And speak your lines as if you've seen a wounded and bloody man, not as if you're talking about the weather. OK, Malcolm.

MALCOLM: "This is the sergeant who, like a good and hardy soldier, fought 'gainst my captivity. Hail, brave friend! Say to the kind the knowledge of the broil as thou didst leave it."

SERGEANT: (word by word) "Dubful, it stood. As . . ."

MALCOLM: That's "doubtful," Matt. "Doubtful it stood as two spent swimmers, that do cling together and choke their art."

SERGEANT: (angrily) C'mon, Tom. That's my part, not yours.

TOM: It doesn't sound like it's yours, Matt. You don't even know it.

MATT: I just haven't had time to study it yet.

TOM: Well, why don't you? It's not that big of a part. We were supposed to have our parts in the first act learned by today. If you're not willing to learn your part, let somebody else do it. You're going to screw up and spoil it for everybody!

TRACY: Tom's right, Matt. If you're willing to learn your part, that's fine. But if you don't have the time, or if you just don't want to, now's the time to tell us so that we can get somebody else to do it.

MATT: (upset) I'm going to learn it! I'll have the whole part learned by our next rehearsal.

TRACY: That's great. We want you to be in the play. But we also want the play to be a really good play.

In the back of the auditorium, Amy is working with the students who are in Scene Three.

AMY: (looking at the witches) You witches did a good job in Scene One. You look ready to go back on in Scene Three. Good. (Loudly) Macbeth, Banquo, Ross, Angus! Where are you? (The four boys come backstage from the seating area.) Good! Do all of you know your parts? (Silence) Oh, no. Don't tell me you haven't learned your lines yet!

MACBETH: I've worked hard on mine, Ms. Pace. But it's a long part, and I haven't memorized it yet. Can you help me learn to memorize? I think I have one of the parts learned, and then the next time I try to say it, I've forgotten it. (The other actors all speak out at once to say that they're having problems, too.)

AMY: Yes, I can help you all. In our next class, I'll teach you some principles of remembering information. Then we'll apply them to our parts.

Throughout the practice, some of the students knew not only their own parts but also several other parts. But a substantial number of the students did not know their parts, when they were supposed to speak, or the appropriate inflection to use.

After school was dismissed, Tracy came to Amy's room and slumped down in a seat as if she were exhausted.

TRACY: What a day! I'm really depressed.

AMY: Let me guess. You're worried about the play.

TRACY: Yes! I don't think that the students will be ready to perform it in May. (Discouraged) We're liable to become the laughingstock of the school!

Figure I–1 Handout on Forgetting from Educational Psychology Class

Why People Forget

1. **Failure to recall:** Not enough associations with information to help them retrieve the information.
   Example: Rod cannot recall the name of a minor character of a story but can recognize it on a multiple-choice test.
   Solution: Help Rod relate the name to the character's actions that are familiar to Rod.
2. **Partial recall:** Can remember parts of information but fills in the remainder based on what seems to be logical.
   Example: Martha remembers some of the character's lines verbatim but ad-libs other lines.
   Solution: Be certain that Martha identifies and learns the exact words of the speaker.
3. **Confusion:** Associations in long-term memory related to similar items interfere with each other.
   Example: Sam recites lines from a play he learned last year instead of similar ones from the play he is learning.
   Solution: Help Sam understand how the character's comments are related to the flow of action in the play he is learning.
4. **Disuse:** Information cannot be recalled because it has not been used regularly.
   Example: Maria is unable to remember her lines because she has not practiced them enough to overlearn them.
   Solution: Review information daily until it is memorized accurately.
5. **Failure to process:** Information was never adequately stored in long-term memory.
   Example: Lois cannot remember her lines because she hasn't learned the play well enough to know what happens next or where her part fits in.
   Solution: Make sure that Lois knows both the context and where her lines fit in.

AMY: Don't give up yet. This was just our first practice. We have six months to get ready for the presentation. I'll admit that I was discouraged this morning. And I think that we're definitely going to have to make some changes if the play is to be a success.

TRACY: I agree. But one of the biggest problems is going to be getting the kids to learn their lines and when to come in. Frankly, Amy, I know we talked about that and you showed me that paper from your class, but what are you going to tell the kids who still haven't learned their lines? What's the best way to memorize stuff like Shakespeare?

Analyzing Cases

Allonache, Bewich, and Ivey (1989), who have conducted workshops on the improvement of decision-making skills, focus on four steps: (1) clearly defining the nature of the problem, (2) generating alternative solutions to the problem, (3) evaluating the positives and negatives of each possible solution, and (4) implementing the solution that is chosen. Step 1, defining the problem, might involve such things as looking at the problem from the point of view of different stakeholders in the situation, such as the teacher, a parent, students, and the principal. It might also mean looking at the problem from the perspective of different theories, models, principles, and values, such as, in the case of educational psychology, different learning theories or classroom management models. Finally, it might also involve examining different kinds of facts or data to help clarify and support the perspective taken. For example, one might focus strictly on observed external behavioral events or give equal weight to more internal, self-report types of data. In any case, Step 1 involves analyzing the case from different perspectives to clarify the nature of the problem.

Step 2 consists of the creative act of generating possible solutions to the problem or problems identified in Step 1. This includes projecting what courses of action the teacher might implement to deal with the situation. Step 3 involves the evaluation of the strengths and weaknesses of the courses of action generated in Step 2. One aspect of Step 3 is forecasting the probable consequence of each course of action. Another aspect would be to consider whether or not a course of action is consistent with or follows from the way the problem is defined in Step 1. For example, suppose a problem identified in Step 1 is that a child's shy, withdrawn, and non-participatory behavior in the classroom is the result of a negative self-concept stemming from an emotionally abusive home environment. Suppose a Step 2 course of action that is proposed involves threatening and, if necessary, punishing the child if she doesn't begin to participate more actively in class. From the standpoint of self-concept theory, such an approach not only is unlikely to work but also is inconsistent with the application techniques associated with that theory.

Another consideration in evaluating courses of action during Step 3 is whether the course of action chosen is practical in terms of the context of the case. Suggesting that the students in a classroom be given an individual intelligence test to assess their intellectual ability is simply impractical, considering the cost of such tests and the demands made in terms of time and personnel.

Participants in case studies do not often get to see Step 4, the implementation of the courses of action chosen. However, they can increase the likelihood of successful implementation by spelling them out as concretely and specifically as possible. Too often teachers are given vague suggestions, such as individualizing instruction by putting the students in small groups. What are the objectives and teaching strategies involved? How should the groups be formed, and what kinds of evaluation procedures should be used? Suggesting that a teacher use the STAD cooperative learning procedures states a course of action in far more concrete and specific terms.

In putting together all four of the steps just discussed, keep in mind that the framework one uses to define the problem in Step 1 is going to affect the choices available for consideration in the other three steps. In an educational psychology course, the theories, models, and principles used as frameworks for analyzing a case are likely to be quite different from those used in such courses as teaching methods, school law, or philosophy of education, to name a few. Different frameworks lead to different courses of action or application procedures.

We suggest that students follow these steps in conducting a case study in an educational psychology course. First, begin by examining the case in terms of your personal belief system and use lay language to define the problem. Second, analyze the case in terms of appropriate course content in the form of whatever psychological theories, models, or principles best explain the problem. Third, defend your analysis by citing evidence from the case to back up your position. The type of evidence you cite would be dictated by the theory used. An operant analysis, for example, would require behavioral data-collection procedures.

Once you have analyzed the case and defended your analysis, the fourth step is to generate courses of action that are likely to solve the problems identified. In a teacher education program, it makes sense to generate courses of action for the teacher in the case to implement. Learning to examine a case from the perspective of parent, principal, and students is important, but ultimately preservice and in-service teachers are learning to look at situations in terms of the teacher being the change agent.

The courses of action that you choose for the teacher to implement for dealing with the problems identified should meet the tests of consistency, operationality, and feasibility. Consistency means, for example, that an operant analysis should suggest operant procedures for the teacher to implement. Operationality means that each course of action should be spelled out concretely and specifically. Feasibility means that each course of action should be practical and possible in terms of the context of the case.

The preceding discussion suggests five criteria for evaluating student efforts at analyzing and resolving a case: (1) accurately and fully applying a theory, model, or set of principles in analyzing the case; (2) supporting the analysis objectively and fully with appropriate evidence cited from the case; (3) choosing courses of action for the teacher in the case to implement that are consistent with the theory used in the analysis; (4) stating the courses of action in an operational form so that specific procedures are spelled out; and (5) stating courses of action that are practical, reasonable, and workable in the context of the case situation. (If the student product takes the form of a paper, the instructor may have a sixth criterion: organizing the paper into a logical and grammatically correct whole.) These criteria will later be further explained and applied to the sample student paper that follows.

The following is an analysis and resolution of the case presented previously. It is an actual paper typical of work done by students in undergraduate educational psychology courses taught by the senior author.

■ Sample Case Analysis and Decision

The case "Learning the Lines" is an example of a student-learning problem. This problem can be analyzed and resolved through the information-processing model of memory. The information-processing model is a "cognitive conception of learning [which] describes how individuals attend to, store, code, and retrieve information" (Gage & Berliner, 1998, p. 613). In this case study, Amy and Tracy, two senior English teachers at Smithfield Consolidated High School, have been asked to put on *Macbeth* as the senior class play. The challenge faced by the two teachers is to teach their students how to successfully store and retrieve the lines of *Macbeth* into their long-term memory. This theory can be used to assist them in teaching their students to memorize their lines.

The students who take on the roles of Duncan, Sergeant, Macbeth, Malcolm and the witches are the focus of the case study. The problems faced by Duncan, Sergeant and Macbeth, as suggested by the text, are those of meaningfulness, retrieval, retention, and nonsensical learning. As Tracy said, "One of the biggest problems is going to be getting the kids to learn their lines and when to come in" (p. 134). On the other hand, it is inferred that Malcolm and the witches have successfully mastered their lines by use of the holistic approach and mnemonic devices, respectively.

Tracy, the more experienced English teacher, attempts to teach her students their lines through the behaviorist approach:

> Copy all your speaking parts in the order that they appear in the play. Then start with the first few lines of the first part. Read them over and over again until you can say them from memory. Then go on to the next few lines. Keep that up until you've memorized the whole thing. You should also identify cues that will help you know when to come in. (p. 131)

Although Tracy uses the approach of rehearsal, it is ineffective in this case. This approach is highly unsuccessful for the high school seniors because they are unable to store and retrieve this information from their long-term memory. This is due to the unfamiliarity of the language spoken in Shakespearean times. Because most high school students are unfamiliar with sixteenth century English, they have difficulty comprehending the words of the play. These inabilities to grasp the meanings of the lines create an inability to memorize and retrieve the information as well. This type of learning problem is referred to as meaningfulness.

On the other hand, Amy uses the holistic approach to teach her students how to memorize their lines:

> I think the best method is to actually try to become the character. Read through the entire play and see what your character does and says. Get a feeling for the type of person your character is. How does your character interact with other characters? How does your character respond to certain things? What is your character's role in the story? Where does your part fit into the plot of the story? (p. 131).

This approach is more successful with some of the high school students because they have a greater understanding of their role as well as the play as a whole. The students are able to better understand the play and retrieve the lines more easily from their long-term memory.

Two of the characters, Duncan and Sergeant, are experiencing encoding failure, as inferred [sic] by the text. Encoding failure is described as a problem with "transforming verbal, visual, musical, and other forms of sensory information, into some system for processing and storing that information" (Gage & Berliner, 1998, p. 609). For example, Duncan says, "What bloody man is that? He can report, as seemeth by his pliget, of the revolt of the newest state" (p. 132). He obviously does not fully understand the meaning of the words he is saying. "The word is 'plight,' not 'pliget.' And speak your lines as if you've seen a wounded and bloody man, not as if you're talking about the weather," says Tracy (pp. 132–133). It can be concluded that a similar problem is seen through the character of Sergeant when he mispronounces the word doubtful as "dubful." A high school senior would know the word doubtful. Therefore, his mispronunciation of the word is due to the lack of comprehension of his part. This is an example of nonsensical learning, where the students are learning their parts without fully understanding the meaning of the lines.

The case study also concludes that both Duncan and Sergeant are experiencing a retention problem as well. "Regardless of whether the stimulus is visual or verbal, its meaning to the person determines how it is stored, retrieved, and used" (p. 262). If the words have no meaning to the students, they [sic] are going to have problems remembering the lines. It can be inferred that this lack of comprehension may be due to a lack of interest. The students may not consider Shakespeare interesting and therefore experience a lack of an orientating response. Without proper motivation, students may never learn their lines.

As [implied] by . . . our course text, the student who plays Macbeth is experiencing encoding and retrieval failure:

> To get material from short-term memory and working memory into long-term memory is not a big problem. It is necessary only to enhance the material in some way or see that it is held as the focus of attention for some period of time. But retrieving information from long-term memory is another matter. (Gage & Berliner, 1998, p. 261)

Macbeth lacks efficient metacognitive skills that would allow Macbeth to be able to regulate his own learning. Macbeth says, "I think I have one of the parts learned, and then the next time I try to say it, I have forgotten it."(p. 133). Obviously Macbeth does not completely understand his own learning process. Macbeth also suffers from a negative transfer of memory. His parts can be very long and the memory of one part may hinder the processing of new information and new parts.

Tom, who plays the role of Malcolm, is one of the few students who knew his lines. In Scene Two, Malcolm is interacting with Sergeant, played by Matt. Matt does not know his lines and Tom corrects him by saying, "That's 'doubtful,' Matt. 'Doubtful it stood as two spent swimmers, that do cling together and choke their art.'" (p. 133). Tom knows his own lines as well as Matt's lines; thus, we infer that Tom is using the holistic approach taught by Ms. Pace to learn his parts. He understands how his lines fit into the play as a whole, and tries to understand his character in various dimensions. By learning the whole play and others' parts as well, it is easier for Tom [sic] to project Malcolm's character and deliver his lines better.

During the first rehearsal of Scene One, the students who play the witches all know their parts. Throughout the play, their lines consist mainly of singing chants or rhymes. It can be inferred that these factors may have made it easier for the witches to memorize their lines. The rhyming words, which act as a mnemonic device, add some organization to the memorization process. The mnemonic devices were most likely in the acoustic-link stage, and hearing the lines and rhyming words helped the students remember more. It is still possible, however, that the witches do not link meaningfulness to their parts, simply because of the content of the material. Shakespeare's style of sixteenth century English is very difficult for the students to read and comprehend.

It can be concluded that the methods taught by the two teachers are not successful in aiding the students in memorizing their lines. It is obvious that other teaching approaches are necessary for the students who are continuing to have difficulty memorizing their lines. "But one of the biggest problems is going to be getting the kids to learn their lines and when to come in. . . . what are you going to tell the kids who still haven't learned their lines? What's the best way to memorize Shakespeare?" (pp. 134–135).

Decision

A learning situation is one in which students' learning strategies are "plans oriented toward successful task performance, or production systems to reduce the discrepancy between their [learners'] present knowledge and their learning goal" (Schunk, 1991, p. 282). In order for learning to take place, there must be tactics known by the learner to help store information in their [sic] long-term memory. However, the ease and speed of learning can vary from student to student depending on the "meaningfulness of the information to that student, the degree of similarity between the pieces of information to be learned, and the length of time between study trials [practices]" (Schunk, 1991, p. 133).

The Information Processing Theory suggests five problems that can be associated with learning information: retention, encoding, orientating response, negative transfer, and metacognition. The first is a problem with retention, which involves information being stored not only visually and verbally, but also with regard to meaning. This obstacle of retention could be corrected if the students knew more background information about the play they were studying and its author. The next problem encountered dealt with encoding the information, entails with the way the students process the information into their long-term memory. An encoding problem can be dealt with by making sure that "the degree to which conditions of retrieval are as similar to the conditions of encoding (as possible)" (Gage & Berliner, 1998, p. 190).

The third problem is with the orienting response, or rather the lack thereof. "An orienting response arouses interest and curiosity, making us (the students) want to know more about the stimulus" (Gage & Berliner, 1998, p. 259). These students are not interested in what they are trying to learn. The teachers failed to intrigue their students with Shakespeare and his plays. Interest could be sparked by showing movies of Shakespeare plays because "film versions of plays and books can bring characters to life and help students recognize universal themes and the human condition" (Considine & Haley, 1992, p. 190). Another idea would be to bring in speakers who know a lot about Shakespeare, his plays, and his life.

The fourth problem has to deal with interference in the way of negative transfer or anxiety. Negative transfer is when "information already learned interferes with the learning of new information" (Gage & Berliner, 1998, p. 623). In this case, knowledge of twenty-first century English is interfering with learning the lines of Shakespeare's play that is [sic] written in sixteenth century English. This obstacle could be countered by giving the students worksheets, or doing fun in-class skits, whereby they can see exactly how sixteenth century English and present day English correspond to each other. Anxiety about failure also interferes with learning. "Students who ruminate about potential failure waste time and strengthen doubts about their capabilities" (Schunk, 1991, p. 291). This could be countered by introducing anxiety-reduction programs to the students.

The fifth and final problem is one of metacognition. Metacognition is the ability to "think about one's own cognitive system" (Gage & Berliner, 1998, p. 270), including "thoughts about what we know, and thoughts about regulating how we go about learning" (Gage & Berliner, 1998, p. 270). Some students believe that they have studied their lines well and have learned them, but when they go to say them they have forgotten what they thought they have already learned. A way to improve metacognitive skills is for teachers to instruct their students to "think in the ways others think when they engage in metacognition" (Gage & Berliner, 1998, p. 271).

Schunk (1991) gives five different learning tactics to help students attain their learning goals: rehearsal tactics, organization tactics, affective tactics, comprehension monitoring tactics, and elaboration tactics. Examples of rehearsal tactics are repeating information verbatim, underlining, and summarizing. Tracy, but not Amy [sic] used these learning tactics. Repeating information aloud to oneself is a tactic commonly used for rote memorization, such as memorizing lines to a poem or a song. This tactic, however, does not link information to what the student already knows. As a result, this information is not stored in any meaningful way in the long-term memory. Underlining improves learning if it is applied constantly, and summarizing involves putting main ideas into your own words. These tactics should only include information that states the most important ideas.

Organization tactics include mnemonics, grouping, outlining, and mapping. Mnemonic devices are good for elaborating information and organizing it in a meaningful fashion. Grouping should be used before any rehearsal or mnemonics, where commonalities should organize information. Outlining improves one's comprehension by requiring the learner to establish headings. Mapping improves a learner's awareness of text structure by creating a hierarchy of points from most important to least important. For these to be affective tactics, teachers need to create a favorable psychological environment for learning. This involves coping with anxiety, setting work goals, developing positive beliefs, establishing a regular time and place for study, and minimizing distractions.

Comprehension monitoring tactics include self-questioning, rereading, checking for consistencies, and paraphrasing. An example of self-questioning may be when students ask themselves questions about what they are reading and then answer those questions. "Elaboration tactics include imagery, mnemonics, questioning, and note taking. These tactics expand information by adding something to make learning more meaningful (to the student)" (Schunk, 1991, p. 286). Imagery is a tactic that adds a mental picture to information you are trying to learn. Mnemonics make information more meaningful by relating the information a student is trying to learn to what a person (student) already knows. There are many types of mnemonic strategies including acronyms, sentence mnemonics, narrative stories, pegword method, method of loci, and the keyword method. All of these types include rehearsal and relating of new information to prior knowledge, which is what most students favor as a way of memorization (Schunk, 1991, p. 287). Questioning requires that learners stop periodically to ask themselves questions about what they are reading. This tactic is most effective if students' questions reflect the type of desired learning outcome. These five tactics are all interdependent on each other; when one uses one technique, they [sic] very often use another simultaneously.

There are three specific students in this case study that are having problems learning their lines: Duncan, Matt who is playing the role of Sergeant, and Macbeth. First, it is inferred that Duncan and Matt are having a retention problem because they are having trouble encoding the information correctly in their memory. This inferred encoding failure is, in part, due to the lack of meaningfulness associated with the Shakespearian text. In addition, the difference in twenty-first and sixteenth century English leads to the problem of negative transfer, where "whenever [they] encounter a text passage [they are not] equipped with a preexisting system of knowledge, concepts, and beliefs" (Gordon, 1989, p. 244).

Combinations of various strategies can be used to solve the above problem. The first step should be familiarizing students with sixteenth century English, culture, and lifestyle. To facilitate proper encoding, Amy and Tracy should go over the entire play with the students and summarize each situation in the play, so that all the students have a clear and consistent interpretation of their own roles as well as the roles of the other students. This will make the play meaningful to the students and thus make it easier to retain information. Here the elaboration tactic of questioning should also be applied, where the student questions what he/she is reading to make sure he/she understands it. Matt, who has problems with his orienting response and finding interest in his character and his lines, should use the elaboration technique of mnemonics or imagery to connect the lines to be learned with something he finds more interesting.

Macbeth is having metacognitive problems where he thinks that he knows his lines, but realizes he has forgotten them when he goes to say them. Here the tactic of comprehension monitoring should be applied. Amy and Tracy should help Macbeth determine whether he is properly applying his declarative knowledge to the material that he needs to learn. They should then evaluate whether he understands the material, decide whether the strategy he is using is effective enough, and help him to know why using a certain strategy will help him improve his learning of his lines. They could ask Macbeth to try to memorize his lines in many different ways, for example, through repetition, imagery, or mnemonics, and then ask him to actively notice the way he remembered the most material so he could use this strategy. Once he knows which strategy works best for him, Amy and Tracy need to make sure that he understands the reason why that certain strategy works, and then incorporate the tactics that most closely deal with that strategy.

We also propose that the whole senior class should rehearse together at least twice a week, with rehearsals being conducted in a setting similar to the actual play setting. This would be beneficial in three ways. First, it will lead to "the success of retrieval [which] depends on the degree to which conditions of retrieval are similar to the conditions of encoding" (Gordon, 1989, pp. 275–76). Secondly, as suggested by the affective technique, familiarity with the setting will reduce anxiety among students during the actual performance. Finally, the act of rehearsing consistently over a period of time will increase the students' memorization. Also, students should have small group practices with the characters they interact with the most in the play.

Finally, in order to enhance the overall performance of the students, Amy and Tracy could do other things to help [the students] be more prepared for rehearsals. Amy and Tracy could register to take a workshop about directing high school plays. They could also hold auditions for the parts so that they know beforehand the motivation and ability of each of the students, instead of "encouraging" certain students to sign up for certain parts. They could also have the students in their classrooms get dressed up in Shakespearean costumes and make up their own skits in sixteenth century English. In this way, they can see how sixteenth century and twenty-first century English correspond.

Amy and Tracy will soon discover that by implementing these different learning strategies into their class curriculum, the students will benefit. One benefit is that when they finally get ready to begin rehearsing the play, there will not be as many problems with the students not having memorized their lines yet. Another benefit is that each student's confidence level and self-esteem will increase. A feeling of group cohesion will arise among the students if they are able to know their part and help other students learn their parts as well.

References

Considine, D. M., & Haley, G. E. (1992). Visual Messages: *Integrating Imagery into Instruction*. Engelwood, CO: Libraries Unlimited.

Gage, N. L., & Berliner, D. C. (1998). *Educational Psychology*. Boston, Houghton Mifflin.

Gordon, W. C. (1989). *Learning and Memory*, Pacific Grove, CA: Brooks/Cole.

Greenwood, G. E., & Fillmer, T. H. (1999). *Educational Psychology Cases for Teacher Decision-Making.* Upper Saddle River, NJ: Prentice Hall.
Schunk, D. H. (1991). *Learning Theories.* New York: Macmillan.

◼ Critique of Sample Analysis and Decision

The preceding analysis and resolution of "Learning the Lines" is typical of higher-quality work at the undergraduate level in the senior author's educational psychology course. Before elaborating on and applying the evaluative criteria mentioned earlier, it should be pointed out that the case could have been analyzed and resolved from the perspective of a number of other psychological theories other than information processing theory. For example, the case could have been approached from the standpoint of constructivism, Vygotsky, Bruner, Ausubel, or even operant conditioning, to name a few.

This does not mean, however, that all theories and models are equally good for analyzing cases. In our experience, the more comprehensive and applied a theory is, the easier it is to use. Analyzing a case in terms of a comprehensive theory that deals with all the problems identified in a case is easier than trying to analyze a case with several minitheories that may or may not integrate well with one another in terms of assumptions, data-collection procedures, and application techniques. Likewise, some theories are replete with application procedures, while others are not associated with any clear methods of application. Operant conditioning theory, for example, is very comprehensive for purposes of analysis and has generated a whole host of application procedures. Motivational theories based on Maslow's need hierarchy are excellent for analysis purposes but weak in terms of application procedures. Bloom's cognitive taxonomy is somewhat limited for analysis purposes, focusing primarily on problems dealing with cognitive classification issues. In short, some theories and models are easier to apply to a case because they are more comprehensive and have generated more application procedures.

The evaluative criteria presented earlier will be used to evaluate the paper. First, is the problem in the case analyzed fully and accurately (from the perspective used and in the language of the theory accurately applied)? Second, is the evidence presented to support the analysis cited objectively, and does it cover the major contentions made? Third, are the courses of action stated for the teacher to implement consistent with the analysis? Fourth, is each course of action feasible (or practical) in the context of the case? Fifth, is each course of action stated in operational form (fully spelled out and specific)? Finally, is the paper well organized and grammatically correct?

It should be obvious from the preceding evaluative criteria that there are no right or wrong answers in doing a case analysis and resolution. A psychological theory, model, or set of principles fits a case if it covers the main issues in the case and if the students demonstrate that it fits by citing in as objective form as possible evidence from the case to support the position taken. The decision part (or resolution or plan) is correct if it consistently follows from the theory used in the analysis and covers the issues identified in the analysis. Also, the decision needs to meet the tests of operationality and feasibility as well. With this in mind, let's examine the previous student analysis and resolution of the case.

Overall the paper is a fine effort. The student chose information processing theory as the frame of reference for analyzing the case, quoted evidence from the case to support his/her information processing contentions, and pretty well covered most aspects of the case with respect to key people and issues. However, the student does make reference to the motivational aspects of the case and then does little with those issues. Also Schunk's five learning tactics are employed quite effectively in the decision but are not used as a framework for analysis. Further, somewhat of an organization problem exists in that some of the analysis regarding Duncan and Matt is presented in the decision part rather than the analysis.

The decision part of the paper is probably stronger than the analysis. It meets the consistency and feasibility criteria quite well. It is a little weak in the operationality area, however. Since the decision part is really a plan for the teachers in the case to follow, how should the teachers apply the tactic of comprehension monitoring and use of declarative knowledge or evaluate whether or not Macbeth understands the material? What should the teachers look for in holding auditions for parts?

The preceding are "picky" points, and generally Information Processing theory is fairly comprehensively applied to the main characters and issues in the case and the analysis is objectively and systematically supported with quotes from the case in the analysis. The decision part systematically applies information processing techniques in a consistent, feasible, and somewhat operational way. The paper is a fairly good overall job by undergraduates in a beginning-level educational psychology course.

◼ Organization of Cases

The 30 cases presented in this book focus on six broad areas of educational psychology:

	Section	*Case No.*
1.	Introduction to Educational Psychology	1
2.	Child and Adolescent Development	2–4
3.	Cultural Diversity	5–9
4.	Learning and Instruction	10–19
5.	Motivation and Classroom Management	20–28
6.	Assessment and Evaluation	29–30

Following each case, additional material is provided regarding the case, such as a teacher's lesson plan or a portion of a student's cumulative record. At the end of each case, "starter" questions are given that may help stimulate case discussion. Each question focuses on the case from the standpoint of a particular psychological theory or principle.

Appendix A provides a theory guide that matches psychological theories, models, and sets of principles with each case. In other words, these are frameworks from the field of educational psychology that seem especially well suited to analyzing and resolving the cases with which they are matched. The course instructor may have other opinions, of course.

◼ References

Allonache, P., Bewich, G., & Ivey, M. (1989). Decision workshops for the improvement of decision-making skills confidence. *Journal of Counseling and Development, 67,* 478–481.

Broudy, H. S. (1990).Case studies—why and how. *Teachers College Record, 91,* 449–459.

Clark, C. M., & Peterson, P. L. (1986). Teacher's thought processes. In M.C. Wittrock (Ed.), *Handbook on research on teaching* (3rd ed.). New York: Macmillan.

Eggen, P., & Kauchak, D. (1997). *Educational psychology: Windows on classrooms.* Upper Saddle River, NJ: Prentice Hall.

Gage, N. (1985). *Hard gains in the soft sciences: The case of pedagogy.* Bloomington, IN: Phi Delta Kappa.

Gage, N., & Berliner, D. C. (1992). *Educational psychology.* Boston: Houghton Mifflin.

Ormrod, J. E. (1995). *Educational psychology: principles and applications.* Upper Saddle River, NJ: Merrill/Prentice Hall.

1

Educational Psychology and Teaching

Key Content to Consider for Analyzing This Case:

1. Research methods
2. Measurement and evaluation (standardized tests, formative versus summative evaluation, observation schedules)
3. Teacher effectiveness (process-product research)
4. Bloom's cognitive taxonomy

Collinsburg is a medium-sized city of approximately 75,000 located in a Midwestern state. The population served by the Collinsburg school system is approximately 75% white, 20% African-American, and 5% other. Mining, agriculture, and several light industries such as clothes manufacturing make up the local economy.

Dr. Arthur Haskins is a professor of educational psychology in the College of Education of the largest, land-grant, research-oriented university in the state. He sits in the office of Dr. Chester Gunn, the superintendent of schools of the Collinsburg school system. Dr. Gunn's office, located in the school board complex in downtown Collinsburg, is large, well lit, and well furnished with artificial plants and wall paintings. Dr. Gunn sits behind his large oak desk while Dr. Haskins sits in a large leather chair facing him.

DR. GUNN: (frowning) Art, I heard about Harry Motto giving you a hard time about whether or not an educational psychologist should be the one to head up and act as consultant to our merit pay committee. I don't know what's wrong with Harry! Sometimes I think that his promotion to principal at CHS has gone to his head. He was clearly out of line to treat you that way, and I told him so.

ART: (smiling) I think that Harry really believes that educational psychologists are ivory-tower researchers who are out of touch with the real world of teaching. While the whole situation made me angry at the time, I've gotten over it and am sure that I can work with Harry as well as the rest of the committee.

DR. GUNN: I'm really pleased to hear that, Art! Where is the committee at this point?

ART: I have all seventeen committee members working in four subcommittees. Luke Melvin [evaluation specialist] is heading a subcommittee to examine the literature on teacher effectiveness. Luke and I talk with each other just about every day.

Dan Burns [assistant superintendent of instruction] and his subcommittee are getting together the literature on merit pay programs around the country.

DR. GUNN: And what committee is Harry Motto heading? If I know you, you put him in charge of one!

ART: (laughing) You know me well, Chester! Harry's subcommittee's job is to collect information from teachers, parents, and students. Barton Richardson's [principal of Collinsburg South High School] committee is collecting information from the school board, school administration, and teachers' union leadership.

DR. GUNN: That sounds like you've covered all your bases, Art. (Pause) What about community people, business leaders, and the like?

ART: Harry's committee is supposed to consult with that group as part of what they do.

DR. GUNN: When do you meet again?

ART: On Thursday the fifteenth, a little over one month from now.

DR. GUNN: Sounds good! Let me know if I can support your work in any way. What you're doing is very important to all of us.

It is more than a month later on a Thursday evening at 7 o'clock. Eighteen members of the Merit Pay Plan Committee sit around a large, oval-shaped table in a conference room. Art sits at the head of the table and presides over the meeting. The other members of the committee are Harry Motto, principal of Collinsburg High School, and Barton Richardson, principal of Collinsburg South High School; Mary Lowe, school board member; Dr. Luke Melvin, head of the evaluation and research division of the local school system; Dr. Dan Burns, assistant superintendent of instruction; Jan Winchester, Lincoln Elementary School Advisory Committee (SAC) member; Alyssa Baker, Collinsburg HS SAC member; four other principals (two from middle schools and two from elementary schools); and six teachers (two each from the elementary, middle-school, and secondary levels).

ART: We have a lot to do, so let's get down to work. (Looking at Luke) Luke, your committee has been pulling together the teacher effectiveness literature. Do you have a report for us?

DR. MELVIN: We aren't finished by any means, but I can go over what we've found so far.

ART: Excellent! Please proceed.

DR. MELVIN: Some of this gets a bit complicated, so don't hesitate to ask questions as we go along. (Pause) I guess we should begin with the process-product literature, where educational researchers, many of whom were educational psychologists like Art, used observation schedules to observe teachers and students interacting in the classroom and correlated their data with various measures of student achievement. Since the observational instruments were used to collect data on the instructional process and the student achievement data were considered the outcome or product of the process, it's generally called process-product in the literature.

MR. MOTTO: Isn't the process part what principals have been doing for a long time when they observe in the classroom and rate the teacher's performance?

DR. MELVIN: Not really. Principals usually use rating scales chosen by the school district, not the more complicated systematic observation schedules used by the researchers. For example, the researchers might record certain numbers every three seconds that would describe what was going on in the classroom. The researchers were concerned with measurement issues such as scoring reliability and various kinds of validity. The rating scales adopted by school districts usually contain items agreed to by various committees and are not so concerned with validity and reliability issues. The items chosen are usually not selected on an explicit theoretical or empirical basis.

MR. MOTTO: (smiling) My, how you research types throw around technical jargon! What do you mean by an explicit theoretical or empirical basis?

DR. MELVIN: By a theoretical basis I mean generating the items from a theory of teaching that is rather clearly spelled out, like that of Dewey, Skinner, or Bloom. By an empirical basis I mean doing what one researcher did by having his grad students place tape recorders in classrooms and then generate items that would describe or code what was going on in the tapes.

MR. MOTTO: Don't the committees have a theory of teaching in mind when they choose items for a rating scale to be used for observation?

DR. MELVIN: Not in my experience. If a theory exists, it's not clearly stated. For example, someone will say that the teacher should be organized. Another will say that the teacher should know her subject matter, while another will say that the teacher should be enthusiastic and that her students should be paying attention and be actively involved in what's going on in the classroom. The rating scale used is either a camel created by a committee or one adopted from another school district and modified a bit.

MR. RICHARDSON: So how did this process-product research come out, Luke? Did it tell us what teacher behaviors are best?

DR. MELVIN: You have to remember now that all this research, years of it, is correlational, not experimental in nature. They were running correlations between categories of teacher behavior and different measures of pupil achievement.

MR. MOTTO: For Pete's sake, Art, what is he saying?

ART: Luke is saying that the data revealed relationships between variables but that you can't draw cause-and-effect conclusions from them.

MR. MOTTO: OK, I understand enough about research to grasp what you're saying: They couldn't put them all in a laboratory and control all the variables that could affect the learning of the students. I also know something about correlations. What kind of correlations did they get when they did this process-product research?

DR. MELVIN: Most of the statistically significant correlations were in the .20, .30 range. Significant, but not large, depending on your point of view.

MR. MOTTO: (intently) What I hear you saying is that these high-powered researchers did years of this kind of research at the taxpayers' expense and ended up finding a bunch of weak correlations for their efforts.

DR. MELVIN: Well, not exactly, Harry. You see some of the studies were better done than others and had very large sample sizes.

MR. MOTTO: (interrupting) Give me the bottom line, Luke. Can these researchers tell us which teacher behaviors are the good or effective ones and which ones aren't?

DR. MELVIN: In a word, no.

MR. MOTTO: (angrily) No offense, Luke, but researchers sometimes make me mad. They are the big experts who get big grants to do studies and come up with nothing. How can you say that the fancy observation schedules that they developed are any better than a lot of the classroom rating scales now in use in a number of school districts around the state?

ART: Luke, I don't want you to think that I'm cutting you off, but why don't we move on to Harry's committee at this point. His committee's job was to collect information from teachers, parents, and students, as well as various community leaders such as businessmen. Is that right, Harry?

MR. MOTTO: Yes, it is.

ART: Perhaps, then, you could go on and tell us what you found when you interviewed these people. We can always come back to the research literature.

MR. MOTTO: I'll attempt to summarize what various people representing all the educational stakeholders that Art mentioned had to say. First, there seemed to be general agreement that most people are able to identify who the good and poor teachers are in a school. Students tell their parents or siblings who to take and not to take. The problem is how to objectify this subjective information. Perhaps you research types could help us develop instruments that we could use to identify our best and worst teachers by surveying parents, students, administrators, and teachers.

DR. MELVIN: You might be able to cut the extremes off from the middle, Harry, but that won't help you with your measurement of teachers who aren't at the extremes.

MR. MOTTO: (frowning) Don't you professors do something like that at the college level, Art? I remember doing student ratings on my professors' teaching when I was a student at State.

ART: That's true, although the validity and reliability of such measures are often questioned. But we don't generally do student ratings of teachers in K-12. The question is whether or not students are capable of judging whether teaching is good or bad.

MR. MOTTO: Well, let me just throw that out as an idea, then, and let it go at that. I strongly feel that we should consider surveying the major stakeholders. However, an idea that everyone seemed to agree on is that of measuring how much a student learns from a teacher.

DR. MELVIN: And how would you do that, Harry?

MR. MOTTO: Simple. Pretest the students at the beginning of the school year, and posttest them with the same or parallel test at the end of the school year. After all, isn't student learning what education is all about?

DR. MELVIN: Your committee isn't the first one to suggest such a plan. What test or tests would you use?

MR. MOTTO: I don't know. That's not my expertise. I'll leave that up to you researchers. I suppose that standardized tests would have to be used.

ART: There are a number of problems in trying to measure pupil learning. One is that most standardized tests don't go beyond the first three levels of Bloom's cognitive taxonomy. We are constantly saying in education how much we regret that American students aren't exposed to higher-order thinking or to the kinds of cognitive processes represented at the three higher levels of Bloom's taxonomy.

MS. WINCHESTER: And problem solving. I was watching a show on TV the other day about how American children are behind Japanese children in problem-solving skills.

ART: Also, Harry, what about classes in art, music, shop, physical education, and the like?

Mr. Motto: OK, so regular achievement tests won't do the job in all classes or measure all the different kinds of learning we want to measure. Aren't there people around who know about other kinds of tests we could use?

Art: Frankly, I don't know of any. But even if we fixed that problem, how would you deal with the problem of student diversity?

Mr. Motto: What do you mean?

Art: How would you collect your pre-post achievement data to take student differences into consideration? You have students from different races, socio-economic backgrounds, ethnic groups, reading abilities, and so forth. How are you going to compare the growth of students in an advanced-placement English class with that of a class that not only contains average-ability students but also has mainstreamed kids with disabilities? It would be like comparing a football coach with highly skilled and highly recruited players with one who has low-ability players. You'd be stacking the deck against some teachers.

Mr. Motto: (frowning) I see what you mean. But isn't there some way to statistically take those differences into consideration?

Dr. Melvin: Not that I know of. The home environment that these kids come from helps produce differences that you can't remove, no matter what you do statistically.

Mr. Motto: What do you mean?

Dr. Melvin: I mean that the parents of kids who are high achievers in school have different values, are more involved with the school, and push their children for good grades. If you're going to evaluate me as a teacher, give me some of those students from strong middle-class backgrounds to teach. The pressure to achieve will come from home as well as from the teacher at school.

Mr. Motto: (in exasperation) Surely you experts can come up with some way of measuring student learning! If you can't, then how is education ever going to be accountable to the public?

Art: Did your committee come up with any other ideas, Harry?

Mr. Motto: Yes, one of our curriculum specialists brought me a copy of an observation schedule used by a school district in another state that has a merit pay plan. I wrote to them and they sent me information on what they do that really impressed me. [Passes out copies of the observation schedule]

Dr. Burns: This is the Jackson School District observation schedule, Harry. That is the kind of thing that my committee is supposed to look into. They sent us their material as well.

Mr. Motto: (with exaggeration and insincerity) I'm really sorry, Dan, if we crossed the boundary and got into your territory. But here is a plan that really works. It was designed by both their administration and teachers' union.

Art: Why don't you go on and tell us about it. We'll let Dan chip in when you're finished.

Mr. Motto: To begin with, they just added a merit step to their salary schedule.

Art: Their salary schedule is a step schedule based on years of teaching experience and amount of education like the one here at Collinsburg?

Mr. Motto: Right. All they did was add a merit step. Of course, you could add as many merit steps as you want, but they added only one.

Mr. Richardson: So how do they decide whether or not a teacher gets the merit step?

Figure 1–1 Teacher Observation Schedule Proposed by Harry Motto

Teacher Evaluation Report
Jackson School District

Teacher's name: _____ School: _____
Evaluator: _____ Date: _____
Grade: _____ Time of observation: _____ _____
                                                     began   ended
                                Conference time: _____ _____
                                                  began   ended

RANKINGS: Outstanding: Performance reflects exceptional qualities of teaching
                         and class management
          Satisfactory: Exhibits expected and desired professional behavior
          Unsatisfactory: Exhibits weak performance and/or teaching
                           deficiencies

Mark X below the appropriate ranking: Outstanding (O), Satisfactory (S), or
Unsatisfactory (U), after each item.

	O	S	U
I. TEACHING PROCEDURES			
A. Evidence of organization and planning			
B. Knowledge of subject matter			
C. Individualization of instruction			
D. Variety of teaching strategies			
E. Effective use of wait time			
F. Encourages good work-study habits			
G. Appropriate practice/review procedures			
H. Evaluates learners effectively			
I. Effective use of class time			
II. CLASSROOM MANAGEMENT			
A. Effective classroom management			
B. Attractive physical setting			
C. Effective interaction with pupils			
D. Maintenance of appropriate records			
E. Positive classroom climate			
F. Appropriate use of group work			
G. Effective monitoring of pupils			
H. Is reasonable, fair, and impartial			
I. Keeps pupils on task			
III. PROFESSIONAL CHARACTERISTICS			
A. Accepts responsibilities			
B. Encourages self-discipline			
C. Continual self-assessment			
D. Keeps abreast of new ideas			
E. Professional appearance			
F. Develops rapport with pupils			
G. Keeps parents informed			
H. Follows school district policies			
I. Poised and self-assured			

MR. MOTTO: I was coming to that. It's simple and elegant at the same time. Each teacher must be observed at least four times over the school year if he voluntarily decides to go for merit that year. And curriculum specialists gather the observation data, so you have a person outside the school collecting the data. The instrument covers most of the important things, as you can see, and is easy to use. You just rate the teacher as outstanding, satisfactory, or unsatisfactory in each category. They set a cutoff score to determine whether you get merit or not. (Pause) I was thinking, folks, if we used something like this, couldn't we adapt it in some way to send it out to the various stakeholders as well? Maybe we could develop a student rating schedule along these same lines and a survey instrument to send out to parents and other teachers.

DR. MELVIN: What about validity and reliability, Harry? Do we know that the items on the instrument really measure good teaching? Would two different raters observing a teacher at the same time agree on their ratings?

ART: Bill Jensen, is there something you want to add as a classroom teacher? You look like you want to say something.

BILL: (secondary teacher) Yes. It so happens that I have a cousin who teaches in the Jackson School District. He tells me that their teachers' union was forced to help develop those merit pay procedures, and especially this rating scale, and that a lot of them resent it. He says that a sizable block of teachers there who are active in the union refuse to participate in their merit plan. They say that it only pits teachers against one another and overlooks the fact that all their teachers do a good job.

MR. MOTTO: (laughing) All of them? That sounds like a bunch of physicians talking.

BILL: If they're not doing a good job, then they should be fired.

MR. MOTTO: That's not so easy to do, Bill, if they have tenure. But if we have some hard data like these to work from, perhaps they could even be used to get rid of some incompetent teachers who hide behind tenure. (Pause) So what I'm recommending—OK, I guess my entire committee is recommending—is the Jackson plan, locally adapted, of course. I know it would take some work, and Luke, you could do validity and reliability studies on it to your heart's content. The only other suggestion I'd make would be to go Jackson one better and find some way to measure student learning and take those data into consideration along with the observed teacher ratings in deciding whether to award merit or not. What do you think, folks? Shall we do it, or does one of you have a better idea?

■ Questions

1. What is the distinction between experimental and correlational research that Luke Melvin mentions? Why is most research on teacher effectiveness correlational in nature? What are the limitations of such research?

2. Who are the "stakeholders" in the field of education that Harry Motto keeps referring to? How much influence should such stakeholders have in influencing school policies and practice? Should stakeholders be surveyed as one source of data for teacher evaluation purposes?

3. What does Luke Melvin mean when he tells Harry Motto that surveys of stake-holders "might be able to cut the extremes off from the middle" but that they wouldn't help with the measurement of teachers who are in the middle? Would such survey data be subjective or objective in nature? What do objective and subjective measurement mean in the context of teacher evaluation?

4. Luke Melvin refers to the "process-product" research. Describe that research literature. Do you agree with Luke's interpretation of that literature and Harry's criticism of its implications? What are the applications of this research to teacher evaluation?

5. Do you agree with the arguments against evaluating teaching through the use of achievement tests given on a pretest-posttest basis as measures of student learning? Why or why not? What are the best such tests available, and what aspects of student learning do they measure? How strongly do such variables as the student's home environment affect student achievement?

6. Describe the teacher effectiveness research mentioned by Art and Luke. Does this literature suggest valid and reliable methods of evaluating teaching?

7. What are formative and summative evaluations? Which is more important when it comes to evaluating effective teaching? Can both formative and summative evaluation be used, or does the use of one preclude the use of the other?

8. What role has educational psychology played in doing research on or developing programs and procedures for evaluating and improving teaching effectiveness? What role might educational psychologists play in this regard in the future?

9. Do you agree with Art's explanation that the role of educational psychology is to make teachers better decision makers? How would teacher effectiveness be evaluated from this perspective?

10. Should the committee accept the plan presented by Harry Motto? Why or why not? If not, what plan should be adopted instead?

2

To Retain or Not to Retain

1. Physical development
2. Social development
3. Language development
4. Cognitive development

Nell Johnson is in her fifth year of teaching first grade. She is completing her first year of teaching at Van Buren Elementary, since she and her husband, Steve, had moved last fall to the large urban area in the Southeast where Van Buren is located. The school serves a primarily lower-middle-class attendance area consisting of an approximately 75% white, 20% African-American, and 5% Hispanic population.

Tyrone Baker is African-American and has been principal of Van Buren Elementary for 16 years. Having put a note in Nell's mailbox that he needed to see her, he invites Nell into his office with a smile, offers her a seat, and closes the door for privacy.

TYRONE: Nell, have you had a good year so far?

NELL: I've had a very good year so far, Tyrone. Are you going to spoil it for me?

TYRONE: (laughing) No, Nell. Not at all. I have nothing but good things to say about your teaching. All the teachers that I've talked to, including the other two first-grade teachers, feel the same way.

NELL: Well, then, I guess I'm a bit curious about why you want to see me.

TYRONE: It's about one of your students, Juan Rodriguez. I see that he's on your promotion list.

NELL: Yes, I recommended that all my first graders be promoted. I didn't see any reason why Juan shouldn't be promoted, too. I know that he isn't into the reading primer yet, but frankly, I feel that it does more harm than good to retain students.

TYRONE: I'm surprised, Nell. Are you saying that you believe in social promotion and are against retaining students under any circumstances?

NELL: Well, no, I guess not. Probably there are circumstances that justify retention, but I guess I'd have to be convinced that it would do the child more good than harm. It certainly doesn't seem to me that it would help Juan to be retained. He's such a small, thin child who constantly needs prodding and reassurance. I really think that it would crush him to make him repeat first grade.

TYRONE: Yes, I was watching him out on the playground the other day trying to play with the other kids. He's the smallest boy in your class, isn't he?

NELL: Yes, I guess he is.

TYRONE: I noticed how poorly coordinated he is when the other boys would let him play ball with them. And that wasn't often.

NELL: What do you mean?

TYRONE: I mean that he doesn't seem to have any close friends. The other boys seem to tolerate him at best, and he seems to play alone a lot.

NELL: Yes, I guess I've noticed that in class somewhat, too. Juan cries easily and sometimes engages in baby talk. I guess that doesn't endear him to most of the boys.

TYRONE: Exactly! I guess we could say that Juan is somewhat emotionally and physically immature.

NELL: That may be true. But how is it going to help him by retaining him? He might get bigger physically in a year, but how is retention going to help his emotional development? You know how cruel children can be to one another! Can't you imagine the kinds of things that they're going to say to poor Juan when they find out he was retained?

TYRONE: I can't deny that point! It's bound to affect his self-concept some, but how much I'm not certain. But we have to look at all the factors involved in deciding whether to promote him or not. How would you assess him academically?

NELL: Well, I'm sure that you know that Juan comes from a large family—I believe he has five or six brothers and sisters—and English is his second language. I spoke to his mother on the phone one day, and I had a difficult time understanding her. It embarrassed me to constantly ask her to repeat herself.

TYRONE: Juan has a real reading problem, doesn't he?

NELL: Yes. He's such a sweet, cooperative child, and he tries very hard. He finished the second preprimer and will probably finish the third. But he won't get to the primer by the end of school. If his second-grade teacher, someone like Mimi Sims, could start him in the reading primer, he would be so much better off! If he repeats first grade, he'll be bored during readiness activities and may fall behind again! It seems such a waste! He knows what sounds are about, and he's ready to read.

TYRONE: But we have got to face the fact that he's way behind academically now, Nell, and I'm afraid he'll be hopelessly lost in the second grade, even if I put him in Mimi's class. He won't be able to keep up, and he'd take up so much of her time that it wouldn't be fair to the other students.

NELL: Then you've made your mind up to retain him?!

TYRONE: No, Nell, I haven't. I want us to look at the big picture and try to decide as objectively as we can on what the best thing would be for us to do. (Pause) Nell, are you crying?! I'm sorry if I said anything to upset you!

NELL: You didn't, Tyrone. It's just that this whole conversation reminds me of Randy Duncan, a boy that I decided to retain during my second year of teaching. A decision I came to regret!

TYRONE: This was when you were teaching in Illinois?

NELL: Yes. The school district had a policy of retaining first graders who couldn't read. Randy was big for his age and came from a family of repeaters. Some of his older brothers and sisters had repeated grades. This was one of those small towns in southern Illinois, and you know what it's like growing up in a place like that!

TYRONE: Yes, as a matter of fact I do. Not in Illinois, but in Alabama. So what happened?

NELL: Randy was slow academically, even though I gave him lots of extra help. I tried to call his parents and sent letters asking for a conference, but they just never responded. It was almost as if they expected Randy to fail and thought nothing of it!

TYRONE: What finally happened?

NELL: My principal looked at Randy's work and test scores and told me to retain him, so I did. I sort of lost track of Randy until the end of the next school year when I talked to Meg Ryan, a friend of mine who taught Randy when he repeated first grade. She told me how Randy stuck out like a sore thumb and how the other children said things like, "There goes that stupid Randy Duncan! He flunked first grade!!!" Meg said that Randy developed into a full-blown behavior problem and was constantly getting into fights with the other children. It just broke my heart when I remembered how cooperative and helpful he was in my class. I may have ruined Randy's life, Tyrone! That's why I think that retention can destroy children's lives!

TYRONE: (sympathetic but businesslike) Nell, I understand how you must feel. And maybe Randy should have been promoted. But maybe there are situations where retention can actually help a child, and that's what we have to decide about Juan. Randy was physically big, and Juan is small, for one thing. And I guarantee you that we'll get his parents involved. Also, I don't think that he comes from a family of repeaters, and this sure isn't smalltown southern Illinois! Tell you what, let's turn all this over in our minds and continue our discussion this Friday after school.

NELL: OK. And I'll bring some information with me that I compile on all my students, mostly from their cumulative records.

TYRONE: Great! Have Mary [the school secretary] make copies for me of anything you have.

It is Friday after school four days later. Nell and Tyrone meet in the principal's office with the door closed.

TYRONE: Mary gave me copies of the information that you compiled on Juan, but I've been so busy that I really haven't had a chance to go over them. Let's see here [looks at papers], he seems to have been absent when we gave the Metropolitan Readiness Test. But he did take the Peabody Picture Vocabulary Test, and he also took the California Test of Mental Maturity and scored in the average range, although he scored higher on the nonlanguage part than he did on the language part. That would suggest reading problems, wouldn't it?

NELL: Yes, I guess it would.

TYRONE: His parents' names are Raul and Maria. He's a janitor at the Ames Corporation, and she's a checker at a supermarket. You said that you talked to them.

NELL: I talked to the mother, but not about retaining Juan.

Figure 2–1 Student Information Sheet for Juan Rodriguez
Compiled by Ms. Johnson

Pupil: Juan Rodriguez
Birthdate: 12/15/92
Age: 6

Metropolitan Readiness Test: Absent
Peabody Picture Vocabulary Test: Scored in the very low, normal range.
California Test of Mental Maturity: Language IQ.:   93
                                                          Nonlanguage IQ.:   107

ACADEMIC RECORD

Grading Periods

	1	2	3	4
Language Arts	U	U	N	
Spelling	U	U	U	
Math	S	S	S	
Science	N	N	S	
Social Studies	N	N	N	

(Grading scale: E = excellent; S = satisfactory; N = needs
improvement; U = unsatisfactory)

Parent Conference Notes:

Talked to Mrs. Rodriguez (Maria) on 10/17/98. She's a checker at Food Giant Supermarket, and her husband (Raul) is a custodian at the Ames Corporation. She said that Juan
has five brothers and three sisters from her first marriage and that she is two months
pregnant. She said that she didn't graduate from high school but that her husband did.
She doesn't seem greatly interested in Juan's schooling.

Comments

Grading period 1—Juan is a shy, immature child who is very small physically. He cries
easily and engages in baby talk sometimes.
Grading period 2—Juan is a sweet, cooperative child who just can't read English. I
thought he might have a learning disability, but he scored low normal on the Peabody.
Grading period 3—Cooperative, immature, still some baby talk, not good at sounds.
However, he is making some progress. He has finished the second preprimer and will
probably finish the third before school ends. But he won't get to the primer this school
year.

TYRONE: Oh, yes, and you said that you had a hard time understanding her.
NELL: Yes, that's right.
TYRONE: Nell, let me call them and talk to them. I'll tell them that we're trying to
do what's best for Juan and wonder how they would feel about his repeating
first grade. In the meantime, I want you to do something.
NELL: What's that?
TYRONE: Talk to Juan. Ask him how he would feel if he had a chance to start over
again in the first grade with new students. Find out a bit more about his broth-

ers and sisters—how they might react if he was retained. Let's meet Wednesday after school and make a final decision. OK?

It is Wednesday after school, and Nell and Tyrone meet in Tyrone's office with the door closed to make their final decision about promoting or retaining Juan.

TYRONE: Were you able to talk to Juan, Nell?

NELL: Yes, but it was very difficult. I thought that we were both going to break down and cry. He's such a sweet, shy child, and those big brown eyes remind me of Bambi in the movie.

TYRONE: Oh my! Then he felt bad about the idea of being retained?

NELL: He wants to go to the second grade with his classmates.

TYRONE: What about his brothers and sisters?

NELL: He said that none of them had ever been retained. He said that they might make fun of him for a while.

TYRONE: (thoughtfully) I see.

NELL: Did you call his parents?

TYRONE: Yes, I did, and it was like you said, difficult to understand their broken English. I talked to both of them at different times. The mother, Maria, seemed to understand the situation and said that she thought that we should do what we think is best for Juan. But the father, Raul, was somewhat upset. He said that he doesn't want his children to fail and felt very strongly that we should promote him and give Juan special attention in the second grade to get him up to speed.

NELL: So where does that leave us, Tyrone?

TYRONE: Nell, where it leaves us is that in my best professional judgment it would be best if you retained Juan. This is the time to do it, in the first grade. If he were in the fourth or fifth grade, I'd say go ahead and pass him. But retaining him now will allow him to develop both physically and academically and catch up with his classmates. I'll see that he gets into Mimi Sims's class. I'll explain it to Juan's father and deal with him. (Pause) So what do you think, Nell?

◼ Questions

1. What kinds of evidence should be considered in making promotion/retention decisions? What kinds of decision-making models exist in the literature?

2. What does the research on promotion and retention say about their effects on student learning and emotional and social development?

3. What impact should Juan's home environment have on the retention decision? How much weight should Nell place on the father's attitude and that of Juan's siblings, for example?

4. How much weight should be placed on Juan's emotional immaturity, such as his crying easily and his baby talk? How much weight should be placed on physical factors, such as his being the smallest boy in the room and his lack of coordination?

5. How much consideration should be given to a child's age, grade level, and gender in making a promotion/retention decision? Would the situation be different if Juan were in the third or fourth grade?

6. What is "social promotion"? How strong is the research support for such a policy?

7. How many times does it make sense to retain a child during the child's academic career? What are the negative effects of retention on a child's self-concept, social interactions in class, sense of efficacy, and locus of control (or attributions)? How do these relate to school achievement?

8. In making a promotion/retention decision, how much relative weight should be placed on child factors (e.g., physical size, psychosocial maturity, neurological maturity, self-concept, independent functioning, and basic skill competency) as opposed to family factors (e.g., parent attitudes, sibling attitudes, bilingualism, and racial/ethnic differences) and school factors (e.g., school and teacher attitudes, availability of personnel and resources to help, and school system attitudes)?

9. Should school districts set standards to guide promotion/retention decisions, or should such decisions be made on a case-by-case basis by the teacher and principal involved? For example, what are the consequences of a policy like that of the school district in which Nell had worked before which required that first graders not be promoted if they can't read at the end of the school year?

10. What response should Nell make regarding Mr. Baker's decision to retain Juan? Why? Should Juan be promoted, or should he be retained? What weight should be given his physical, language, and cognitive factors in making the decision?

3

Baiting the Hook

Key Content to Consider for Analyzing This Case:

1. Constructivism
2. Cognitive development (Piaget)
3. Information processing theory
4. Motivation (mastery versus performance goal-orientation, sense of efficacy, underachievement)
5. Self-concept
6. Social development
7. Home environment (including parenting styles)

Wilson Middle School is located in a large urban area in the southwestern part of the United States. Its attendance area serves a population that is approximately 55% white, 25% Hispanic, and 20% African-American.

Tony Green, a graduate of a teachers college in the Midwest, is in his second year of teaching experience at Wilson. It is three and a half months into the first semester, and it is almost the end of third period on a Thursday morning. Tony has just asked the 31 students in his Math 8 class to turn in their weekly tests on positive and negative numbers.

MR. GREEN: Okay, gang, pass 'em up to the front row and then down to Rae Ann. Rae Ann, will you collect them for me? [Rae Ann smiles and nods her head.] Wayne, I need to talk to you for just a minute when the bell rings.

WAYNE: OK. I have study hall next period anyhow.

MR. GREEN: And it's my planning period. I'll give you a note to take to your study hall teacher if you're late. (Bell rings.) See you all in math lab tomorrow, I hope! (Holds test papers up high as he speaks. Several students laugh.) Pull a chair up to my desk, Wayne, so we can talk. (All other students leave the room.)

WAYNE: (pulling a chair up to the teacher's desk) What did you want to talk to me about, Mr. Green?

MR. GREEN: Your grades, Wayne. (Pulls out Wayne's test paper and grades it as they talk) Wayne, I was talking to several of your teachers about you the other day in the teachers' lounge. We were all in agreement that you're a very bright guy, but your grades don't seem to show it.

WAYNE: I do OK. I'm getting C's in most of my classes, and that's average. That suits me just fine.

MR. GREEN: You're right on target, Wayne. I just graded your test, and you got a C.

WAYNE: See! That's just fine. I get to go to math lab tomorrow just like the other guys.

MR. GREEN: That's true, Wayne. You would even have gotten to go if you had made a D, but why do you set such a low standard for yourself when you have such potential?

WAYNE: I'm not that good at math, Mr. Green.

MR. GREEN: Not that good, or is it that you just don't want to work that hard? I have no doubt that you could be making A's in here if you set your mind to it.

WAYNE: I study the stuff hard enough. Math isn't exactly easy for me.

MR. GREEN: That's what I wanted to find out from you. Is it that the material is hard for you, or you just put out enough effort to make C's?

WAYNE: No, math isn't exactly easy. Take negative numbers. I may have passed the test, but the idea of not only not having anything left but going into the hole by so much still confuses me. Like if I go fishing and catch five fish and the game warden comes along and says that the five fish that I caught are illegal and that I not only have to give those five fish back but also five others that I haven't caught yet—you know that example you gave in class—well, I guess it's OK and I understand that example OK. It's just when you start giving us numbers by themselves that I get confused. When you take the examples away and I have to work with the numbers by themselves, that not only confuses me but bores me, Mr. Green. I'm an action person, not an Einstein.

MR. GREEN: Is that why you've been turning in some of your assignments but not others? You like the concrete examples but not abstract numbers?

WAYNE: I don't know what you call it, but those assignments with just numbers bother me and I guess bore me too much to try to figure them out. Some of the earlier stuff I could think out how they apply to fishing, but it gets hard with some things like negative numbers.

MR. GREEN: Why fishing?

WAYNE: Just because I go fishing all the time. That's my favorite thing to do. Dad and I go out about every weekend to one of the four or five lakes we fish.

MR. GREEN: That's great, Wayne! I used to do a little fishing myself when I was a kid. But you say that you go with your dad? That's great!

WAYNE: Yeah. Dad works in an office all week, and we like to get out together as often as we can. He finally bought an eighteen-foot aluminum boat and put a fifty-horse Mercury engine on it so we can move right along! The boat's real stable, too. You can stand almost anywhere in it and cast a line without feeling like you're losing your balance!

MR. GREEN: It sounds like you're quite a fisherman, Wayne. What does your dad do?

WAYNE: He's an accountant. Has his own business downtown.

MR. GREEN: Is that what you want to do when you graduate?

WAYNE: I don't know. I haven't given it much thought. I don't think I want to go to college, though, not unless they'd let me major in fishing! (Both Wayne and Tony laugh.)

MR. GREEN: Well, I don't know. I'm sure there must be a lot of careers you could explore that involve fishing and the sea. Have you done any saltwater fishing?

WAYNE: (eagerly) No, but Dad and I have been planning to! Dad says we need to go down to the Florida Keys during his next vacation and rent a boat and go after those big marlins! Do you have any idea how big those marlins get, Mr. Green?

MR. GREEN: Yes, I've seen pictures on TV. But what else do you like to do besides fish, Wayne?

WAYNE: Oh, not much. I'm not interested in much of anything else.

MR. GREEN: What about sports?

WAYNE: Dad thought I should try out for the basketball team. I wasn't much good.

MR. GREEN: What do you like to do with your friends?

WAYNE: I don't hang with the guys much. Sometimes John Bailey and I go to the mall and mess around awhile, but I mostly just like to stay home and read.

MR. GREEN: Oh. What do you like to read?

WAYNE: Mostly just books and magazines about fishing. Dad's bought me subscriptions to practically all the good magazines, and that one bookstore in the mall gets a lot of good books on fishing. Dad lets me charge all the books I want. He says that books are one thing that you shouldn't be cheap about.

MR. GREEN: I couldn't agree with your dad more! (Pause) Well, Wayne, this has been very interesting getting to know you a little better and to find out that you're such a fisherman and all. But I'm still convinced that you can make better grades than you are making, and I want to work with you more on helping you understand abstract numbers better. Will you work with me?

WAYNE: Sure, Mr. Green. Anything you want. Just let me know what you want me to do.

MR. GREEN: OK, Wayne. Let me get a little more information and we'll set something up. Here, let me write you a study hall pass, since the bell has already rung.

As soon as Wayne left the room, Tony walked down the hall to the counselors' office and walked up to the open door of the office of Kimberly Crandall, who is looking at some forms she is filling out.

TONY: Hello, Kim.

KIM: (startled and looking up) What!? Oh, hello, Tony!

TONY: (smiling) Sorry to startle you. Do you have a minute?

KIM: (putting away the forms and her pen) Sure. Come on in. (Motions to a wooden chair) These forms will keep. What's up?

TONY: I wonder if you can tell me who's Wayne Conner's counselor. I'd like to look at his folder.

KIM: You've come to the right person. I was making some entries in some of the folders yesterday, and Wayne's was one of them. (Pulls a folder out of a large stack of folders and hands it to Tony) As a matter of fact, I talked to Wayne's mother on the phone last week about where Wayne ought to go to high school.

TONY: Oh, really?! What was her concern?

KIM: You'll see my note in the folder. Basically, I think that she's a bit concerned about Wayne and just wanted to talk to me about it. In a nutshell, I think she believes that Wayne is an underachiever, and both she and her husband feel that he's college material and are disappointed that his grades are so, well, average.

TONY: That's really interesting. I just came from a conference with Wayne where he and I discussed these same issues. I got the feeling that Wayne is perfectly content to make C's and has no real ambitions to attend college. All he really seems to be interested in is fishing.

KIM: Yes, Marie—that's Wayne's mother—said that Wayne and his father go fishing together all the time. You'll note from the folder that Wayne is their only child, and they may be a bit overprotective. Marie was describing Wayne's room at home, and it sounds like he has everything money can buy.

TONY: He doesn't seem to have many friends his own age, though. Sounds like his dad is his best friend.

KIM: I hear that sometimes happens with only children.

TONY: His dad's an accountant or something? (Looks at the folder) Oh, yes, here it is. His dad's a CPA, and his mother is an elementary teacher. Now, this is interesting: He was tested last year, and his IQ is 128. I thought he was bright! And he's at the seventh stanine on the math portion of the Metropolitan Achievement Test. I compiled this information on all my third-period students over a month ago in order to assign them to groups and had forgotten about it! This just reinforces my belief that Wayne should be doing a whole lot better than he is in my class!

KIM: And not just in math, I might add. He's pretty much a C student in all his classes. Do you think it's a lack of motivation, Tony?

TONY: I'm not sure. Partly, I guess. But he also seems to have a problem with abstract material, at least in math. In my class he does only the assignments that interest him. But the only ones that interest him seem to be those dealing with concrete material or material he can relate to fishing examples. I don't know how his algebra teacher is going to get him interested in algebra when he takes it next year!

KIM: Let me know if I can help in any way, Tony.

TONY: Thanks, Kim. This helps a lot.

It is late on a Friday afternoon about two weeks later. School has ended, and most of the students have already left the building. Tony has arranged a conference with Wayne's parents, Wayland and Marie Conner. They sit in movable desks in Tony's classroom facing each another.

TONY: I really appreciate you two taking the time to come in and meet with me. I have been wanting to talk to you about Wayne.

MARIE: (with concern) And we have really wanted to talk to someone here, Mr. Green. Wayne has told us that you've tried to help him.

TONY: I think what it comes down to, Mr. and Mrs. Conner, is that Wayne isn't working up to his potential. I've talked to a number of his other teachers and to his counselor, Ms. Crandall, and I've gone over his cumulative record with his test scores and all. All the information seems to point to Wayne's being what we call an underachiever. He seems to be willing to settle for C's when he could be making A's in his classes, including mine.

WAYLAND: I think you've sized Wayne up rather accurately, Mr. Green. He does just enough work to get by with C's but just isn't interested enough in his schoolwork to put forth the effort to make A's. I go over this with him just about every time he brings home a report card. (Pause) You know, Mr. Green, I'm a CPA and have a rather well-established and profitable business. We just hired another young man yesterday who is fresh out of college who reminds me a lot of Wayne. Wayne could fit right in and take over my firm when I retire if he wanted to. The opportunity is there for the taking. But when I talk to him about it, he just says that he isn't sure whether he'd like being a CPA or not. When I ask him what he'd like to do if he could do anything he wanted to, he just says that he isn't sure. It seems like fishing is the only thing that really interests him. (Smiling) He doesn't even seem to have really discovered girls yet.

MARIE: We have talked to him about his grades and his future a lot, Mr. Green. But he's our only child, and all we really want is for him to be happy. We don't want to put too much pressure on him. After all, he's only thirteen, and sometimes I think that's too young for anyone to be making decisions about what he wants to do with the rest of his life. We're disappointed that he isn't making better grades but hope he'll improve as he gets older and matures a bit. If he doesn't, maybe he can go to a community college later on and take some courses in things that interest him. (Pause) I know Wayland wants him to eventually step into his firm and take it over, but that may not be what Wayne wants to do or would be good at. Wayne has to find himself first before he makes big decisions about his life. He's still really just a little boy in many ways.

WAYLAND: (with annoyance) Yes, all that may be true, Marie. But when I was thirteen I at least had a desire to make something of myself and had a little ambition. Wayne doesn't seem to have any drive at all. And what worries me most is that he's such a loner. He doesn't seem to have people skills. You have to learn to relate to other people if you're going to be a success in life.

MARIE: (animatedly) Wayland, you have to learn to look at the good side of things more! Wayne has a wonderful relationship with you, and he is a good boy. I'm glad that he's not into that adolescent drug and party scene. I'm real glad that we don't have the kinds of problems with Wayne that the Masons have with their son.

TONY: One of my concerns as Wayne's math teacher is that he seems to have trouble learning abstract concepts. If he can't relate what he's learning back to concrete examples, he has real difficulties. The only way he could deal with negative numbers, for example, was to relate them to catching fish. This concerns me because he's going to have to grasp abstract concepts when he takes algebra next year.

WAYLAND: (frowning) See! That's what I mean, Marie! Wayne's not dumb! He just doesn't try to use his brain! (Smiling) No offense, Mr. Green, but I think that he has his teachers fooled into believing he can't think in abstract terms. He sure doesn't have any trouble figuring out abstract issues when it comes to fishing! (Eagerly) He's really quite an expert when it comes to fishing, you know. He can tell you all about the habits of various fish, the effects of lake temperatures on the eating habits of the fish, what lure to use under what circumstances. And you ought to see him cast! He can put it anywhere he wants it! It's amazing. (Pause) No, Mr. Green, I think he just doesn't want to think abstractly about certain subjects.

TONY: (frowning) You may be right, Mr. Conner. It may be more of a motivation problem than an abstract thinking problem. All I can say is, if it's true, he sure had me fooled!

WAYLAND: (smiling) Believe me, he's no dummy, Mr. Green! Well, Marie and I do appreciate all that you're trying to do for Wayne. If he could just get into his schoolwork the way he's into fishing, he would end up as valedictorian when he graduates. But I guess he has to decide that his schoolwork is important to him. Well, thanks again, Mr. Green, and if there's anything we can do to help, please let us know.

MARIE: (smiling) Yes, thanks so much, Mr. Green. I want you to know that we do talk to him about his schoolwork at home, but Wayland is right. Wayne is evasive and doesn't want to talk about it. (Pause) But I don't know about the abstract thinking thing you were talking about. I've noticed that several times when I've sent him to the store for me, he has trouble with simple things like making change and figuring out in his head how much things cost. If he and I shop together at the supermarket, I always get one of those shopping carts with a calculator on it so Wayne won't get confused.

WAYLAND: (interrupting) He just doesn't pay attention, Marie! Believe me, if he wanted to, he'd become an expert in no time.

MARIE: But like the other day when you and Wayne were making that new lure.

WAYLAND: You mean the yellow jacket?

MARIE: Yes, the black and yellow one. Wayne couldn't follow what you were telling him until you drew it up on a piece of paper. Then he put it together without any problem.

WAYLAND: (reflecting) Yes, that's true. But didn't you have to take a picture of the hairdo that you wanted to your beautician the other day so she could get it the way you wanted it? It's the same thing.

MARIE: (puzzled) Maybe you're right. I don't know. (Pause) Well, thanks again, Mr. Green. We appreciate your helping Wayne.

TONY: And thank you both for taking the time to come in and talk. Let's keep in touch. I'm sure that the three of us can figure out ways to help a bright guy like Wayne do better in school.

It is the following Monday afternoon after school has ended. Tony sits in the classroom of Ramon Garcia, chair of the math department. Tony and Ramon sit in chairs facing each other.

TONY: Ramon, I need to ask your advice about one of the students in my Math 8 class.

RAMON: Your third-period class?

TONY: (smiling) Yes. How did you guess? I seem to have more trouble with that class than all my others, don't I?

RAMON: Who's the student?

TONY: Wayne Conner. He's a classic underachiever. He has an IQ of 128 and works just hard enough in his classes to make C's. His dad's a CPA, and his mom's an elementary teacher. We had a conference about Wayne last Friday. The picture that emerges is a thirteen-year-old kid who is a loner and spends all of his spare time with his father fishing. Wayne's a real expert on fishing. His mother seems a bit overprotective but cares a lot about Wayne. I think that Wayne's father thinks that Wayne's just unmotivated about schoolwork and could do better if he really tried.

RAMON: And what do you think, Tony?

TONY: I don't know, Ramon. Something tells me that it's more than just motivation. I think that Wayne may have some difficulty in the area of abstract thinking. He has to relate abstract concepts to concrete examples, usually fishing, before he can understand them. His dad thinks this is just a game that Wayne plays with his teachers to avoid working too hard. His mother isn't so

Figure 3–1 WILSON MIDDLE SCHOOL
Cumulative Record

Name:	Conner, Wayne Lynne	Home Telephone:	555-318-1423
Address:	6023 Robin Lane Rd.	General Health:	Good
Father:	Wayland D. Conner	Occupation:	CPA
Mother:	Marie R. Conner	Occupation:	Elementary Teacher
Siblings:	None	Handicaps:	None
Former Schools:	Blaine Elementary	Date of Birth:	11/13/86
Date Entered Wilson:	8/30/92	Age:	13 years

TEST RECORD

Intelligence Tests	IQ	Date	Grade
Otis-Lennon Mental Ability			
Elementary I	121	9/1/94	3
Intermediate	128	9/5/98	7

Achievement Tests

	Math	Basics Total	Complete Total
Metropolitan Advanced (in stanines)	7	7	7

ACADEMIC RECORD

Grades 1–6 (year averages)	1	2	3	4	5	6
Language Arts	A	A	B	B	C	C
Reading	A	A	B	B	B	B
Writing	A	A	B	C	C	C
Spelling	A	A	B	C	C	C
Social Studies	A	A	B	C	C	B
Arithmetic	A	A	B	C	C	C
Science & Health		A	B	C	C	C
Music	A	A	A	A	A	A
Citizenship	A	A	A	A	A	A

Grade 7 (year average)	
English	C
Geography	C
Arithmetic	C
Phys. Ed.	C
Science	C
Exploratory	C
Pers./Social Dev.	C

sure and says that she has noticed some abstract thinking problems at home. (Pause) I guess that my instincts tell me that Wayne's father is wrong and that Wayne's abstract thinking problem is real.

RAMON: This is a difficult and unusual situation, Tony. Did you look up his records or talk to his counselor to get additional information on this?

TONY: Yes, I did. And guess what! He's at the seventh stanine on the math subtest of the Metropolitan. I almost forgot that bit of information. Maybe his dad is right after all.

RAMON: Maybe. Maybe not. What's your next step, Tony? Or is that why you came to see me?

TONY: (smiling) That's why I came to see you, Ramon. We're starting square root this week. How would you go about teaching square root to a student who is an expert on fishing but who may have an abstract thinking problem? Are there some tests he can take that would help me figure out how to help him?

Questions

1. What is an underachiever? To what extent is an IQ score a good predictor of student ability or potential? Is Wayne an underachiever?

2. Is Wayne's problem motivational or cognitive, or both? What type of motivational or cognitive problem does Wayne have? What can be done about such problems?

3. Describe teacher expectancy theory. Is there a self-fulfilling prophecy at work in Wayne's case? What expectations or beliefs seem to be influencing Wayne's behavior?

4. How would you describe Wayne's home environment and his relationship with his parents and his peers? Are Wayne's parents overprotective? How would Erikson's theory of personality development explain the development and effects of parental overprotectiveness?

5. From Baumrind's perspective, what parenting style do Wayne's parents exhibit: authoritarian, authoritative, or permissive? How does such a parenting style relate to school achievement?

6. What are concrete and abstract learning? Given that Wayne is 13 years old, does he seem to exhibit problems in making the transition to formal operations (from the standpoint of Piaget's theory of cognitive development)?

7. From the standpoint of constructivism, does Wayne seem to be "in the zone" with regard to learning Math 8 concepts such as negative numbers? What type of learning scaffolds would be helpful to a student like Wayne?

8. From the motivational perspective of Ames's mastery learning versus performance learning, does Wayne seem to be more oriented to mastery or toward performance in his schoolwork? In the area of fishing? How can Tony take advantage of this information?

9. From a social development frame of reference, is Wayne's mother correct in her belief that society puts too much pressure on students to make early career choices? Should such choices be made at the middle school level? What pressure is being put on Wayne, and how is he responding to it? What can Tony do?

10. What advice should Ramon give Tony about teaching his unit on square root so as to involve Wayne? Can Wayne's interest in fishing be utilized in some way? How can Wayne's abstract thinking skills be developed?

4

Honesty or Maturity?

Key Content to Consider for Analyzing This Case:

1. Moral Development
2. Observational Learning
3. Parent Involvement

Lakewood Elementary is a new school with an excellent physical plant and abundant facilities that are only 2 years old. It is located in an upper-middle-class suburb of approximately 60,000 people on the West Coast of the United States. Its attendance district is approximately 80% white, 15% African-American, 3% Hispanic, and 2% Asian-American.

Akia Brown is an African-American teacher with 5 years of teaching experience, the past 2 years at Lakewood. She is currently teaching a third-grade class with 24 students evenly divided between boys and girls.

It is early in the school year, and Akia has introduced her students to the multiplication tables, twos through nines. She has put the multiplication tables in large block symbols on a large piece of white construction paper, which she has placed on an easel at the front of the classroom. As she talks she uses a wooden pointer to point to the particular item she is talking about.

Ms. Brown: Now, children, there are a lot of ways to learn the multiplication tables. You can learn them by using them over and over again, or you can learn them by thinking of a picture of something that goes with each number. But no matter how you do it, you have to practice. Yes, Sarah?

Sarah: What do you mean pictures?

Ms. Brown: That's a good question, Sarah. I was just coming to that. In a class I took as a college student a long time ago, I learned a system of using pictures in your mind as a way of remembering things. (Goes to the blackboard, picks up chalk, and writes the numbers from 2 to 9 in a vertical column) Now here are the pictures of things I think of when I see each number. I want you to close your eyes and imagine that you see two pennies. Can you all see two pennies? Who doesn't see two pennies in their mind? (No hands go up.) Now those two pennies form a group of two. We could use real pennies, but we won't always have real pennies with us, so it's better to use your imagination. Yes, Brad?

BRAD: Is one penny a group?

MS. BROWN: That's a very good question, Brad, and I promise that I'll answer it later. But ones and zeroes are a little more difficult, so I want to do them after we learn twos through nines first. Now look at the chart (points to $2 \times 1 =$ with the wooden pointer). Think of the 2 as the number in a group, as in this case, two pennies. Think of the 1 as the number of groups. So class, if you have a group of two pennies and only one such group, that means $2 \times 1 =$ what?

CLASS: (in unison) Two!

MS. BROWN: Right! Who doesn't understand? Roger, you're frowning.

ROGER: Well, I was thinking that one penny would be a group of one and 1×1 would be the same as one group of one penny. But then 1×0 would be one group of one penny times no groups. I don't get it. (With sudden insight) Oh, I get it! No groups of even one penny, so $1 \times 0 = 0$!

BRAD: (without raising hand) Wait a minute! What did he say?

MS. BROWN: Yes, that's very good, Roger. But how many of you understand what Roger just said? (Six hands go up, one hesitantly.) Well, we'll come back to the ones and zeroes like I promised. But for now close your eyes again, class, and imagine a group of two pennies again. (All students close their eyes.) Now imagine two groups of two pennies. How many do you have?

CLASS: Four!

MS. BROWN: So (using wooden pointer), $2 \times 2 = 4$. Right?

CLASS: Right!

MS. BROWN: Yes, Annmarie?

ANNMARIE: I understand it all right. When you multiply, it's the number of times you increase the groups. But I just tried to imagine nine groups of nine pennies and I couldn't hold them still in my mind so I can count them. I keep losing track. How am I going to remember all those pennies?!

MS. BROWN: (smiling) I was just trying to explain to you what you are doing when you multiply. There's only one way to remember them, though. You have to memorize them and practice repeating them often. When you get stuck, though, you can always figure it out using the method that I just taught you. (Passes out papers) Now, everybody take one of these. We call this a pretest. See how many of the multiplication tables you can do now on your own. Do your own work and keep your eyes off other people's papers. Now start.

As all the students get down to work, Akia begins to do her own work but looks at what the students are doing from time to time. One time when she looks up she notices that Brad is looking at Roger's paper. She quickly looks back down at her work so that Brad won't know that she's seen him. She covertly watches Brad's copying of Roger's answers from time to time.

MS. BROWN: OK, children, turn in your papers. (Collects papers as they are passed in) By the way, Brad, I need to see you for just a minute when school's out. So don't run away without seeing me. OK?

BRAD: OK.

The school day has ended, and Brad remains after school to talk to Ms. Brown. Akia sits behind her desk, and Brad sits in a chair in front of the desk. Akia pulls out Brad's and Roger's papers and lays them side by side so that she can compare the answers.

Ms. Brown: Brad, I watched you when you were doing your multiplication tables and saw you copying Roger's answers.

Brad: (angrily) I did not! I looked over toward Roger's paper, but I didn't copy his answers.

Ms. Brown: There's no need to lie to me, Brad. I watched you do it for some time. Also, here are your two papers. Every answer is exactly the same. I'm really disappointed in you, Brad! Don't you know better? You never learn anything when you copy someone else's work except how to cheat.

Brad: (contritely) I'm sorry! I just wanted to get a good grade! I didn't know how to do them!

Ms. Brown: Brad, you can't pretend that you know the multiplication tables by copying someone else's answers. Even if I hadn't caught you, you still wouldn't be able to do them on the next test unless you cheated again.

Brad: (looking down at the floor) I know.

Ms. Brown: Have you cheated in here before, Brad?

Brad: (sternly) No! And I won't do it again.

Ms. Brown: I hope not, Brad. Next time I'm going to have to talk to your parents about it. OK?

Brad: (dejectedly) OK.

It is two weeks later. Akia has asked her students to bring in either a picture or an action figure of their favorite cartoon or television character for a sharing and writing assignment. Brad has brought in the blue Power Ranger to share with the class. He concludes his explanation of the history and powers of the superhero and goes back to his seat. Roger is called on next and goes to the front of the class and takes an action figure out of a box he is carrying.

Roger: (holding the action figure up high for everyone to see after placing the box on Akia's desk) I'll bet everybody knows this one. He's called Wolverine and is one of the X-Men.

Brad: (without raising his hand) Cool! He's really big! Where did you get him?

Roger: My dad got him for me on his last trip to New York. You can't get them here. I looked. (Pause) Now watch this. (Roger pushes a button on the action figure's back, and "claws" pop out, then retract from the action figure's hand. Several boys, including Brad, shout exclamations of wonder and disbelief.)

Ms. Brown: That's really interesting, Roger. What does Wolverine use the claws for? (Several boys, including Brad, shout out that Wolverine uses them to fight the bad guys with.) OK, well, now will you be able to write me a paper about Wolverine and the X-Men and explain how they fight against the bad guys?

Roger: Oh, yeah! That's one of my favorite things! I really like this assignment!

Ms. Brown: OK, Roger, we're about out of time. Why don't you put Wolverine back in the box and you can tell us more about him later.

Roger: OK. (Puts action figure back in the box and leaves it on the teacher's desk.)

It is later that same day, and Akia is listening to the students take turns reading. Brad has just finished.

Ms. Brown: OK. Annmarie, it's your turn next. Yes, Brad?

Brad: I have to go to the bathroom real bad! I can't wait!

Ms. Brown: OK, Brad. Go ahead and come right back. (Pause) Go ahead, Annmarie.

Akia listens to Annmarie read, but some intuition tells her to watch Brad out of the corner of one eye without turning her head. As Brad walks by her desk on the way to the bathroom, Akia sees him quickly pick up the box with Roger's action figure in it and put it under his shirt. Brad continues on into the bathroom. Akia continues with the reading.

Ten minutes before the school day is over, Akia tells the students to pick everything up, clean up the room, and get ready to go home. There is considerable hustle and bustle as students move around the classroom. Roger walks over to Akia.

ROGER: Ms. Brown, I can't find my Wolverine! It was on your desk.

MS. BROWN: (loudly) Has anyone seen Roger's action figure that was in a box on my desk? (Students shake their heads or say no quietly.) Would Brad, Jeremy, and Annmarie please help Roger look. Look everywhere and see if you can find it. Roger doesn't want to lose what belongs to him! Now look hard!

After 5 minutes, the three students and Roger come over to Akia and tell her that they couldn't find the action figure.

MS. BROWN: OK. Thanks for looking children. (Turns to Roger) Roger, I'm sorry this happened, but I'll bet that your action figure shows up. (Pats him) Don't worry about it now. (Children begin to move away from her to go to their desks.) Brad, I need to see you for a minute after class is dismissed. Please don't leave.

All the students have left except Brad. Akia motions for Brad to sit in a desk at the front of the classroom, and she leans against the edge of her desk looking down at him.

MS. BROWN: (in a serious tone) Brad, where's Roger's action figure?

BRAD: (looking down) I don't know! We couldn't find it! We looked all over!

MRS. BROWN: Brad, I deliberately gave you a chance to return it. Now you are lying on top of stealing it. I saw you take it off my desk and stick it under your shirt on the way to the bathroom. Now, you get Roger's action figure right now or we're going down to the principal's office and call your parents right now!

BRAD: (tearing up) Oh, OK. (Leaves the classroom and returns in a couple of minutes with the box containing the action figure. He hands it to Akia, who lays it on the desk. Brad sits back down at the desk and hangs his head.)

MS. BROWN: (quietly) Brad, why did you steal this from Roger?

BRAD: (crying) I don't know! I just wanted it real bad! I knew that I'd never find one that good!

MS. BROWN: Brad, do you think you can go through life stealing whatever you want? Don't you know what happens to people who live that way?!

BRAD: Yes, I know it's wrong. I would have given it back to him after I played with it for a while.

MS. BROWN: Maybe you would and maybe you wouldn't. But let me ask you this. Suppose that the action figure you took belonged to you and you brought it in to share with the class and another student stole it from you. How would you feel?

BRAD: Bad.

MS. BROWN: That's called the Golden Rule, Brad. Do unto others as you would have them do unto you. Have you ever heard of it?

BRAD: Yes.

Ms. Brown: But you don't think these things through before you do them, do you?

Brad: No.

Ms. Brown: Brad, I'm worried about you. As far as I'm concerned, you're on probation. The very next time I catch you stealing or cheating or lying in my classroom I'm going to involve the principal and your parents. Do you understand me?

Brad: Yes. I'm sorry. I promise I won't do it again. (Wipes a tear from one eye)

Ms. Brown: OK, Brad. This is your last chance. Go on home.

It is one month later and the school day has just ended. All the students except Annmarie have left the room. Akia sits at her desk, and Annmarie walks over to talk to her.

Ms. Brown: Annmarie, don't you have to catch your bus?

Annmarie: Yes, but there's something important I have to tell you, Ms. Brown.

Ms. Brown: Oh! What is it?

Annmarie: Well, you know when they called you down to the office today?

Ms. Brown: Yes, what about it?

Annmarie: Well, I saw Brad go up to your desk and take your purse out of the drawer. He took some money. I told him to put it back, but he wouldn't.

Ms. Brown: (shocked) What! Are you sure? (She opens the drawer, opens up her purse, takes out her billfold, and sees that the 5-dollar bill, the only paper money she had, is missing.) Oh, my goodness! He took my five-dollar bill. (Calms down) Thank you so much for telling me, Annmarie. It shows that you are honest and have a lot of courage.

Annmarie: My mother says that you are supposed to tell when you see something bad.

Ms. Brown: Your mother is so right, Annmarie. Now please, let me handle this. Don't talk about this with the other children.

Annmarie: OK, I won't. Can I tell my mother?

Ms. Brown: That would be OK, but tell her I want to handle this my own way and that I'd appreciate it if she kept it to herself. And thanks again so much!

Annmarie: OK. Goodbye, Ms. Brown.

The next morning Akia sends Brad to the principal's office with a note in a sealed envelope for the principal. When the principal talks to Brad, he denies taking the money. The principal calls Brad's mother, has her take Brad home for a couple of days, and schedules a conference for the next day after school. However, the principal is called to an emergency meeting downtown and suggests that Akia go ahead and meet with Brad's parents, Charles and Gloria Downing, in Akia's classroom after school. Before the conference Akia has a chance to look at Brad's cumulative record and notices that his father is an attorney and his mother is a high school social studies teacher. Brad also has a sister who is 2 years younger than he. The parents seem very friendly and concerned as they sit in movable desks facing Akia, who also sits in a student desk.

Gloria: We were very surprised—I guess shocked might be more accurate—when Ms. Martin (the principal) called us and told us that she thought it best for Brad to stay home until we had all talked about this. What's this about Brad stealing from your purse, Ms. Brown? We just can't believe that he'd do something like that. We give him a good allowance. Why would he need to steal money? Did you actually see him take it out of your purse?

AKIA: I'm afraid that this isn't the first situation that has come up, Ms. Downing. (At this point Akia reiterates the details about Brad's cheating on the test, stealing the action figure from Roger, and taking the money from her purse.) And in all these cases he tried to lie his way out of the situation until he was confronted with the facts. Perhaps I should have contacted you earlier about these things, but I kept trying to give Brad another chance. But this time I knew that I had to do something.

CHARLES: (smiling reassuringly) And we're really glad you did, Ms. Brown! What a stupid way for Brad to behave. We give him a more than generous allowance, and you should see his room! He has everything a child his age could want. Why he feels a need to go around stealing toys and money is beyond me! Really stupid! And his copying the other kid's answers! Now that really bothers me! I have no doubt that Brad has what it takes to get a college scholarship and get accepted to law school one day. A bright kid like Brad should have other students copying answers from him!

AKIA: Well, Mr. Downing, I don't think that any student should cheat, or steal for that matter!

CHARLES: Oh, of course. I was just making a point. I am really disappointed in Brad, and he's going to catch it at home, I can guarantee you!

AKIA: My concern is that Brad is at a formative age and seems to value lying, cheating, and stealing as acceptable ways of getting along in the world.

GLORIA: Yes, I know what you mean. I see the results of that in some of the adolescents that I teach in high school. I think that a lot of it goes back to changes in our society since the 1950s. The emphasis on competition and getting your own way by walking over other people that starts with our politicians and state and federal government has filtered down even to the children in our elementary schools. Get your own way at any cost!

CHARLES: Regrettably, that's the way the world is now. (Reaches for his wallet and takes out a 20-dollar bill) Ms. Brown, we're really sorry that Brad stole the five dollars out of your purse, and we insist on reimbursing you with some extra for damages. (Handing the money to Akia) Brad never does these kinds of things at home, and I can't understand why he does them at school. I guarantee you that we'll get to the bottom of it before we're through. (Pause) I hope that as Brad's teacher you'll be able to put his immature and thoughtless behavior in perspective. I'm sure that he's going through a phase, and I'm certain that we'll all be glad when he gets through it. (Extends his hand to shake Akia's hand and stands up; Gloria does likewise.) Thanks so much for talking with us and for helping Brad.

GLORIA: Yes. Thank you, Ms. Brown, and don't hesitate to let us know if he does anything further. We need to nip this thing in the bud right now!

AKIA: (also stands up) Yes, well, OK, Mr. and Mrs. Downing, and thanks for coming. I'm sure we'll be talking to one another again.

It is the next day after school, and Akia sits in the office of the school principal, Celia Martin.

CELIA Tell me, Akia. How'd your conference with the Downings go yesterday?

AKIA: My impression was that they weren't all that concerned. They took a sort of "kids will be kids" position and implied that Brad is going through a phase they hope he'll outgrow. Can you believe that Mr. Downing gave me a twenty-dollar bill to make up for a five that Brad stole from my purse?! They say they're going to give Brad a good talking to at home. Apparently Brad's behavior makes no sense to them, since he has about anything money can buy at home.

CELIA Yes, he's an attorney isn't he? And she's a teacher at Lincoln High. So you don't agree with their analysis or approach to handling Brad?

AKIA: Of course not! The problem is going to get worse unless somebody does something! I'm not sure I handled the conference with the Downings well. I wish you could have been there, Celia. But Brad will be back in my class tomorrow. What am I going to do with him, Celia? How can I get his parents involved?

Figure 4–1 Lakewood Elementary School Cumulative Record

Name: Downing, Bradley Omar
Address: 3221 Elm Road
Father: Downing, Charles B.
Mother: Downing, Gloria A.
Siblings: Downing, Elizabeth, Age 6
Former Schools: None
Date Entered Lakewood: 8/30/96

Home Telephone: 408-472-1411
General Health: Excellent
Occupation: Attorney-at-Law
Occupation: Secondary Teacher
Handicaps: None
Date of Birth: 03/13/91

TEST RECORD

Intelligence Tests	CA	MA	IQ	Date	Grade
California Test of Mental Maturity				5/14/97	1
Language	6-9	7-6	111		
Nonlanguage	6-9	7-10	116		

ACADEMIC RECORD

Grades 1-6 (year averages)	1	2	3	4	5	6
English						
Reading	3	3				
Writing	3	3				
Spelling	3	3				
Social Studies						
Arithmetic	3	3				
Science & Health						
Music	3	3				
Citizenship	2	1				

KEY:
1. Child is working below grade level
2. Child is working below grade level, but is making progress
3. Child is working at grade level
4. Child is doing excellent work at grade level
5. Child is working above grade level

▪ Questions

1. At which of Kohlberg's stages of moral development does Brad seem to be operating? What moral education methods seem to work best with children at that stage? How effective are they?

2. At which of Erikson's stages of personality development does Brad seem to have unresolved crises? What techniques work best in such cases?

3. From the standpoint of Ames, does Brad have a mastery or performance goal orientation toward learning? How does such an orientation develop, and what can be done to help children move toward a mastery orientation?

4. From an observational learning perspective, what kinds of behaviors are modeled by Brad's parents? What can a classroom teacher do to change a child's behavior that stems from patterns of modeling and imitation that originate in the home?

5. In terms of cooperation versus competition, what kind of classroom environment has Akia established in her classroom? Would the establishment of cooperative learning teaching methods in her classroom help in Brad's case?

6. From a cognitive learning perspective, how effective is Akia's "imaging technique" in getting her students to learn the multiplication tables? What method would have been more effective?

7. How effective was Akia's conference with the Downings? What should she have done differently?

8. What method(s) of classroom management would be most useful to Akia in this situation? What are the relative merits of reality therapy, teacher effectiveness training, and behavior modification in this situation?

9. What parent involvement techniques might Akia consider using in this situation? How effective are such techniques?

10. What advice should Celia give Akia about working with Brad when he returns? About working with Brad's parents?

5

Potpourri

Key Content to Consider for Analyzing This Case:

1. Cultural Diversity
2. Intelligence
3. Cognitive Style (Field Dependence/Independence)
4. Exceptionalities
5. Bloom's Cognitive Taxonomy

North Middle School is 25 years old and is located in a low socioeconomic neighborhood that is many years older than the school. The community in which the school is located is part of a large metropolitan area in the eastern United States. The student population comprises approximately 70% white, 20% African-American, 7% Hispanic, and 3% Asian-American.

Abe Goodman, who is 23 years old, is beginning his first year at North as an eighth-grade American history teacher. Last year Abe taught eighth grade in a small rural middle school in the southern part of the state, near the prestigious private university from which he graduated with a B.S. in education and a major in social studies.

It is the sixth period of the first day of school, and the American history class is entering the classroom. There is much talking, pushing, and laughing, but the pupils quickly find seats. Abe notices immediately that there is a wide diversity of pupils in the class and that they have segregated themselves into ethnic groups. As Abe makes eye contact with pupils who are talking, the students continue to talk. It is not until he taps a paper weight on his desk that the pupils gradually quiet down and give him their attention.

ABE: (smiling) Welcome to American history class. As you've probably noticed, I'm a new teacher here. Last year I taught in Bowen Middle School in the southern part of the state.

ELIJAH: (speaking out) Man, what kinda name is dat fo' a school?

ABE: It's the last name of a man. Frank Bowen was the superintendent of schools for many years and a leader in that community. Everybody liked him and appreciated what he did both for the schools and for the community. The school was built shortly after he died, so the people in town agreed that they should name the school in his honor. The full name of the school is the Frank E. Bowen Middle School.

ELIJAH: That's cool! I'd like a school named after me. (Much laughter and derision from the class)

ABE: (holding up his hand for silence) What's your name?

ELIJAH: Elijah.

ABE: Elijah what?

ELIJAH: Elijah Duwaine Jackson (More laughter from the class. Some pupils say "Wow, Duwaine," "What a classy name for such an unclassy guy," etc.)

ABE: (holding up his hand for quiet) That sounds pretty good to me—Elijah Duwaine Jackson Middle School. (More laughter and derision from the class. Abe quiets the laughter and speaks seriously.) Maybe someday you'll have a school or some other public building named after you, Elijah. If you work hard in your community and people appreciate what you do, it can really happen. (While some of his friends point at Elijah and jeer, Elijah sits quietly as if he is pondering this possibility.) It could happen to anyone else in this class, too—if you help people in your community. That's how people get buildings, roads, parks, libraries, and other public properties named after them. As we study American history in this class we'll learn about many people who've become famous because they helped other people. These are names that you and I know even though the people have been dead for hundreds of years. (A girl near the front raises her hand. Abe looks her way.) What's your name?

ANGELA: I am Angela Aguila, and I know people like you talk about. Like Thomas Jefferson, and Ben Franklin, and J.C. Penney—people like that. (Some pupils laugh.)

ABE: That's great, Angela! Those are people who are part of our history. In this class we'll learn about people who helped to develop our country.

MOSES: You ain't gonna make us memorize lots of names and dates, are you? I hate that. I just can't remember names and dates. (Several other pupils support Moses, saying, "Cool, Moses," "Ya," "That's right," etc.)

ABE: Well, I'll want you to know some of the people who were famous for certain accomplishments, Moses. For instance, you probably know the name of the sailor who's given credit for discovering America, don't you?

MOSES: (exuberantly) Right on! That would be Columbus!

ABE: (smiling) That would be the right answer.

JANET: What other kinds of assignments will we have?

ABE: Basically, I'd like you to know about the discovery and settlement of our country, winning our independence from England through a revolution, establishing our own government, the westward movement, the Civil War, Reconstruction, the Industrial Revolution, and the westward expansion.

IONA: (sounding discouraged) That sounds like a lot of work. (Other pupils agree.)

ABE: But remember, we're talking about a year's work. And I plan to have you do most of that work in groups. Each group will research a different part of the topic and report on it.

BARBARA: I hate doing reports. I always read everything we're supposed to read, and then I can't figure out what to put in the report.

ABE: Don't become discouraged just yet. I can show you how to outline your reports so that you'll know what information you should include. (The bell rings.) OK. Class is over. I'll see you tomorrow (Pupils leave. Many of them complain to each other about the proposed class assignments)

The following Wednesday Abe is in the guidance office recording information from the cumulative records of the pupils in his sixth-period American history class. Sherry Matson, the guidance counselor, is working at her desk.

SHERRY: Are you finding everything you need, Abe?

ABE: I'm not finding what I wanted to find, but I'm finding what I need.

SHERRY: What did you want to find?

ABE: I wanted to find that the children in my sixth-period class were all like the children from Lake Woebegone—cooperative, attractive, and all above average in intelligence. Alas! That isn't what I found.

SHERRY: Why doesn't that surprise me?

ABE: I guess it's because you've been here longer than I have. (Handing the paper on which he's been writing to Sherry, who holds it so that they can both see it) Here's the information I took from the folders of my pupils.

SHERRY: (after perusing the list of names) Yes, I know all these pupils. And, indeed, some of them are quite challenging. And what a range of abilities you have—from Moses Gully to Chan Yin!

ABE: And the sad part is that Moses seems to try as hard as anyone else in the class. But he just doesn't seem to have enough background information to carry it off.

SHERRY: Yes, I know about the home situation. The father left the family years ago. The mother seems to be gone most of the time. Moses has both an older and a younger sister, and the three of them survive the best way they can. None of them does well in school, but to their credit, they've managed to stay out of serious trouble.

ABE: I don't know other members of the family, but I like Moses. He really tries hard but has trouble learning. Then he becomes frustrated and disruptive. I need to find a way to keep him occupied.

SHERRY: (looking at the list) I see that Kevin Felton and Connie Petty are both in that class. They're probably difficult to deal with also. You probably already know that Kevin Felton's been diagnosed as socially maladjusted and Connie Petty as having attention deficit hyperactivity disorder.

ABE: I wasn't informed of this, but they've demonstrated their disabilities. Kevin wanders around like a lost soul, and Connie's usually out of her seat wandering around the room at least half the period. I walk her back to her seat and sit her down, but she's up again before I can get back to the front of the room. Knowing that they have disabilities will help me to be more patient with them. (Begins to walk toward the door) And thanks for making your records available to me. I'm going to use the information to form heterogeneous groups.

SHERRY: (walking beside him) You're welcome. I've enjoyed talking with you. If there's anything else I can do to help, let me know.

During his planning period the following day, Abe went to the teachers' lounge and found two other teachers there, Mary Johnson and Don Bradbury, both of whom teach English.

ABE: (feigning surprise) There must be something special happening in the lounge today.

MARY: Yes, we heard you were planning to grace us with your presence during your free period. To what can we attribute this honor?

ABE: Ordinarily, I'd come here regularly on my free period, but I've been busy trying to figure out how to deal with my sixth-period American history class.

DON: What's so special about that particular class?

ABE: They're a wild and crazy bunch of eighth graders with a wide range of intellectual and cultural diversity, and many of them don't want to do any work at school, it seems. Other than that, they're fine.

MARY: When you get a combination like that, it usually complicates your life. Have you come up with any creative ways of dealing with them?

ABE: I'm working on one. Yesterday, I went to the guidance office, and Sherry let me collect information about my pupils from their folders. Having seen how diverse they really are, I've decided that the best way to work with them would be to divide them systematically into heterogeneous groups and have the groups work together on projects.

DON: How did you decide to divide them up?

ABE: I thought about that a lot while I was reviewing their records, so when I went home yesterday, I wrote each pupil's name, ethnic background, IQ score, and social studies and total score on the Metropolitan Achievement Test, whether the pupil qualifies for free lunch, and whether he or she prefers to work alone or in a group.

MARY: (enthusiastically) Wow! I'm really impressed. I can hardly wait to see how you used all that information! I divided my pupils into groups, but I used only their reading level.

ABE: Well, it really helped to have the information on cards because I decided that it would be manageable to have six groups of six pupils each. I began by identifying the six brightest pupils. I put one in each group. Then I found the six poorest pupils and put one in each group. Next, based on the remainder of the information on the cards, I added the other four pupils so that the groups would be fairly mixed in terms of ability, SES [socioeconomic status], work preference, and racial or ethnic group.

DON: I'm impressed too. How long did it take you to assign pupils to the six groups?

ABE: It really took me longer than I anticipated. I started as soon as I got home from school. Then I ate dinner. After dinner, I went through the piles several more times and rearranged them. Then, I took some time to consider several types of assignments. After that, I went through the cards one more time and made a few changes. By then it was almost bedtime. I spent more than five hours in all. But I really consider that to be time well spent.

MARY: Now that you've arranged the class into heterogeneous groups, what kinds of assignments are you going to give them?

ABE: (hesitating) I'm not really sure. In fact, I was planning to ask you what kinds of assignments you gave to the pupils you grouped by reading levels.

MARY: I grouped my pupils by reading levels because in my class we read literature. I found that their reading levels ranged from Grade two through Grade nine, with more than half of them below sixth grade. You'll probably find the same situation in your class.

ABE: I imagine I will. But how did you use this information to make class assignments?

MARY: That's the beauty of reading-level grouping. After I assigned them to groups by their reading levels, I was able to let them choose their own books to read. Our library has a great collection of trade books, and Susan, our librarian, has them grouped by levels of reading difficulty. You might consider allowing your pupils to read trade books in history instead of the textbooks. That way, Susan could help them select books at their own reading level.

ABE: (apologetically) I'm embarrassed to have to ask this, but what are trade books?

MARY: (smiling) Well, we English types know what trade books are because they make life easier for us and our pupils. Trade books are literary selections not written primarily for instructional purposes. I'm sure there must be thousands of trade books that would be appropriate for teaching history. What are you teaching now?

ABE: The discovery of America.

MARY: Wow! There must be zillions of trade books you could use for that— biographies of Christopher Columbus, Amerigo Vespucci, Queen Isabella, Indian chiefs, books about ships, explorers, and stories of the various Indian tribes that were living in America then. (Pauses) See, I just thought of these books instantly, without half trying. I'm sure that with your knowledge of history, you could find enough trade books to teach your entire course. They're written at all levels of difficulty and are really interesting for kids.

ABE: Trade books sound interesting. There's no question that my pupils would have an easier time reading them than they're having with the text we're using now. (A bell rings signaling the end of the period.) Thanks to both of you for the great suggestions!

Several days later the pupils in Abe's sixth-period class enter the room, sit with the other members of their group, and begin to work on reports that they have negotiated with Abe. Each group had chosen a major topic related to the discovery of America. Each major topic was divided into six subtopics. Each group member was responsible for a report and presentation on the topic he or she had chosen.

ABE: I'm really proud of this class. You're becoming good workers already. I'm sure your reports will be excellent. Today I'll visit each group and see how the research on your topics is coming. If you have questions, ask me while I'm with your group. (He walks over toward the closest group. Just then there is a loud noise followed by shouting.)

EDWARD: (loudly) Connie, what's wrong with you! That globe'll break if you drop it on the floor!

CONNIE: (on the verge of tears) I was just looking at it.

EDWARD: I'm using that globe for my report! You don't need to be messing with it!

CONNIE: (shouting) I said I'm sorry. I didn't mean to drop it. (Begins to cry)

EDWARD: So what! Just leave my stuff alone. (Connie returns to her seat and continues to sob.)

ABE: (walks to Connie's chair) You're all right, Connie. Ed was just upset that you dropped the globe that he needs to write his report.

CONNIE: (sobbing almost out of control) Everybody's so mean to me. I didn't mean to do anything wrong. I'm just so upset. I need to go to the office.

ABE: Why do you need to go to the office?

CONNIE: My mother gave Ritalin tablets to the principal so that his secretary can give me one when I need it. (Sobbing) I need one now, I'm so upset.

ABE: I don't know anything about this arrangement, Connie. You just sit here until you feel better. Then join your group and work on your report. I'll walk with you to the office as soon as class is over and find out about these arrangements you mentioned.

CONNIE: (sobbing again) But I'm telling the truth. My mother came in this afternoon and made the arrangements.

ABE: I believe you, Connie, but I don't know anything about these arrangements. As soon as I find out what they are, I'll be happy to let you go. (Connie continues to cry. Abe walks back to the group he was approaching before the fall of the world. He stops beside Barbara.) Wow, Barbara! You really have a pile of information there. Are you planning to go on a cruise?

BARBARA: (smiling) No, these travel brochures are for my report on the differences between the lives of Columbus's sailors and the lives of sailors today. I went to the Star Travel Agency and found all these brochures on some of their cruises. They give good information on the size and equipment of their cruising ships.

ABE: That's a great idea, Barbara. Do you have the same type of information on Columbus's ships?

BARBARA: Yes, I found a book in the library that described them.

ABE: Terrific! So now all you need to do is write a report comparing the life aboard one of Columbus's ships with life on a modern ship.

BARBARA: (with resignation) I just can't do it. I have all the information about the ships, but it doesn't tell anything about the lives of the sailors. I haven't been able to find any books that tell about sailors' lives.

ABE: But Barbara, you have all the information you need right here to compare the sailors' lives. Make a list of some of the things today's sailors can do because they have electricity, motors, navigational equipment, and radios that Columbus's sailors couldn't do. Just use your own ideas.

BARBARA: I just can't make things up out of my mind. I need information that I can see.

ABE: Let's think about this for a minute. Did the early sailors have air-conditioning?

BARBARA: No.

ABE: Then how would that make their life different from today's sailors?

BARBARA: I don't know. I can't think that way.

ABE: Well, what does air-conditioning do?

BARBARA: (on the verge of tears) I don't know. I just don't know! Don't ask me all those questions. I can't work this way. You expect me to figure out all these things by myself, and I can't. Teachers are supposed to tell us what we need to know and then test us on it to see if we learned it. (Puts her head facedown on the desk and covers it with her arms. Abe stands by her desk for a while, but she won't look up, so he moves on to Aaron's desk.) Aaron, you're writing on the Indian tribes who lived in eastern America around the time of Columbus, aren't you?

AARON: (pointing to a pile of trade books on his desk) Yes. I found all these books on these five different tribes that were in America. I read them and learned a lot about how Indians live, but I'm really having trouble writing a report that tells the differences between the tribes. I just get all mixed up when I try to separate them from each other.

CONNIE: (stomping her foot and screaming loudly) Kevin! Let me alone! Go away! You're bothering me!

KEVIN: (getting out of his seat and confronting Connie) Shut up and go back to your seat, stupid! You're a real nerd! You walk up and down the aisle poking me with your finger while I'm trying to work. Then you scream bloody murder when I tell you to stop! (Turning to Abe) Mr. Goodman, can't you do something about this pest?

ABE: (sternly) Both of you—calm down. Connie, what are you doing on this side of the room? Your desk is way over there. (Connie hangs her head and remains silent.) Kevin! Why do you have to yell out and disturb everybody in the class?

KEVIN: (yelling) I get tired of her bothering me when I'm trying to work!

ABE: Connie, I want you to move your desk to the front of the room next to my desk. I don't want to see you up walking around unless you raise your hand and get permission from me. Do you understand me?

CONNIE: (shouting) It's your fault! You wouldn't let me get my pill!

ABE: (slowly and sternly) We're going to talk about your pills after class! Now do as I asked! (Turning to Kevin) Kevin, go back to your seat and continue your work. Connie won't bother you anymore. (At this point, the bell rings and Abe gratefully dismisses the class.)

During his free period the following day, Abe enters the office of Mark Reid, the curriculum supervisor.

ABE: (extends his hand) Mark, I'm Abe Goodman, the new eighth-grade teacher. I appreciate your seeing me so quickly. As I told you when I called yesterday, I'm looking for some suggestions that'll help me be more effective with my sixth-period American history class. A number of teachers have recommended you highly and suggested that I talk with you.

MARK: Well, I'm pleased that some of our faculty think I'm doing my job well. How can I help you?

ABE: My sixth-period American history class is extremely diverse. They're generally pretty well behaved, but some of them just seem unable to learn the material. For instance, one of the girls did research on the differences between Columbus's three ships and modern-day ocean liners. She'd written several pages of statistics, but she was unable to use them to write a comparison between the old and new ships. Another pupil had a similar problem. He found quite a bit of information on various Indian tribes. He's very well informed on the common characteristics of those tribes but isn't able to tell how they differ. He just couldn't see the forest for the trees.

MARK: I guess all classes have pupils who are better analyzers than others and respond better to certain approaches to teaching, such as problem solving, drill, individual reading, group reading, or lecture.

ABE: Yes, but in my class this is a major problem.

MARK: I see. Have you considered using grouping procedures for dealing with your students' analyzing differences?

ABE: Well, I recently divided them into heterogeneous groups, hoping that the good pupils would help some of the poorer ones. But most of the poorer pupils have such poor backgrounds that they seem to be beyond help. Other pupils prefer to work independently.

MARK: Have you considered homogeneous grouping—putting the analyzers and nonanalyzers in different groups? Or perhaps put the nonanalyzers together and work with the analyzers on an independent study basis, since they're often more self-directing. The nonanalyzers often need more structure and support, in my experience.

ABE: No, I really didn't consider grouping the students that way. I guess I have a bias when it comes to homogeneous grouping. Somehow that approach seems undemocratic. Maybe I'm wrong, but it seems to me that part of our job as teachers is to help kids from varying backgrounds and ability levels learn to get along and work with one another. Somehow homogeneous grouping doesn't seem compatible with that goal.

MARK: I understand your position, Abe, and I respect it. Perhaps we should consider, then, how to make your heterogeneous grouping approach work more effectively.

ABE: I don't want you to think that none of my groups are working. Some of them work quite well.

MARK: Can you put your finger on what makes your good groups work well?

ABE: Now that I think about it, in the good groups the stronger students help the weaker ones. I don't know, maybe it is the analyzers helping the non-analyzers. Also, thanks to Mary Johnson, I learned about trade books, which helped me meet the various reading needs of some of my weaker students.

MARK: Well, it seems as if you're experimenting with several approaches to teaching. But with regard to pupils helping other pupils, sometimes that helps the good pupils as well as the slow ones.

ABE: Perhaps some of my groups aren't working because of other differences in the class besides the analyzer/nonanalyzer one we've talked about.

MARK: Oh? Such as?

ABE: There are so many differences that I don't know where to begin! I've gathered information on my students' differences from their cumulative records. I used this information to group them. (Hands sheet to Mark) Besides racial and ethnic differences, there are IQ differences, plus I have two exceptional students, Connie Petty and Kevin Felton. You'll also notice differences in work preferences, which I got from a questionnaire I gave them.

MARK: Do your analyzers prefer to work independently and your nonanalyzers in groups?

ABE: Yes, that's the general pattern.

MARK: Tell me about your exceptional students. What kinds of disabilities do they have?

ABE: Connie Petty is ADHD, and the other day she announced that her mother had made arrangements with the principal to allow her to take a Ritalin pill twice a day when she or I decide that she needs one. But I hadn't even been consulted. I checked with the front office after class, and indeed, this is the case. I'd already recognized that Connie has trouble sustaining her attention. In fact, I had just this morning moved her seat close to my desk, away from other pupils.

MARK: And the other student? I believe you said his name is Kevin?

ABE: Yes, Kevin Felton. He's diagnosed as socially maladjusted. When he's annoyed he goes out of control, and this happens several times a day.

MARK: Let me ask you this, Abe: Are Connie and Kevin in the groups that you are having trouble with?

ABE: Oh, yes. They had a big blowup in class the other day. But as I've been saying, they aren't the only ones having trouble in my sixth-period class. (Pause) What do you think, Mark? Do you think I should change my grouping procedures, or even get rid of them? But what can I do to deal with so many differences in one class?

Figure 5–1 Information Collected by Mr. Goodman on His Sixth-Period History Students

Name and Ethnic Origin[1]	IQ[2]	Total Score[3]	Soc St. Subtest[3]	Eligible for Free Lunch	Work Preference[4]
1. Adams, Anthony (W)	110	5	5	No	I
2. Aguila, Angela (H)	90	3	3	Yes	G
3. Brown, Lamar (AA)	90	3	2	Yes	G
4. Edwards, Elaine (AA)	95	4	4	Yes	G
5. Castillo, Maria (H)	90	3	4	Yes	G
6. Collins, Horace (AA)	80	2	1	Yes	G
7. Davis, Terry (W)	96	3	4	No	G
8. Edmonds, Edward (W)	84	3	3	No	I
9. Epling, Sally (W)	102	4	4	No	I
10. Espinoza, Edwardo (H)	96	3	1	Yes	G
11. Evans, Christina (W)	105	5	5	No	I
12. Felton, Kevin (W)	95	3	3	Yes	I
13. Griffith, Lawanda (AA)	88	2	1	Yes	G
14. Gulley, Moses (AA)	80	2	1	Yes	G
15. Ho, Wan (A)	110	5	5	No	I
16. Jackson, Elijah (A)	100	2	1	Yes	G
17. Jarvis, Robert (AA)	95	3	3	Yes	G
18. Johnson, Sarah (W)	103	4	4	No	I
19. Kane, Charles (W)	100	4	3	No	I
20. Lake, Sharon (W)	97	3	3	Yes	I
21. Matthews, Elaine (W)	101	4	4	No	I
22. Nazario, Merida (H)	96	3	2	Yes	G
23. Nero, Charles (AA)	96	3	2	No	G
24. Norton, Pearl (AA)	98	4	4	No	G
25. Owens, Janet (W)	106	5	5	Yes	I
26. Patrick, Natasha (AA)	94	3	2	Yes	G
27. Petty, Constance (W)	98	3	2	Yes	I
28. Rozelle, Patricia (W)	102	3	3	No	G
29. Samuels, Barbara (W)	89	2	1	Yes	G
30. Thompson, Martha (W)	107	5	5	No	I
31. Vaughn, Paula (W)	89	2	1	No	G
32. Velasques, Iona (H)	85	2	1	Yes	I
33. Williams, Victoria (W)	109	5	5	No	I
34. Wilson, Aaron (AA)	105	5	2	Yes	G
35. Yin, Chan (A)	115	5	6	No	I
36. Zimmer, Karl (A)	102	4	4	No	G

[1]W = Non-Hispanic white; H = Hispanic; AA = African-American; A = Asian-American
[2]IQ = Total IQ on California Test of Mental Maturity
[3]Total and Social Studies subtest stanine scores, Metropolitan Achievement Test
[4]I = Individual work preference; G = Group work preference

■ **Questions**

1. What is diversity in the field of education? What kinds of diversity are portrayed in this case? What kinds of diversity exist in this situation that Abe recognizes, and what kinds does he not recognize?

2. What are ethnic differences, and how do they differ from racial differences? What kinds of ethnic differences exist among students in this case? Do students prefer to work with students from the same or a similar ethnic background? Why? What is the best way for teachers to deal with biases toward certain ethnic groups?

3. What are racial differences, and which ones are portrayed in this case? What teaching methods work best with students from different racial backgrounds? How can teachers cope with racial biases?

4. Two of Abe's students have trouble "seeing the forest for the trees." What are field dependence and field independence in the cognitive style literature? Do field dependent/independent students prefer to work independently or in groups with structure?

5. Two of Abe's students have disabilities. What kinds of disabilities do they have, and what is the most effective way to work with these students? How well did Abe handle them? What effect is Ritalin supposed to have on persons with ADHD? How effective are such drugs?

6. Abe tries to deal with his class by setting up heterogeneous groups based on information that he obtained from his students and their cumulative records. Is this the best way to group these students in this situation? What might be a better way?

7. In terms of teacher expectancy or self-fulfilling prophecy theory, does Abe evidence any biases toward any of his students? What are the best ways to deal with such biases?

8. How would you describe Abe's view of the nature of learning? Would a cognitive or behavioral model best fit his learning orientation? What model of learning would you advise Abe to consider applying in this situation?

9. What is Bloom's cognitive taxonomy? At which of Bloom's levels are Abe's students able to work? At which levels are Barbara and Aaron not able to operate? How can a teacher help students move to higher levels of thinking?

10. What advice should Mark give Abe? What teaching methods might work in this situation? What should Abe do differently?

6

Double Trouble

Key Content to Consider for Analyzing This Case:

1. Exceptionalities (Especially ADHD, Behavior Disorders)
2. Behavior Modification
3. Observational Learning
4. Classroom Management

Martha Thompson is a 27-year-old African-American who joined the faculty of Jackson Elementary School as a fourth-grade teacher upon graduating from college a year ago. Jackson Elementary School is located in an old section of a large metropolitan city in southeastern United States. The school has a student population of approximately 900 pupils and has four sections at each grade level from K-6. This population represents an equal mix of low-SES residents and upper-SES families who have restored large old homes located in the district served by the school.

Martha married her college sweetheart during her final year of college. Her husband works in an accounting firm on the same side of town as the school. The Thompsons reside in a large old home which they bought last year with the intention of gradually restoring it while they live in it.

It is Monday morning of the second week of school. Martha's 24 fourth-grade students are reading independently from the trade books they have selected from the classroom library. There is a knock on the door. As Martha walks toward the door, Art Hagstrom, a special education teacher, opens it and smiles. He has two boys with him.

ART: Good morning, Ms. Thompson. Nice to see you again.

MARTHA: Hi, Mr. Hagstrom. To what do I owe this pleasant surprise? And who are the young men accompanying you?

ART: (nodding toward one of the boys) This young man's Bill Matz, and (nodding toward the other boy) this young man's Evan Carter.

MARTHA: (smiling) Hello, Bill. Hello, Evan. Why don't you boys take a seat? (She looks towards Art for an explanation as the boys move away.)

ART: If you recall during the pre-school workshops three weeks ago, Ms. Jamison [principal] told us that our school district's making an effort this year to mainstream more special needs pupils out of separate special education classes and into regular classes.

MARTHA: Yes, I do recall that. I assumed that this was to be done the first day of class.

ART: (apologetically) We tried to place the students before school started, but the criteria for placement are pretty complicated, and we just finished making the assignments last week.

MARTHA: (smiling at the boys, who are seated) And Bill and Evan are going to be in my class?

ART: Yes. They'll be in your class all year.

MARTHA: (walking over and shaking each boy's hand) Bill. Evan. Welcome to my class (Pointing to different seats) Bill, this can be your seat. Evan, that can be your seat. (Evan flops down in his seat with great fanfare.) Is there anything else you can tell me while you're here, Art? I'd like to get these boys started on some reading.

EVAN: (shouting loudly) Oh, no! I hate reading!

ART: (ignoring Evan) No, it looks to me like you're doing fine. I'll come to your room to help you work with these boys. We can set up a regular schedule after they get settled.

MARTHA: That's good. I'll probably need some help, because I haven't had much instruction on working with special education students.

ART: (reassuring her) I'm sure you'll do fine. I'll be in touch real soon. (Leaves the room)

MARTHA: Now, class. I want you to continue reading your books. (To Bill and Evan) Come with me to the bookshelves, and we'll find you books to read.

BILL: That's OK. I don't want a book. I don't like to read. I can't read very good.

EVAN: Me neither.

MARTHA: You don't need to worry about that in this class. I've arranged all the books on these shelves from easy to hard. (Pointing to the K-3 bookshelf) These are the easiest books on the bottom shelf. The hardest are on the top shelf. The others are in between. Pick your books from this shelf here (points to the K-3 bookshelf). These are fairly easy books you can start with. Then you'll find out whether you can read harder ones. Take a few minutes to find a book you want, then show it to me. (Walks to the center of the room to see that everyone is reading. After a few minutes, Evan leaves the book corner and walks toward Martha.)

EVAN: Ms. Thompson, I'm not gonna read a book. I don't like to read, and I can't do it very well. Can't I do something else besides reading? I'm a good drawer. Could I draw instead of reading?

MARTHA: (enthusiastically) That's great that you can draw, Evan. I like to have somebody who can draw in my class, and you'll be able to get grades sometimes for drawing. But you'll also have to read. That's one of the main things people learn in school—to read. Maybe you can draw scenes from stories you read.

EVAN: (just about to cry) But I can't read. I get upset when I try to read.

MARTHA: (enthusiastically) I know what you can do, Evan. Find a book on this shelf [pointing] that has an interesting cover. Then you can draw the scene that's on the cover. After that, maybe I can help you read the book.

BILL: (interrupting) Ms. Thompson. Here's a book I'm going to read.(Evan takes a book off the shelf and walks back to his seat.)

MARTHA: (reading the title of Bill's book) *Daddy Is a Monster . . . Sometimes.* That's a neat title. Why'd you pick this book?

BILL: I don't know. It just sounded good. I looked at a couple of pages in it, and I can read them.

MARTHA: (handing the book back to Bill) Great! It sounds interesting. I hope you like it. (Bill takes the book and walks back toward his seat. On the way he hits Malcolm hard on the back of the head with the book.)

MALCOLM: (jumping out of his chair and knocking it over) Hey, why'd you hit me! I didn't do anything to you!

BILL: (shoving Malcolm down over his upturned chair) Because I don't like the way you look! You look like a wimp!

MALCOLM: (scrambling to get up off the floor) What's the matter with you? You're crazy!

BILL: (shoving him over the chair again before he can regain his footing) Who're you calling crazy? Not me! Nobody calls me bad names! (Malcolm falls hard again.)

MARTHA: (Rushing over to the boys, Martha grabs Bill and pushes him toward his chair.) (Crossly) Go sit down this instant! (She helps Malcolm get untangled from his desk.) Are you all right, Malcolm?

MALCOLM: (rubbing his elbow) I skinned this elbow when I fell, but I'm all right, I guess.

MARTHA: That's good. I'm glad you're not hurt seriously, but I'm not sure what happened between you two.

MALCOLM: I didn't do nothing! That new guy's really a creep!

At the end of the following school day, Martha goes to see Art Hagstrom in the special education office. Since she had made an appointment the previous day, he is expecting her. The door is open when she arrives. Art sees her approaching and motions her to come in.

ART: I'm glad you called about Bill and Evan. I wanted to talk with you at length before I put them in your class, but as I told you, the placements for the mainstreamed students were made the same morning that I brought them to your class.

MARTHA: (sighing) Well, the two of them together are really challenging. They take more of my time than all the other pupils in the class put together. The two days he's been in my class, Bill's started three fights. He seems unable to relate either to adults or to age-mates. On Monday, he was all over the classroom annoying other students. He got into three fights. Today, he sat and stared at the wall all day and totally ignored the other students and me.

ART: (smiling) I was afraid of that. He's been diagnosed as having a behavior disorder.

MARTHA: (exaggerated) Well! Great! But I'm not really interested in what they've labeled him. I want to know what I can do to help him learn something!

ART: I know, and I intend to help you to teach him. But first, tell me about Evan.

MARTHA: Evan worries me more than Bill does. He's so disorganized he can't do anything. He forgets what the assignment is, even before he begins. He doesn't listen well. He can't concentrate. He can't even copy information accurately. He just seems like a zero personality. He can't stay on task or sit still for thirty seconds. He's constantly out of his seat disturbing other students or messing around with objects in the room.

ART: Evan's been diagnosed as having attention deficit hyperactivity disorder, better known as ADHD. As you know, such disorders can't be corrected easily or quickly, but there are some things we can use to help these students learn to take some responsibilities for their actions.

MARTHA: (relieved) That's welcome news. I've never had any courses in special education. I don't feel confident in working with these two students.

ART: (smiling) From the little I've observed in your class, you seem to be quite sensitive to the needs of all your students. That's half the battle. When I brought Bill and Evan to your class, I told you that I'd help you work with them. I have free time from 9 o'clock to 10 o'clock on Monday, Wednesday, and Friday mornings. Would it be OK if I come to your class at those times to help with Bill and Evan?

MARTHA: (delighted) Would it! You've made my whole day! As you work with them, maybe you could make specific suggestions to me on how to change their behavior.

ART: I'm sure that we'll find something that works if we try enough different strategies. They've had a lot of success using behavior modification with behavior disorders, and drugs like Ritalin can help with ADHD students.

MARTHA: I've tried to work on classroom management this week. I had the class establish behavior guidelines and penalties for violating them. They're working well for everyone but Bill and Evan.

ART: That's good. That way Bill and Evan won't feel discriminated against if we enforce those rules. Evan's records indicate that his doctor prescribed Ritalin for him. Has he gone to the school nurse to take it?

MARTHA: He has some, but he often forgets to take it, and frankly, I've forgotten to remind him.

ART: Well, let's make out a schedule and post it to make sure he takes it at regular intervals. That'll probably help him control his outbursts.

MARTHA: That's a good idea. I'll look for you tomorrow morning, then?

ART: Yes, I'll be there around 9 o'clock as usual.

MARTHA: I'll see you then, Art.

The following morning Art comes to Martha's class a little before nine. Martha suggests that he might like to help Evan read a story. He finds that although Evan can say most of the words, he can't follow the meanings of the sentences.

The more Evan reads, the more frustrated he becomes. He loses his place in the story, mispronounces words, and can't remember what's happened earlier in the story.

The other students are working quietly in groups on social studies units. Martha is moving among the groups to help them as needed. Suddenly, the hum of conversation among the students working on their projects is shattered by a loud exclamation.

JACK: (jumping from his chair after Bill jabbed him with a pin) Damn you, Bill! You're really a jerk! (He grabs a handful of Bill's hair and pulls him out of his chair onto the floor.)

BILL: (screaming at the top of his lungs) Let go of my hair, jackass! Let go of me or I'll kill you. (He throws his weight against Jack and drives him against the wall. He repeatedly lunges into Jack with his shoulder.)

ART: (jumps out of his chair and runs toward Bill and Jack) Bill! Stop that immediately!

MARTHA: (running toward the struggling boys) Boys! Stop that! Take your seats immediately!

Martha and Art reach the boys at the same time and manage to separate them. Martha takes Jack to his seat, and Art escorts Bill to the principal's office.

That same day, immediately after the students are dismissed, Art sticks his head into Martha's classroom.

ART: Anybody home?

MARTHA: (coming out from beside the bookshelves) Yes, I'm straightening out the books. How're you doing?

ART: I came to see if you had time to talk about the fiasco this morning and to see what we could do to avoid future problems of that type.

MARTHA: Sure. I've been thinking about that incident since it happened. I think Bill's a dangerous person, and I'm worried about what he could do in my class.

ART: I agree. And that's one of the reasons why I'm here. The other reason is that I have some information about Bill that I haven't shared with you yet.

MARTHA: I'm certainly interested in learning all I can about Bill. Tell me what you know.

ART: Well, I think that Bill may come by his abusive tendencies naturally.

MARTHA: Why do you say that?

ART: Well, one day last year after classes were over, I left the building and saw Bill on the basketball court shooting baskets with two or three other guys. Then I saw a man that I later found out was Bill's father striding quite purposefully across the field. He walked to the basketball court, grabbed Bill by the shoulders, and shouted at him at the top of his voice that Bill was supposed to be waiting in the parking lot. He shook Bill pretty hard, and then literally threw him toward the parking lot. Bill almost fell to the ground. Bill's father then unlocked the car door on the passenger side, opened it, grabbed Bill's arm, and shoved him roughly across the seat. He then went to the driver's side, started the motor, and burned rubber for about thirty yards as he squealed out of the parking lot.

MARTHA: Sounds as if I'm dealing with a "like father, like son" situation. Maybe Bill's selection of the book *Daddy Is a Monster . . . Sometimes* wasn't just a coincidence.

ART: I'd say based on what I saw that's definitely the case.

MARTHA: Then, I guess I'd better forget my plans to call his father. He probably wouldn't be willing or able to offer me much support with Bill. I think we're better off making our own plans.

ART: I think so, too. And I think it's important for us to consider using a behavior modification procedure like time-out with Bill the minute he begins to get out of control.

MARTHA: That's fine with me! We just can't have him disrupting the entire class every day and give him an opportunity to seriously injure one of the other students. What kind of time-out procedure do you have in mind? How do you use time-out? I've never tried it.

ART: Well, I checked with Ms. Jamison, and she told me that the small room adjoining her office is vacant all day and that we can use it as a time-out room. I could take Bill there, and he would be monitored by the principal and the secretaries while he's there.

MARTHA: (excited) That's perfect! Let's do that! How long will he stay there?

ART: Let's start with fifteen minutes. We can lengthen it, if necessary.

MARTHA: I'm glad we're going to help Bill develop some self-control. Let's begin the time-out as soon as you come in on Friday. We'll need to explain it all to Bill first.

ART: That's fine with me. (Enthusiastically) Friday's the day!

Before the pupils arrive on Friday, Martha arranges the chairs in circles for the groups and lays out their project materials. She notices that Bill has taken some notes relating to a group project. She puts Evan's book on his desk.

When Art arrives a little before nine, the groups are busy at work. Bill is taking notes from a reference book. Evan is at his desk with his book open, looking around.

ART: (smiling, nods toward Martha and sits down beside Evan) Good morning, Evan. How're you coming with your book?

EVAN: Not too good. I have trouble reading it.

ART: Do you like the book so far?

EVAN: Yes, I like the book, but I just can't stay in the right place.

ART: How would it be if I'd read the book to you for a while.

EVAN: (smiles) (enthusiastically) I'd like that!

ART: Good. Here we go. (Begins to read with much expression)

As Martha circulates from one group to another, she is pleased at how well the class is going. Then, she remembers that she and Art haven't told Bill about the time-out procedure. She looks in Bill's direction and sees that he is not working on his assignment but is staring into space. She walks over toward him.

MARTHA: (softly) Bill, I need to talk to you about something. (Pauses) Bill, you've gotten into a lot of fights lately, and that has to stop. The next time that happens, I'm going to say "time out" to you and you'll need to leave the room with Mr. Hagstrom for fifteen minutes. He'll tell you when you can come back to class. Do you understand?

BILL: I guess so. Can I go out in the hall and get a drink?

MARTHA: Yes, that'll be all right. But come right back. (Martha circulates from group to group answering questions and observing their progress.)

Art stops reading and gives the book to Evan to read aloud. As he is listening to Evan try to figure out the pronunciation of words in the story, he glances out the window at the playground equipment. He catches sight of Bill furtively coming out of a door and going around a corner of the building. He immediately tells Evan to read silently, gets up, and walks over to Martha.

ART: I just saw Bill leave the building. I'm going out to get him.

MARTHA: (angrily) It's my fault. I guess I felt sorry for him when I told him about time-out and let him go. I'm sorry.

ART: (reassuringly) Don't take the blame for a student who deliberately breaks rules. Don't worry. I'll get him back.

Art walks quickly out of the building in the direction he saw Bill take. As he rounds the building, he sees Bill walking quickly down the street away from the school building. Since Art is behind Bill, he can run toward him without Bill's seeing him. He comes within reach of Bill before Bill is aware of his being there.

ART: (taking Bill firmly by the arm) You need to come back to class with me, Bill. Walking away from school is considered truancy. You don't want to be truant. That's breaking the law.

BILL: (jerking his arm away from Art) Lemme go! Keep your hands offa' me, man!

ART: (taking a firmer grip on Bill's arm and pushing him forcefully toward the school) I'm taking you back to your class right now!

BILL: (runs forward, then twists quickly and breaks Art's grip) Leave me alone! Let me go! (He runs away from Art.)

ART: (catches up with Bill and grabs him) You're coming with me!

BILL: (Spins around and hits Art hard on the jaw) I'm not going back to school! Leave me alone!

ART: (Hurt and infuriated, he grabs Bill around the neck from behind with his left arm and twists Bill's right arm up behind his back with his right arm.) Now you've done it! I'm tired of being gentle with you. (Shoves him forward) Now march back to the school and be quick about it!

BILL: (walking ahead of Art reluctantly) What are you going to do to me when we get back?

ART: I don't know yet. But whatever it is, you won't like it! I could have you arrested for assault.

BILL: (quite upset) You won't do that, will you?

ART: Probably not, but it might be good for you. It would teach you to respect other people's rights.

BILL: If I promise not to run away, will you let me walk by myself into the school?

ART: Are you embarrassed to have me hold onto you when we enter the building?

BILL: Yeah, everyone would make fun of me.

ART: (smiling) Yeah, that'd be bad. OK, it's a deal. (Releases his hold on Bill. They walk into the classroom together.)

After classes are dismissed the following Monday afternoon, Martha and Art meet with Carolyn Nevin, a school psychologist, in her office.

MARTHA: Thanks for seeing us on such short notice, Carolyn. We need some help dealing with the two special education students in our class.

CAROLYN: (smiling) That's why I'm here. The two students we're talking about are Bill Matz and Evan Carter, right? (Hands both teachers a sheet of paper) I've been looking at their IEPs [individualized education programs], and I've prepared a handout on their disabilities that I hope will be helpful.

MARTHA: Good. We've had them in class for a week now, and frankly, we don't know what to do with them. Everything we've tried has failed. Art and I spend ninety percent of our time working with those two, and we've been unsuccessful most of the time.

CAROLYN: Describe "unsuccessful" for me.

ART: The most notable "unsuccessful" for me was getting hit by Bill on Friday afternoon. I chased him down when he was trying to run away from school.

CAROLYN: (sympathetically) Yes, I'd call that unsuccessful.

MARTHA: Neither of these boys is learning a thing. Bill physically abuses other students regularly, and Evan's like a loose cannon rambling around the classroom unable to attend to anything for more than five minutes or so. And that's with one-to-one tutoring. We were going to try time-out with Bill, but we never had the chance before he ran away.

Figure 6–1 Handout Prepared by Carolyn Nevin, School Psychologist, on Behavior Disorders and ADHD

Behavior Disorders

Symptoms of pupils who are diagnosed as having behavior disorders:

1. inability to learn that cannot be explained by intellectual or health problems
2. poor relationships with others
3. extreme reactions to ordinary events
4. moodiness or depression
5. fear or physical problems related to school difficulties

Recommended teacher strategies for working with pupils who have behavior disorders:

1. explain to pupils how they cause negative reactions from classmates
2. assure pupils that others have similar problems
3. model appropriate responses to frustrating situations
4. praise desirable behavior when it occurs
5. clearly state expectations
6. realize that improvement is a long-term project

Attention Deficit Hyperactivity Disorders (ADHD)

Symptoms of pupils diagnosed with ADHD:

1. excessive general activity (haphazard climbing, crawling, or running)
2. difficulty in sustaining attention, remaining seated, being attentive
3. forgetful
4. impulsive, talks excessively, intrudes on others, and engages in dangerous activities such as dashing into the street without looking

Recommended treatment of pupils diagnosed with ADHD:

   The use of stimulant drugs such as Dexedrine and Ritalin has been found in some experiments to be twice as effective for treating pupils diagnosed with ADHD as behavior modification strategies.

ART: What we're saying is that we really need help. We need help in controlling the boys. We need to figure out how to help them get themselves under control and how to help them learn. We also want to turn the classroom back into a good learning environment for the other children in the class.

MARTHA: I think Art said it well. Can you help us, Carolyn?

Questions

1. How have the Education for All Handicapped Children Act (P.L.94-142) and the Individuals with Disabilities Education Act (IDEA) changed special education? What kinds of disabilities, ages, and types of diagnoses do these laws address? What educational treatments do they prescribe? How was special education conducted in the public schools prior to the passage of these laws?

2. What is a behavior disorder, and what forms can behavior disorders take? What are the signs and symptoms? What treatments are most effective with a behavior disorder like Bill's? How effective is behavior modification?

3. What is ADHD, and how does it differ from ADD? What are the signs and symptoms of ADHD? How well do drugs like Ritalin work with a student like Evan? How well does behavior modification work?

4. What is an IEP? Is such a program being followed by Art in working with Bill and Evan? Who designs an IEP? Who is responsible for its implementation?

5. Bill and Evan have been mainstreamed into Martha's class. How is mainstreaming supposed to work? What does the research say about the effectiveness of mainstreaming in terms of its effect on regular students as well as on the mainstreamed students? What attitudes do teachers, administrators, and parents have toward mainstreaming?

6. What are school psychologists, and what role do they play in special education? How does a school psychologist differ from a guidance counselor in a school or an educational psychologist?

7. Examine the relationship between Bill and his father from an observational learning perspective. Can children learn aggressive behavior from their parents? What can the teacher do in such cases?

8. Martha seems to have developed a classroom management procedure that worked with her regular students. What classroom management model would you recommend in her new situation?

9. Cooperative learning methods have been found to work well in some mainstreaming situations. Would you recommend them in this case? If so, which cooperative learning program?

10. Art and Martha decide to use a behavior modification technique called time-out with Bill. What is time-out, and how is it supposed to work? What mistakes do Art and Martha make in their attempts to use time-out? For example, what are differential reinforcement of other behavior (DRO) and differential reinforcement of low rates of responding (DRL), and how are they supposed to be used in conjunction with time-out?

7

Withdrawn Wanda

___

Key Content to Consider for Analyzing This Case:

1. Self-Concept
2. Learned Helplessness
3. Sense of Efficacy
4. Attribution Theory
5. Maslow's Need Hierarchy
6. Operant Conditioning
7. Child Abuse

Karen Young has taught social studies at Fairmont Middle School for 5 years. She also taught for 2 years at another middle school in the same city, Midland, which has a population of about 60,000 in a Midwestern state. Fairmont's attendance district is approximately 75% white and 25% African-American.

It is sixth period of the second day of classes, and Karen leads a discussion of prehistory with her ninth-grade world history class. The class has 32 students.

KAREN: We've all had a chance to read this interesting chapter on prehistory. I know that the dinosaurs always fascinate people because of movies like *Jurassic Park,* but we want to focus on people today or, to be more technical, Homo sapiens. Let's review a little from yesterday. Roger, how old is the earth?

ROGER: Four and a half billion years.

KAREN: Right! Now how long have human beings been on the earth? (Several hands go up.) Gloria?

GLORIA: About a million years, but I'm not sure that all those prehistoric people were human beings.

KAREN: Good answer, Gloria. Yes, certainly Homo sapiens haven't been on earth that long. What are the names of some of Homo sapiens' predecessors? Wanda? (Wanda stares at the floor and shakes her head.) You don't remember any of them, Wanda? (Wanda continues staring at the floor.) Barry, can you remember any of the names of our prehistoric ancestors?

BARRY: Yeah. Neanderthal man, Java man, and, what's that, oh, yeah, Peking man.

KAREN: Yes, Barry, very good! I'll bet you all remember Neanderthal man from *The Clan of the Cave Bear*. But the Neanderthals weren't our immediate ancestors, were they? (Hands go up.) Yes, Marilyn?

MARILYN: No. Cro-Magnon man was, and he lived about 25,000 years ago.

KAREN: Excellent, Marilyn. You people have really been working hard, I can tell! But think about this, people—Homo sapiens haven't been on earth very long. If the earth is four and a half billion years old and Cro-Magnon man has been here for only about 25,000 years, we are real new on the scene. Barry?

BARRY: My dad says that we've probably done more damage to the environment and killed more animals and people than all those early guys combined.

KAREN: I couldn't agree with your dad more, Barry. Homo sapiens may be a relatively new species on this planet, but we sure have caused a lot of trouble in that short period of time. (A few laughs) What do you think, Wanda? Can you think of some ways that Homo sapiens have either helped or harmed the earth? (Wanda looks down and shakes her head. Karen counts off 5 seconds to herself as she waits for Wanda to answer.) OK, Kristen, what do you think?

It is one week later. Karen has noticed Wanda's failure to participate in class in any way. She has resolved to draw Wanda out during class discussion.

KAREN: OK, people. We talked the last time about the end of the New Stone Age around 5000 B.C. Around that time civilization began. Wanda, do you remember that we talked a little about the rise of civilization? We said that certain developments took place that brought about the beginning of civilization. Can you name one of those for us? (Wanda frowns and looks down at the floor. Several hands go up. Karen counts off 5 seconds to herself.) OK, think about it, Wanda, and I'll come back to you in a minute. Yes, Donna?

DONNA: The development of writing was one of them.

KAREN: That's right, Donna, and maybe that's the most important one. Ray, what's another?

RAY: The development of metal tools.

KAREN: Absolutely! Wanda, have you thought of one yet? (Wanda stares at the floor.) Maybe one relating to what we would call business today? (Wanda just frowns.) OK, the development of trade, weren't you thinking of that, Wanda? (No response) Well, uh, Gloria, can you give us a more exact date for the beginning of civilization besides 5000 B.C.?

GLORIA: Yes, 4241 B.C. is the oldest date in recorded history.

KAREN: Very good, Gloria. What is that date from?

GLORIA: I'm not sure—I've forgotten.

KAREN: (moves directly in front of Wanda) I'll bet you can tell us where that date comes from, Wanda. Think now. (Wanda stares at floor as Karen counts off 5 seconds to herself.) OK, Barry?

BARRY: It's from the first calendar. It was developed by the Egyptians.

KAREN: (still in front of Wanda, speaks quietly) I'll bet you knew that, didn't you, Wanda? (Wanda nods her head.) OK, then, Toni Sue. Besides writing, metal tools, and the development of trade, what else had to develop before civilization could begin?

TONI SUE: Government.

KAREN: Absolutely. And we've had problems ever since, haven't we? (Several students laugh.)

It is Friday after school during the same week. Karen sits in her classroom talking to Mark Harris, a school psychologist in the local school system.

KAREN: Thanks for coming, Mark.

MARK: My pleasure, Karen. You said that you wanted to talk to me about Wanda Loveless. Are you considering referring her? I didn't get a chance to look at her cum record. We had a long staff meeting about farming out some of our testing, and I came directly here from the meeting. I do know a little about Wanda though. Several of her teachers consider her very shy and withdrawn. Is that the problem?

KAREN: I'll say! I've tried every trick in the book to draw her out, and she just won't participate. I sense she knows the answers, but she just won't talk!

MARK: Have you given any tests yet?

KAREN: Yes, and she does just fine on them—low B, high C range.

MARK: Sounds like she primarily has a social problem then.

KAREN: Yes, I guess so, but we're going to be working in groups soon, and I wonder if Wanda is going to be able to contribute.

MARK: That will be a good test, won't it? My guess is, based on her past behavior, that she won't participate much more working in a group with her peers than she did during class discussion.

KAREN: That's discouraging, Mark! But what do you think is going on here? Should she be referred to some program?

MARK: Let me look into her case a bit, Karen, before we do anything. Between you and me, it's possible that she's emotionally disturbed. But I don't want to jump the gun. Once you label a child as exceptional, the stereotype can be as bad as the disease, if you know what I mean.

KAREN: Not really.

MARK: What I mean is that teachers, other students, and sometimes even parents begin to relate to the child differently.

KAREN: I see what you mean.

MARK: I just want to take my time and be certain before we do anything.

KAREN: Of course. However, I have done one thing I hope you approve of.

MARK: What's that?

KAREN: I called Wanda's mother and asked her to come in for a conference.

MARK: Oh, boy! Mrs. Loveless?

KAREN: Yes. Why do you say it that way?

MARK: Did she agree to come see you without any protest?

KAREN: Yes, of course. Parents don't usually object to having a conference about their child. I guess she thinks it's about grades. But why, Mark?

MARK: Mrs. Loveless is a real battle-ax. Talking to her is a little like talking to a truck driver who's busy and in a hurry. Good luck!

KAREN: (smiling) Well thanks, Mark, for your good wishes! But seriously, she didn't protest, she seemed reasonable enough, and I just don't expect any trouble.

MARK: (smiling) OK. Let me know how it comes out, and meanwhile I'll look into Wanda's situation.

It is Wednesday of the next week, and students are working in small groups of six to nine members. Each group is focusing on a different cradle of civilization that developed around certain river valleys during the dawn of civilization around 5000

B.C. One group is working on Egypt, another on the Fertile Crescent, a third on India, and a fourth on China. As each group busily works on its report, Barry leaves the ancient Egyptian group and comes up to Karen's desk.

KAREN: Yes, Barry? What is it?

BARRY: Ms. Young, you said that everyone in the group will get the same grade for the group report?

KAREN: Yes, that's right.

BARRY: Well that doesn't seem fair! Some people aren't hardly doing anything, and they're going to get the same grade as me!

KAREN: Who are they, Barry? I'll talk to them.

BARRY: Well, it's mostly one person. Wanda.

KAREN: Really? Wanda? Well, you go back to your group, and in a little bit I'll call Wanda up and talk to her about it. And I'd appreciate it, Barry, if you'd do your very best to work with Wanda. I think she's shy.

BARRY: (leaving) I think she's lazy! (Five minutes later Karen calls Wanda up to her desk. She motions for Wanda to sit in a chair next to her desk. Wanda looks away from Karen's eyes as Karen talks to her.)

KAREN: Wanda, I've been wanting a chance to talk to you, and this is the first real class time we've had. (Pause) Wanda, I've tried to call on you in class several times, and I'm certain you know the answer, but you just don't seem to want to talk. Why is that?

WANDA: I don't know.

KAREN: But you do know, don't you, Wanda? Like the other day when I asked you who developed the first calendar. You knew the answer, didn't you? (Wanda nods her head.) Is it hard for you to talk to me, Wanda?

WANDA: (speaking barely above a whisper) No.

KAREN: Wanda, I want you to do well in here, and I know you are capable. Can't you tell me why you won't talk more?

WANDA: I don't know the answers. I can't remember all this stuff! It's too hard!

KAREN: Wanda, you've been getting good grades on the tests. You got nine out of ten on the last one. Don't you remember that?

WANDA: Yes, but I really didn't understand it. Sometimes I just seem to get it right.

KAREN: Well, Wanda, tell me about your group. Do you like working with the other students? (Wanda shakes her head.) Why not, Wanda?

WANDA: They just don't like me. They don't really care what I think.

KAREN: Well, Wanda, when you don't say anything, the group may begin to think that you don't know anything when you really know as much as any of them. Why don't you try to contribute more? Why don't you go back to the group now and see if you can't contribute at least three ideas. Will you do that for me?

WANDA: If I can.

KAREN: Did your mother tell you that she's coming in to have a conference with me next week?

WANDA: (with fear in her eyes) No! Why? I haven't done anything wrong, have I?

KAREN: (taken aback) No, Wanda, you haven't. But I like to meet the parents of as many of my students as I can. Since your mother has known you longer than I have, I thought that she might tell me some things that might help me get to know more about you so I can do a better job of teaching. That's all. Nothing to worry about.

WANDA: (frowning) Can I go back to my group now?

KAREN: Well, yes, I guess so. But Wanda, don't be afraid to speak up and let other people know what you know. OK?

WANDA: OK.

It is Friday of the next week after school. Karen meets Wanda's mother in her empty classroom. Ms. Loveless is a tall, heavy woman dressed in jeans. She shakes Karen's hand and takes a seat next to Karen's desk.

KAREN: Thanks for coming, Ms. Loveless. I wanted to talk to you about Wanda.

MS. LOVELESS: Is she doin' something wrong? Don't remember her bringin' home any bad grades.

KAREN: No, that's not the problem. Wanda can make B's when she applies herself.

MS. LOVELESS: Well, that's just it. Wanda can be lazy when she wants to. You just have to keep after her and not cut her any slack. I'll guarantee you she's not lazy around home. It's just her and me, you know. Her dad ran off with some young chick when Wanda was four.

KAREN: Oh, I didn't realize that you were divorced.

MS. LOVELESS: Yes, and I love it that way. I don't have to listen to some man tellin' me how to live my life. But I work at Central Electric and often get a lot of overtime. So Wanda has to pitch in and do her share. Of course, from what I've seen of a lot of kids these days, it's clear that a little discipline would do them good. So I guess what I'm tellin' you is that if Wanda slacks off in her work, just let me know. I'll back you up at home. I didn't get to be the only female foreman at Central by bein' lazy, and I'm not goin' to let Wanda learn bad habits.

KAREN: Well, Ms. Loveless, it isn't laziness that worries me. Wanda is just so shy and withdrawn. She just won't answer questions during class discussions, and she even seems to have trouble talking with other students when they are working in small groups.

MS. LOVELESS: (pondering) I guess I can see how she might be a bit shy. She and I don't get out much—maybe to church some Sundays. We mostly stay home nights and watch TV. She doesn't have any regular friends that come over. But I always make her do her homework first before she does her chores around the house. (Pause) But I think all you need to do is tell her that it's important to talk out and draw her out a bit. If that doesn't work, let her have it. I'll back you up.

KAREN: Yes, well, I have talked to her and have tried to draw her out as you put it. But, Ms. Loveless, she acts fearful, like she's scared of making a mistake all the time. I guess she doesn't try talking so she won't fail.

MS. LOVELESS: Like I said, just explain to her that it's important for her grades that she talk and don't mince any words. Really crack down on her if she doesn't do what you want. I'll guarantee you that it'll work. I do it at home with her all the time.

KAREN: (hesitantly) Ms. Loveless, I was wondering if that might not be part of the problem? Your coming down so hard on her at home all the time might be causing her to be fearful around other people.

MS. LOVELESS: (angrily) It sounds to me like you're telling me I'm a poor parent! I'd like to point out to you that you don't see Wanda goin' around beatin' up, insulting, and robbin' other folks! There are a lot of parents out there not doin' their jobs, but I'm not one of them! Even though I have to do the job alone, I do it right, and I don't need you tellin' me otherwise! You take care of the teachin' and I'll take care of the parentin'. (Storms out)

KAREN: Ms. Loveless, I . . .

It is Tuesday of the next week, and Karen meets with Wanda in her classroom alone after school.

KAREN: Wanda, I just wanted to compliment you on the score you made on the test that I gave Friday. I guess that you know by now that I talked to your mother that same day, and I would have told her about your good grade if I'd had a chance to grade them.

WANDA: Yes, I guess I got real lucky on that one.

KAREN: Wanda, do you really think that getting 87 of 100 points was just luck? Don't you think your hard work had something to do with it?

WANDA: That's just it. I have to work twice as hard as the other kids because I'm just so dense. I'm so envious of someone like Gloria Ashton—she doesn't need to study hardly at all and gets straight A's.

KAREN: Wanda, you're smart, too. It exasperates me that you keep putting yourself down like that all the time. Believe me, as your teacher who has taught a lot of students, you're not dumb! (Silence) Did your mother say anything about our conference?

WANDA: Yes.

KAREN: What did she say? Won't you tell me?

WANDA: She said that you told her that I'm as lazy at school as I am at home and that I'd better get busy and get my grades up or she'll come down on me. I don't think she likes you either.

KAREN: What did she say?

WANDA: She said that you're a know-it-all and she doesn't want any more to do with you.

KAREN: Oh, goodness! Now I wish I'd had some really good news to tell her, like your test score. Maybe that would have helped.

WANDA: No, she really wouldn't have cared. She would just have told me that I should try to do better. I really wish you hadn't talked to her.

KAREN: Why not, Wanda?

WANDA: Because she blames me for causing trouble and making her come to school to talk to you. It always turns out to be my fault! I just wish everybody would leave me alone!

Karen meets with Mark Harris, the school psychologist, in his office located in the district school board building downtown.

MARK: Come in, Karen. I'm sorry that you had to meet me here, but I had an important staff meeting before our appointment. Finances, you know. Thought we were never going to finish!

KAREN: Mark, I needed to talk to you about Wanda Loveless so badly that I would have agreed to meet you anywhere!

MARK: (laughing) Sounds really serious! What's going on?

KAREN: I met with Wanda's mother, and the conference turned into a real disaster. I think I may have hurt Wanda more than I helped her by talking to her mother.

MARK: I was afraid of that. What happened?

Figure 7–1 Fairmont Middle School
Cumulative Record

Name: Wanda M. Loveless	Home Phone: 384-5768
Address: 1423 Herera Avenue*	Former School: Rawlings Elementary
Father: Dewey J. Loveless	General Heath: Good
Occupation: Unknown	Handicaps: None
Address: Unknown	Date of Birth: 9/14/82
Mother: Rita L. Loveless	
Occupation: Forewoman	
Central Electric	
*Mother's address: parents divorced	

TEST RECORD
INTELLIGENCE TESTS

Test	Form	IQ	Date	Grade
	Elementary I	116	9/8/84	3
Otis-Lennon School	Intermediate	106	9/14/88	7
Ability Tests	Advanced	111	9/1/90	9

ACADEMIC RECORD

	Grades 1-6 (Year Averages)							Grades 7-9 (Year Averages)		
	1	2	3	4	5	6		7	8	9
Reading	B	B	B	B	B	B	English	B	English	B
Mathematics	C	C	C	C	C	C	Geography	B	U.S. History	B
Science/Health				B	C	C	Mathematics	C	Mathematics	C
Social Studies				B	B	B	Science	C	Earth Science	C
Language Arts	B	B	B	B	B	B	Phys. Ed.	C	Phys. Ed.	C
Spelling	A	A	A	A	B	B	Conduct	A	Conduct	A
Music/Art	C	C	C	C	C	C				
Citizenship	A	A	A	A	A	A				

KAREN: I tried to discuss Wanda's withdrawn behavior with her, and she thought I was criticizing her parenting skills.

MARK: (smiling) Were you?

KAREN: (laughing) Yes, I guess maybe I was. She's so demanding and thinks punishment is the solution to every problem.

MARK: (seriously) Do you think there's physical abuse going on there?

KAREN: Not physical—mental maybe. But I'm not real sure what abuse is anymore.

MARK: Well, certainly the scars of mental abuse are sometimes more difficult to detect than those of physical abuse.

KAREN: I just don't know what to try next, Mark. Ms. Loveless has certainly made it clear that she doesn't want anything more to do with me. I had some idea about involving her as a classroom volunteer, but that will never work.

MARK: I agree. At least, I'd hate to try that if I were in your position.

KAREN: Mark, I wonder if Wanda would be better off in another class, like a class for exceptional children. Wouldn't you say she is emotionally disturbed, or handicapped, or whatever the current label is?

MARK: Honestly, I'm not sure yet, Karen.

KAREN: How do you determine that?

MARK: It isn't an easy evaluation procedure. There are behavior checklists that we use, and I plan to evaluate Wanda as soon as I can schedule it. But what it comes down to is a matter of degree. Is the problem behavior a consistent and persistent pattern, or not? Is Wanda overinhibited, or not? That is, is she excessively withdrawn and shy? Once we label her and put her in a special program, it is likely to follow her the rest of her school days. So it's a serious call. Based on what you know now, Karen, what call would you make?

KAREN: I'm not certain, Mark. But what am I going to do with her in the classroom if you decide she isn't emotionally disturbed?

Questions

1. What is self-concept, and how does it differ from self-esteem? Is it a unidimensional or multidimensional construct? How is the self-concept formed, and under what conditions can it change? How do your answers to the above questions explain Wanda's self-concept?

2. What is self-efficacy, and how does it differ from self-concept? In what areas does Wanda have a low sense of self-efficacy? How can one's sense of self-efficacy be raised?

3. What are internal and external attributions? Are Wanda's attributions external? Does Wanda exhibit a learned helplessness pattern of beliefs? What are attribution training programs, and do they have implications for Wanda's situation?

4. What is child abuse? Is Wanda a mentally abused child? Why?

5. At what level of Maslow's need hierarchy is Wanda primarily functioning? Wanda's mother? How could Karen have taken advantage of that information?

6. What is discipline? Does it differ from punishment? What relationships exist between punishment and withdrawal behavior? What forms can punishment take? At what point does corporal punishment begin to become physical abuse?

7. What are Baumrind's parenting styles? What parenting style best fits Ms. Loveless? How do parenting styles relate to a child's success in school?

8. What is a withdrawn child? Are such children usually viewed as discipline problems? What teacher strategies are most effective in working with withdrawn children? In working with the parents of such children?

9. What are the characteristics of an emotionally disturbed child? What are the characteristics of an overinhibited child as opposed to a child who is just unusually shy? What techniques work best with such children?

10. What are the principles involved in conducting an effective parent-teacher conference? How good a job did Karen do? What could she have done differently?

To Start off with Something positive

8

Guys and Dolls

Key Content to Consider for Analyzing This Case:

1. Gender Differences
2. Teacher Biases/Self-Fulfilling Prophecy
3. Cultural Diversity
4. Home Learning Environment
5. Parent Involvement Methods

Patricia Renfroe is a doctoral student at Midwest State University. She has completed all her coursework, has passed her qualifying exams with flying colors, and is making arrangements to collect the data she will need to complete her dissertation, "An Investigation of Teacher Gender Biases in Elementary School Instruction." Shortly after school started in the fall, Pat made an appointment with Dr. Lois Freeman, principal of Shadyside Elementary School, which Pat would like to use in her data collection.

Shadyside Elementary School is located in an upper-middle/lower-middle-class community of 20,000, approximately 50 miles from Midwest State. It has three classes at each K-6 grade level, with a school population of approximately 600 pupils, of which approximately 65% are white, 25% African-American, 5% Hispanic, and 5% Asian-American.

PATRICIA: I'm Pat Renfroe, a doctoral student in educational psychology at Midwest State. I appreciate your seeing me this morning, Dr. Freeman. As I told you in my letter, the title of my doctoral dissertation is "An Investigation of Teacher Gender Biases in Elementary School Instruction." I've drawn a stratified random sample of elementary and secondary schools based on size, ethnic composition, and geographic location. Your school met our criteria. And perhaps even more significant is the fact that Dr. Thomas Riley, the chair of my doctoral committee, said that he's worked with you and knows you'd be interested in the results of the study.

LOIS: It's nice to meet you, Pat. Please call me Lois. I'm delighted that you're working with Tom Riley. I earned an EdD in Educational Administration from Midwest State several years ago, and Tom was my favorite professor. I enrolled in two of his courses, and they were the best courses of my entire college experience.

PAT: That's interesting! He's the best teacher I've had, too! And when he said that he knew you, I just knew that you would certainly be a good person to work with.

LOIS: Thank's for the compliment. I've always tried to run a good school, and I'd be pleased to have you collect your data here if it would help you. Your study sounds really interesting and should certainly make an important contribution. I think all professional women should be interested in gender issues. But if you're looking for gender bias in instruction, you'd probably find more at another school. I'm quite aware of gender stereotyping and can assure you that you'll find very few such practices in my school.

PAT: It will be wonderful if that happens. The major purpose of my study is to investigate instances of gender discrimination, classify them as to type, and then attempt to determine whether gender bias has increased, decreased, or remained relatively constant since we became aware of its existence several years ago. I'd like to be able to conclude that it's decreased.

LOIS: Let's make arrangements, then. Here's an application to conduct research in this school district and a copy of the procedures that must be followed. If you'll fill out and sign the application, along with the enclosed agreement stating that you'll follow the procedures stated in the procedures booklet, I'll sign to indicate that I'm willing to have you work in this school. Then I'll forward both documents to the superintendent's office. When he signs them, approved copies will be sent to both of us. Then you're in business. I'm certain that the superintendent will sign them, providing the research and evaluation people approve.

PAT: You've really been a big help, and I appreciate it. I'm sure I'll enjoy working with you and hope that the data I collect in your school will be of use to you, the teachers, and the pupils.

LOIS: I hope so, too. Let me know when you'd like to begin collecting data in the classes, and we'll plan a schedule together.

Near the end of the school year, Pat is in Dr. Riley's office with the first draft of her dissertation.

DR. RILEY: You were really efficient in your dissertation research, Pat, and you've done a good job of writing it up.

PAT: I couldn't have been so efficient without all your help.

DR. RILEY: It's always a pleasure for me to have a student like you who knows what she wants to do and how to go about doing it. It's one of the great rewards of being a professor.

PAT: It's nice of you to say that. Thank you. I still have some loose ends to tie up. I've shared the results with most of the principals who allowed me to observe in their schools, but I haven't talked yet with Dr. Freeman at Shadyside Elementary School. And I promised her that I'd do that.

TOM: Yes, you should at least let her see the observational data you collected in her school. In fact, she'd probably appreciate a copy of the entire study if you have an extra one.

PAT: I'll make her a copy and talk with her this week about a convenient time that I could visit with her.

Two weeks later, Pat and Lois Freeman are sitting in Lois's office at Shadyside Elementary School. Pat has just presented Lois with a copy of her study, and they are going over it together.

PAT: The classrooms I used in the study have been identified by grade level, but I didn't identify the schools, teachers, or students. In your copy of the study, I put a tab on each page that contains Shadyside Elementary School data. Thanks again for allowing me to make observations here. It helped me tremendously and contributed significantly to my study.

LOIS: I'm glad it did. I believe we all should support research in our profession whenever we have an opportunity to do so. Can you stay for a few minutes until I read the observational data? I'm interested in gender issues. There may be some things in the study that we can discuss.

PAT: Yes, I'd like to do that. In fact, I was going to suggest it.

The following are transcripts of "raw" observations made at Shadyside Elementary School before systematic analysis.

Observation One: A kindergarten class taught by a female teacher. The bell has rung and the pupils are entering the classroom.

TEACHER: Good morning, Girl One and Girl Two. Don't you look pretty this morning. Is that a new dress, Girl Six?

GIRL SIX: Yes, I got it for my birthday.

GIRL NINE: I got my dress to wear to Mary's birthday party.

TEACHER: Well, you both look very pretty. Good morning, Boy Four. I see you're wearing new basketball shoes. Do you think you'll play basketball for our school when you get to fifth grade?

BOY FOUR: Maybe. (After all the pupils have entered the room and gone to their seats, the teacher begins class.)

TEACHER: I'm glad to see all of you this morning. The first thing we'll do is to go to the centers for a while. You girls can go first. Ladies first, you know. (Girls all select centers.) Now it's the boys' turn. (Boys go to various centers, including the doll center.) Boy Ten, you and Boy Seven would probably enjoy the building center more than the doll center. Here, let me take you there with the other boys.

BOY TEN: Why can't we stay here?

TEACHER: You don't see men playing with dolls, do you? But men do build roads and buildings and other things.

BOY TEN: My dad takes care of my baby sister a lot. (Teacher ignores the comment and takes the boys to the building center. While there, she sees Girls Three and Four in the building center.)

TEACHER: You girls come with me to the art center. You'll probably use art skills much more than you'll use building skills.

(Now the building and science centers are occupied by boys only. The doll center and kitchen are occupied by girls only. Both boys and girls are working in the art center, reading center, and toy center and at the water table. Pupils work in the centers for approximately 45 minutes.

TEACHER: Now let's sit in the reading circle and I'll read you a story. Boy Three, would you bring the chair behind the desk to me?

GIRL NINE: I can get it, Teacher.

TEACHER: No, Girl Nine. Carrying heavy loads is an easier job for a boy. (Boy Three brings chair to the teacher, who sits in front of the reading circle.)

Observation Two: A male physical education teacher has taken a fourth-grade class of 18 boys and 12 girls to the playground for physical education.

COACH: OK, class, I want all the girls on the grass over there in front of the gym. Girl One, take four jump ropes out of the carton sitting over there. There are twelve of you, so you'll all have something to do. You'll work in four teams. Each team will have two turners and one jumper. Four teams of three are twelve, right? Take turns jumping and turning the rope so that everybody will have a turn at both jobs. You boys go out to the field. We're going to have a game of kickball. It has the same rules as baseball, but it's a little easier because the ball's bigger. Each team will have nine players: three fielders, three basemen, a shortstop, a pitcher, and a catcher. Three strikes and you're out; four balls and you walk.

GIRL ELEVEN: Why can't we play kickball, too, Coach?

COACH: With all that running around, I worry that one of you might get hurt. Besides, if you girls played, there would be too many players to deal with. Baseball and kickball teams have nine members. That's the number we have if the boys play. Each team would have fifteen if the girls played, and that's too many.

GIRL ELEVEN: You could let the boys jump rope and let us play kickball.

COACH: Then there wouldn't be enough players on the kickball team. Anyway, boys don't jump rope. That's more of a girl's game. Besides that, I'm going to coach the boys' baseball team in the spring. I want to watch the boys in the different classes play so that I'll be able to pick out the ones who can catch, throw, run fast, and understand the game. Then I'll know who the real players are.

GIRL SIX: My dad said there's a baseball program for girls in the spring, too. Will you watch the girls in this class to pick out the girls who are good players, too? My dad showed my brothers and me how to play.

COACH: I don't know anything about a girls' team. There wasn't one last year. But if there is one this summer, I won't work with it, because I'll be working with the boys' team. What's wrong with jumping rope? Jumping rope is good exercise for you. It makes your muscles strong, improves your breathing, and helps you to work in rhythm.

GIRL FIVE: It might be good for the boys, too. It might help them be good baseball players.

COACH: It might. One of these days I might have the boys skip rope. Maybe you can demonstrate how to do it right when I do.

Observation Three: A fifth-grade science class has a female teacher. In this class the boys are all seated on one side of the room and the girls are on the other. The teacher is using a reading strategy known as KWL, designed to help pupils comprehend written selections more effectively. She has written the following diagram on the chalkboard:

KWL Strategy

K—What we know   W—What we want to know   L—What we learned

TEACHER: Now I'm going to ask you to give me some information that can be put under *K*. This is information you already know about bats. That's what this *K* stands for, *know*—what we know. If you know something that we should list under *K*, "What we know," raise your hand. When I call on you, you can tell me what it is. OK, who wants to tell us something about bats? (Several girls and a few boys raise their hand.)

BOY TEN: (shouting out) Bats aren't birds. They're animals.

TEACHER: That's right, Boy Ten. Bats are mammals. Who else knows something about bats? (More pupils raise their hand.)

BOY TWO: (shouting out) They sleep in the day and come out at night.

TEACHER: Good, Boy Two. Do you know what we call animals who sleep in the day and come out at night?

BOY EIGHT: (shouting out) Nocturnal.

TEACHER: Right. That's a big word, Boy Eight. (The teacher is standing in the aisle that separates the boys' and girls' side of the room, but she's facing the boys' side and not looking at the girls.) Who else knows something about bats that you can tell us?

GIRL SIX: (shouting out) Bats eat insects.

TEACHER: That's right, Girl Six, but let's remember to raise our hand if we want to talk.

The pupils continue to list things they know about bats until they can't think of anything else. The teacher continues to face the boys' side of the room and allow the boys to shout out information. Only one girl shouts out. The teacher calls on three girls, but eight boys shout out answers.

TEACHER: That's very good. You know many things about bats. Now let's move on to the *W* part of the chart. The *W* stands for *Want*—things that we don't know now but *want* to know.

Who can think of something you would like to know about bats that you don't know now? (No response) Sometimes it's hard to think about what we don't know, isn't it? Boy One, tell us something that you could learn about bats that you don't know now. (Waits for about 5 seconds)

BOY NINE: Do bats really attack people?

TEACHER: Good. There are books and movies about bats who do attack people, aren't there? (Writes question on the board below the *W* section) Who else can think of something to list under *W*? Girl One? (Waits about 1 second, then calls on another pupil) How about you, Boy Five? (Waits for 6 seconds)

BOY FIVE: Where do bats live?

TEACHER: That's an interesting question, Boy Five. I'm sure we'll find out the answer when we read the selection. (Writes question on board)

BOY THREE: (shouting out) I'd like to know what bats eat.

TEACHER: It seems to be an important question that should be included, doesn't it, Boy Three? (Writes question on the board)

The teacher continues to stand in the center aisle facing the boys' side of the room. Two boys shout out questions. Four more raise their hand. Eight girls sit with their hand up, and two are called on. One shouts out successfully. All questions are listed on board.

TEACHER: Now we'll take turns reading aloud the article on bats. After each section of the story, we'll list all the information that we learn below the *L,* which stands for what we *learned.* Girl Two, please read the first two paragraphs of the article.

For the remainder of the period the teacher faces the girls' section and calls upon girls to read. But when she asks questions, she turns to the boys' section and calls on them to answer the questions about what they learned from the reading selection.

Observation Four: A male sixth-grade teacher is beginning a social studies unit.

TEACHER: Today we begin a study of famous Americans. You'll remember that last week I asked each of you to list three Americans whose contributions have made them famous. As you give your names, I'll write them on the board. If someone else gives a name that's on your list, cross that name off. We don't want to list any name more than once. When all the names are on the board, you'll all vote to decide the fifteen famous Americans we'll study in depth. Boy Seven, tell us your three choices.

BOY SEVEN: I picked George Washington, Abraham Lincoln, and Bill Clinton, because they were all presidents.

TEACHER: Yes, Boy Seven, those are good choices. Tell us the names of your three famous Americans, Girl One.

GIRL ONE: I think that Martin Luther King, George Washington Carver, and General Colin Powell are good Americans.

TEACHER: Yes indeed. I agree. Girl Two, who are your famous Americans?

GIRL TWO: I chose John F. Kennedy, Robert Frost, and Garth Brooks.

TEACHER: A president, poet, and singer, a variety of different talents. Good choices. Who are your famous Americans, Boy Two?

BOY ELEVEN: Magic Johnson, Muhammad Ali, Arthur Ashe.

TEACHER: Aha! A sports fan—basketball, boxing, and tennis. And those are three great athletes.

As the pupils present their choices, the teacher lists them on the chalkboard. Duplicate choices are eliminated. After 15 of the 27 pupils have responded and more than 40 names have been listed, the teacher makes an observation.

TEACHER: Wait a minute. What's happening here? Do you see what I see? There's something unusual about this list. What is it? (There is a long silence. Finally a boy raises his hand.) Boy Three, what have you noticed?

BOY THREE: There aren't any women on the list.

TEACHER: Bingo! That's right. Look at that! Forty names of famous Americans, and not a woman among them! Have you all learned to be prejudiced against women? Do any of you have women on your list? (Two girls raise their hand) Good for you! What women do you think are famous Americans, Girl Ten?

GIRL TEN: I have two women on my list: Eleanor Roosevelt and Hillary Clinton. Then I listed a male poet, Robert Frost. He's my favorite poet.

TEACHER: Let's get those names up here on the board, especially the women, before someone passes by in the hall and thinks that I'm brainwashing you to ignore women. (Students laugh.) Tell us who your famous Americans are, Girl Fourteen.

GIRL FOURTEEN: I selected three African-American women: Coretta Scott King, Rosa Parks, and Maya Angelou.

TEACHER: (Writes the names on the board) And all of them wonderfully talented. Thank you, Girls Ten and Fourteen. You saved our class from being guilty of gender discrimination. Now, let's discuss why only two of us listed women as great Americans.

GIRL FIVE: When you asked for famous Americans, I think you cut down the choices. In the past, famous people were mostly men. Most of the books tell about men who were presidents, explorers, politicians, inventors, and athletes. I think we did the same thing. Maybe we've been taught to think like that.

TEACHER: Thank you, Girl Five. Your comments show much insight, and I agree with you. You've been taught that famous people are people who do the things men typically do. And I was taught the same thing when I was in school.

BOY THIRTEEN: But that idea seems to be changing now. We have women astronauts, soldiers, athletes, and politicians. Hillary Clinton is a politician.

GIRL FIVE: But doesn't that mean that women have to do men's jobs to be famous? What about Rose Kennedy? I heard on TV that she really influenced all the members of her family. All her sons became what they are because she was such a strong person in their lives. Doesn't that make her a famous American? Coretta Scott King helped Martin Luther King at tough times. Abraham Lincoln said his mother helped him a lot. We have a book of sayings at home. One goes, "All I am or ever hope to be I owe to my mother." All through history there are examples of women helping their husbands and sons. Aren't these women as famous as some of the men in history? (A bell rings.)

TEACHER: There's the bell. I'm sorry that we have to stop. However, you certainly raised some issues that are important to our society and, I might add, I didn't expect to come up in class today. You're a good class, and I promise you that we'll continue this discussion later.

Lois finishes her reading of the "raw" observations that Pat made in the four classrooms at Shadyside.

LOIS: I've read these observations several times, but they don't seem to get any better no matter how many times I read them! (Pause) I'm sure that I don't need to tell you how disappointed I am and how ashamed I am that some of my teachers are so insensitive to gender differences! I had no idea. I'm shocked! (Pause) In fact, I remember suggesting to you when we first met that perhaps you'd be better off observing in another school if you were looking for gender discrimination. And here you have found blatant examples of it in all four of the classrooms you visited in my school. I'm mortified!

PAT: Would it be of any comfort to you to know that your school was about average in comparison with the other schools I observed?

LOIS: (smiles wanly) Not very much. For years I've taken pride in the fact that I spend at least one meeting each year with my faculty discussing school problems. We always talk about avoiding any kind of discrimination based on gender. It appears that my time and effort have been wasted! You must think that I'm a really poor principal! Please help me! Tell me what I can do about these gender problems!

PAT: It just so happens that as I analyzed the data from the various schools, I grouped them into different categories. Then I suggested ways that these categories of teacher bias could be reduced. I titled this document "Strategies Teachers Can Use to Reduce Gender Bias." [See list on next page] I hope to be able to expand it into a short article for one of the educational journals. Here's a copy that you may have. It might at least be a starting point for you to work from.

LOIS: (after reading the page with the five strategies) The examples of gender bias that appeared in my classes certainly fall into these categories. It's a good list.

Figure 8–1 Strategies Teachers Can Use to Reduce Gender Bias

Research studies and observations of gender bias in classrooms have clearly identified inequities that exist in the treatment of boys and girls. The following suggestions for classroom teachers are based on the results of these studies:

1. Assume that both boys and girls are equally capable of learning all subjects. Currently, after Grade 4, girls are less likely to have an interest in science and math, elect a science or math class, or experience success in these fields. Women now represent only 9 to 10% of the science and engineering workforce in the United States, Great Britain, and Canada.
2. Provide boys and girls with equal amounts of attention and recitation time in class. Research indicates that boys are currently called on up to three times more frequently than girls and are given as much as one third more wait time to answer questions.
3. Avoid gender-biased actions or comments, such as "throw like a girl," "boys don't cry," "girls are pretty and frilly," "boys are tough and manly," "girls clean house, cook, do laundry, and raise children," "boys play sports, bring home the paycheck, and discipline the children," "girls are sweet and docile," and "boys are strong and assertive."
4. Avoid using books that have strong gender bias. Research conducted by Women on Words and Images, Princeton, N.J. (1972), included an analysis of 2,760 stories from 134 children's books. The ratio of boys' stories to girls' stories was 5 to 2. The ratio of adult male main characters to adult female main characters was 3 to 1. Male biographies outnumbered female biographies 6 to 1. Male animal stories outnumbered female animal stories 2 to 1. Male folk or fantasy stories outnumbered female folk or fantasy stories 4 to 1. Although this research resulted in a general reduction of these ratios, more recent research indicates that pupils are still exposed to more stories about men and boys than about women and girls. Teachers should make a conscious effort to expose pupils to literature that describes both successful men and successful women. Avoid using textbooks that stereotype gender roles.
5. Provide equal recreational opportunities for boys and girls. At present, public schools and universities have approximately 70% more athletic teams and intramural activities for men than they do for women.

But how do you think I can apply these strategies here at Shadyside? How can I get the teachers to become aware of what they're doing and begin to use strategies like these every day? And the parents, the homes that children come from—doesn't gender bias begin there? How can I change the behavior of the parents? I just feel overwhelmed!

▉ Questions

1. What are the origins of gender discrimination? What role does the family play? How does the school, especially the teachers, reinforce such discrimination? Why are the teachers biased?

2. How do ethnic, racial, and social class influences differ with regard to gender biases? When do gender biases begin, and who is responsible for them? Are all

gender biases against females? Are there courses and types of teachers that favor girls over boys?

3. What types of parent involvement techniques can Dr. Freeman and her teachers employ in this situation? How could parent volunteering, parent classes at school, home visits, and parent participation in advisory committees, open houses, and parent-teacher conferences be used to reduce gender bias?

4. What kinds of things can teachers do in the classroom to reduce gender biases? Can you suggest curriculum and textbook changes? What subjects lend themselves to the greatest amount of bias? Why?

5. How did Boy Ten innocently reject a gender stereotype suggested by the kindergarten teacher's remark that men don't play with dolls?

6. What message did the physical education teacher send to the pupils by his assignment of activities? How did the fourth-grade girls challenge the physical education teacher's gender bias?

7. What message did the fifth-grade teacher send to the boys by calling on them more frequently and allowing them to shout out answers to questions without raising their hands? By the way she positioned herself in the classroom? What message did these practices send to the girls?

8. What is the significance of wait time (time allowed to students to answer a question) in sending messages to the boys and girls in the fifth-grade class?

9. What is the significance of the fact that neither the boys nor the girls in the sixth-grade class noticed that their list of famous Americans included no women? React to the explanation of Girl Five regarding why the class did not include women in their choices of famous Americans. What criteria does she believe should be used to designate famous women?

10. Describe the kind of program that Principal Lois Freeman should implement to reduce gender bias in her school. Describe some specific activities that would be appropriate in such a program.

9

Parent Power

West Hills Elementary School is located in a residential area outside a large urban area in a northeastern state. The district that this K-6 school draws from consists of 67% white, 20% African-American, 10% Hispanic, and 3% Asian-American students. Roughly 60% are from low-income families. The school building is 8 years old and is well maintained.

It is the first day of a 2-week preplanning session for teachers prior to the opening of school. Ann Riley, a white fourth-grade teacher, and Tara Hill, an African-American third-grade teacher, are sitting in Ann's classroom talking during the afternoon. The two teachers have become close friends during their 5 years of teaching at West Hills.

ANN: I tell you, Tara, I've never taken a course that I've gotten so much out of! My head is just brimming with ideas!

TARA: What did you say the course was called? I never get in a course like that!

ANN: "Parent Involvement in Education."

TARA: Who was the professor?

ANN: Dr. Saunders. Boy, was he full of information! It has to be the best summer course ever!

TARA: What did you learn?

ANN: For one thing, did you know that a lot of studies have been done that show that when a child's parents are involved in school, the child is likely to learn more in school and be more motivated? Programs for involving parents have existed for a long time, especially in elementary schools, but we just haven't heard about them.

TARA: Why not?

ANN: I wasn't real clear on the answer to that. I think a lot of the programs have been experimental, and they just haven't done a good job of disseminating the information about them.

TARA: Who hasn't?

ANN: Well, I guess the federal government and other agencies that have funded them and teacher education institutions.

TARA: That sure sounds right! I never heard of a course like the one you took or of a parent involvement program. I mean, I guess I've heard of the ideas, but I've never visited a school that actually had such a program. (Pause) Tell me, Ann. What did you learn about parent involvement that we could be doing here?

ANN: Plenty. I learned that parent involvement can take many forms besides the traditional ones of classroom visitation, open houses, and parent-teacher conferences. Parents can be encouraged to help their children with their schoolwork at home by receiving visits at home from trained home visitors. They can also work in the classroom as volunteers or as paid paraprofessionals. Parents can participate in school decision-making activities through parent advisory committees, and they can become adult learners through school-based classes like literacy and parenting.

TARA: (excitedly) Whoa! Stop, Ann! I can't follow all that! Just tell me about home visits. Wouldn't they take a lot of a teacher's time? And how often would you make home visits? What would you take to the parents, homework?

ANN: It turns out that people other than teachers make good home visitors, maybe better.

TARA: Really?!

ANN: Yes. For example, in one federal program they put two teacher aides in each classroom. Each aide worked in the classroom half-time and made home visits half-time. That way, there was at least one aide in the classroom at all times, and every child's home got visited every week.

TARA: Then the teacher didn't actually make home visits?

ANN: No, although she could go with the aide anytime she wanted to, and usually did two or three times a year for each child. But the aides were selected so that they came from the same background as the parents they were visiting. If the children were low-income African-Americans, for example, a low-income African-American aide was selected and trained to make the home visits. The teacher's role was to plan the visits with the aides and help develop the home learning activities that the aide demonstrated to the parent each week.

TARA: What kind of activities?

ANN: They grew out of what was being taught in the classroom at the time but weren't just homework. They were more like enrichment material—games, puzzles, and other kinds of follow-up activities.

TARA: That is an exciting idea, Ann! But what were you talking about involving parents in decision making? What kinds of decisions?

ANN: I learned that some states have passed laws requiring school districts to set up parent advisory committees involving parents in making decisions about things like school budgets, zoning issues, and curriculum changes. The interesting thing is that some of the parents who become leaders are from low-income backgrounds.

TARA: You mean low-income African-American parents were involved?

ANN: Not just low-income African-Americans but, yes, many of them were African-American.

TARA: That is exciting, and you say it helped the African-American children's achievement test scores?

ANN: Yes, it helped the achievement test scores of a lot of the low-income children to have their parents involved.

TARA: Why aren't we doing some of these things here at West Hills? We pride ourselves on being progressive.

ANN: I guess it comes down to a lot of teachers and administrators either not knowing about or being afraid of parent involvement programs. Probably a lot of them think they know more about education than the parents. In other words, they're the experts and don't want to be challenged by people with less education. Then too, I guess some teachers just don't want any other adults in their classroom. Can you imagine Bessie Moran working with either aides or parent volunteers in her classroom?

TARA: (chuckling) No, I really can't. She doesn't even like it when Marie Allen, the music teacher, shows up once a week.

ANN: (laughing) That's right.

TARA: (seriously) But you know, Ann, I think she's the sole exception here at West Hills. I think most of the teachers here would appreciate more parent involvement. (Pause) Why don't we go talk to Marguerite about it and see if we can't bring it up at the next teachers' meeting and see how many teachers would want to get involved.

ANN: (smiling) Now wait a minute, Tara! You're trying to get me in trouble again, aren't you? I have enough to do as it is!

Tara and Ann sit in the office of Marguerite Fleming, the building principal, and discuss with her some of the ideas that Ann disclosed to Tara the day before.

MARGUERITE: (frowning) Saunders. Is that Richard Saunders?

ANN: Yes, I believe Richard is his first name.

MARGUERITE: I remember him well. We were in an educational administration course together when I was working on my EdD. (Pause) A bright man, at least when it comes to theory. But you'll notice he went on to become a college professor instead of getting down here on the firing line like us. (Pause) So he really impressed you, Ann?

ANN: Yes he did, and so did his ideas.

MARGUERITE: To be honest with you, I've seen a lot of these theoretical ideas come and go. Personally, I think parents need to be involved by visiting the school, through conferences, and as supporters of our activities. We certainly couldn't put on our annual school carnival without parent help. And our new softball diamond wouldn't exist if it hadn't been for some of the dads, especially Billy Oeffer's father. But I'm not too sure about some of these ideas like home visits, parent volunteers, and parent advisory committees. Not only do we not have enough money for a lot of these ideas, but I wonder if you two realize how much work would be involved in trying to involve parents in these ways?

ANN: What do you mean?

MARGUERITE: Suppose, for example, we found the money somewhere to put two teacher aides in each classroom. Do you have any idea what it would take to train these parents? Do you realize how much time you'd have to spend planning with them for home visits and developing the home learning curriculum materials? Ideas like that may work in federally funded programs, but they just aren't cost-effective in the real world.

TARA: But Marguerite, most of us already have one aide. Can a second one cost that much? Some of the parents of our children would jump at the chance at being employed as a teacher's aide. As for the training, I think that Dr. Saunders would help us with that at very little cost. I had him for a course once, too.

MARGUERITE: Even if we got a home visitation program going, why would you want the aides to make the visits instead of doing it yourselves?

ANN: Because they are from the same backgrounds as the parents they are visiting. They share the same values, language, and subculture. I sometimes don't know what to say on a home visit after being introduced to a low-income parent. We don't dress alike, we don't share the same problems, and often our values about school are different. Sitting in a home without rugs, with old furniture, and a number of dirty children running around often leaves me speechless.

MARGUERITE: I see what you mean. But do you really think that such parents should be advising the building principal regarding such things as the school budget? We have a very active PTA, which does a good job of supporting our activities. But frankly, the real leaders of that organization are white, upper-middle-class housewives who have the time and know-how to get the job done. Many of them are also active in other community organizations. How can you expect low-income parents who haven't had that kind of experience—and many of whom didn't even graduate from high school—to take an active decision-making role?

TARA: Marguerite, just because many of those parents don't have high-school diplomas does not mean that they don't have any ideas about how the school is affecting them or their children. It might do us good to listen to low-income as well as middle-income parents. It might also help the parents develop a different view of school. The only time we contact some of them is when their child is in trouble.

MARGUERITE: Yes, I see what you mean. Perhaps I could talk to Mary Clark, the current PTA president, and see if we can figure out how to encourage a few low-income parents to attend meetings. But I'm afraid that transportation and babysitting will be big problems.

ANN: (interrupting) Marguerite, can we present our parent involvement ideas to the other teachers at the first teachers' meeting and see how many of them might want to try out some of these ideas? If you want, I could even call Dr. Saunders and see if . . .

MARGUERITE: Ladies, I think we're being a bit premature. I'll agree that the two of you can go ahead and try out some of these ideas, provided you work with me as you develop them. But I don't want to make this a school project this year. I don't want to jump into the development of such a program on a schoolwide basis without exploring it more. You two can develop a kind of pilot program and present it to me, and we'll go from there. I do want to support teacher innovations like this, but I'm not prepared to involve the entire school staff at this time.

It is the next-to-last day of preplanning, and five other teachers spontaneously join Ann and Tara in the teachers' lounge during the late afternoon. These teachers are teaching children at the K-2 and 5-6 grade levels.

MEG: So Tara, what's this thing you're doing with the parents? Everyone's talking about it! How come Marguerite didn't bring it up at the teachers' meeting?

TARA: It's as much Ann as me, maybe more so. She took this parent involvement course this summer, and we got the idea of going beyond open house to involve parents. In the course, she learned that there are parent involvement techniques that even work with low-income parents and increase student achievement. Marguerite agreed to let Ann and me try them out this year and see how they work.

CORRINE: (with much indignation) Well, I like that! How come we all get left out! Anything that gets the home and school working together to benefit the child sounds like something I want to try too!

OTHER TEACHERS: (chorus) Yes. Tell us about it, Ann. What Marguerite doesn't know won't hurt her. Yes. Tell us.

ANN: Well, . . .

It is the first regular faculty meeting of the new school year. Marguerite presides over the meeting in the school library.

MARGUERITE: I think that pretty well covers my agenda, folks. Are there any questions before we adjourn? Yes, Meg?

MEG: I'd like to hear more about the pilot project that Ann and Tara are doing this year.

MARGUERITE: (slightly flustered) Yes, well, I didn't plan to bring it up, since it's a project that involves only the two of them. I thought we'd see how it worked before I reported on it to you.

MEG: Several of us, I would say most of us, heard about their project and are eager to try out some of the parent involvement procedures. I, for one, think the home visitation and parent volunteering ideas are great! I also think that more parents, especially parents from low-income backgrounds, should be involved in school decision making. After all, it's their school as well as ours. (Many teachers nod their head in agreement at Meg's remarks.)

MARGUERITE: (recovering quickly) I agree with the concept as well, Meg. But I feel that we should try out these new ideas slowly and see what the problems and costs are before we make it a school program.

CORRINE: Couldn't some of the rest of us participate in the experiment as well. After all, only two teachers isn't a very large study.

MARGUERITE: I know, but the bottom line is that I'm not going to commit our staff and financial resources to a large-scale parent involvement program until we all do our homework. Such a program may be quite costly in more ways than one. (Many teachers frown or look away.) Look, I'll tell you what I'm going to do. We'll bring up our pilot program at the parent open house and tell them what we're trying to do. (Looking at Ann) Ann, would you and Tara do that?

ANN: Yes, Marguerite. We'd be glad to.

MARGUERITE: Also, the room across from the library, Room 121, is large and not being used right now. We'll turn it into a "parents' room" that can serve as a meeting and organizing place for our parent involvement activities this year. I'll let Mary Clark know about this and ask her to help us organize it. Also, let's all do our research on these programs so we know what we're talking about before we get too far along. (A general chorus of teacher approval and agreement)

It is November of the same school year. Marguerite sits in the office of Dr. Brad Sutton, the superintendent of schools.

BRAD: What's up, Marge?

MARGUERITE: Brad, some of the teachers at West Hills have gotten bees in their bonnets about involving parents. Seems one of them took a course and has convinced most of my teachers that unusual kinds of parent involvement will increase student learning. I've tried to get them to try out a limited version of the program, but a large number of the teachers are feeling left out and are demanding to be involved. I just wanted you to be fully informed as to what is going on.

BRAD: Whoa, Marge! What do you mean by "unusual kinds of parent involvement?"

MARGUERITE: It grew out of a course taught by Rich Saunders.

BRAD: (interrupting) Oh, yes. I know him. A bright guy!

MARGUERITE: (frowning) Yes. Well, he advocates involving parents through home visits, as volunteers in the classroom, in parent advisory committees, and as adult learners in school-based programs.

BRAD: That's a bit unusual, but overall sounds innocent enough. Open houses, PTA, and parent-teacher conferences aren't enough for Rich, huh?

MARGUERITE: It's more than that, I'm afraid, Brad. He especially advocates reaching out to low-income parents and getting them involved. Also, the kind of home visitation he advocates involves putting two teacher aides in each classroom as home visitors. My teachers, especially Ann Riley and Tara Hill, the two ringleaders, don't seem to realize the costs and training problems that would be involved if the whole school adopted this program.

BRAD: (with a twinkle in his eye) What's the real problem, Marge?

MARGUERITE: (with anger) Brad, those parents aren't capable of advising me on how to run my school! Also, I feel like the teachers are railroading me into a potentially dangerous situation. I've talked to Mary Clark, our PTA president, and she agrees with me that some of these parents can be real troublemakers if given half a chance. What do you think I should do, Brad?

BRAD: (soothingly) Marge, how many times have I told you that things are never as bad as they seem? I've seen these kinds of movements come and go before. Just go along with it as best you can and drag your feet. Both the parents and teachers will tire of this before the year's over. I don't see any problem, budgetwise, with your putting an extra aide in the classrooms of the teachers who insist on having one. If you have an empty room, tell the parents they are welcome to meet and organize their activities there. Put a big "Parents' Room" sign over the door.

MARGUERITE: I've already done that.

BRAD: Good. Call Rich Saunders and ask him to come work with them for free. Tell him we have no consulting money, but the staff will be eternally grateful. (Pause) Don't worry about the low-income parents. After a little flurry of interest, they'll get tired and fade away. Maybe Mary Clark can help you with that.

MARGUERITE: (smiling) Brad, you're wonderful! I knew you'd know how to handle things! I feel better already.

BRAD: (smiling) Just remember that half the things we worry about never come to pass.

It is halfway though the school year, and Ann sits in her classroom at the end of the school day planning with her two African-American teacher aides, Rose Brown and Vanette Sanders.

ANN: I really feel good about the way we have been able to organize things this year so that you can make your home visits in the mornings, Rose, and you can do yours in the afternoon, Vanette. That way, I have one of you here in the classroom all day. Can we keep to that schedule the rest of the year? (Rose and Vanette nod in the affirmative.) Good.

ROSE: What did you think of the home learning activity we did on reading, Ann?

ANN: (picking up and looking at a sheet of paper) Good. Very good. This follows up nicely on the vocabulary activity you took into the homes last week. How is Mrs. Jackson responding to your home visits, Rose?

ROSE: Great! She even has punch and cookies ready for my visits now. She told me last week that although she enjoys working with Jerome on the home learning activities during the week, the thing she likes best is my telling her what's going on at school. She said she didn't know much about the school before. Now she even knows who Mrs. Fleming is when she sees her. The other day Mrs. Fleming recognized her as she passed the parents' room and called her by name. It just thrilled her to death. She says Mrs. Fleming is the first principal she has ever really gotten to know.

ANN: (with eyes watering up) That's a sad and wonderful story at the same time! (Pause) Do you think she'll come to a parent advisory group meeting and maybe get involved?

ROSE: I asked her, and she said yes, if I would pick her up and give her a ride.

ANN: (with emotion) That's wonderful! I don't know how I ever taught without the two of you!

Seven teachers, including Ann, Tara, Corrine, and Meg, sit in the teachers' lounge after school one month later.

CORRINE: (excitedly) I just can't believe how involving the parents has affected the behavior of the children this year! Even though I have only one teacher aide and she can make only biweekly home visits, it has made all the difference in the world! I've never seen such a hard-working and happy bunch of kids! (Other teachers voice their pleasure and agreement with this report.)

MEG: I hear from the grapevine that a lot of parents, including a number of low-income parents, are really getting involved and vocal in both the PTA and the school advisory committee. I understand that Mary Clark is having a real problem trying to keep PTA from becoming more of a political group than a support group. (Laughter and exclamations of surprise follow.)

ROYANE: (conspiratorially) Do you know what I heard last night? The SAC [School Advisory Committee] elected a low-income parent, Arlene Jackson, as its president, or is it chair? (Exclamations of surprise)

MEG: Chair. That's true! Isn't change wonderful and exciting? (Exclamations of agreement and delight)

ROYANE: And the parents' room. Talk about a beehive of activity, with Dr. Saunders in and out of there all the time!

CORRINE: You know what else I heard? I heard that Marguerite got him to help without giving him a consulting fee. How do you suppose she did that?

MEG: (with a puzzled look) That's a good question. Maybe the man is just dedicated to getting parent involvement going.

ANN: (assertively) Definitely. Doesn't surprise me at all.

MEG: (looking directly at Ann and Tara who are seated next to each other) You two! You really got something going, didn't you? (Exclamations of praise and support)

It is seven months into the school year, and Marguerite has asked Ann and Tara to meet her in her office after school. After the two are seated, she closes her office door, sits down at her desk, and tries to control her anger.

MARGUERITE: Are you two aware of what happened at the board meeting last night? I didn't see either of you there, so I'm not sure.

TARA: (puzzled) No, what happened?

MARGUERITE: A whole block of your new PTA and SAC parents showed up and accused, in rather vulgar language I might add, the school board of being racist. They demanded rezoning of the schools. I would have liked to have disappeared when Dr. Sutton asked them to introduce themselves and tell what school their child attended, mainly to reduce the tension, I think, and about three fourths of them were West Hills parents. Dr. Sutton and the members of the school board all looked at me and glared! I would liked to have died!

ANN: (sympathetically) That was terrible for you, Marguerite!

MARGUERITE: (angrily) Well, don't you two think you had something to do with it? I told you that I wanted to move slowly with this thing and just try it out in your two classes! But, no, you two had to get the rest of the teachers involved, and now look at what has happened!

TARA: (both surprised and angry) That's not fair, Marguerite. We did tell the other teachers what we were doing, but you agreed to let the other teachers develop their own programs.

Figure 9–1 Home Learning Activity for Ann Riley's Class

A–Reading We Will Go

Why?   For development of vocabulary.
What?   Several short story books.
How?

1. You and the child should look through the books, checking the pictures to see which book appeals to the child.
2. After he has decided on one, find a quiet time and place for you and the child to be alone so you may read it to him.
3. Have him tell you something about the cover picture.
4. Let him discuss the pictures in the book as you read to him.
5. Read about two pages. Then ask him questions about what has been read. Give him time to think about his answers. Accept his answers only if they have been given in complete sentences.

After you are finished with the complete book, ask

Who was the main character in the story?
What was she trying to do? Why?
Which part of the story did you like best? Why?
Do you suppose you would have liked another book better? Why?

What then or what else?

Have the child write his own story from an experience he has had. Encourage him to use new words and use your dictionary to check the spelling of them so he will learn that it's always good to use the dictionary to find new words.

MARGUERITE: I agreed reluctantly, and now I wish I hadn't. But that's not all!

ANN: (anxiously) What else?

MARGUERITE: Mrs. Jackson, the chair of the SAC, came in to pay me a visit this morning. The SAC is demanding, let me emphasize demanding, that they be allowed to go over every inch of the school budget and be given a summary of West Hills' students' test scores in relation to other schools. Finally, ladies, they want to assist me and Dr. Sutton in developing procedures for evaluating teachers, with a view toward implementing merit salary procedures in this county. (Ann and Tara look at each other with shock and surprise.) (Marguerite pauses as she struggles for self-control.) It's all happening too fast!

TARA: What are you going to do, Marguerite?

MARGUERITE: (controlled) Well, let me ask you two a question. You two started this whole thing. Do you see any reason why I shouldn't close down the parents' room? Can you give me any reason why I shouldn't ask you two and the rest of the teachers to stop this experiment in parent involvement right away? Don't you agree that the whole thing has been one tragic mistake?

Questions

1. What is parent involvement in education, and how strongly is it related to student achievement? What are the different forms that parent involvement can take, and how relatively effective is each (for example, home visits, parent volunteering, parent advisory committees, parent adult learning activities, parent-teacher conferences)?

2. What is socioeconomic status (SES)? What is its relationship to racial and ethnic differences? How do upper- and lower-SES groups differ in their participation in various types of parent involvement activities? Why is it more difficult to involve parents from low-SES and culturally different backgrounds? What attitudes and values do they hold toward the school? How can parent involvement programs help change parents' negative attitudes?

3. What home and parental variables have been found to relate to a child's success in school? How can the school and other community institutions help compensate for the lack of such influences in a child's life?

4. What federally sponsored research and development programs like Project Head Start and Project Follow Through have been developed to help compensate for home and parental differences in children's lives and success in school? What are the components of such programs, especially with regard to parent involvement? How successful have they been?

5. What are the barriers to getting successful parent involvement programs started in schools? What kinds of things can teachers and administrators do to help get such programs started and to sustain their growth? What kinds of contributions can successful parent involvement programs make in turn to the school and the school district?

6. What kinds of school-sponsored parent involvement activities are most effective in helping the parents as learners? For example, are such classes as parenting, human growth and development, literacy, and employability successful? How well does involving parents as classroom volunteers work? As paid

paraprofessionals? Can field trips include as many parents as possible and make an impact on them as learners as well as the children?

7. What is the purpose of home visitation? What are the characteristics of a successful home visitor? If the purpose of the home visit is to encourage the parent to work with the child at home, what kind of home learning material is most appropriate? What is the best way to deliver such material to the parent? How can such home visitation activities affect other children in the family? How could home learning material be delivered to a parent who is illiterate or who doesn't speak English?

8. How would you describe the principal's leadership style? What type of school climate has she helped create, and why? How might a different principal have functioned differently, especially in relation to parent involvement? How might personnel at the school district level have helped?

9. Who are the key persons in this case? What primary need levels are operating that explain their behavior from the standpoint of Maslow's motivational need hierarchy? Under what conditions can people and schools become more self-actualizing?

10. What response should Ann and Tara make? Can and should the school's fledgling parent involvement program be saved? Do its potential benefits outweigh its problems? What changes will have to be made if the program is to be saved?

Life in an Elementary Classroom

1. Instructional Evaluation
2. Instructional Objectives
3. Classroom Questions
4. Group Dynamics

Lincoln Elementary School is located on a quiet, tree-lined street in Mountainview, a city of about 50,000 in a northwestern state. It is early in the fall, and the morning air is filled with the sweet smell of pine. Within a two-block radius of the school, several children can be seen as they slowly make their way to school. Like children the world over, they are easily diverted by objects attractive to the young eye—a strange insect on a tree stump, or perhaps a shiny piece of metal on the sidewalk.

Mountainview is the home of one of the regional campuses of the state university, and most faculty children of elementary age attend Lincoln. The school, which spans kindergarten through fifth grade, has an enrollment of just over 450.

Linda Walker graduated from the university last June and began teaching second grade this year at Lincoln. Though she had a high grade-point average at the university and received a very favorable recommendation for student teaching from her cooperating teacher at another elementary school in Mountainview, Linda feels lucky to have begun her teaching career at Lincoln. The school is generally regarded as the best in the city. Parents take an active role in school functions and try to support the teachers' efforts at home. Real estate agents make it known to potential home buyers with elementary-age children that homes in the Lincoln area are more desirable than homes near other schools.

As Linda nears the main entrance to the school this morning, a small boy dressed in blue jeans and a red shirt calls to her from high atop the jungle gym.

TIMMY: (calling out) Hey, Miss Walker, come over here and see what I got.

LINDA: (stopping) What is it, Timmy? (She leaves the sidewalk and begins to walk across the playground toward Timmy.)

TIMMY: (climbing down) You'll never guess. (He runs the few steps to his books and lunch box, which are stacked on a window ledge of the school building.)

LINDA: I don't have the slightest idea, Timmy. (Timmy opens his lunch box and pulls out a small white cardboard box. He removes the lid and then, smiling, looks up at his teacher.)

TIMMY: It's a meteorite. I got it from my uncle.

LINDA: (touching the small orelike rock in the box with her right index finger) This is wonderful, Timmy! Do you know what a meteorite is?

TIMMY: Yeah, it's from outer space.

LINDA: Right.

TIMMY: (excitedly) My uncle, he lives in California!

LINDA: He does? (Pausing) Timmy, why don't you show your meteorite to the class today during our science lesson?

TIMMY: (agreeably) Okay. (He replaces the lid and then tosses it back in his lunch box.) I gotta get back to the monkey bars. (He looks over toward the jungle gym.)

LINDA: (smiling warmly). Okay, Timmy. I'll see you inside real soon.

TIMMY: Bye. (He turns and runs back to the jungle gym.)

As Linda walks the remaining 50 feet to the main entrance of the building, she encounters three more of her students.

LINDA: (waving to the three girls who are busy writing something on a sheet of notebook paper) Hi, Mary. Hi, Cathy. Hi, Heather. What are you girls up to this morning?

HEATHER: (excitedly) Hi, Miss Walker. We're writing a secret code so the boys can't get into our club.

LINDA: That sounds like a good idea! What's the name of your club?

MARY: We're the Power Dreamer Girls, and we have magic powers.

LINDA: (continuing to walk toward the main entrance) It sounds like the boys better be careful. I'll see you girls soon. Bye-bye.

THREE GIRLS IN UNISON: Bye-bye, Miss Walker.

Inside the building, Linda first stops in the main office to sign in and check her mailbox. Mrs. Flanigan, the principal, stands at the counter and greets the teachers as they sign in.

MRS. FLANIGAN: Good morning, Linda.

LINDA: Morning, Mrs. Flanigan. Isn't it a beautiful morning?

MRS. FLANIGAN: The prettiest we've had in a long while. I was beginning to wonder if that drizzle would ever stop. (Clearing her throat) I put a note in your box, Linda, as a reminder that I'll be coming by first thing this morning to observe a reading lesson. We set up the time and date at our preobservation conference, remember?

LINDA: (enthusiastically) Oh, I haven't forgotten! I'll be working with the children in their reading groups.

MRS. FLANIGAN: Good. I'll be down there in just a few minutes. I'll be using the same observation form I used last time.

LINDA: Good. See you soon.

A short time later Mrs. Flanigan arrives at Linda's classroom as the students are filing into the room. Linda is standing behind her desk arranging papers.

LINDA: (looking up) Hello, Mrs. Flanigan. (Points to a full-sized student desk at the back of the room) You can sit there. It's right next to the table we use for the reading groups.

MRS. FLANIGAN: Thank you, Linda. That'll be just perfect.

As Linda's students continue to enter the room, they take their seats obediently. The room holds 30 desks arranged in five rows of 6 desks each. Only a few students seem to notice Mrs. Flanigan, who is now seated at her desk. Within a few moments, Linda's 24 students are at their desks waiting for her to begin. Linda moves around in front of her desk; she smiles at a blonde-haired girl who sits directly in front of her.

LINDA: Okay, children, today we have a visitor. Mrs. Flanigan, our principal, will be observing us during reading.

Nearly every child turns to look at Mrs. Flanigan, who looks up from her notebook and smiles broadly. Almost immediately the boys and girls turn back toward their teacher.

LINDA: (in a sweet, bubbly voice) Is everyone here today?

CLASS IN UNISON: Yes.

LINDA: Good. (Writes the attendance figure on the small yellow pad she holds in her left hand) Does anyone know what day it is? (Several students' hands go up.) Mary?

MARY: The tenth?

LINDA: The tenth is the date. What day of the week is it? Carol?

CAROL: (proudly) Monday.

LINDA: That's right. Today is Monday the tenth, the first day of the week. And everyone's here. (Enters the date on the yellow pad) How many are not eating in the cafeteria today . . . either you brought your lunch or you're going home? (Four students raise their hands.) Okay, that's four. Twenty-four minus four is how many? (Three students raise their hands.) Timmy, do you know?

TIMMY: Twenty.

LINDA: Very good, Timmy. Twenty-four minus four is twenty. (Enters this number on the yellow pad) By the way, boys and girls, Timmy has something very special that he wants to show us during our science lesson. Right, Timmy? (Smiles at him)

TIMMY: (with energy) Right! It came from way far away!

LINDA: (chuckling) Now don't give it away, Timmy. (Continuing) Paul, would you put this lunch count outside on the door? (Tears off a page from the pad and hands it to Paul, who does as requested. Places the pad on the corner of her desk, picks up a stack of papers, and then turns to her class.) This morning, boys and girls, I have three stories that I want you to read. Read them very carefully. At the end of each story are several questions. They check to see how well you understand the story. (Moves over to the first row on her left) I'll hand out the three stories now. You may read them in any order you want. Everybody will need a pencil. When you're finished answering the questions for all three stories, you may color the picture that goes with each story. (Counts out enough papers for the children in the first row and hands them to the first student, an African-American girl, in the row. Whispers to the girl) Take one and pass the rest back, please. (Moves on to the next row)

Within a minute or two, each student is busily at work. Linda moves up and down the rows checking on each student's progress. She stops to help a boy in a green plaid shirt.

LINDA: (softly) Let's read it together. (Pointing with her pencil) "The boy wanted to take a boat and a pail and shovel to the beach. But his mother could not find the boat. 'Maybe you will find a friend at the beach who has a boat,' said his mother. So the boy just took his pail and shovel to the beach." Now, the question here asks "What did the boy take to the beach?"

GARY: A boat and a pail and a shovel?

LINDA: No, Gary. Remember, his mother couldn't find the boat. So he just took his pail and shovel. See, in the picture he just has his pail and shovel. Now you try the next question, and I'll come back to help you if you need me. (Addressing the entire class) Okay, boys and girls, would Group I please go back to the reading table. Everyone else keep working on your stories until it's time for your group to go to the reading table.

At Linda's instructions, eight children get up from their desks and walk to the large, round table at the back of the room. Two boys at the front of the room and behind Linda also get out of their seats momentarily, pretending as though they are going to join the group at the back of the room. When Linda happens to turn in their direction, however, they dart back into their seats. Linda sees this but does not comment on their behavior. Meanwhile at the back of the room, a boy hands out hardcover dictionaries as the children take their seats. Linda scans the 16 students who are working on the three stories, and satisfied that they are on task, she joins the eight children at the round table.

LINDA: (taking her seat) Does everybody have a dictionary? Okay. Gwen, do you want to scoot over here so everyone can see the flannel board? (Gwen moves her chair closer to her teacher.) Everybody sit up nice and straight. Let's say the days of the week beginning with Monday. (Beginning slowly until all eight children are responding in unison) Monday, Tuesday, Wednesday, Thursday, Friday, Saturday, and Sunday. Very good. Now, who remembers which day of the week starts with one of the consonant digraphs we've been studying? Beth?

BETH: Thursday.

LINDA: Thursday. And which consonant digraph does it begin with? Bill?

BILL: (softly) TH.

LINDA: Very good. Now this morning, boys and girls, we're going to begin with the four consonant digraphs we've been studying. As I put them on the flannel board, would you say them with me.

CHILDREN IN UNISON: (Linda places the letters on the flannel board.) SH. TH. WH.

LINDA: Okay. As we all know, a consonant digraph is when we take two consonants and put them together so they make a brand new sound. It doesn't sound like either one of the consonants usually sounds. All right, I'm going to call out several groups of words and you're not going to know whether they have a CH, an SH, a TH, or a WH. Listen carefully. (Slowly, emphasizing the consonant digraphs) Children. Champ. Church. Chirp. Checkers. Chair. Cheese. Who knows the answer? Raise your hand. Cathy, which two letters? The CH, the SH, the TH, or the WH? (As Cathy begins to formulate her answer, Linda glances quickly at the rest of her class. Satisfied that they are all busy, she turns back to Cathy.)

CATHY: The CH.

LINDA: Good. Every one of those words began with a CH. Now sometimes a consonant digraph comes where? At the beginning of a word. (Several children try to provide the answers along with their teacher.) Sometimes it comes at the middle. And sometimes . . . at the end. Now we're going to use our magic hat. (From a shelf to her right, Linda takes a large black top hat made out of construction paper. She places the hat in the middle of the table.) In the hat, boys and girls, are words that have the CH in them. Some are at the beginning of the word. Some are at the middle of the word. And some are at the end. Also some words may even have more than one CH. I'm going to shake up the words, and then each of you will draw a word and tell us where the CH is: at the beginning, the middle, or the end. Okay, Timmy, you look ready. You go first. Read the word and then tell us where the consonant digraph is. (Linda pushes the hat over toward Timmy, who gingerly sticks his hand into the hat and pulls out a word. Linda again glances back at the rest of her students to check their progress.)

TIMMY: Church.

LINDA: Where's the consonant digraph?

TIMMY: (softly) At the beginning . . . and at the end.

LINDA: Very good, Timmy. At the beginning and at the end. Let's put your word right up here on the flannel board. (Moving from left to right, slowly scans the small group of children) I like the way Beth is sitting . . . would you like to choose next, Beth?

BETH: Okay. (Reaches into the hat and pulls out a word) Cherry.

LINDA: Cherry. And where's the consonant digraph in cherry?

At this moment, one of the two boys who earlier had started to join this first reading group appears at Linda's side.

LINDA: Frank, what do you want? You're in the next reading group.

FRANK: (lethargically) I'm tired, Miss Walker.

LINDA: Go back to your desk and finish your work, and then you can rest.

FRANK: (insolently) All right. (With greatly exaggerated fatigue, he walks back to his desk.)

LINDA: Okay, let's see . . .

BETH: At the beginning.

LINDA: Very good, Beth. The digraph's at the beginning. Let's put your word up here next to Timmy's. Bill, why don't you choose a word. (Pushes the hat toward Bill)

BILL: (weakly) Peach.

LINDA: Peach. How many of you like peaches? (Five children raise their hands.) Okay, where is the consonant digraph in your peach, Bill?

BILL: (tentatively) At the end.

LINDA: Yes, at the end. (Places the word *peach* on the flannel board) All right, Mary, do you want to take a word out of the hat?

MARY: Yes.

LINDA: Take a word out and read it to us, and then tell us where the consonant digraph is.

MARY: Chicken.

LINDA: Yes, Mary pulled a chicken out of the hat. (Several children giggle.) And where's the consonant digraph?

MARY: The beginning.

LINDA: Good, Mary. Let's put your word right here. (Pausing) Annie, why don't you take a word out of the hat.

ANNIE: (trying to pronounce ketchup) Ker . . .

LINDA: Sound it out. It's something we like to put on hot dogs and hamburgers.

ANNIE: (suddenly) Ketchup

LINDA: Good, now, where's the consonant digraph?

ANNIE: At the end?

LINDA: No. It's in the middle. See? (She points to the letters.) Okay, let's put Annie's ketchup right here. Gwen, why don't you take a word now. (Pushing the hat toward Gwen)

GWEN: (in a strong voice) Chief.

LINDA: Right. Chief. Where's the consonant digraph?

GWEN: At the beginning.

LINDA: Right, Gwen, at the beginning. And let's put your word right here on the board. Rusty, you get to take the next-to-last word out of the hat. (Once again glances at the rest of her students and notices that Frank has his head on his desk and is not doing anything)

RUSTY: (with a surprised look on his face) Champ. It's at the beginning.

LINDA: Right. Champ. Let's put Rusty's word here. Now, Cathy, you get to read the very last word in the hat. What is that word?

CATHY: (proudly) It's chair.

LINDA: Right. And where is the consonant digraph in the word *chair*?

CATHY: At the beginning.

LINDA: Very good, Cathy. (Places Cathy's word on the flannel board) Now we have all eight words on the board. OK. I have a silly tongue twister here. (Takes a one-by-two-foot piece of poster board from the shelf to her right, careful not to let the children see what is written on it) Do you know what a tongue twister is?

CHILDREN IN UNISON: Yes.

LINDA: (slowly) After church, Charles had a lunch of cheeseburgers and cherries. How many CH's do you hear? (With emphasis) Everyone's hand went up. Timmy?

TIMMY: Five.

LINDA: Let's see if Timmy's right. Let's read the sentence together.

ALL IN UNISON: After church, Charles had a lunch of cheeseburgers and cherries.

LINDA: Let's count the CH's.

ALL IN UNISON: One, two, three, four, five, six.

LINDA: There are six CH's. Church had two, and that was hard to catch, wasn't it? Very good. (Removes the words from the flannel board) Okay. Now we're going to work with another pair of letters that we met last week. The O and the A. Remember, there's a rule for when two vowels go side-by-side in a word. Can anyone remember that rule? (Silence) When two vowels go walking, the first one does the talking. Let's all say that together.

ALL IN UNISON: When two vowels go walking, the first one does the talking.

LINDA: What does that mean when two vowels go walking, the first one does the talking? Mary?

MARY: You hear the sound of the first one.

LINDA: Very good. You hear the sound of the first vowel. The O says its name. The O is first, so that's what you hear. You don't hear the A. All right, all of the words that we're going to look at today say O. The O and the A go together, but we just hear the O. Now, look at these words on this chart. (Takes a two-by-three-foot piece of poster board from the shelf and holds it so her students can see) Let's read the words on this chart. (Begins pointing with her pencil) Timmy, what's this word?

TIMMY: Boat.

LINDA: Good. Gwen, what's this one?

GWEN: Float.

LINDA: Good, Gwen. Cathy, what's this word?

CATHY: Road.

LINDA: Yes, that's road. Let's see. Annie, can you read this word?

ANNIE: Toad.

LINDA: Very good, Annie. Okay, Mary, can you read this word?

MARY: Goat.

LINDA: Good, Mary. That's goat. All right, Bill, can you read this last word?

BILL: Load.

LINDA: Very good, Bill. Now let's all say the words together.

ALL IN UNISON: Boat. Float. Road. Toad. Goat. Load.

LINDA: Okay. Very good, children. The next thing we're going to do this morning is work with some vocabulary words. Each of you has a dictionary in front of you, right?

CHILDREN IN UNISON: Yes, Miss Walker.

LINDA: Dictionaries can be used for several different things. Can somebody tell me what we use dictionaries for? Gwen?

GWEN: To find out things.

LINDA: Okay, we can find out things. What kind of things can we find out? Gwen?

GWEN: The meaning.

LINDA: All right, the meaning of what?

GWEN: The meaning of words.

LINDA: Right. If you want to know the meaning of a word, you can look up that word in the dictionary and find out what it means. Can a dictionary do anything else? Rusty?

RUSTY: How to spell a word.

LINDA: Right. If you know the first couple of letters of a word you can find out how it is spelled. Mary?

MARY: How many syllables.

LINDA: Good, Mary. The dictionary will tell you how many syllables or how many parts a word has. Also the dictionary will tell you where the accent mark goes. What does that tell you? (No response) Well, it tells you what part of the word you pronounce the loudest. Now, can a word have more than one meaning?

CHILDREN IN UNISON: More than one.

LINDA: Okay, it can have more than one meaning. It could have several meanings; it just depends on how the word is used. (Holding up her dictionary) This is a thick book, isn't it? (Students murmur their agreement.) Is there a quick way to find a word in the dictionary? If I give you a word to find, do you have to look at every page in the dictionary to find the word? Is there a quick way to do it?

Figure 10–1 Teacher Summary Evaluation Report

Name _____

College _____

School _____ Date _____

Grade or
Subject _____

Period of
Sept.-Dec. ☐

Period of
Jan.-March ☐

Period of
Apr.-Dec. ☐

Observation Time _____ Conference Time _____

Check on March
and Dec. Report

Check on
March Report Only

Contract Status

☐ Outstanding
☐ Satisfactory
☐ Unsatisfactory

☐ Recommended for first
   one-year contract
☐ Recommended for
   second one-year contract
☐ Recommended for
   initial four-year
   contract
☐ Recommended for third
   one-year contract
☐ Not recommended for
   reappointment

☐ First-year contract
☐ Second-year contract
☐ Four-year contract
☐ One-year contract
☐ Continuing contract
☐ Long-term substitute
   (60 or more days)

*OUTSTANDING: Performance shows exceptional professional qualities and growth.
*SATISFACTORY: Performance at expected and desired professional qualities and growth.
*UNSATISFACTORY: Performance shows serious weaknesses or deficiencies.
*For more complete definition refer to page 12 in The Toledo Plan.
*Unsatisfactories and/or outstandings must have a written supportive statement.

	Out-standing	Satis-factory	Unsatis-factory
I. TEACHING PROCEDURES			
A. Skill in planning			
B. Skill in assessment and evaluation			
C. Skill in making assignments			
D. Skill in developing good work-study habits			
E. Resourceful use of instructional materials			
F. Skill in using motivating techniques			
G. Skill in questioning techniques			
H. Ability to recognize and provide for individual differences			
I. Oral and written communication skills			

	Out-standing	Satis-factory	Unsatis-factory
J. Speech, articulation and voice quality			
II. CLASSROOM MANAGEMENT			
A. Effective classroom facilitation and control			
B. Effective interaction with pupils			
C. Efficient classroom routine			
D. Appropriate interaction with pupils			
E. Is reasonable, fair and impartial in dealing with students			
III. KNOWLEDGE OF SUBJECT-ACADEMIC PREPARATION			
IV. PERSONAL CHARACTERISTICS AND PROFESSIONAL RESPONSIBILITY			
A. Shows a genuine interest in teaching			
B. Personal appearance			
C. Skill in adapting to change			
D. Adheres to accepted policies and procedures of Mountainview Public Schools			
E. Accepts responsibility both inside and outside the classroom			
F. Has a cooperative approach toward parents and school personnel			
G. Is punctual and regular in attendance			

_____

Evaluator's Signature   Teacher's Signature   Principal's Signature
(when required)   (when required)

_____

Evaluator's Position

Date of Conference _____

DIRECTIONS
1. Rate all categories, bold face and subcategories.
2. Attach all supporting documents that have been signed or initiated.

SOURCE: The Toledo Plan: Intern, Intervention, Evaluation. Toledo Public Schools, 1986, p.13. Reprinted by permission.

BETH: (tentatively) Maybe.

LINDA: You're right, Beth, there is a quick way. What is that?

TOMMY: Use the guide words at the top.

LINDA: Okay. How do you use those guide words? Cathy?

CATHY: They show you . . . Like if you're looking up the word *boat,* you find B O and then . . .

LINDA: (interrupting) All right. The first guide word on a page is the first word on that page, isn't it? (Students murmur in agreement.) What's the last guide word on that page?

TIMMY AND ANNIE IN UNISON: The last word.

LINDA: All right. It's the last word. So the guide words tell you what word that page is going to begin with and what word it'll end with. Now I'm going to give you each a sheet with five new words on it. These are words that we haven't seen yet. I want you to see if you can find them in the dictionary. When you find the word, write down the page number that the word is on in the dictionary. Then we'll talk about those words.

Linda gives each child a sheet with the words on it. After making certain that the children have started their work, she leaves the round table and begins to walk up and down the rows checking on the progress of her other students. She notices that Frank now appears to be working on his assignment. Satisfied that all her students are on task, Linda walks over to Mrs. Flanigan's desk.

LINDA: (whispering) I'll be finished with this reading group in just a few minutes. Then I'll take the second group and we'll go over the same material. If I have enough time before science, I'll work with the third group.

MRS. FLANIGAN: (softly) That's fine, Linda. I've seen enough. (Begins to return her papers to her notebook) The children seemed to respond well. I would like to talk to you, though, about the lesson. Could you come by tomorrow for a postobservation conference during your preparation time?

LINDA: Sure, that'd be fine. (Hesitating) I always get so anxious. . . . Could I ask you what you thought about the lesson? How do you feel things went?

Questions

1. How effective was Linda at beginning class on that Monday morning? What specific things did she do that were effective? Ineffective?

2. Just after Linda gives instructions to students in Group I to go to the reading table at the back of the room, two boys not in Group I pretend they are going to join the group. When Linda turns in their direction, however, they return to their seats. Why do you suppose Linda does not comment on their behavior?

3. What steps does a teacher need to take to work with a small group while the rest of the class works independently?

4. What strengths does Linda have as a teacher? In what areas might she try to improve?

5. If you were to observe Linda's teaching using the teacher summary evaluation report at the end of this case, how would you rate her performance?

6. If you were to use a systematic observation schedule, such as Flanders' Interaction Analysis, to observe Linda's interactions with her students, what conclu-

sions would you draw about the interactions? For example, what conclusions would you draw about the amount of teacher talk and student talk? About the amount of teacher direct and teacher indirect behavior? How do such interaction patterns relate to student outcomes such as achievement? What are some other systematic observation instruments that could be used to observe teacher-pupil interactions?

7. What kinds of classroom questions does Linda ask? How do the questions distribute themselves in terms of Bloom's cognitive taxonomy? To what kinds of student outcomes (for example, achievement or creativity) do such questions relate? How effectively does Linda question her students in the small reading group? For which specific interactions might she have been more effective?

8. How well does Linda's teaching style take into consideration the backgrounds and characteristics of her students, especially in terms of socioeconomic status and grade level?

9. What instructional objectives does Linda seem to be pursuing? State two or three of her objectives in behavioral terms. How well do her instructional strategies fit her objectives?

10. Do most of the students in Linda's class evidence mastery or performance goal orientations? What teaching techniques foster mastery goal orientations in second graders?

Life in a High School Classroom

Key Content to Consider for Analyzing This Case:

1. Instructional Evaluation
2. Instructional Objectives
3. Classroom Questions
4. Kounin's Principles
5. Intrinsic Versus Extrinsic Motivation

After being let out at the curb by the driver of a newer model pickup, two boys dash up the sidewalk to McKinley High School in Centerville trying to escape the bitter early morning cold. The hard-packed snow makes a squeaking sound under their feet. With hardly a pause in their mad charge, they burst through the green double doors and then slide to a halt in the hallway, laughing wildly and stamping the snow from their feet.

Mr. Swenson, the school's only assistant principal, is standing nearby. During bad weather he monitors students who may wait in the hall by the entranceway until the first-period bell. About 25 students stand around in clusters of two to four talking animatedly about the things that matter most to young people in this rural area of a Midwestern state—sports, cars, and, depending upon their sex, girls or boys.

MR. SWENSON: Cold enough for you fellas?
TWO BOYS IN UNISON: Yeah!

McKinley High has an enrollment of 670 students, most of whom live on the farms that surround Centerville. The town has a population of 4,500 and is the hub of most of the newsworthy events that happen in the county. All of McKinley's students are white, with almost equal proportions from families with German or Scandinavian ancestry.

After a hotly debated school bond issue was passed in the early 1980s, the school was built at the north end of town, two blocks east of the state highway. The school grounds cover just under 4 acres and appear exceptionally barren after the previous day's 4-inch snowfall.

Later that day John Andrews, a 35-year-old mathematics teacher who has been at McKinley for 7 years, walks into the main office for his 12:20 P.M. appointment with Mr. Swenson. He places both his hands on the counter and leans over to speak to Brenda, a clerical worker.

JOHN Hi, Brenda. Is Mr. Swenson in? He said he wanted to see me at 12:20.

BRENDA: (picking up the telephone) Let me see. I'll give him a buzz. (After a moment, she speaks to Mr. Swenson.) Mr. Andrews is here to see you . . . OK . . . I'll send him in. (Hanging up the receiver and gesturing toward Mr. Swenson's office.) Go on in, Mr. Andrews. He's expecting you.

JOHN: (turning toward Mr. Swenson's office) Thanks.

A moment later John enters Mr. Swenson's office. On the wall behind Mr. Swenson's desk is a red-and-white banner that reads "McKinley Wildcats." Mr. Swenson is seated behind a moderately cluttered desk.

MR. SWENSON: (noticing that John is about to close the door) No, that's all right. This'll only take a minute. Besides, it gets darn cold in here when that door's closed. (Motions to John to sit in one of the two chairs on the other side of his desk)

JOHN: (sitting down) You wouldn't think a building this new would have cold spots in it.

MR. SWENSON: Well, when it gets below zero like it is today . . . (Clearing his throat) I just wanted to let you know that some time next week I'll be dropping by to make this semester's observation. Is there a class that you'd like me to visit?

JOHN: Really, any one's fine. (Pausing) You might like to see my third-period general math, though. They're a good bunch of kids.

MR. SWENSON: That sounds fine. So I'll make it some day third period next week. Remember, nothing special—just business as usual.

JOHN: (getting up to leave) Oh, don't worry about that. This group of kids wouldn't let me get away with doing something out of the ordinary to impress you. (Chuckling) They'll let you see them and me, warts and all.

MR. SWENSON: (smiling) That's good.

That next Wednesday Mr. Swenson arrives at John's classroom just as John's third-period students are filing into the room. He nods and smiles at John, who stands in the hallway by his door. Mr. Swenson enters and takes a seat at the back of the room. He removes a district observation form from the manila folder he has with him and begins to enter John's name, the period, date, and other standard identifying information at the top.

The bell rings, and two boys run up and squeeze through the door just as John is about to close it.

JOHN: (sternly) I've told you fellas you're gonna have to get here on time.

PAUL: (breathlessly) Coach Walker didn't let us out of gym on time.

CECIL: Yeah, he didn't.

JOHN: All I know is I can't have you guys waltzing in late like this. Go ahead, take your seats.

John walks over to his desk and flips open the record book that lies on top of his desk. Pointing with his right index finger, he scans the list of the 28 ninth graders in his class, looking up occasionally to determine whether a student is present. As he takes attendance, about half the students are arranging their materials—snapping and unsnapping three-ring binders, shuffling papers, thumbing through pages in the math text, or pulling all the contents out of a backpack to find the right pencil.

Another eight students scattered about the room in pairs talk and giggle in low tones. The students seated at the front of the four rows of desks sit and wait silently for the lesson to begin.

JOHN: (looking up) What about Molly? Has anyone seen Molly? She's been out three days now.

BARBARA: She rides my bus. Haven't seen her since last Friday.

PATRICIA: I talked to her last night. She has the flu. She said she'd try to come today or tomorrow.

JOHN: (continuing with the attendance) Thanks, Patricia.

Two boys on opposite sides of the room nod to each other and then get up in unison and walk over to the pencil sharpener mounted on a bookcase at the back of the room. One of them inserts his pencil in the sharpener and begins turning the crank lazily while he chats softly with the other. After a few moments, he glances furtively over his left shoulder at his teacher and at Mr. Swenson, who is seated nearby. Satisfied that neither is paying attention to them, he returns to his conversation.

JOHN: (looking up) Hey, Sam and Dale, sit down right now. We're going to get started.

SAM: (with irritation) OK, OK. I was just sharpening my pencil.(He and Dale walk slowly back to their desks.)

JOHN: (moving around in front of his desk) All right, before we learn how to figure out the volume of different objects, I think we should review how we figure out the area of plane figures. I'm not sure all of you know that, and you'll need to know it for next week's test.

At the mention of a test, several students make various noises of protest and exhibit a variety of pained expressions for their teacher.

SHERMAN: Aah, Mr. Andrews, we don't want no test again. We had one last week.

JOHN: That was two weeks ago. (With irritation) We are going to have a test on area and volume next Friday. Now let's get with it.

KEVIN: Couldn't we just use our homework grades?

JOHN: (rapidly) No. No. No. (Walking up to the blackboard) Now everyone look up here. You should know every one of these formulas.

John quickly writes the following on the board, reading each statement aloud as he writes it:

Area of rectangle =

Area of square =

Area of parallelogram =

Area of triangle =

Area of circle =

JOHN: OK. Who knows the area of a rectangle? (Stands ready with the chalk to write in the correct answer. Seven students raise their hand.) Come on now. Everyone should know this. (Another four hands go up.) Ray, what is it?

RAY: (loudly) You multiply the length by the width.

JOHN: (writing the correct answer on the board) Good. Length times width. (Turning to face his students) So what is the area of a square? Robert, do you know? (Robert sits erect and stares straight ahead, but he does not answer.) If the area of a rectangle is the length times the width, what's the area of a square? (Robert still does not answer, though he eventually shakes his head.)

ANNIE: (calling out) Length times width.

JOHN: OK. Length times width. (Writes this answer on the board) Is there another way to write it? (Turns toward his students)

CAROL: (calling out) The side squared.

Suddenly a female student appears at the door and knocks loudly. John walks over to the door, opens it, and, standing in the open doorway, begins speaking to the girl. A moment later, he turns toward his students.

JOHN: Did anyone find a pink fanny pack from last period?

Several students blurt out that they have not. A few others slide back their chairs to get a good look at the bookshelf beneath their desks. Still others look on the floor around their desks. When these efforts fail to turn up the missing fanny pack, John turns back to the student.

JOHN: Maybe you'd better try the Lost and Found. Sorry. (Closes the door and walks back to the blackboard) Let's see, Carol, you said it was the side squared?

CAROL: Yeah.

JOHN: (adding this answer to the one he has already written on the board and then turning toward his class) Actually, the formula for finding the area of a square is the same as finding the area of a rectangle. A square is just a special kind of rectangle. Now what about a parallelogram? (Two students, Paul and Jim, raise their hand.) Oh, come on, you know this. What is a parallelogram? Do you remember that? Karen? (No response) Agnes? (No response. By now four more students hold their hands aloft.) OK, Cecil, what is it?

CECIL: (softly and without assurance) It's a four-sided figure that's parallel . . . uh, no . . . that has opposite sides that are parallel.

JOHN: Are you asking me or telling me?

CECIL: That's it. It has parallel sides.

JOHN: Good. Cecil got part of it. Besides opposite sides that are parallel, what else does a parallelogram have? (Several students blurt out answers simultaneously.)

LUCY: Equal sides.

JIM: The opposite angles are equal.

JOHN: Great. Now we've got it. The opposite sides are equal *and* the opposite angles are equal. Hmm . . . who could come up here and draw one on the board for us? (He surveys the room. Three students have their hand raised.) All right, Dale, you try it. (He holds out his piece of chalk and motions Dale to come up to the board. Dale gets out of his chair and begins walking to the front of the room. Just then a heavyset boy at the back of the room turns to say something to the girl behind him.) Henry, you'd better pay attention here. I might have you up here next. (Several students laugh.)

Dale takes the piece of chalk from his teacher's hand and swiftly draws a parallelogram with remarkably even parallel sides.

JOHN: Good. Thanks, Dale. (Dale returns the chalk and walks back to his seat.) See, the sides are parallel . . . (Traces the sides with his right index finger) And the opposite angles are equal . . . (Outlines the two pairs of equal angles) Now, how do we figure out the area of a figure like this? (Three students raise their hand. John ignores the students' hands and continues.) Suppose we let the base of this figure be twelve inches. (Writes this number beneath the base of the parallelogram) And suppose we let the height be ten inches. (Draws a dotted line from the base to the top of the figure and labels this ten inches) How do we figure out the area? (Three more students raise their hand. John surveys the room for a moment before deciding to call on a student whose hand is not raised.) Ron, you look like you have the answer.

ALAN: He don't know nothing.

JOHN: (sharply) All right, Alan, zip it up. Ron?

RON: (quickly) It'd be the base times the height.

JOHN: Absolutely. (Writes this answer on the board) It'd be the base times the height. (Pausing) Does everyone see that? (Continuing) OK, now that we know how to find the area of a parallelogram, it should be easy to figure out how to find the area of a triangle. (Points to the statement "Area of triangle =" and then looks out at his students) Who knows how to find the area of a triangle? (Four students blurt out different answers simultaneously.)

PERRY: Base times height.

JUDY: You add the sides and then take half of that.

LOUIS: You multiply the sides.

JIM: Half the base times the height.

JOHN: Attaboy, Jim. (Writes this on the board) I don't know where you other guys got those strange answers. (Several students laugh, and two point accusing fingers at the three who gave incorrect answers.) That's enough of that; everybody makes mistakes. (Pausing) Now we have one more plane figure, a circle. Who remembers the formula for that?

MIRIAM: (waving her hand excitedly) Oh, I know.

JOHN: Let's see, everyone's hand should be up. (Pausing) I think I'll call on someone whose hand is not raised. (Several more hands shoot up.) Kevin, what's the area of a circle?

KEVIN: But my hand is up.

JOHN: (smiling) I know.

KEVIN: You weren't supposed to call on me.

JOHN: I thought if you had your hand raised you'd know the answer. You wouldn't raise your hand if you didn't know the answer, would you? (Several students laugh.)

KEVIN: Uh, I don't know what it is.

JOHN: Well, know it by next week. (To the entire class) What's the area of a circle? (Nearly all the students blurt out something. John cups his hand to his ear as though he cannot quite make out the correct answer.) What was that? (Again the students blurt out answers.) I think I heard pi r squared, but I'm not sure what that other stuff was. (Moves a few steps and writes this final formula on the board) What is the value of pi? Who knows that? (Turns toward the class) Dale, what is it?

DALE: Uh, 3.1416.

JOHN: Good. Everyone remember that. (Steps back and makes a sweeping gesture to take in the five formulas he has written on the board) You all better know these by next week. OK? Now let's turn in our books to page 88 and find out how to figure out the volume of objects. (Picks up a text on his desk and opens it) Who'd like to begin reading near the bottom of page 88, right where it says "the volume of objects?" (Two students raise their hand) All right, Beth. Read to the top of page 90.

As Beth reads, John walks up and down the aisles making sure that each student is following along. He stops to get a boy to turn to the correct page.

JOHN: (softly) Page 88. You're on the wrong page.
SHERMAN: Oh.

John waits until Sherman turns to the correct page and then moves on. Another boy has his book open to the correct page but appears to be staring out into space. As he passes the boy's desk, John taps on the open book with his right index finger. With a sigh the boy begins to look down at his book. After checking each student, John returns to the front of the room. Beth continues to read. A boy at the back of the room continues to sink lower in his seat until he is able to avoid John's gaze by hiding behind the student in front of him. He places his chin on his open book and stares ahead vacantly.

JOHN: OK, you can stop there. So when we figure out the volume of something, we find out how much it can hold . . . what its capacity is. Uh . . . what are some things that we'd want to know the volume of? (Pointing to a student whose hand is raised) Karen?
KAREN: A box.
JOHN: Yes, we might want to know how much a box would hold. Ray?
RAY: What about a swimming pool?
JOHN: Good. We'd want to know how much water it would hold. Anyone else? Yes, Perry.
PERRY: A drum. (Two students giggle.)
JOHN: A drum?
PERRY: Yeah, a drum like you'd put oil in.
JOHN: Oh, OK. Isn't that usually called a barrel?
PERRY: I don't know.
JOHN: Well, you're right. We might want to know how much oil a drum would hold. (Continuing) Any other objects we'd want to know the volume of? (No response) Actually there are hundreds of objects that we'd want to know the capacity of. How many of you have a silo at your place? (A few hands go up.) I'm sure your dads know the capacity of them. How many of you have helped your parents move furniture in a rental truck? (Again a few hands go up.) You have got to know how much the truck holds. (Pausing) Now, how do we measure volume? What did Beth just say? Patricia?
PATRICIA: You measure it in cubes.
JOHN: (chuckling) Not quite. In cubic units. Cubic feet. Cubic inches. (Noticing Ron's hand) Ron?
RON: How come they measure engines in cubic inches? It's not a container.
JOHN: Good question, Ron. Who knows the answer?
ALAN: It's like how much space it takes up.
JOHN: Exactly. So a 400-cubic-inch engine takes up a lot of space . . . and (chuckling) a lot of gas. (Pausing) Now, what is a cube? (No response) A cube is a solid shape with six square sides. The length, width, and height are all equal. And all the angles are what kind?

SEVERAL STUDENTS IN UNISON: Right angles.

JOHN: Good. They're all right angles. Now, a cubic inch is the space occupied by a cube that is one inch long, one inch wide, and one inch high. So what is a cubic foot? (Several students blurt out the correct answer but at different tempos.) Wait, wait. Let's just have one answer so we can all get it. Beth?

BETH: It's one foot long, one foot wide, and one foot high.

JOHN: OK. Everyone got that? (A few students nod.) Now look on page 90. The picture shows how many cubic inches there would be in a cubic foot. Everyone look. Does everyone see that there'd be 144 cubic inches in each one-inch layer of the cube? (Holds his open book to his left side and points to the illustration) Then to fill in the cube it'd take 144 times 12, or 1,728 cubic inches. Right? (He looks at his students; a few nod to indicate that they understand.) Now there's an easier way to do this, isn't there? Instead of counting all these little one-inch cubes, we could just multiply the length times the width times the height, couldn't we? (Again only a few students nod. John goes to the board and writes the formula $V = l \times w \times h$ in large letters. He then draws on the board a rectangular box that is 6 inches long, 3 inches wide, and 4 inches high.) Now look at this rectangular box, which is a rectangular solid. Figure out the volume of the box. How many cubic inches would it be? (Waits for a minute while his students do the calculation) OK. What did you get? Helen?

HELEN: Seventy-two?

JOHN: Seventy-two what?

HELEN: Uh . . . cubic inches.

JOHN: How many of you got seventy-two cubic inches? (About half his students raise their hands.) Good. Just remember the formula, volume equals length times width times height. OK? (Pausing) All right. We have one more formula to learn. The volume of a cylinder. (Goes to the board and draws a cylinder) Everyone look up here. We have a cylinder, and we want to find its volume—how much it'll hold. We do just like we did for finding the volume of a cube or a box. We take the area of the base times the height. (Pointing to the base of the cylinder) What kind of plane figure is the base? Cecil?

CECIL: It's a circle.

JOHN: Exactly. So we just take the area of the base, or this circle, times the height. Let's write it as a formula. What would it be? (Slowly writes on the board "$V = \pi r^2 h$" and then draws a line under it) That's all there is to it. (He places the chalk back on the chalk tray and then picks his book up off his desk. He walks around in front of his desk and sits on the edge.) All right, listen up. Here's what I want you to do for homework. Page 91. One through twenty. These are story problems, but if you set them up right, they'll be easy. I'll give you the rest of the period to work on them.

PERRY: We have to do all of them?

JOHN: What did I just say?

PERRY: I was just asking.

ALAN: You want us to show our work?

JOHN: Yes. I can't tell what you did wrong if you don't. It'll help if you make a little drawing for each one. Try to do that. Oh, and remember to give your answer in cubic units. You're figuring out the volume for all of these.

JIM: What time is it?

JOHN: Sh! Get to work. It's time to work.

SHERMAN: (to Jim) Hey, man, quiet. I'm trying to do my work.

HENRY: Yeah, you guys shut up.

JOHN: All right, let's be quiet. (Notices a girl next to the window with her hand raised and walks over to her desk to see what she wants) Karen, having trouble?

KAREN: I can't do this one.

JOHN: What don't you understand about it?

KAREN: I don't know what to do.

JOHN: Well, read the problem. What does it ask for?

Suddenly two boys seated across from each other and about 8 feet behind John begin squirming violently trying to contain their laughter. In an attempt to camouflage his laughter, one boy begins coughing loudly. Two other students nearby, a girl and a boy, turn to see what the noise is about. After a quick glance, they return to their seatwork. At this moment, John turns and snaps his fingers for silence. The two culprits' clowning lessens somewhat, but neither one makes an attempt to resume work on the assignment.

KAREN: (reading) The body of a truck is eight feet long, six and one-half feet wide, and four feet deep. What is its capacity?

JOHN: What shape is the truck body?

KAREN: A cube?

JOHN: Are all the sides equal?

KAREN: (hesitating) No.

JOHN: Well, then, it can't be a cube, can it?

KAREN: (softly) No.

JOHN: So what shape is it?

KAREN: (slowly) I don't know.

JOHN: Look, it's eight feet long, six and one-half feet wide, and four feet deep. What does that describe?

KAREN: A rectangle?

JOHN: (becoming frustrated) No, that's a plane figure. (To the entire class) Class, in number one, what kind of solid is the truck body? Jim?

JIM: A rectangular solid . . . like a box.

JOHN: Right. Right. I even drew a picture of one on the board. (Points to the drawing on the board) That's what the truck body looks like. (To Karen) Do you see that?

KAREN: That's what I said.

JOHN: No, you said it was a rectangle, not a rectangular solid.

KAREN: Oh.

JOHN: Now I want you to go back and read page 89 where it talks about how to find the capacity of a rectangular solid. Then see if you can work it.

John turns the page of Karen's book and points to the appropriate section. Then he steps back a couple of paces from Karen's desk and surveys the rest of the class. Apparently satisfied that everyone is working on the assignment, he walks to his desk and sits down. He opens one of his desk drawers, removes some student papers, and thumbs through them. After glancing at the papers for a few seconds, he returns them to the drawer and then removes another set of papers from another drawer. After making a slow row-by-row scan of his class, he begins to grade the papers.

Nearly all John's students are working quietly now. A boy leaves his desk at the front of the room and walks back to sharpen his pencil. The two boys who had been laughing uncontrollably a minute ago work on their assignments, occasionally stopping to exchange a whispered comment. A girl in the middle of the row by the window rests her chin on her left palm and stares out the window.

For the remainder of the period, John grades papers at his desk, looking up periodically. From time to time students go up to his desk to ask for help. The room is now very quiet, and the voice of the world history teacher across the hall occasionally drifts into the room.

After about 15 minutes, a boy sitting near the front finishes his assignment. He matter-of-factly closes his math book and takes out a paperback book, which he begins reading. John notices that the boy is reading a book, but he allows him to continue.

About 5 minutes before the bell rings, the noise level gradually begins to increase as students disengage from their work. Several pupils start gathering their books and chatting softly with one another. John looks up more frequently now but does nothing to prevent the gradual escalation of noise and activity.

A few minutes later nearly every student is prepared for the bell to ring. Books piled on top of their desks and restlessly drumming their fingers or tapping their feet, the students watch the red sweep second hand on the room's clock as third period draws to a close. With about 20 seconds remaining, John gets up and walks around in front of his desk.

JOHN: Remember to finish your homework tonight if you didn't finish it in class today. And also check your work. Check your work. Everyone should get a perfect paper. There's no excuse. (The bell rings. John begins speaking in a loud voice to compete with the noise of students who immediately begin to leave.) Tomorrow we'll check your homework in class, and then we'll learn how to figure out the volume of triangular prisms. (Fading out) See you tomorrow.

As his students leave the room, John walks back to where Mr. Swenson is seated.

JOHN: Well, that was third period.
MR. SWENSON: (getting up from the student desk) Good class.
JOHN: Today was typical . . . some really understood, and then, a few didn't.
MR. SWENSON: They seemed to be pretty responsive. As you said, they're a good group of kids.
JOHN: Yes, they try.
MR. SWENSON: I was wondering . . . do you have lunch right now?
JOHN: Yes I do.
MR. SWENSON: I thought we could go to the faculty lunchroom and talk about what I observed. You did a lot of good things, and I want to go over those. Also I have some questions about the way you handled a few of the

Figure 11–1 Centerville School District
Teaching Observation Form

Teacher's Name: _____   Date: _____

Class: _____   Period: _____

Observed by: _____

	Poor, needs Improvement	Weak	Acceptable	Very good	Excellent
1. Introduction of lesson					
Comment: _____	1	2	3	4	5
2. Organization of content					
Comment: _____	1	2	3	4	5
3. Clarity of instructional objective(s)					
Comment: _____	1	2	3	4	5
4. Pacing of lesson					
Comment: _____	1	2	3	4	5
5. Variety of activities during lesson					
Comment: _____	1	2	3	4	5
6. Corrective feedback given to students					
Comment: _____	1	2	3	4	5
7. Praise and/or support to students					
Comment: _____	1	2	3	4	5
8. Interaction with entire class					
Comment: _____	1	2	3	4	5
9. Interaction with small groups					
Comment: _____	1	2	3	4	5
10. Interaction with individual students					
Comment: _____	1	2	3	4	5
11. Monitoring of seatwork					
Comment: _____	1	2	3	4	5
12. Pleasant room atmosphere					
Comment: _____	1	2	3	4	5
13. Classroom management procedures—roll taking, etc.					
Comment: _____	1	2	3	4	5
14. Teacher's acceptance of individual differences					
Comment: _____	1	2	3	4	5
15. Overall effectiveness of lesson					
Comment: _____	1	2	3	4	5

Additional Comments: _____

_____

_____

interactions with the kids . . . some situations you might have handled differently.

JOHN: OK.

MR. SWENSON: I'd also like to get more of your reactions to the class . . . what you thought went well and what didn't work out so well.

JOHN: Great. But how do you feel it went overall?

Questions

1. As John spends the opening minutes of this class period taking attendance, his students for the most part sit and wait for the lesson to begin. Critique John's performance in terms of "academic learning time."

2. For the most part, does John try to motivate his students extrinsically or intrinsically? What other motivational techniques might he have used?

3. How effectively does John use praise? What specific suggestions would you have for him?

4. Following the large-group lesson, Karen asks John for help in determining the capacity of a truck body. Critique the interaction John has with Karen. How might he have been more effective in working with Karen?

5. If you were to observe John's teaching using the teaching observation form at the end of the case, how would you rate his performance? What are his overall strengths and weaknesses?

6. If you were to use a systematic observation schedule, such as Flanders' Interaction Analysis, to observe John's interactions with his students, what kind of picture would emerge about his teaching? For example, what is the ratio of pupil talk to teacher talk? What is the ratio of teacher indirect and direct behaviors? How do such interaction patterns relate to student achievement, particularly in ninth-grade math? What other systematic observation instruments could be used to observe teacher-pupil interactions?

7. What kinds of classroom questions does John ask? How do his questions relate to the different levels of Bloom's cognitive taxonomy?

8. How well does John's teaching style take into consideration the backgrounds and characteristics of his students, especially in terms of socioeconomic status and grade level?

9. What instructional objectives does John seem to be pursuing? Could you state two or three in the form of behavioral objectives? How well do his instructional strategies fit his objectives?

10. How well does John deal with disruptions? In terms of Kounin's theory of classroom management, does John exhibit withitness? Does John respond appropriately to Paul and Cecil, who enter the classroom just after the bell rings? How else might he have handled their tardiness? Critique John in terms of "overlappingness," "maintaining momentum," "smoothness," and "group-alerting" skills.

Fractions and Interactions

Key Content to Consider for Analyzing This Case:

1. Instructional Evaluation
2. Instructional Objectives
3. Cognitive Taxonomy
4. Classroom Questions
5. Kounin's Principles

Sherry Anderson is 28 and in her fourth year of teaching mathematics at a junior high school located in a small community in a southwestern state. About half the school's 850 students are from families that are involved in farming or ranching; the other half, from families that live in the community of less than 8,000.

It is three-thirty on a Monday afternoon, and Mrs. Anderson has just entered the office to sign out for the day. Arnold Grimes, the school's principal for the past 8 years, stands behind the counter, greeting teachers as they sign out. He is handsome and in his late fifties.

MR. GRIMES: Hello, Sherry. How'd it go today?

MRS. ANDERSON: Pretty well, Mr. Grimes. You know how Mondays can be.

MR. GRIMES: (sympathetically) Right. (Pausing) Say, Sherry, do you have a minute? I'd like to set up a time for me to observe one of your classes next week.

MRS. ANDERSON: (somewhat uneasily) Oh, it's that time already?

MR. GRIMES: I need to observe everyone at least twice this year, so I better get started next week. (Removes a small appointment book from the inside pocket of his sports coat) What would be a good time for you?

MRS. ANDERSON: Hmm. How about fourth period? I have a seventh-grade general math class then.

MR. GRIMES: Good. What day would be best?

MRS. ANDERSON: How about Wednesday?

MR. GRIMES: (looking at his appointment book) Wednesday'd be fine. (Writes her name and the time in his appointment book)

MRS. ANDERSON: Is there any kind of lesson you'd like to see?

MR. GRIMES: (chuckling) No, Sherry, just business as usual. Of course, I'll be interested in the interactions between you and your students. I'm using a slightly different observation form this year.

MRS. ANDERSON: They're not hesitant to interact. You'll see a lot of that.

MR. GRIMES: Good. I look forward to my visit.

It is Wednesday of the next week, and the bell signaling the end of third period has just rung. As soon as Mrs. Anderson's third-period students begin to stream out into the hallway, Mr. Grimes, who had been standing just outside the door, enters and walks to the back of the room. He selects a student desk seat and pulls it into a far corner. After sitting down, he removes an observation form from a manila folder and, in pencil, begins to enter information, such as the date, teacher's name, and subject. When finished, he looks up and begins his observation.

Mrs. Anderson is seated at her desk arranging the handouts she plans to use this period and checking her record book. It is 10:26, two minutes before the bell that marks the start of fourth period will ring. Fourteen students are already in their seats arranging their books and materials. Occasionally some of them turn to look at Mr. Grimes. Two girls stand near the pencil sharpener talking with each other. Two boys pause for a moment in the doorway surveying Mrs. Anderson's classroom before they turn and dart off down the hallway. In spite of the random individual activity and the fairly high noise level in the room, Mrs. Anderson continues to work at her desk. A girl enters the room and stops at Mrs. Anderson's desk before taking her seat.

GIRL: What are we going to do today?

MRS. ANDERSON: (looking up) We'll get started in just a moment. (This response seems to satisfy the girl, who walks to her desk.)

Students continue to file into the room. At 10:28 the bell rings. Mrs. Anderson looks up and surveys her class. Twenty students are in their seats. Several of them are just sitting looking around the room. Two students are lined up at the pencil sharpener. Another three students are walking toward their desks. A boy suddenly leaps up and runs to the pencil sharpener.

BOY: (to the other two students at the pencil sharpener) Come on, hurry up! (The girl at the pencil sharpener turns and gives the boy a sneer.)

GIRL: (angrily) Just wait your turn! (Casts a quick glance at Mr. Grimes)

MRS. ANDERSON: (noticing the students at the pencil sharpener) Hurry up back there. We need to get started.

This warning seems to have little effect on the students, who continue to talk. Mrs. Anderson turns to a girl seated just in front of her desk.

MRS. ANDERSON: Pam, would you give each person one of these worksheets? (Holds out the set of papers)

PAM: Okay, Mrs. Anderson. (Gets up and takes the worksheets.)

Mrs. Anderson continues to work in her record book, looking up every 15 seconds or so to see how many of her students are present and in their seats. The two boys who appeared momentarily in the doorway minutes earlier now reenter the room and, as if to acknowledge their lateness, begin to tiptoe to their desks. When they see Mr. Grimes, however, they stop tiptoeing and quickly take their seats. Pam continues to move up and down the five rows of desks, passing out worksheets and pausing every now and then to say something to a fellow student.

At 10:31 Mrs. Anderson opens her record book to the page with her fourth-period roster. Pointing at the names with a ballpoint pen held in her right hand, she scans the list.

MRS. ANDERSON: Amy? Does anyone know anything about Amy?

ALICE: She's still out. I think she has the flu.

MRS. ANDERSON: OK. (Continuing to scan the roster) What about Ralph? He was out yesterday, wasn't he?

DAVID: (from the back) Yeah, he ain't here.

MRS. ANDERSON: All right. (Continuing) Harold not here?

HAROLD: (from the pencil sharpener) Hey, I'm over here! I ain't absent.

MRS. ANDERSON: Well, that's what happens when you're not in your seat. (Takes a book from the top of her desk and holds it aloft) Did anyone leave this book in here? I found it after class yesterday.

DICK: (calling out) What's the name of it?

MRS. ANDERSON: Let's see. *The Red Badge of Courage.* It's from the library. (Opening the cover) It's overdue. Due November 10th. (No one claims the book, so Mrs. Anderson places it back on her desk.)

At 10:33 Mrs. Anderson gets up and walks over to the door and closes it. She then walks back to her desk and stands in front of it.

MRS. ANDERSON: Let's get started, class. I've given each of you a worksheet on adding fractions. You have twenty-five addition problems. I've checked your papers from yesterday, and I wasn't too pleased.

SEVERAL STUDENTS IN UNISON: Ohhh nooo.

MRS. ANDERSON: It seems like we don't understand fractions. But maybe we'll do better today.

BILLY: (calling out) Are we gonna get our papers back?

MRS. ANDERSON: I'll return them later. (Pausing) Open your books to page 39, and let's go over some of this again. (Takes her book from her desk and opens it to page 39) Look at the sample problem at the top of the page: $\frac{1}{2} + \frac{1}{2}$. Why is that equal to $\frac{2}{2}$ and not $\frac{2}{4}$? A lot of you made that mistake yesterday. (Noticing Beverly's hand) Beverly?

BEVERLY: Cause when the numbers on the bottom are the same, that's what you put on the bottom of your answer.

MRS. ANDERSON: OK. But what do we call the number on the bottom? Who remembers? Stanley?

STANLEY: The denominator.

MRS. ANDERSON: And the number on the top?

FIVE STUDENTS IN UNISON: The numerator.

MRS. ANDERSON: Good. OK. What do we call it when we have two denominators that are the same? (Three students raise their hand.) Look back on page 38. (Turning the page in her book) What is the third key term it defines there in red type?

EIGHT STUDENTS READING IN UNISON: Common denominator.

It is 10:37, and Billy walks back to the pencil sharpener and begins slowly sharpening his pencil. Mrs. Anderson notices him but does not say anything.

MRS. ANDERSON: Right. Common denominator. Once we have that, we can add or subtract. So whenever we have fractions with unlike denominators, the first thing we need to do is what?

CAROL: (blurting out) Find the common denominator.

MRS. ANDERSON: Right. Now let's look at exercise 1 on page 39, finding the common denominator. Let's just do this out loud real fast. There are only ten of them. Number one—$\frac{1}{4}$ and $\frac{1}{8}$.

SEVERAL STUDENTS IN UNISON: 8!

MRS. ANDERSON: Good. Now $\frac{1}{3}$ and $\frac{1}{6}$.

SEVERAL STUDENTS IN UNISON: It's 6!

MRS. ANDERSON: Good. What about $\frac{1}{5}$ and $\frac{1}{10}$?

SEVERAL STUDENTS IN UNISON: That's 10!

MRS. ANDERSON: And $\frac{1}{5}$ and $\frac{1}{25}$.

SEVERAL STUDENTS IN UNISON: (after a slight pause) It's 25.

MRS. ANDERSON: Good. Number five—$\frac{1}{7}$ and $\frac{1}{3}$.

WANDA: (in a loud voice) It's 7.

MRS. ANDERSON: No. Who knows?

PAM: It's 21.

MRS. ANDERSON: Good, Pam. How'd you get that?

PAM: I multiplied.

MRS. ANDERSON: Multiplied what?

PAM: The denominators.

MRS. ANDERSON: OK. Number six—

DICK: (calling out) Why didn't she divide three into seven?

MRS. ANDERSON: That's a good question, Dick. That's how we test to see if we have the *lowest* common denominator. We ask if we can divide one denominator evenly by the other. So will three go into seven an even number of times?

DICK: (tentatively) No.

MRS. ANDERSON: Right. So we need to find the smallest number that can be evenly divided by *both* of the denominators. And to get that we multiply three times seven. That gives us what?

DICK: Twenty-one.

MRS. ANDERSON: Right. And both 7 and 3 will go into 21 an even number of times. Right?

DICK: Right.

MRS. ANDERSON: Look at number six. This one's tricky—$\frac{1}{3}$ and $\frac{3}{27}$. (Noticing Heather's raised hand) Heather?

HEATHER: Eighty-one.

MRS. ANDERSON: Is that the *lowest* common denominator?

HEATHER: (slowly) No. I guess not.

MRS. ANDERSON: What is it?

HEATHER: I don't know.

MRS. ANDERSON: Does anyone know? Who can help Heather?

ERIC: (calling out) Nine.

MRS. ANDERSON: Good, Eric. Nine is the lowest common denominator. Let's look at number seven. (Noticing Heather's raised hand) Heather, you have a question?

HEATHER: How'd he get nine?

MRS. ANDERSON: Eric, you want to answer that?

ERIC: First you change $\frac{1}{3}$ to $\frac{9}{27}$. Then you can divide everything by three to get ninths.

MRS. ANDERSON: Good. Does everyone see that?

HANK: But why didn't he just multiply the denominators and get 81 like we did on the other one?

MRS. ANDERSON: You can do that, but what you get is a common denominator of 81. It doesn't give you the *lowest* common denominator. (Moves to the blackboard and quickly writes $\frac{1}{3}$ and $\frac{3}{27} = \frac{27}{81}$ and $\frac{9}{81} = \frac{3}{9}$ and $\frac{1}{9}$) Does everyone see that? (No response) OK. Let's take a look at the next one—$\frac{1}{81}$ and $\frac{1}{9}$. What's the lowest common denominator there?

ERIC AND PAM IN UNISON: Eighty-one.

MRS. ANDERSON: OK. Number eight—$\frac{1}{8}$ and $\frac{1}{5}$. What's that one? Let's see. Cecil?

CECIL: Thirteen?

MRS. ANDERSON: No. You added the denominators. You multiply them. What do you get then?

CECIL: Forty.

MRS. ANDERSON: Right. (Pausing) Number nine—$\frac{1}{2}$ and $\frac{1}{7}$.

PAM: Fourteen.

MRS. ANDERSON: Good. And the last one—$\frac{1}{3}$ and $\frac{1}{9}$.

PAM: (quickly) Nine.

MRS. ANDERSON: All right. Now when we add or subtract fractions, our first step is to see what the lowest common denominator is. Once we have that, the problem is half solved. Right? (Mrs. Anderson then walks up to the blackboard, picks up a piece of chalk, and turns to face her students. The time is 10:41.)

MRS. ANDERSON: Now let's try a few addition problems.

She turns and quickly writes the following problems on the board:

$\frac{1}{4} + \frac{1}{8} =$ $\qquad\qquad$ $\frac{1}{5} + \frac{1}{4} =$ $\qquad\qquad$ $\frac{1}{18} + \frac{1}{6} =$

$\frac{3}{4} + \frac{1}{2} + \frac{1}{3} =$ $\qquad\qquad\qquad$ $\frac{1}{5} + \frac{1}{10} + \frac{7}{20} =$

As Mrs. Anderson is writing on the board, a chubby boy on the window side of the room casts a quick glance at Mr. Grimes and, seeing that he is looking in another direction, throws a paper wad at a boy seated two desks in front of him. The missile, right on target, hits the boy on the back of the head and falls to the floor. The victim bends over, picks the paper off the floor, and shakes his fist good-naturedly at his grinning assailant.

MRS. ANDERSON: (now facing her students) Look at the first one. (Points to the first problem) Everyone look up here please. What is the lowest common denominator? Ricky?

RICKY: Four. No, no, eight. Eight.

MRS. ANDERSON: OK. It's eight. So $\frac{1}{4}$ becomes how many eighths? Ricky?

RICKY: Ah, two.

MRS. ANDERSON: (rewriting the problem as $\frac{2}{8} + \frac{1}{8}$) So now we have $\frac{2}{8}$ plus $\frac{1}{8}$. What's that?

RICKY: It's $\frac{3}{8}$.

MRS. ANDERSON: Good. (Writes the answer on the board) Let's take a look at the next one—$\frac{1}{5}$ plus $\frac{1}{4}$. The lowest common denominator, what is it? (Several students' hands go up.) Pam?

PAM: Twenty.

MRS. ANDERSON: Right. So $\frac{1}{5}$ would give us how many twentieths? Randy?

RANDY: Two.

PAM: (spontaneously) That's wrong. Should be four.

MRS. ANDERSON: Right, Pam, $\frac{4}{20}$. Then how many twentieths would $\frac{1}{4}$ give us, Randy?

RANDY: (softly) I don't know.

MRS. ANDERSON: (slightly impatiently) Well how many times will 4 go into 20?

RANDY: (slowly) Five.

MRS. ANDERSON: OK. So you'd have $\frac{5}{20}$, right? (Continuing) And $\frac{4}{20}$ and $\frac{5}{20}$ is how many twentieths? All right, Billy?

BILLY: Nine.

MRS. ANDERSON: (writing Billy's response on the board) Right. Now let's look at the next one. (Pointing to the next problem) $\frac{1}{18}$ plus $\frac{1}{6}$. What's the lowest common denominator here? (Five students who have been participating most raise their hands.) Come on, what about the rest of you? Randy, can you tell us? (Randy doesn't respond.) Can someone help Randy? Pam?

PAM: Eighteen.

MRS. ANDERSON: OK. And what do we do next?

PAM: Change $\frac{1}{6}$ to eighteenths.

MRS. ANDERSON: (beginning to write on the board) So we get $\frac{1}{18}$ plus how many eighteenths?

PAM: Three.

MRS. ANDERSON: Plus $\frac{3}{18}$. That gives us $\frac{4}{18}$. (She writes $\frac{4}{18}$ on the board.) Can we reduce this any further? Billy?

BILLY: Yeah. It's the same as $\frac{2}{9}$.

MRS. ANDERSON: Good, Billy. (Writes $\frac{2}{9}$ on the board) Now let's look at the next one. Here we have three fractions, but it's really just the same as the other problems, isn't it? (A few students nod their heads) We have $\frac{3}{4}$ plus $\frac{1}{2}$ plus $\frac{1}{3}$. The lowest common denominator is what? (Stands with chalk in hand, poised to write)

PAM: (calling out) Twelve.

MRS. ANDERSON: So that would give us how many twelfths here? (Points to $\frac{3}{4}$).

ERIC: Nine.

MRS. ANDERSON: (writing on the board) So $\frac{9}{12}$ here. And here?

ERIC: Six.

MRS. ANDERSON: Yes, $\frac{6}{12}$ here. And for the last one?

PAM: It's $\frac{4}{12}$.

MRS. ANDERSON: (writing Pam's response on the board) OK. So all
we have to do now is add the three numerators. Nine plus six plus four are what?

ERIC: Are 19.

MRS. ANDERSON: OK. (She writes $\frac{19}{12}$ on the board.) And what can we reduce $\frac{19}{12}$ to?

DICK: 1 $\frac{7}{12}$.

MRS. ANDERSON: (writing Dick's response on the board) All right, 1 $\frac{7}{12}$ (Turning to the class) Does everyone see that? (A few students nod their head.) OK. We have one more up here. (Pointing to the last problem) $\frac{1}{5}$ plus $\frac{1}{10}$ plus $\frac{7}{20}$ (Slowly and with emphasis) First of all, what do we look for? Cecil?)

CECIL: (softly and with difficulty) You reduce.

MRS. ANDERSON: No, that might come later. What do you do? What's the first step? (No response from Cecil) Well, what have we been doing with all these problems? (Points to the work on the board) What have we been talking about?

CECIL: (shrugs his shoulders) Numerators and denominators?

During Mrs. Anderson's exchange with Cecil, a boy at the end of the row on the window side of the room begins a long yawn, his outstretched arms reaching toward the ceiling. Suddenly his yawn becomes noticeably audible, a change that causes him to stop yawning and start giggling. Two students turn and look in his direction. He smiles at them and then glances at the clock on the wall to his right. It is 10:50.

MRS. ANDERSON: Yes, but we've been working on finding the *lowest common* . . .

CECIL: Denominator?

MRS. ANDERSON: Right! The lowest common denominator. (Sighing) So what's the lowest common denominator here? (Points to the three denominators in the problem on the board)

CECIL: Uh, 20?

MRS. ANDERSON: Good! So we have 20 as our denominator in all three fractions. (Rewrites the three fractions, converting each to twentieths) That would give us $4/20$ plus $2/20$ plus $7/20$, right? (Looks at Cecil, who nods his head, and then points to the three numerators) And four plus two plus seven is how much? Cecil?

CECIL: (after a long pause) Thirteen.

MRS. ANDERSON: All right. That gives us $13/20$. (Writes this fraction on the board) Now is everyone clear about how we got that? Does everyone understand? (Seven students respond by nodding their head; the rest sit woodenly staring at their teacher.) OK. (Glances at the clock, which reads 10:54.) We have about twenty minutes left. That will give you a good start on tonight's homework. (A few students moan.) I want you to do the twenty-five problems on the worksheet Pam handed out. If you work fast, you might be able to finish before the period is over. (Noticing David's raised hand) David?

DAVID: Is this the right worksheet, Mrs. Anderson? These problems aren't like the ones we just did.

Mrs. Anderson goes over to Pam's desk and glances down at her worksheet. Three students get up and walk over to the pencil sharpener, where they begin talking in low tones as one of them slowly sharpens her pencil.

MRS. ANDERSON: (chuckling to herself) Oh, I see what I did. I gave you the worksheet with mixed numbers to add. (Speaking to the entire class) Class, you have the wrong worksheet. It's one on mixed numbers. We'll go over that tomorrow, so just hold on to it. (Walks over to her desk and picks up a set of papers) Here's the one I want you to do for tomorrow. (Walking back to Pam's desk) Pam, would you please pass these out?

PAM: (taking the papers from Mrs. Anderson) OK.

MRS. ANDERSON: Please take your time as you work these problems. I think a lot of your mistakes are the result of carelessness. Take your time. Check your work. Everyone should be able to get a perfect paper.

As Pam goes up and down the rows passing out the correct worksheet, the room is filled with the sounds of students moving papers and books, snapping three-ring folders, sharpening pencils, and talking softly with one another. Mrs. Anderson takes a seat at her desk, where she begins to enter homework grades in her record book.

Two boys in the middle of the room sit sideways in their seats and lean toward each other, engrossed in animated talk. One of them playfully punches the other in the shoulder and starts giggling. When Pam comes by and places a worksheet on their desks, they try to strike up a conversation with her. Pam, however, continues to move down the row. The boys then turn around in their seats and begin to examine the worksheet.

At 10:59 Mrs. Anderson looks up and surveys her class. Her students are working quietly now.

MRS. ANDERSON: If you have any questions, be sure to come up and ask me. (A few students look up from their work.)

Mrs. Anderson closes her record book and takes a set of papers, which she begins to grade. Moments later Billy gets up and walks to her desk.

BILLY: (softly) May I go to the washroom?
MRS. ANDERSON: (looking at the clock, which says 11:01). Can you wait? The bell's going to ring in about fifteen minutes.
BILLY: (frowning) Oh, all right. (He turns and walks back toward his desk. As he passes Carol, he grabs a pencil out of her hand and then flips it back on her desk.)
CAROL: (in a loud whisper) Stop that, you creep!

Billy continues sauntering toward the back of the room. When he arrives at his desk, he makes two complete turns on his heels before dropping into his seat. He then emits a loud yawn, which causes two nearby students to look in his direction. Billy looks at his worksheet and then decides to put his head on his desk.

Three minutes later two boys walk up to Mrs. Anderson's desk for help. Mrs. Anderson talks to them in low tones, using her red pen to point out the errors on their worksheets. As she speaks to them, a girl, also needing help, arrives at her desk. The girl stands in line behind the two boys.

While Mrs. Anderson is working with the students at the front of the room, David takes this opportunity to turn around in his seat and begin copying the paper of the girl behind him. As he copies the work, the girl follows Mrs. Anderson's moves closely. The girl also checks on Mr. Grimes and sees that he, too, is also watching Mrs. Anderson.

When Mrs. Anderson is finished helping the students at her desk, she stands and begins to arrange the papers on her desk. Moments later she begins to walk up and down the aisles checking on her students' progress. Those students who previously had been daydreaming or visiting now begin to work.

MRS. ANDERSON: (continuing to walk) I notice that several of you didn't get too far. (Two boys behind her giggle at her observation.) That means you'll have homework tonight.

Mrs. Anderson spends the next few minutes walking around the room, stopping occasionally to answer a student's question. With the period drawing to a close, the noise level gradually increases as students prepare to leave.

At 11:17 the room is quiet. Twenty-five students sit with their books on their desks waiting for the bell to ring. Mrs. Anderson stands in front of her class. Most eyes are on the clock, watching the sweep second hand as it moves. With seconds remaining in the period, two boys who apparently know exactly where the second hand is when the bell rings begin counting backwards from ten.

BOYS: (in unison) Four, three, two, one!

At the appointed instant, the bell rings, and amidst much chatter and the harsh sounds of moving desks and chairs, most of Mrs. Anderson's students dash from the room. The two boys and three girls who are left behind gather up their books and follow their classmates at a much more leisurely pace.

As soon as the room is empty, Mrs. Anderson walks back to the corner where Mr. Grimes is seated. Mr. Grimes stops sorting through the papers on his desk and motions to her to pull a nearby chair up next to his desk.

MR. GRIMES: (smiling) They're an energetic bunch, aren't they?

MRS. ANDERSON: (sighing) You're right about that.

MR. GRIMES: You have a lunch period now, don't you?

MRS. ANDERSON: Yes, I do.

MR. GRIMES: Well, I won't hold you up. I'll just leave a copy of this completed observation form with you and you can look it over between now and our postobservation conference. OK?

MRS. ANDERSON: That sounds good. (Takes the observation form from Mr. Grimes and glances at it) This may tell me more about my teaching than I want to know. (Chuckles nervously) Could you . . . could you just give me your reactions? How do you think it went? Did I have good interactions with my students?

■ Questions

1. Review the opening minutes of Mrs. Anderson's class period. How might she have begun class more effectively?

2. Should a teacher respond to *every* instance of misbehavior during a class period? What criteria should a teacher use in deciding whether or not to respond to a student's misbehavior?

3. Research has shown that teacher expectations have a significant influence on student achievement. What expectations does Mrs. Anderson convey to her students, and what effects do these expectations appear to have on students?

4. If you were to use a systematic observation instrument, such as Flanders' Interaction Analysis, to record the interactions between Mrs. Anderson and her seventh graders, what kind of picture would emerge? For example, what is the ratio of teacher talk to pupil talk? What is the ratio of teacher indirect and direct behaviors? How do such interaction patterns relate to student achievement? What other systematic observation instruments could be used to observe teacher-pupil interactions?

5. How effective is Mrs. Anderson in the area of classroom management? From the standpoint of Kounin's classroom management theory, how well does Mrs. Anderson deal with disruptions like those involving the pencil sharpener, paper wad throwing, and shoulder punching? To what extent does she demonstrate

withitness? Overlappingness? Smoothness? Group alerting skills? Momentum maintenance? Desist strategies?

6. How efficient is Mrs. Anderson in terms of her use of class time? Critique her performance in terms of academic learning time.

7. What are Mrs. Anderson's instructional objectives? State two or three in the form of behavioral objectives. What levels of Bloom's cognitive taxonomy do Mrs. Anderson's objectives seem to involve? Do her instructional strategies fit her objectives?

8. What kinds of classroom questions does Mrs. Anderson ask? What levels of Bloom's cognitive taxonomy do her questions seem to involve?

9. How would you evaluate Mrs. Anderson's performance as a teacher? What do you base your judgment on? Could Mr. Grimes have collected other data on Mrs. Anderson's teaching besides his observation of classroom interactions?

10. To what extent do the students in Mrs. Anderson's class evidence mastery versus performance goal orientations? What can Mrs. Anderson do to foster mastery goal orientations? Is there anything she can do to make the material more interesting?

Different Strokes

Key Content to Consider for Analyzing This Case:

1. Instructional Evaluation
2. Instructional Objectives
3. Objective Versus Essay Tests
4. Norm Versus Criterion-Referenced Evaluation
5. Grading
6. Operant Conditioning

Sandford Middle School is in the Jackson School District on the north side of a large metropolitan city in a southern state. The primarily middle-class population served by SMS is 65% white, 20% African-American, 10% Hispanic, and 5% other ethnic groups.

Two of the five sixth-grade teachers are first-year teachers. One of the new teachers, Maria Velez, graduated this past May with a BA from a private liberal arts college located within 20 miles of SMS. Maria majored in history and completed an education program leading to certification as an elementary teacher. The other new teacher, Emma Chen, graduated last May from the College of Education with a BSEd, with a specialization in elementary education at State University in the eastern part of the state.

Both teachers attended the pre-school workshops held the week immediately before classes began. It is now Monday of the fifth week of school. Two weeks ago, Esther Starks, the building principal, had notified both teachers that she planned to observe their classes in accordance with the district policy that all first-year teachers be observed and evaluated three times during their first year of teaching to help administrators determine whether or not they should be reemployed the following year. She had given them the teacher evaluation form designed by the Jackson School District so that they would be aware of the behavior she was planning to observe and informed each of them of the day and time she planned to visit their class. She scheduled Maria's observation for the first period today. Last Friday, she left a note in Maria's mailbox as a reminder. Esther plans to observe Emma's class during the first period next Monday.

Esther comes to Maria's room prior to the ringing of the first bell, which signals that the pupils are to enter the building and proceed to their classrooms.

MARIA: Good morning, Esther.

ESTHER: Good morning, Maria. I came a bit early so that I'd have a chance to look around your room before the pupils arrive. (Looks at commercial posters related to ancient Greece, such as the Parthenon, Apollo's temple, a sculpting of Zeus, and photographs of paintings by famous Greek artists, hung from the crown molding around the room. The bulletin boards display commercially prepared maps of early civilizations. No pupil efforts are displayed in the room.) What attractive posters and bulletin board displays! You must be planning to study ancient Greece.

MARIA: Thank you. I bought them at the college bookstore my last year of college. I've always enjoyed the study of ancient Greece and thought that since I'm a history major, I'd someday teach about ancient Greece and have an opportunity to use these posters. Fortunately, the fourth unit in our social studies book, which we are beginning to study today, is about ancient Greece. I'm really excited about it! (A bell rings and the sounds of pupils entering the building grow louder and louder. Soon the pupils enter Maria's room. They greet both Maria and Esther enthusiastically.

MARIA: Good morning, class. Ms. Starks is visiting our class for a while this morning.

MARTIN: (politely) Welcome to our class, Ms. Starks.

ESTHER: Thank you, Martin. Thank you, girls and boys. I appreciate Ms. Velez' invitation to visit with you this morning.

The pupils sit in their seats, which are arranged in two curved rows of 15 chairs, one row in front of the other. Both rows are in the shape of a U.

MARIA: (walking to her desk, which has nothing on it except a file folder containing the lunch tally and attendance report) Let's see, now. There are no empty seats, so no one is absent. (Marks the attendance sheet) Now, how many of you are buying the school lunch today? (Counts raised hands) OK, twenty-one of you are buying lunch. (Marks the lunch tally sheet, walks to the door of the classroom, and inserts both papers into the clip outside the door, then returns to the opening at the mouth of the U and faces the class) This morning we begin our study of my favorite civilization—ancient Greece. But before we begin, I want to review with you briefly the beginnings of civilization so that we can place the development of ancient Greece in the proper time frame. Martha, what do we mean by civilization?

MARTHA: (pause) It's people who are advanced in the way they live.

MARIA: (enthusiastically) That's right. Warren, what do advanced, or civilized, people have that uncivilized people don't have?

WARREN: (looks at his hands on the desk and remains silent)

MARIA: (waits one second) Warren, do you want to give an answer?

WARREN: I can't remember.

MARIA: Vernon, will you help Warren with the answer?

VERNON: (sits silently at his desk)

MARIA: (waits one second) Vernon? (Waits another second) Vernon, are you there?

VERNON: I didn't hear the question.

MARIA: How can we recognize a civilized society, Sam?

SAM: (looking in his book) They have a writing system.

MARIA: Good, even though you had to look in your book! What else do they have? (Pause) Juan?

JUAN: They have a government to keep order.

MARIA: That's great, Juan. Can you tell me another thing they have, Juan? (Maria looks to the back row, where Vernon has just knocked Warren's books off the arm of the chair.) Vernon! Get up out of your chair and move it to the side of the room over by the bookcase. You obviously aren't participating in the class anyway!

VERNON: But Warren took my pencil! It's his fault!

MARIA: Vernon, I asked you to move your chair, and I expect you to do so right this minute without any further discussion! (Warren gets up slowly and moves his chair. He sits down and looks at his book.) Juan, have you thought of another thing that helps us identify a civilized society?

JUAN: Well, let's see. (Pause) Civilized people make tools.

MARIA: What kind of tools? (Noticing a pupil dozing off) Laura? (Laura opens her eyes, startled, and sits up straight.) Were you up too late last night, or are you bored with the lesson?

LAURA: (embarrassed) No ma'am, I'm not bored. We went to dinner at my aunt and uncle's home in Smithfield. It was after midnight when we arrived home. I think the lesson is interesting.

MARIA: Good. I hope you'll be able to stay awake for the rest of the day. We're doing a lot of important things today. Now, Juan just told us that civilized people have tools. I want somebody to tell me what kind of tools they have. Laura, can you do that?

LAURA: Yes. Their tools are made of metal.

MARIA: (enthusiastically) That's right! Good! Now, there's something civilized people can do that uncivilized people haven't been able to do. (Looks around the classroom) Tina, tell us what that is.

TINA: Civilized people are able to move supplies across the land and water.

MARIA: (pleased) Bingo! These are four ways we can identify civilized people. They have a system of writing, make metal tools, have a government that protects people and property, and are able to transport goods. Tell us about one of the earliest civilizations, Matt.

MATT: The first one was called Mesopotamia, which meant "between two rivers." It was where Iraq is now. The two rivers were the Tigris and Euphrates. The soil was very fertile there, so the people began to farm, raise cattle, and grow many of the crops we grow today.

LAMAR: (speaking out) All the early civilizations were located in river valleys. The Hebrews and Phoenicians settled in the Nile Valley, which was also near the Mediterranean Sea.

MARIA: That's right, Lamar. But please raise your hand if you want to speak! But since you brought it up, why did these civilizations spring up in river valleys?

LAMAR: I guess because there was always a water supply for their farms.

MARIA: I'd like it better, Lamar, if you remembered what we studied and didn't have to guess. What are other reasons that civilizations sought out river valleys, Tim?

TIM: Rivers bring rich soil to river valleys. And water makes the climate warmer.

MARIA: Good answer, Tim! Now, tell us what other civilizations began about that time? (Pause) Rosalyn?

ROSALYN: A civilization was formed along the Hwang Ho River in China, and the fourth was in the Indus River Valley in India.

MARIA: Very good, Rosalyn. That covers all four locations: in Mesopotamia between the Tigris and Euphrates, in the Nile River Valley, in central China in the Hwang Ho Valley, and in Northwest India in the Indus River Valley. (Pauses) Now, what were some of the major contributions to civilization that were made during this period? Warren? (Warren stares blankly at his book and does not respond.)

MATT: (calls out) Religions. The Hebrews developed Judaism, Egyptians developed nature worship, Aryans developed Hinduism, and a Hindu named Gautama developed Buddhism. These civilizations also developed writing, medicine, and a calendar. They built pyramids, ships, and temples and used irrigation.

MARIA: Excellent! You must have been interested in this section, Matt.

MATT: Yes, I had never thought about how these things came about! It's really interesting.

ROSALYN: (speaking out) Will we have a test at the end of Unit 4 covering the whole unit, like we did with the other three units?

MARIA: Yes, Rosalyn, we'll have just one test covering ancient Greece.

ROSALYN: Will the test be about the same as the tests we have had on the other units?

MARIA: Yes. Since this is a long unit, the test will probably have fifty multiple-choice questions worth two points each. The grading scale will be the same as it was on the previous three unit tests: A = 92–100; B = 84–91; C = 76–83; D = 68–75; and F = 67 or lower. (Vernon raises his hand.)

MARIA: Yes, Vernon?

VERNON: (haltingly) I made bad grades on the tests we've had. Can I earn points by making some kinds of projects?

MARIA: What kinds of things do you mean, Vernon? Reading about things is usually the best way to learn about them.

VERNON: Well, when my brother was in this class two years ago, he made a building with steps all around it out of cardboard and tape. The Sumerians built buildings like that. They were where people had religious ceremonies. But there were also storage warehouses for grain and other food that belonged to the people.

MARIA: Are you talking about a ziggurat, Vernon?

VERNON: Yes, that's what they're called. I couldn't think of that name. There's a picture of a ziggurat in our book. My brother learned all about the Sumerians when he built the ziggurat. But he's like me—not a good reader, and his teacher gave him points for making projects. That way when he made a low grade in a test, he could bring it up with his project points.

MARIA: But he must have read about the ziggurats if he learned all that information about them.

VERNON: Maybe, but he wouldn't have read it if he hadn't been interested in building the ziggurat.

MARIA: I'd rather have you get interested in becoming a better reader. Then you wouldn't have to spend all that time building something. You can learn anything better by reading about it. Reading is our most important learning tool. Would you be willing to do that?

VERNON: I don't know. I'll try. But I'm not a good reader.

MARIA: Good. And thank you for telling us about the ziggurat, Vernon. Now we need to turn our attention to the magnificent civilization of ancient Greece. If you'll look at the posters I hung around the room last Friday after school, you'll see some of the magnificent architecture the Greeks used in their buildings, which are still standing today. (Pointing) This building is the Parthenon, which is a temple in Athens constructed to honor Athena, the patron goddess of the city. It was constructed entirely of white marble. This building is a temple dedicated to Apollo, who was the Greek god of the sun. This is a statue of Zeus, who is the primary god who rules over all the other Greek gods, so you can see what the sculptor thought he looked like. These posters over here are various paintings by famous artists who lived in ancient Greece.

LAMAR: (speaking out) Their gods looked like real people, just like us!

MARIA: Yes! Some people want to know what their gods look like, so they make them look like humans. Other religions believe that gods are different from people, so they don't show what their gods look like.

LAMAR: I never thought that gods would look like people.

MARIA: I think there are so many interesting questions that are answered as we study history. That's why I love history so much. Well, the time's really flown by. It's just about time for us to move on to reading class. We'll end class today by talking about our history assignment for tomorrow. (A few of the pupils groan discreetly.) These assignments should be interesting. First, I want you to study the map of Greece carefully. Notice how it is surrounded by different bodies of water. Read the section of the chapter that describes the climate of Greece, along with the section that describes the early Aegean world, and be prepared to answer these questions tomorrow. Write them down in your notebooks. (States each question very slowly)

1. How do the bodies of water near Greece affect its climate?

2. On the climate map in your text, locate the five areas in the world having a Mediterranean climate.

3. Explain how this climate affects the life of the people living in these areas.

4. Use the population map in the text to find where most of the people in Greece live. Explain why they live where they do.

5. How did the Lydians and Phoenicians contribute to the development of Greece?

6. Contrast the lifestyles of the citizens of Sparta and those of Athens.

7. What were the major strengths and weaknesses of the democratic government established in Athens?

8. How did personal freedom help to place the Greeks among the most original thinkers in history?

9. Briefly describe the three great Greek philosophers: Socrates, Plato, and Aristotle.

10. List who you believe are the five most important Greek statesmen and tell why you think they were most important.

(At that point a bell rings.) All right, let's take a break. I want you all back in your seats in ten minutes, and we'll begin our reading class.

The pupils get up from their chairs. Some mingle inside the room. Others go into the hall to get a drink, go to the bathroom, etc.

ESTHER: (rising from her chair and stretching) Thanks for allowing me to observe your class. It helped me recall interesting information that I haven't thought about for years. I'll fill out the evaluation form that I gave you a copy of a couple of weeks ago. Can you meet with me after classes end a week from today?

MARIA: Yes, that's a good time for me.

ESTHER: Great! I'll see you then, if not before. (Leaves the room)

The next Monday, Esther enters Emma Chen's sixth-grade classroom approximately 15 minutes before the pupils are scheduled to arrive. Esther had made arrangements for the visit 2 weeks before, and had left a note in Emma's mailbox in the office the previous Friday reminding her of the visit.

ESTHER: Good morning, Emma.

EMMA: Good morning, Esther. I've been expecting you. Is there anything you'd like me to show you or tell you about?

ESTHER: Thanks. Your room is so interesting. I'd appreciate it if you could take me on a guided tour until the pupils arrive. I may not be able to absorb it all in the time available.

All the bulletin boards are completely covered with pupils' work neatly displayed. The tables are covered with models of buildings, bridges, and other structures, along with various kinds of artwork. The chairs are arranged in circles, with five chairs in each circle. A bookcase in the corner is filled with a variety of art materials and supplies.

EMMA: There are many hours of pupil effort represented in each of those displays. There's such a wide range of ability in my class that the only way I can encourage pupils to work at their own level is to allow them to select individual projects, as well as work in groups. These projects are usually a component of a larger project that a committee is working on.

ESTHER: That seems like quite a reasonable way to proceed. But how do you ever manage to think of all these different projects?

EMMA: I don't think of the projects. As we discuss a topic, the pupils select what they think is important information that they should learn. They research this information and develop a strategy for presenting it to the rest of the class. (Pointing to a two-foot wide strip of wrapping paper on the floor extending from the back wall to the front wall on one side of the room) That's a time line. The first week of school we began our study of history. Barry, one of the most immature pupils in the class, thought it was important to demonstrate in some manner how many years were involved in the development of civilization. I allowed that to be his project, and he began to work with that time line. We're now beginning our fourth unit, and he extends the time line appropriately with each unit. I'm sure he'll continue it for the entire year. Eventually it will extend clear around the room. But all of us have learned from that project, especially Barry. I learned about teaching through the use of thematic units when I was at State College, but no one in the school at which I did my internship used this approach. When I first saw our social studies book, it occurred to me that it was organized in such a way that it could serve as the framework for a thematic unit on civilization that could continue all year. I've collected many literature books that deal with ancient history. Some are fiction based on fact, and others are factual. But they serve a dual purpose. They enrich our social studies, and they help pupils realize that they can do their own research through reading. (At that point a bell rings.)

ESTHER: Oh, now the pupils will arrive. I was hoping to find out more about how you manage a thematic unit.

EMMA: That's no problem. Ask the pupils. Any one of them can tell you how he or she selected a project, researched it, and presented it to the class. Today we're going to begin the study of how Greece was settled and the many contributions the Greeks made to civilization. But this will really be a continuation of many of the projects the pupils have already begun, such as the time line and the evolution of agriculture.

The pupils enter the classroom, go to their respective seating areas, and begin to work on their projects. One pupil is taking the class roll and the lunch orders simultaneously. When she finishes, she fills out the two forms and inserts them in the clip outside the door. Then she returns to her group and begins to read a book.

EMMA: Boys and girls, I'm sure that you all know our principal, Ms. Starks. She is visiting us this morning because she is interested in what we are doing in class. I hope that she'll ask you lots of questions about what you're doing and that you'll be able to answer them all. (Some pupils groan at the last remark. Esther and Emma both smile.) Today, we're beginning the study of a new civilization. Have any of you looked ahead to see what it is? (Several hands go up.) Martin, what is it?

MARTIN: Greece.

EMMA: Good. How did you know that?

MARTIN: I read the first part of the chapter last night.

CHARLIE: (whispering to Doug) What a nerd, reading ahead in the book! (Doug chortles.)

EMMA: (pleasantly) Doug, do you have something you'd like to say to the class?

DOUG: No ma'am. I just coughed. (Becomes interested in looking at his book)

EMMA: (looking back at Martin) It's good that you're reading ahead, Martin! Reading ahead shows that you're interested in learning. Can you tell us something interesting you learned about Greece?

MARTIN: I read about the location and climate of Greece and learned that there are only five places in the world that have the same type of climate as Greece. I thought the geography group might be interested in that information.

EMMA: Good thinking, Martin! It's good that you're aware of what topics other people in the class are working on.

THERESA: I read part of the new chapter, too. I noticed that there are two new groups of people that the culture committee can give a report on.

EMMA: Good, Theresa. You're helping another group, too. Do you remember who these new people are?

THERESA: They are the Achaeans and the Mycenaceans. I'm not sure I pronounced them right.

MARK: (waving his hand enthusiastically) Ms. Chen?

EMMA: (equally enthusiastic) What is it, Mark!

MARK: I thought of another work group we'll need to have!

EMMA: OK. Tell us what group we need.

MARK: We'll need an important people committee, because this unit begins to talk about important people, like Homer, Pericles, Socrates, Plato, and Aristotle. I think I've heard of some of these people, but I don't know anything about them. So someone should make a book of important people in the different civilizations.

EMMA: That's an excellent suggestion, Mark. Is this a group that you'd like to work on?

MARK: Yes. I think that would be cool.

EMMA: Good! I'll appoint you chair of the important people committee. I'm sure there will be other people in the class who would like to work on that committee. If there are, they can tell you. (Four people raise their hand) Probably two or three others would be enough for that committee right now, but we may need more people on it when we begin to learn about more and more important people. Thanks for that suggestion, Mark.

Now, let's all skim the entire unit on ancient Greece to identify important information that needs to be presented to the class. By Wednesday you should be able to tell me what projects you want to do for this unit. We'll probably spend two weeks on it.

Barry, you'll begin to have more and more entries on your time line because more things are happening in the world now than were happening when civilization was just beginning.

BARRY: That's OK. I'll get them all recorded.

EMMA: I hope so, because that time line is important for all of us. (Barry beams.) Let's see, we already have a culture group, a religion group, a geography group, and a government group, don't we? (Pupils answer affirmatively.) Can any of you think of any other groups we need to form?

SYLVIA: There are at least two wars that I read about. Maybe we'd better form a war group.

EMMA: You're right, Sylvia. That's a good suggestion, because from now on the number of wars will increase. And wars do have a big influence on civilization. Would you like to chair that group, Sylvia?

SYLVIA: Yes, I think it would be interesting to learn about what causes wars and how they could be avoided. Consuela wants to be on the war committee, too.

EMMA: That's fine. You could use four or five people on that committee. (Four hands go up.)

GEROME: Ms. Chen, is it OK if Sam and me go to the library for a while?

EMMA: You and Sam were at the library for at least two hours Friday afternoon. Why do you need to go again today?

GEROME: We found a lot of books about ancient Greece Friday and gave them to Ms. Simpson to check out to us. But she said that there were some other books that we could use in our study of ancient Greece. She said that if we come to the library this morning she'd have them all checked out to us. And since there would probably be at least fifty altogether, she'd stack them on a library cart that we could use to bring them to our room.

EMMA: (pleased) How nice of Ms. Simpson! You and Sam must behave yourselves nicely in the library for her to give you such special attention.

GEROME: (embarrassed) She's a nice lady. But we don't do anything bad in the library.

EMMA: Good! I'm glad to hear that. And, yes, you and Sam may go to the library. We might be able to use some of the books for book reports in our English class. All right, class, it's just about time for the break. When you come back, I want you to meet with your groups and plan the reports and projects you want to prepare for this unit. In addition to your planning the reports, I want you all to read the entire unit on the ancient Greeks. Be aware of who settled that area, how the Mediterranean climate affected the settlers, what caused the

Figure 13–1 Teacher Evaluation Report
Jackson School District

			O	S	U
Teacher's name _____ School _____					
Evaluator _____ Date _____					
Grade _____ Time of observation _____ _____					

Teacher's name _____ School _____

Evaluator _____ Date _____

Grade _____ Time of observation _____ _____
                                                          began   ended

                                     Conference time   _____ _____
                                                          began   ended

RANKINGS: Outstanding   Performance reflects exceptional qualities of teaching
                          and class management.
           Satisfactory   Performance exhibits expected and desired
                          professional behavior.
           Unsatisfactory Performance exhibits weak performance and/or
                          teaching deficiencies.

Mark *X* below the appropriate ranking: Outstanding (O), Satisfactory (S), or
Unsatisfactory (U), after each item:

	O	S	U
I. TEACHING PROCEDURES _____			
A. Evidence of organization and planning _____			
B. Knowledge of subject matter _____			
C. Individualization of instruction _____			
D. Variety of teaching strategies _____			
E. Effective use of wait time _____			
F. Encourages good work-study habits _____			
G. Appropriate practice/review procedures ____			
H. Evaluates learners effectively _____			
I. Effective use of class time _____			
II. CLASSROOM MANAGEMENT _____			
A. Effective classroom management _____			
B. Attractive physical setting _____			
C. Effective interaction with pupils _____			
D. Maintenance of appropriate records _____			
E. Positive classroom climate _____			
F. Appropriate use of group work _____			
G. Effective monitoring of pupils _____			
H. Is reasonable, fair, and impartial _____			
I. Keeps pupils on task _____			
III. PROFESSIONAL CHARACTERISTICS _____			
A. Accepts responsibilities _____			
B. Encourages self-discipline _____			
C. Continual self-assessment _____			
D. Keeps abreast of new ideas _____			
E. Professional appearance _____			
F. Develops rapport with pupils _____			
G. Keeps parents informed _____			
H. Follows school district policies _____			
I. Poised and self-assured _____			

various wars that broke out, contributions that the ancient Greeks made to civilization, what caused the Greek dark age, how Greece became a democracy, what the major cities of Greece were, what Greek life was like during the Golden Age, and who Alexander the Great was and what he did. Members of the study groups will need to begin researching the information related to your groups and prepare reports for the class to study. (Enthusiastically) OK. Break time. When you return, you'll have an hour to meet with your groups. (Pupils get up from their seats. Some leave the room, some walk to the bookcase and look at the new books, others stand in groups and converse.)

ESTHER: (to Emma) This was a most interesting experience for me. I've read about thematic units and heard them discussed at workshops, but I've never seen one in operation. I'm astounded at how much work your pupils are doing. And they seem to enjoy it.

EMMA: This is a brand new experience for me, too. So far, I'm really pleased with the outcomes. But sometimes I think it's too good to be true. Maybe the pupils will become bored with it or get tired of doing so much work. But so far, they've actually become more enthusiastic as we continue to implement the unit.

ESTHER: I'm really interested to see how it works out!

EMMA: You're certainly welcome to come to my class anytime. You don't have to be a spectator. You can pitch right in and work with the pupils. Drop in anytime. You don't need to give me any kind of notice. We pretty much do what you saw this morning every day. Except that in a week, the different groups will present reports to the class and turn in written work to me to be graded.

ESTHER: I wanted to ask you about grades. How do you decide what they will be?

EMMA: I've examined all the pupils' records and have a pretty good idea of the level on which they function. They select their own projects and pretty much seek their own level. If they select something I think is too hard, I make suggestions that will make it easier, and vice versa. I don't want the assignments to be either too easy or too hard. If the final report or project is really excellent, I give it an A. If it's better than average, I give it a B. Average is C. Below average, D. I don't give below D if they turn in something. This system isn't infallible, but it takes individual ability as well as effort into consideration, and I think it is fair. (At this point the bell rings and the pupils rush back to their groups.)

ESTHER: Thanks for letting me observe your class. I really enjoyed it. Can you meet with me in my office next Monday after the pupils leave? I'd like to go over the evaluation form with you.

EMMA: Sure, that's a good time for me. I'm anxious to see my evaluation.

ESTHER: Good. I'll see you then, if not before.

■ Questions

1. How would you describe the student evaluation system used by Maria? By Emma? Which system do you prefer? Why?

2. What are cognitive and affective behaviors as defined in the *Taxonomy of Educational Objectives* by Bloom et al.? Which teacher's questions encouraged pupils to respond on higher levels of the cognitive domain? Of the affective do-

main? Give one example of the highest-level assignment made by each teacher for each domain related to teacher-pupil dialogue, discipline, or academic assignments.

3. In her questioning technique, Maria Velez usually called a pupil's name before she asked a question. Emma Chen sometimes asked the question before she called the pupil's name. Which of these is the better technique? Why? Both teachers provided reinforcement to pupils who answered a question correctly. How did the reinforcement differ? Which teacher's reinforcement was more effective? Why?

4. Both Maria and Emma were studying the same historical periods and using the same textbook, yet their approaches were quite different. Compare and contrast the types of information Maria's and Emma's pupils would learn about ancient Greece. Which information would you prefer your pupils to learn? Why?

5. Compare and contrast the instructional objectives and teaching methods of Maria and Emma. What different curriculum models were involved? Which will have the greatest impact on student learning? Why?

6. Critique the teacher evaluation report. Does it really relate to effective teaching? How would you change the instrument? What would you add or subtract? Should such rating scales be used to determine merit pay for teachers?

7. What are formative and summative evaluation? Which type of evaluation is the principal making in this case?

8. At what levels of Maslow's need hierarchy are Emma and Maria primarily operating? How does this help explain their differences in teaching procedures?

9. Compare and contrast Emma and Maria in terms of their use of academic learning time, the classroom climates, their learner accountability and monitoring strategies, and their practice and review procedures. Who is more effective and likely to have the greatest impact on student learning? Why?

10. To which teacher would you give the highest overall ratings on the teacher evaluation report? On what categories would they be most similar? Most different?

14

A Class Divided

Key Content to Consider for Analyzing This Case:

1. Group Dynamics
2. Intrinsic Versus Extrinsic Motivation
3. Classroom Management
4. Instructional Objectives
5. Operant Conditioning
6. Observational Learning

Central Elementary School is in a working-class neighborhood in a Midwestern city of about 75,000. Built in the early 1970s, the school was designed to handle a K-6 student body of about 600. Before the end of the decade, however, Central experienced a large influx of students whose parents had taken jobs at three new plants that had opened on the edge of the city. To handle the enrollment that had now mushroomed to over 800 students, a new wing for fifth- and sixth-grade students was added in the early 1980s. The school's student body is approximately 80% white, 15% African-American, and 5% Hispanic.

Karen Ellison has been teaching sixth-grade reading and language arts at Central Elementary for 8 years. She is 33 and a graduate of the state's major university. At this moment, she is seated at her desk, spending the remaining minutes of her lunch period reviewing materials for her next class—a group of 27 students, two thirds of whom are reading at or near grade level, and the remaining one third, 2 to 3 years below grade level. This latter group of low-ability students has been especially difficult to work with during the past few class meetings. Karen knows that these students are frustrated by having to read materials that are beyond their independent reading levels.

Two days ago, Karen introduced a unit from the new district-adopted reading text organized around the theme of courage. She announced to the class that they would spend about a week reading several short stories dealing with that theme and exploring what it means to be courageous. Almost immediately, her lower-ability students began to grumble about having to read stories that were "boring" and "stupid." They wanted to continue doing the exercises in the reading workbooks they had been using.

Karen has just finished skimming today's story—about an Eskimo boy who kills his first polar bear—when the passing bell rings. She gets up from her desk and moves out into the hallway to stand next to her classroom door. Throngs of noisy, excited fifth and sixth graders have already poured out into the hallway. There is a lot of good-natured kidding and shoving as the youngsters work their way to their next class.

Karen notices two of her students who are getting too excited as they wrestle playfully, each trying to prevent the other from getting into his locker.

KAREN: (loudly) Come on, Kevin and David. You can play around all you want after school. Right now, though, you have reading, and you both better be in your seats by the time the bell rings. (Motions them into the room)

KEVIN: (in a voice filled with exaggerated despair) But Miss Ellison. He won't let me in my locker. This creep just keeps messing with me. (Takes another playful swipe at David, who is fumbling with the key to his padlock)

Karen senses that the two boys will get to class faster if she ignores them and does not give them an opportunity to draw her further into their harmless squabbling. She gives both boys a stern, authoritative frown and then turns to direct a trio of girls just entering the room to take a reading book from the stack on her desk.

About 5 minutes into the class period—after students have finished getting their books and papers organized, sharpening pencils, and generally winding down from the hustle and bustle of the passing period—Karen stands in front of the group ready to begin the lesson.

KAREN: \ Everyone open your books to page 99. We're going to read a story about a boy who lives in the Arctic and shows a very special kind of courage. Remember we said yesterday that a person can show courage in many different ways. Who remembers how we defined courage? (Beth and Mary raise their hands.)

BILLY: (blurting out) Hey, I ain't got no book.

KAREN: (with irritation) I told you to take one off the desk as soon as you came into the room, Billy. Now hurry up and get one. (Motions with her left hand toward the few books that remain on her desk) Mary, what did we say courage is?

MARY: It means being able to do something without being afraid of getting hurt.

KAREN: That's part of it, Mary. Can you give us an example?

MARY: Like that guy that jumped in the river last week and saved that little girl who was drowning. He wasn't afraid.

KAREN: Good example, Mary. But you mean jumped into the river, don't you? Beth, what were you going to say?

BETH: (loudly and clearly) Well, sometimes being courageous means that you're willing to stand by what you believe. Even though other people might criticize you, you do what's right.

Suddenly Billy, who is returning to his seat with his reading book, engages in a brief bit of horseplay with Wally, who has stuck his foot out in a halfhearted attempt to trip Billy. Everyone's attention momentarily turns to the two boys.

KAREN: (angrily) Get back to your seat immediately, Billy. If I have any more problems from either of you, you're staying after school. (Before proceeding, she looks around the entire room to make certain that all eyes are on her.) Now,

Beth, you've said that someone can be courageous without necessarily facing physical danger. (Beth gives an affirmative nod.) Can you give us an example?

BETH: Well (hesitating), I remember this basketball coach on TV who made his team give up the state championship it had won because one of his players was ineligible. (Several of the boys break into exaggerated expressions of disbelief at what their classmate said.)

KAREN: That certainly took courage, didn't it? Well, the story that we're going to read now involves an Eskimo boy who shows that kind of courage. As we read, be thinking about how today's story shows a different kind of courage from what we saw in yesterday's story. Okay, who'd like to begin reading on page 99?

About seven students raise their hand; another five or so stare off into space or fidget restlessly. The rest appear ready to follow along as soon as someone else begins reading aloud. Karen is surprised to see John, one of her poorer readers, with his hand held aloft, urgently waving it back and forth. She hesitates for a moment, considering whether to call on John or Judy, perhaps the best reader in the class. Karen decides to let John begin reading.

KAREN: Okay, John.

JOHN: Miss Ellison, do we have to read these stories again? I don't like these stories. They're dumb.

SEVERAL OTHER STUDENTS: (echoing) Yeah!

JOHN: These stories are boring. Why can't we do more of the vocabulary worksheets and the stuff in the workbooks?

KAREN: Now wait a minute. (Gestures with her right hand to calm her students) We've spent two weeks in the workbooks, and now it's time to read and put into practice the things we've learned.

SCOTT: I don't want to work in the workbooks again; that's *really* boring.

MICHAEL: Right, these stories give us something to talk about. We learn how different people live and stuff. When we're in the workbooks, we just fill in the blanks, check your work, fill in the blanks, check your work.

Karen realizes that her students are divided—about one third want to return to the drill-and-practice exercises in the workbooks, another third want to get on with reading the story, and the remaining third are seemingly content to do either one. She also notices that those who do not want to read the story are all reading well below grade level. Because she believes that her students will not learn to read better by working exclusively on exercises pertaining to prefixes, suffixes, and so on, Karen resolves that all her students are going to read the stories in the unit.

KAREN: (firmly) We *are* going to read and then discuss the stories in this unit on courage. When you get to junior high, and definitely by high school, you will have to read and talk about different kinds of literature. Now, Judy, I believe you were ready to read. (A few resistant students scowl and slouch down provocatively low in their seats, making every effort to use body language to express their disagreement with the teacher.)

JUDY: (in a singsong voice) "The polar bear is the king of the Arctic. Among land animals, it is the largest predator in the world. For the people who live in the Arctic, hunting the polar bear is the truest test of a man's courage. . . ."

After Judy reads about four paragraphs, Karen calls on Michael, who she knows reads well. After Michael, she calls on Elizabeth, also a good reader. To keep the class moving ahead and to build up some interest in the story, Karen has her stronger readers read before calling on those who do not read as well.

KAREN: Okay, John, now would you like to read a bit from the top of page 102?

JOHN: Okay. (Stumbling and in a low voice) "Though a . . . polar bear might look . . . white, its skin . . . is really black . . . and its hair has no color at all. Each hair is really a hanging . . . uh, a hollow tub . . . uh, a hollow tube. Sunlit . . . ah, sunlight . . . reflects . . . off the hair, and this makes the bear . . . white . . . ah, look white.

As John is reading, several students are becoming noticeably restless and fidgety. Three students are looking around the room. One boy is writing something on his desk. A girl seated in the row by the window is reading a magazine. Four students are whispering in low tones at the back of the room. Suddenly the four begin laughing. Nearly all the students turn to the back of the room. John, however, continues with his slow, labored reading.

KAREN: (irritated) John, stop right there. We have some people who can't seem to follow along. (Walks to the back of the room) What seems to be the problem here? (All four students stare at the open books on their desks, avoiding eye contact with the teacher.) Is there any reason you can't follow along? (Three of the students shake their head; the fourth, Allen, begins to speak.)

ALLEN: It's just when some people read you can't hear them, and they go so slowly. (Several students nearby giggle.) It's really hard to follow along.

KAREN: Well, you'll just have to concentrate. (Points down to the open book on Allen's desk) You never know when I might call on one of you to read. All right, John, would you continue, please.

JOHN: I don't want to read any more of this. It's a dumb story. Why can't I work in the workbook?

KAREN: (obviously frustrated) Listen, everybody, we *are* going to finish this story and this unit together. (Begins to move to the front of the room to be easily visible to everyone in the class) I know that most of you are eager and ready to move ahead. If you're not, be patient and do your best to follow along. It won't be long before we start doing something in class that you like and maybe some other people won't. (Before returning to the story, she surveys the class carefully to make certain that each student is paying attention.) All right, everyone, we're right in the middle of page 102. I'll read to the top of page 104, and then I'll have someone else read from there.

For the remainder of the period, the atmosphere in Karen's room is tense. To avoid the risk of another disruption, Karen only calls on her better students to read. She walks up and down the aisles, carefully checking to see that each student is paying attention. After finishing the story, Karen conducts a brief discussion that focuses on several questions she prepared beforehand. Her better students respond enthusiastically and animatedly, while her slower readers sit silently with blank expressions on their faces. During the final 10 minutes of class, Karen has her students write a paragraph on "My Most Courageous Moment."

Two days later, just after the students have left for home, Karen decides to drop by the office of Claudia Jenkins, the school's curriculum coordinator. Claudia has just hung up her phone when Karen arrives.

KAREN: Do you have a minute, Claudia? I'd like to get your advice about one of my sixth-grade classes.

CLAUDIA: Sure. My husband's not picking me up until five. Come on in. Have a seat. Is this about your sixth-period class?

KAREN: You've got it; that's the one. They're really good kids—all of them. It's just that I don't know if I'm giving all of them the right curriculum. My real problem is that I actually have two classes in there—the kids who read at or near grade level, and then those who are two or more years behind. I can't seem to come up with a curriculum that suits both groups.

CLAUDIA: I know what you mean.

KAREN: For a few weeks we did workbook exercises—you know, phonics drills, word attack skills, and so on. The kids were staying together pretty well, though I sensed that the kids at grade level were getting a bit bored. I figured their turn would come when we started reading in the new readers that just came in.

CLAUDIA: I know the book you're talking about. It's a good one; it has some excellent stories.

KAREN: Right. It's really a good book. No book is perfect, but this one is close. So ever since we started in the readers—I put together a unit on courage—my low-ability kids don't want to read. They want to keep doing the workbooks! I guess the structure and always having to look for the *right* answer to fill in the blank with gives them security. But their comprehension scores aren't going to improve unless they actually start reading.

CLAUDIA: (with concern) It's hard to work with a group of kids if some of them want to be doing something else. Have you thought about grouping them?

KAREN: I thought you might suggest that. And to be honest, that was my first reaction. But I really don't believe in tracking or grouping; there's enough research out there to show that it doesn't work. And, darn it, someone's got to wean these kids from always doing worksheets and filling in the blanks. That's not reading, but some of the kids seem to think it is. (With determination) But I'm not going to teach in a certain way just because it'll make some of the kids happier. If I don't push them to read now, they're just going to get further and further behind.

CLAUDIA: (nodding her head) I agree with what you're saying. I think it's important that all students get beyond drill and practice exercises.

KAREN: Also I think it's important for my kids to learn to function in a group situation—where the group focuses on something that *everyone* has read. I think that's the best way for them to learn higher-order thinking skills. (Sighing) But, oh, it's certainly not easy. Sometimes I wish I could design a separate curriculum for each child, but that's not realistic.

CLAUDIA: What I hear you asking, then, is how can you develop a curriculum that challenges your more able students and doesn't turn off the less able ones. Right?

KAREN: Yes, I guess that's what it comes down to. Really, how do you meet the needs of all students? It's a real dilemma, because no two kids are at the same place.

CLAUDIA: I think you've done a good job clarifying your problem. It seems to me that the logical thing to do now is to ask, given all the facts and given your views about what an effective teacher does, what are you going to do? What options are open to you?

Figure 14-1 Central Elementary School
Reading Comprehension and Vocabulary Grade
Equivalent Scores

Class: Sixth Grade Reading
Teacher: Karen Ellison
Period: Sixth

Name	Reading Comprehension*	Vocabulary Grade Equivalent*
1. Ahrens, Kevin	5.6	5.8
2. Anderson, Jan	5.5	5.6
3. Baker, David	5.7	5.8
4. Becker, Hannah	4.5	4.5
5. Boyer, Mary	5.0	4.9
6. Byrne, Ann	5.1	5.0
7. Dukes, Walter	3.4	3.5
8. Green, John	3.5	3.6
9. Gunn, Amy	5.2	5.6
10. Hahn, Elizabeth	5.4	5.7
11. Harrison, William	3.8	3.9
12. Herring, Lynn	3.4	3.6
13. Holt, Anita	3.7	4.0
14. Jarvis, Nicki	5.8	6.0
15. Jennings, Judy	6.5	6.7
16. Munson, John	6.2	6.7
17. Murray, Michael	6.5	7.0
18. Newberry, Scott	5.7	5.7
19. Neff, Rachel	3.1	3.3
20. Payne, Cyndi	3.9	4.1
21. Peacock, Beth	4.8	5.1
22. Reynolds, Annie	5.7	5.7
23. Rodriguez, Alfredo	4.7	4.9
24. Schmidt, Carol	5.7	5.6
25. Sontag, Allen	5.9	6.2
26. Yang, Ming	5.5	5.8
27. Zimmerman, Martha	6.0	6.4

*Scores are for the Test of Academic Progress given during the fifth month of the fifth grade. Decimal scores refer to months; e.g., 5.9 = fifth year, ninth month.

Questions

1. Is a teacher with a group of students of varying ability levels justified in giving better students more opportunities to participate in class so as to avoid disruptions? What are the possible advantages and disadvantages of grouping students according to ability? Does educational research generally support or refute the practice of grouping? What procedures can be used to form and work with ability groups?

2. Are there techniques—such as small-group instruction, peer tutoring, learning centers, individualized instruction, or mastery learning—that might be effective for Karen's situation? How realistic would it be for Karen to implement each of these strategies?

3. Are Karen's more able students motivated intrinsically or extrinsically? Her less able students?

4. From the standpoint of a motivational theory like Maslow's need hierarchy, what needs seem to be operating? Can the differing reactions of the students to the use of the courage theme be explained by their different need levels? Do frustration and aggression help explain such disruptive behavior as Kevin and David's wrestling? How might Karen lessen the tension between the two groups of students?

5. How would you explain Karen's attempt to have her stronger readers read first in terms of observational learning? Does this strategy seem to be working? Why or why not?

6. Explain the disruptive behavior in the classroom, such as the horseplay between Wally and Billy, in operant conditioning terms. What reinforcers seem to be maintaining the behavior? Can behavior modification techniques be used to modify the behaviors being emitted?

7. What instructional objectives does Karen seem to be pursuing? To what levels of Bloom's cognitive taxonomy do Karen's objectives relate? What recommendations would you give Karen regarding her instructional objectives?

8. What are some of the ways that individual students in the class might view the reading material Karen is using? How do some of the individual students view themselves (self-concept)? What criteria do individuals among the two groups of students use to determine whether an activity is meaningful and worthwhile?

9. Can Karen's students be analyzed in terms of their being field-dependent or field-independent learners? What instructional procedures work best with the two types of learners?

10. What is the best interpretation that Karen can make of the reading comprehension and vocabulary scores?

15

Keeping Your Eyes Open

Michael Groza is a 22-year-old senior at Zane State College and is majoring in elementary education. He is currently serving an internship in an eighth-grade class at Fort Henry Middle School, a multicultural urban middle school located in Bridgeton, a city on the Ohio River about 20 miles from his college.

Bridgeton is an old city that was settled by the early explorers as a port city. It quickly grew into a thriving community because of its location. It now has a population of approximately 85,000, approximately 50% white, 20% African-American, 15% Hispanic, and 15% Asian-American.

As Michael drove to Bridgeton to report for his internship experience, he was awestruck by the rural scenery surrounding his college town. However, as he neared the outskirts of Bridgeton, it seemed as if he were entering another world. The winding road on which he had been driving widened into an access road entering an expressway stretching over what once had been a thriving manufacturing center.

But then the many deserted brick skeletons of what once were active, busy, industrial factories that manufactured electrical apparatus, glassware, batteries, good china, metal parts, and other products gave testimony to the death of the economy of this area. The demise of these factories was also apparent in the boarded-up doors, broken windows, and graffiti exterior of these buildings.

As Mike's route took him closer to the downtown section near the river, Mike came upon what had once been an affluent suburban area dotted with beautiful mansions. But these mansions had long ago been converted to apartment houses, which were in bad repair, with chipped paint, broken windows, and trash scattered about the bare lawns, with no evidence of plant life, with the exception of a few clumps of weeds here and there.

Later, the mansions gave way to decaying tenement apartment complexes, small dilapidated houses, and abandoned brick buildings that had once been successful manufacturing plants, now with broken windows and boarded-up doors. After driving for three or four miles on the expressway, Mike saw a sign pointing to the exit ramp that led to Fort Henry Middle School. Obviously, some of his students would be residents of the area he had just driven through.

As Mike enters the parking lot behind the school, he notices that several sections of the chain-link fence are pulled apart and leaning askew. The cement driveway is cracked, with chunks of cement uprooted. The back of the large, old building is covered with graffiti, and selected words, evidently obscene, had been painted over with black paint. The paint on the wooden trim is discolored and chipped off.

Mike opens the back door of the school and walks into the hallway. He is gratified to notice that the hallway has been recently painted a light blue and the composition floors are clean and shiny. He follows the room numbers to the classroom to which he has been assigned and sees that his supervising teacher is already in the room.

MIKE: Ms. Rudner, I'm Michael Groza. I've been assigned to you for my internship.

MS. RUDNER: Welcome, Michael. Please call me Roz. I'm delighted that you're here. I requested an intern this semester because I'm introducing a reading and writing workshop into my English curriculum. Our classes have met for two weeks, and the pupils have pretty much gotten into the swing of things.

MIKE: It's nice to meet you, Roz. I go by Mike. I'm really glad that you're using reading and writing workshops. We studied those strategies in my reading and language arts methods courses. Based upon my limited knowledge of them, I think they are the approaches I'd like to use. Now I'll have an opportunity to actually use them.

ROZ: Good. How about you observing all my classes this week? Then if you feel comfortable with the idea, you can take over one of the classes next Monday. It might be a better experience for you to do the writing workshop. It's more open to innovations than the reading workshop. I think both reading and writing workshops are especially appropriate for a school population like ours.

MIKE: In what way?

ROZ: Our classes generally follow the ethnic make-up of Bridgeton. For instance, the writing class you'll be teaching comprises fifteen whites, six African-Americans, five Hispanics, and four Asian-Americans. There's a wide range of ability among the pupils. By using the workshop approach, we can allow each of our pupils to work at his or her level in both reading and writing. That allows each of them to have an opportunity to succeed.

MIKE: I didn't expect to jump into teaching so quickly, but I'm delighted that I can. The writing workshop's fine with me, because I became really interested in it when we studied about it in our language arts method class. But I haven't ever taught before, so I may goof up a little here and there.

ROZ: I'm not worried, Mike. Both of us are going to be operating on a trial-and-error basis for a while. But when you experiment with new teaching strategies, that's the only way you can go. Our school district has an observation instrument we use. I have a copy here in my desk. Yes, here it is. (Instrument shown at end of case) Go over it briefly, and that'll give you a clue regarding the things that we'll discuss about your teaching. I'll fill it out as I observe your class Monday.

MIKE: That's fine with me. Let's go for it.

Soon, the first-period eighth-grade class comes into the room, visiting with one another, pushing, shoving, and generally acting like eighth-grade students. Mike's mind automatically calls up the name of the singing group The Motley Crew. This class exemplifies a motley crew. It has 31 pupils, whose dress ranges from Ivy League to dire straits. The majority wear either boots or basketball shoes. Long, un-washed hair seems to be the norm, along with gold jewelry and tattoos.

ROZ: All right, class. Please take your seats and quiet down. I want to introduce you to Mr. Groza, our intern from Zane State College. (Uproar from the class. "Zane State College, Rah, Rah, Rah." Jeers from the boys. "A college gentleman. Woowee, a brain! Look at the suit and tie." From the girls, "Whatta hunk. Sexy. Spend some time with me, Mr. Groza.") That's enough! You're being rude, and you all know better than that. (The class quiets down quickly.) Mr. Groza's your intern for the remainder of this semester, and he'll be in charge of your writing class beginning next week.

STUDENTS: "All right! Great! What a writing teacher! I'm gonna like writing!"

MIKE: I'm happy to be here, and I'm looking forward to working with you in the writing class.

ROZ: We're happy you're here, too, Mr. Groza. It's always good to have interns from Zane.

It's Monday, and Mike arrives at school earlier and more excited than usual. Today he's taking over the writing workshop. He's studied the various components of the workshop and mentally rehearsed the strategies he plans to use throughout the period. By mutual agreement, Roz will be a silent observer of the class and not interfere in the instruction or classroom management. During this period, she will evaluate Mike's performance using the teaching observation form they have already discussed.

After what seems to be an eternity to Mike, the buses arrive and the pupils in his writing class begin to enter the room.

JAMAL: You're the man today, ain't ya', Mr. Groza!

MIKE: Yes, I'm the man, Jamal. Thanks for remembering.

Other pupils enter, greet Mike, and visit with one another. When the bell rings, Mike starts the class.

MIKE: Let's get right to work now, class. During the mini-lesson this morning I'm going to review for you the three ways that direct quotations are written. In re-viewing your writing Friday, I noticed that some of you aren't punctuating di-rect quotations correctly. I'm going to write some examples on the board, and I want you to copy them in your writing journal. (Mike writes these examples on the board):

Mary said, "Wait for me."

"Wait for me," said Mary.

"Wait," said Mary, "until I come."

As he is completing the third sentence, a rubber eraser hits the chalkboard just to the left of his head. Mike whirls around.

MIKE: (angrily) Who threw that?

TOD: Cathy threw it.
CATHY: I did not. You know I didn't, Mr. Groza!
JASON: Tod did it!
TOD: Not me.

Several pupils begin to accuse other pupils. Some stand up and point to others.

MIKE: Stop it! Get back in your seats and be quiet. (After order is restored, angrily) There will be no more throwing of objects! You know that's against the rules! (Pause and quiet) Now, look at these three sentences. These are basically the only way you can write direct quotations. Notice that in sentence one, the direct quotation's at the end of the sentence. In sentence two, the direct quotation's at the beginning of the sentence. In sentence three, the name of the speaker separates the words of the direct quotation. The end punctuation's inside the quotation marks, and the first word of the direct quotation's capitalized.

MATT: I always put the periods outside the quotation marks. Why's that wrong?

MIKE: Punctuation marks are called conventions. Because true language is the spoken language, punctuation marks were invented by printers after the printing press was invented. Eventually, rules for punctuation were agreed on by all the printers and became the accepted rules. This doesn't mean they're better than other ways, Matt, like your putting the periods outside the quotation marks, but they're the accepted way. Other ways aren't accepted by writers and printers, which, I guess, does make them wrong. One of the things we'll do in writing workshop is to learn accepted grammar, usage, and mechanics like punctuation.

SID: Why can't we just go ahead and punctuate the way we want to?

MIKE: You can, if you want to have points taken off for doing it incorrectly.

SID: But you just said that the conventional way isn't really more correct than other ways.

MIKE: But it is the only way accepted by literate people, and I'm trying hard to help you all become literate. (Looks at his watch) I've already exceeded the time set aside for the mini-lesson, so we need to go on to the state of the class conference. As I call your name, if you're writing a first draft, say *one*. For a second draft, say *two*. If you're conferencing, revising, proofing, or publishing, just say the word. Ted?

TED: The word.

MIKE: What?

TED: You said if we're conferencing, revising, proofing, or publishing, just say the word. I'm revising, so I said, "The word."

MIKE: Very funny. You're the type of commodian who needs to be flushed. (Appreciative laughter from the class)

Mike polls each class member and indicates his or her activity for the day on the chart he has prepared. He records on the chart as follows:

STATE OF CLASS CHART

Name:	M	T	W	Th	F
Ted	RV				
Cathy	2				
Jamal	1				
Lee	C				

MIKE: OK, now. We have forty minutes to work on our writing. Let's get to work. Those of you who are conferencing with each other, do it quietly. Those of you who are conferencing with me, come to my desk one at a time. I'll see Lee first. (Lee comes up and takes a seat next to Mike, and they begin to discuss his writing. Other conferencing pupils take their chairs and sit by their conferees. Mike is so absorbed in his conference with Lee that he fails to notice a paper airplane sailing from one side of the room to the other. Tod leaves his seat and walks toward the pencil sharpener.)

JAMAL: Ouch! What in hell wrong wit'chu, man? (He jumps out of his seat and shoves Tod off balance.)

TOD: Watch it, Jamal.

JAMAL: You watch it, man. You kick me in the leg.

MIKE: (jumping up out of his seat) What's going on back there?

JAMAL: This honkie jes' walk down the aisle and kick me in the leg.

TOD: He jumped out of his seat and shoved me halfway across the room.

JAMAL: You kick me again, man, and I break yo' head. Maybe I do it anyway jes' for sport.

TOD: I don't want no trouble with you, Jamal.

JAMAL: Then you jes' keep yo' hans and feet to yo'self.

MIKE: Tod, what're you doing out of your seat, anyway? You're supposed to be working on your second draft.

TOD: I needed to sharpen my pencil.

MIKE: You took sort of a long, out-of-the-way route to the pencil sharpener, didn't you? You go back to your seat. If you need to sharpen your pencil from now on, you ask permission first.

TOD: That's not fair! (Looking at Ms. Rudner) Ms. Rudner lets us sharpen our pencils without asking. You're treatin' us like babies. (Ms. Rudner remains silent.)

MIKE: Maybe you don't kick people on your way to the pencil sharpener while Ms. Rudner is teaching. When you stop acting like a baby, maybe I'll stop treating you like a baby—if, indeed, asking you to get permission to sharpen your pencil is treating you like a baby.

TOD: I didn't even kick Jamal. He just made that fuss to get me into trouble.

JAMAL: Yeah, man. And pigs fly, too.

CYNTHIA: He did kick Jamal, Mr. Groza. I saw him.

TOD: You lie, Cynthia!

CYNTHIA: You're the liar, Tod!

MIKE: OK. That's enough, both of you. Tod, go back to your seat and get to work. (Mike gets back to his conference with Lee. As Mike reads Lee's composition, two more paper airplanes fly across the room. Sid's reading a comic book, and Juan has his head down on his desk with his eyes closed.)

KEVIN: (bursts into laughter even though he tries to control it)

MIKE: What's going on, Kevin? You and Jason are supposed to be conferencing.

KEVIN: We are, Mr. Groza.

MIKE: Then what's all that laughter about? That's not part of your conferencing, is it?

KEVIN: It's my fault, Mr. Groza. I told Jason a joke.

MIKE: Then you go back to your seat, Jason, and you boys can work alone. You don't seem to be able to work together quietly. (Notices Juan's head on the desk) Juan, what are you supposed to be doing?

JUAN: I'm writin' the first draft.

MIKE: Then get your head up off the desk and write!

JUAN: I'm tryin' to think of what to write.

MIKE: Then do it sitting up so that I'll know you're not taking a nap.

Mike goes back to his desk and continues to work with Lee. Almost immediately, he hears talking and follows the sound. Juan and Kevin are talking across the aisle.

MIKE: Juan! Kevin! You're not working. Bring your writing journals to me. I want to see how much you've done. You're both supposed to be working on a first draft today. Let me see how much you've written.

JUAN: I didn't write nothing yet. I've been thinkin' in my head what to write.

MIKE: And what did your head decide you should write?

JUAN: I'm still thinkin'.

MIKE: You've been thinking now for twenty minutes. You probably need to begin writing some of your thoughts down on paper. How about you, Kevin? Let me see your journal.

KEVIN: I've been thinkin' too.

MIKE: But you don't have anything written yet?

KEVIN: No.

MIKE: Well, then. You probably don't have any time to waste talking to people, do you?

KEVIN: No.

MIKE: Good. I'll expect to see you begin on that first draft soon.

CATHY: Mr. Groza, you've been conferencing with Lee for almost twenty minutes! The conferences are only supposed to last for five minutes. We're worried that we won't get a chance to conference with you today!

MIKE: You're right, Cathy. I've spent too much time with Lee. There've been too many interruptions. I'll finish with Lee quickly and still have time to meet with the rest of you. Sorry I got off track. Thanks for reminding me.

CATHY: Good. Thank you.

MIKE: OK, Lee. I think the main thing you need to do is make the beginning of your story more interesting. You can ask the reader a question, or make a dramatic statement, or jump right into the high point of the action. You also need to show the reader that you're angry rather than write, "I was angry." Then you can begin to tell about the events that led up to the action. Is there anything else you want to ask about while you're here?

LEE: No, it's the beginning of the paper that's weak. Those're really good ideas, Mr. Groza. I already know what I'm going to do with the beginning of the story, and that'll give me a chance to show the reader that I'm angry. Thanks for your help!

MIKE: Anytime, Lee. That's why I'm here. Cathy, come on over, and we'll see what you need to do next.

Just as Cathy is walking toward the desk, a marble rolls across the floor.

MIKE: (angrily) I saw that, Jason! You come up here!

JASON: Sorry. That dropped out of my hand as I was gettin' up from my desk.

MIKE: Good try, Jason, but I saw what happened! You deliberately rolled that marble across the floor! I think you'll have to lose about five points on your writing grade to pay for the disruption.

JASON: That ain't fair, Mr. Groza! Since class started this morning, a fight happened between Jamal and Tod, Kevin's sailed three paper airplanes that you didn't even notice, Kevin and Juan've been talkin' the whole period, hardly no one's written a word in their writing journal, and nothin's happened to no one. And now, I roll a marble across the floor and get dropped five points for it. That ain't fair!

MIKE: You've no doubt heard about the straw that broke the camel's back. Your rolling of the marble was that straw. I've been working ever since the period started to have the pupils in this class behave themselves and get to work. Finally, just as things seemed to be settling down, you rolled the marble. Maybe that's why you rolled it. If nothing else, your five points off represent a penalty for using bad judgment and having bad timing.

JASON: That still ain't fair! (Turning around) Ms. Rudner, that's not fair, is it?

ROZ: Jason, I'm not here today. I promised Mr. Groza that I would observe his class today but wouldn't say anything or participate in any way. I've said something in response to your question, but I'll say no more.

MIKE: Thank you, Ms. Rudner. Now, we have just five minutes left, which is how much time we schedule for group sharing. Who has something he or she'd like to share with the group?

LEE: (after a long period of silence) I'd like to read my story. I changed the opening as you suggested.

MIKE: That's quick work, Lee. I'm anxious to hear how you changed it. The floor's yours.

LEE: This story's called "My Inconsiderate Sister." (Reads aloud)

MY INCONSIDERATE SISTER

As I was eating breakfast yesterday morning, I looked up and saw my sister coming down the stairway. She was wearing my brand new sweater. "Dammit," I thought. "Why's she have to wear my clothes without even asking me if it's OK? I haven't even worn that sweater myself yet."

This is my main problem with my sister. She's inconsiderate about my things. Otherwise, she's a good big sister. My friends think she's really pretty, and they think she's very nice. She has many friends in her class at school. She also belongs to many groups and is in charge of some of them. So the people she works with must like her.

I have to admit that she's nice to me. When something bad happens to me and I'm sad, she always comes to my room and talks with me about it and helps me realize that I'm still OK. When I need help with my homework, she's always willing to explain it to me. She also comes to see my team play baseball and cheers for us.

Now that I've thought about my sister and all the nice things she does for me, I've decided that maybe I should be glad that she can wear some of my clothes. I should probably tell her that she can wear any of my clothes anytime she wants to. As nice as she is to me, if I get angry because she wears my new sweater, I would be an inconsiderate brother.

JAMAL: (applauding) Great story, my man! You sound like a real writer.

CATHY: Yes, Lee. I liked it a lot! It was clever how you changed your opinion when you began to think about what your sister is really like. I liked the beginning, too. It really lets the reader know you are mad. (The bell rings)

MIKE: Well, we timed it perfectly. Think about your writing when you're at home this evening. We'll have the same schedule tomorrow. You have time for a five-minute break while the other classes change. When you return to the room, Ms. Rudner'll resume her role as teacher for your reading workshop next period, and I'll be the silent observer. (The pupils leave the class for their 5-minute break.)

Roz: (to Mike) You're welcome to contribute to the reading workshop, Mike, whenever the spirit moves you. What do you think of your first day of teaching?

Mike: I think I screwed up royally in many different areas. Basically, I'm disappointed in myself. What did you think of my first day of teaching?

Roz: I thought you did what most first-day teachers would do. You did some things right and some things wrong. And I'm optimistic that over the course of the semester you'll increasingly do more things right and fewer things wrong. I have to get ready for the reading workshop now. Can we talk about your writing workshop after the last period today?

Mike: Yes, I'd appreciate the advice.

Roz: Great. See you then.

After the sixth-period class has ended and all the pupils have gone, Roz and Mike are sitting in their classroom.

Roz: How would you evaluate your performance this morning, Mike?

Mike: As I mentioned to you, I'm disappointed. I let the class get out of hand several times. It just seemed to me that so many things were happening at once that I couldn't keep track of them all.

Roz: A lot of things happen in the classroom at once, and it isn't easy to keep track of everything that's going on.

Mike: Definitely. But today, there were a lot of things that happened that I could've and should've stopped before they got started.

Roz: Why do you think you let them go without stopping them?

Mike: I guess it was because they were all happening at once. I wasn't able to attend to all of them.

Roz: Is there something you can do to help yourself attend to many different events at the same time?

Mike: (long pause) There must be. You're able to do it.

Roz: While you were teaching, I filled out the observation form that I gave you this morning. Let's go over it, and maybe you'll find classroom management strategies that you can use. (Hands Mike a completed copy of the teaching observation form)

Roz: As you can see, Mike, I evaluated you as acceptable or better on all the topics except those under classroom management. I thought your help for individual pupils was relevant to writing, and your obvious interest in all the students was impressive. To me, those are two of the most important factors on the list. I think you have the potential to achieve an excellent rating on all these topics if you can develop effective strategies in classroom management. Do you agree?

Mike: That's my goal, and I think I can achieve it with your help. Do you have any suggestions that will help me improve my classroom management?

Roz: The first item under classroom management is awareness of classroom behavior. I gave you the lowest rating on this item. Jason was right. Many examples of unacceptable behavior took place in the class that you didn't even notice.

MIKE: Did you notice them?

ROZ: Yes, I did. But our agreement was that I don't take any part of the class. Besides, you won't learn where you need help if you aren't allowed to get into trouble. Look at all the things you learned about yourself in just fifty minutes of teaching.

MIKE: Yes, I can see that my major problems are awareness of what's happening in the class, being constant and fair in my discipline, and redirecting unacceptable behavior. I guess the awareness part is most important, because I think that was the basic cause of all my other classroom management problems.

ROZ: Yes, definitely. If you don't know what's going on, you can't do much about it. Also, in redirecting behavior, be sure that you don't scold pupils in front of the class. Just tell them to get to work on whatever their assignment is. In that way, you don't offend the pupils, yet you focus their attention on why they are here in school. They know they're supposed to do schoolwork at school.

MIKE: I really appreciate your advice. I see what you're saying. It makes a lot of sense.

ROZ: Good. Now, before you leave, I want you to write down what classroom management strategies you're going to use in your writing workshop tomorrow to become aware of all the things happening in the classroom and how you plan to handle them.

Figure 15–1 Teaching Observation Form
Bridgeton Middle School

Teacher: <u>Michael Groza</u>   Date: <u>9/12/94</u>   Class: <u>Writing Workshop</u>   Period: <u>1</u>
Observed by: <u>Ms. Rudner</u>
Ratings: 1—Poor, needs improvement; 2—Weak; 3—Acceptable;
              4—Very good; 5—Excellent

Topic	Rating
A. Teaching Procedures	
1. Presentation of lesson	4
2. Good motivational techniques	3
3. Good questioning techniques	3
4. Provided for individual differences	3
5. Used a variety of activities	3
6. Clarity of objectives	4
7. Relevance of lesson to objectives	5
8. Overall effectiveness of lesson	3
B. Classroom Management	
9. Awareness of misbehavior	1
10. Consistency in handling misbehavior	1
11. Fair and consistent discipline	1
12. Redirects behavior rather than scolding	2
13. Disciplines with dignity	3
14. Maintains good classroom organization	3
15. Demonstrates interest in all pupils	5

Questions

1. What are the differences between intrinsic and extrinsic views of motivation? Does the writing workshop focus on intrinsic or extrinsic motivation techniques? Explain.

2. In writing workshops, pupils may be required to include examples of specific writing genres but they choose their own writing selections. How can Mike evaluate each pupil's writing proficiency fairly? How can he report his evaluations to the pupils' parents? How can he defend a grade that a pupil or parent protests?

3. What social class, racial, and home environmental differences exist among the pupils in Mike's writing workshop? Identify some examples of how these differences affected both student and teacher behavior in Mike's class. Does Mike deal with these differences acceptably? Explain.

4. What is Kounin's model of classroom management? What is "withitness," and how does it apply to the way Mike related to his class? What should Mike do differently?

5. What other models of classroom management could Mike have used with his class? How effective would (1) behavior modification, (2) teacher effectiveness training, (3) assertive discipline, and (4) reality therapy have been as methods of classroom management? Which would you recommend to Mike, and why?

6. What other teaching methods could Mike have used that might have allowed him to be more aware of what the students in the class were doing? How might he have used visual aids to accomplish this purpose?

7. If you were to use a systematic observation schedule (e.g., Flanders' Interaction Analysis) to observe Mike's interactions with his students, what conclusions would you draw? For example, what conclusions would you draw about the amount of teacher direct and indirect behavior? How do such interaction patterns relate to student achievement? What are some other systematic observation instruments that could be used to observe teacher-student interactions?

8. What could Mike's supervising teacher, Ms. Rudner, have done to make him aware of the types of behavior she planned to observe to help her evaluate his teaching?

9. How effectively has Mike planned for instruction? How clear are his objectives? How effective are his rule-setting and enforcement procedures? How adequate is the amount of student-engaged time? What improvements can Mike make?

10. What are some of the strategies that you think Mike will suggest to help him deal with the discipline problems in his classroom? How should he handle his writing workshop differently?

What If They Can't Read?

1. Constructivism
2. Language Development
3. English as Second Language
4. Instructional Objectives
5. Meaningful Verbal Learning (Ausubel)

Victor Burns, a 35-year-old social studies teacher, has taught at Gulf Coast High School for 7 years. Gulf Coast is located in a small coastal town in a southwestern state. The school has an enrollment of about 900 students, two thirds of whom are from low-income families. Of the students at GCHS, 70% are white, 20% Hispanic, 7% African-American, and 3% Vietnamese.

The attendance of many GCHS students is irregular because about one third have parents who are migrant farmworkers while another one fourth have parents who are involved in the Gulf Coast shrimp industry. GCHS administrators and teachers therefore work closely with the state's Department of Health and Rehabilitative Services to ensure that the educational needs of these students are met.

GCHS teachers also face a challenge in the language abilities of their students. About 20% of the students have been classified as limited-English-speaking and another 5% as non-English-speaking. To address the special needs of these students, the school has one English as a second language (ESL) teacher, who teaches three classes and acts as a resource person for regular classroom teachers.

On an unusually warm October day, Victor and Helen Watkins, another social studies teacher, are sitting in Victor's classroom at the end of the day discussing the reading abilities of their students.

VICTOR: I've been here seven years, and I don't think I've ever seen so many reading problems. I mean, usually it's one or two kids per class who have problems with the text. But this year it seems like half my students can't read the book!

HELEN: (with sympathy) I've noticed the same thing, Vic. It seems to be getting worse.

VICTOR: (with a long sigh) Take my fifth-period world history class. That's probably the worst. They're a good bunch of kids. I don't have any discipline problems really. But how can I teach if my kids can't read? (Shrugs his shoulders) So what I end up doing is lecturing the entire period, telling them what the book says. They're ninth graders, and their reading levels range from the third grade to about the seventh or eighth.

HELEN: (nodding her head) Hmm. Right.

VICTOR: I have a degree that says I can teach history, not reading. (Becoming more emotional) I had one reading course as an undergraduate. Is that supposed to make me a qualified reading teacher? No. I'd be the first one to admit it.

HELEN: Maybe the workshop we're having next month with the reading specialist will give us some ideas.

VICTOR: I hope it does. But I don't know. How much difference can one three-hour workshop make? We really need to have a full-time reading specialist at the school.

HELEN: Now, Vic, you know the chances of getting a reading specialist assigned to GCHS are about zero.

VICTOR: Maybe so, but I don't see why the district can fund some things and not others. I think it's all politics anyway.

HELEN: Yes, but—

VICTOR: (interrupting) I'm going to talk to the principal about it. We'll never get a reading specialist unless we ask and put some pressure on.

Three days later Victor is visiting with Mr. Henderson, the principal of GCHS. The door to Mr. Henderson's office is closed. Mr. Henderson is seated behind his desk, and Victor sits in a chair in front of the desk.

VICTOR: (with emphasis) How can we teach if the kids can't read? I know I'm speaking for all of the social studies teachers when I say we *desperately* need a reading specialist here.

MR. HENDERSON: I'm glad that you and the others recognize the importance of reading, Vic. I've always felt that every teacher needs to be a teacher of reading.

VICTOR: But that's just it, Mr. Henderson. We're *not* reading teachers! We teach world history, American history, and geography, not reading.

MR. HENDERSON: (somewhat testily) I understand that. What I mean is, you should stress basic reading skills *while* you teach your content. You stress vocabulary, reading for the main idea, and outlining and skimming, don't you?

VICTOR: Well, yes.

MR. HENDERSON: Then you are teaching reading. Every teacher has to do that.

VICTOR: I agree with you, but the reading problems this year seem to be worse than ever. It's really overwhelming. In my fifth-period world history class, for example, at least half the kids can't read the book. We simply need a full-time reading specialist!

MR. HENDERSON: I understand your frustration, Vic, but the district couldn't even come close to funding a position. We're lucky we have an ESL teacher.

VICTOR: Something has to be done, though. We have the state assessment tests coming up in March, and the tests are based on textbooks half our kids can't read. We really need some help!

MR. HENDERSON: You're forgetting that we have the reading-in-the-content-areas workshop coming up next month. That's one of the topics you teachers voted to have a workshop on.

Victor: (solemnly) I know. I just wish we could get more than a one-shot workshop. You don't think there's *any* chance we could get a reading specialist assigned to the school?

Mr. Henderson: I'm sorry, Victor. I've seen the district budget through next year, and it's really tight. Maybe the year after that. Until then we'll have to do the best we can.

Several weeks later Victor and Helen are in the social studies office enjoying a cup of coffee 20 minutes before the start of first period. The room is small, barely large enough to hold the two desks Victor and Helen are seated at. Beneath the only window in the room is a worktable on which sits a copy machine and a large electric coffeepot. The top three shelves of a large metal bookcase to the left of the door hold the department's collection of social studies textbooks and curriculum guides. The bottom three shelves are filled with copy paper, toner, and miscellaneous office supplies. The door opens and Karen Sanders, another social studies teacher, enters. She puts her books on Helen's desk and then sits on the end of the worktable.

Victor: Karen, we missed you yesterday at the workshop.

Karen: Jamie had a fever of 102, and I had to take him to the doctor. But he was fine this morning. You know how kids that age bounce back. (Pausing) I hated to miss the workshop. How was it?

Helen: This presenter from the university gave us a lot of materials.

Victor: She spent most of the time showing us how to prepare different kinds of study guides for the kids to use.

Helen: I think she had some good ideas.

Victor: (tilting his chair back) You're not going to believe this, but I stayed up past midnight last night making study guides for my fifth-period world history.

Helen and Karen in Unison: Wow!

Victor: Here, take a look at these.

Victor removes several pages from a foot-high stack of papers. Helen scoots her chair close to Victor while Karen hops down from the worktable and walks over to Victor's desk.

Karen: (looking down at the pages Victor holds) You've been busy.

Victor: I have three kinds of study guides for the chapter we're starting on Roman civilization. First I made this overview guide. (Holds up a page with two paragraphs on it) I summarized the chapter in two paragraphs. We'll read this and discuss it before they actually start to read the chapter.

Karen: That sounds like a good idea.

Victor: Then I made a vocabulary guide with all the key words. (Holding up a two-page handout and pointing as he continues) See, I gave the new word, a definition, the page where it first appears, and then a sentence in which the word is used. (Reads several of the vocabulary words on the handout) Plebeian. Tribune. Republic. Patrician.

Karen: I like that, too.

Victor: This last guide we learned how to make is called a learning-from-text guide. (Shows Helen and Karen his third handout) Kids fill this out as they read the assignment. See, I have questions plus the page numbers and paragraphs where the answers can be found.

HELEN: (with excitement) These study guides just might be the answer we've been looking for!

VICTOR: I'm going to start using them today. I'll let you know how they work.

Later that same day Victor is teaching his fifth-period world history class. He stands in front of a world map on the side wall of his classroom. Twenty-six ninth graders are seated at moveable desks arranged in a large circle.

VICTOR: OK. Does everyone have a copy of the overview study guide? (Holds his copy aloft as several students nod their heads) The overview guide is to give you an idea of what chapter 4, "The Rise and Fall of Rome," is all about. This chapter tells us how the city of Rome grew and conquered an empire that stretched from Spain on the west to the Caspian Sea on the east. (Sweeps his right hand across the map to indicate the approximate size of the Roman Empire) And who knows what happened to the Roman Empire? Where is it today? (Noticing Juan's raised hand) Juan?

JUAN: It collapsed—just fell apart.

VICTOR: Exactly. So what we're going to read about is the fantastic story of Rome. Who would like to begin reading from the study guide, just the first short paragraph. (Harold is first to raise his hand.) Harold, would you start?

HAROLD: (slowly and with moderate difficulty) At the start of the fifth . . . uh . . . century, Rome was a small . . . (Stops at the next word)

VICTOR: (encouragingly) Italian . . . Italian town.

HAROLD: (continuing) Italian town. During the next several centuries, the Roman Empire became even more powerful . . . uh . . . (correcting himself) larger and more powerful than Alexander the Great's empire. The Romans were great . . . What's that?

VICTOR: Sculptors.

HAROLD: Sculptors and . . .

VICTOR: Architects.

HAROLD: And architects and . . .

VICTOR: Philosophers.

HAROLD: And philosophers. The Roman civi . . . (slowly) civilization was known for its system of laws based on the will of the people.

VICTOR: All right. Who'd like to read the next paragraph? (Sheila raises her hand.) Sheila, would you read then?

SHEILA: (also reading with difficulty) The greatest Roman leader was . . . what's that name?

VICTOR: (slowly) Julius Caesar.

SHEILA: (haltingly) Julius Caesar. He was commander of all the Roman . . .

VICTOR: Legions. Those were the Roman armies.

SHEILA: Legions. The Roman sentence . . . uh, senate tried to get. . . . What's his name?

VICTOR: Caesar.

SHEILA: Caesar to give up command of his army. Instead Caesar marched on Rome and a civil war began. Caesar defeated the senate's armies and became the leader of the Roman Empire. He was a wise and just ruler who fought cor . . . (She stops.)

VICTOR: Corruption.

SHEILA: Corruption and tried to improve life for all Romans. On March 15, 44 B.C., however, he was . . . (She stops again.)

VICTOR: Assassinated. He was murdered.

SHEILA: He was assassinated.

VICTOR: OK. Thank you, Sheila. That was a very quick overview of what chapter 4 is about. Now I have another kind of study guide here. (Hands a set of the vocabulary guides to the nearest student) Here, John, take one and pass the rest on. (Waits while the vocabulary guides are being passed around) Does everyone have one? (A few students nod their head.) Now this guide has all the key vocabulary words from chapter 4 on it. (Holds his copy up and points to the first page) See, it gives you the new word and a short definition for the word. Then it also gives you the page number in the chapter where the word first appears. And the last thing it gives you is the sentence where the word is used. We have thirty-two vocabulary words in chapter 4. Let's go through the guide and pronounce each one of them. I'll pronounce the word first, and then you repeat it after me. OK? (A few students nod their heads.) Republic.

CLASS IN UNISON: Republic.

VICTOR: Patrician.

CLASS: Patrician.

VICTOR: Plebeian.

CLASS: Plebeian.

Victor continues pronouncing the words, and his students repeat after him. By the time Victor gets to the end of the list, his students are repeating the words with energy.

VICTOR: OK. Good. Keep this list and use it as you read the chapter. Now I have one more kind of study guide to help you. (Hands a stack of the learning-from-text guides to a student) Take one and pass the rest. This study guide has several questions based on chapter 4. For each question you also have the page and the paragraph number where you can find the correct answer.

Victor waits until all his students have a copy of the study guide before he continues. As the papers are being circulated, he walks to the front of the room and sits on the edge of his desk.

VICTOR: Everyone take a look at the first question. (Reads the question slowly) It says, "What two groups of people influenced the early Romans?" Then it tells you the answer is on page 57, the first paragraph. So let's look that one up. Who can find it? (Calling on Sharon) Sharon?

SHARON: (reading slowly from her book) The early Romans were influenced by two peoples who had settled in the Italian . . . (Hesitates)

VICTOR: Peninsula.

SHARON: Peninsula—the Greeks and the . . . (Stops this time)

VICTOR: That's Etruscans.

SHARON: (very slowly) Etruscans.

VICTOR: OK. There's the answer—the Greeks and the Etruscans. Now I want you to begin reading chapter 4 and filling out the study guide. I want you to fill out the guide as you read the chapter. But be sure to read the chapter. Don't just answer the questions. I'll come around to see how each of you is doing.

It is 3 weeks later, and Victor, Helen, and Karen are having their morning coffee in the social studies office.

Figure 16–1 Gulf Coast High School

Class: Ninth-grade world history
Teacher: Victor Burns
Period: Fifth

Name	Eighth Grade Percentile	Reading Stanine*	Reading Comprehension**	Vocabulary Grade Equivalent
1. Andrews, John	33	4	5.7	5.9
2. Arciero, Tony	4	1	3.2	3.3
3. Azar, Juan	15	3	4.7	4.8
4. Baber, Sharon	55	6	7.9	8.1
5. Bailey, Heather	29	4	5.4	5.5
6. Becker, Jill	42	5	5.7	5.7
7. Booth, Jane	5	1	3.4	3.6
8. Bowen, Harold	9	2	4.0	4.1
9. Burrows, Sheila	18	3	4.8	5.0
10. Colton, John	19	3	4.8	5.2
11. Diaz, Ernesto	11	2	4.5	4.6
12. Dill, Scott	30	4	5.1	5.2
13. Espitia, Enrique	27	4	4.9	5.0
14. Fan, Kuo-Chin	49	5	7.7	7.8
15. Fernandez, Carlos	30	4	5.2	5.2
16. Foster, Amy	36	4	5.3	5.7
17. Gilbert, Kim	24	3	4.8	4.9
18. Gutierrez, Jose	29	4	4.9	5.2
19. Kee, Chang	51	5	7.8	7.9
20. Kerr, Brian	28	3	5.2	5.3
21. Lawson, Buck	5	1	3.5	3.6
22. Mercer, Cecil	10	2	4.4	4.8
23. Nguyen, Thuy	39	4	5.9	6.0
24. Platt, Karen	35	4	5.4	5.4
25. Sanchez, Dolores	43	5	6.0	6.0
26. Wilson, Tommy	28	4	5.0	5.1

SOURCE: *Eighth grade *Metropolitan Achievement Test.*
**Decimal scores refer to months, e.g., 7.8 = seventh year, eighth month.

KAREN: So tell us, Vic, how's it been going with the study guides? (Chuckling) I don't believe I've ever seen anyone run off so many materials on the copy machine. You're going to burn this thing up! (Gives the copy machine next to her a tender pat)

VICTOR: (glumly) I'm about ready to give it up. I've been killing myself writing these study guides! (Pausing) I'm beginning to think it doesn't make any difference.

HELEN: Are you sure they're not helping the kids?

VICTOR: I gave them a unit test this Monday, and the grades weren't any better than they were before I started writing all these study guides. Oh, I think they might be helping a few of the kids, but just a few. Most of the kids have just as much trouble reading the guides as they do the book. I just feel like I'm creating a lot of work for myself. What about you, Helen. Did you try the study guides?

HELEN: I put together one set that I tried out in my American history classes. (Shakes her head) Like you, I didn't think they made that much difference. And frankly, they take a lot of time to write. If I'm going to spend that much time on something, I want to see a bigger payoff.

VICTOR: Exactly. (With frustration) I don't know what to do. The only thing I can think of is rewriting the book, but that doesn't make much sense. I don't know. What do you do when the kids can't read the book?

Questions

1. What special techniques should teachers employ to be more effective in working with limited-English-speaking students? With non-English-speaking students?

2. Do you agree with Mr. Henderson that "every teacher needs to be a teacher of reading"? Why or why not?

3. What can a teacher do when students are unable to read the text?

4. What pupil characteristics are related to success in reading?

5. What are the pros and cons of encouraging a student to use his or her special language or dialect? How can this best be done in the school?

6. Should every secondary teacher be a reading teacher as well as a subject-matter specialist? What role could a reading specialist play at Gulf Coast High School that an ESL teacher could not play? Is high school too late to begin working on reading with students like those at GCHS?

7. How could Victor have taken advantage of the cognitive theory of David Ausubel in designing his overview guide? How could he have taken advantage of Robert Gagne's five types of learning in developing his vocabulary guide and learning-from-text guide?

8. What interpretation can be made of the data presented at the end of the case on the reading abilities of Victor's fifth-period class? What are percentiles and stanines? What is a grade equivalent? What are reading comprehension and vocabulary?

9. Should all students be made to learn standard English regardless of their racial or ethnic origin? How can this be done without destroying students' native language competency, self-image, or cultural identity? When such students constantly make errors in reading, speaking, and writing English, what are the best procedures for a teacher to use for correcting the errors?

10. Examine this case from a constructivist standpoint. What teaching and evaluation procedures should Victor use?

17

Token Learning

Key Content to Consider for Analyzing This Case:

1. Operant Conditioning
2. Behavior Modification
3. Observational Learning
4. Intrinsic versus Extrinsic Motivation
5. Parent Involvement Procedures

Maplewood Elementary School is located in the quiet residential community of Midville, a New England community with a population of approximately 25,000. The student body of the school is primarily from middle-class backgrounds, with an 80% white/20% African-American racial mix.

Sharon Davis has just received tenure in the school district by signing her current contract. She is a product of the College of Education at a nearby land-grant state university and is full of energy, enthusiasm, and ideas. Sharon is particularly happy to be teaching at Maplewood, since it is generally considered to be the best, most progressive school in the city. The physical plant is modern, up-to-date, and immaculately maintained.

Sharon is in her room the last day of preplanning, talking to her friend Mary Jean, who teaches second grade in a room down the hall. Although classes begin the following Monday, Sharon has her room and materials well-organized enough that she can stop and chat with Mary Jean.

SHARON: I can't wait until Monday to meet my new third graders! I finally finished getting my materials together. At least I think I have.

MARY JEAN: How many will you have this year?

SHARON: Twenty-four. How about you?

MARY JEAN: Nineteen—and I think that's plenty!

SHARON: I know what you mean, but I think I can easily handle twenty-four this year. I'm going to use some of the techniques that I learned at State and have always wanted to try. Jessica [the building principal] has always wanted us to be on the same page as a faculty, with only a few experimental things going on that she approves in advance. This year I told her that if I was going to

164

teach twenty-four third graders, I would like to use behavior mod procedures, and she said that made sense.

MARY JEAN: You mean behavior modification classroom management procedures?

SHARON: Yes, but I mean precision teaching—both academically and discipline-wise. You know, the token economy approach using the Premack Principle and all!

MARY JEAN: Boy, you sound like you are really into it—using the behavioral lingo! Weren't those behavioral techniques popular back in the seventies and early eighties? I don't know of any other teachers here at Maplewood who are using behavioral techniques, except maybe for some of the special ed people. I'm sort of surprised that Jessica approved them, since she's always seemed to be kind of a humanist.

SHARON: She agreed with me that token economies have a long history and seemed to work well. I also pointed out that Sherrie and Arica [two other teachers] are both using assertive discipline, which is very similar to behavior modification. Just more emphasis on punishment. Jessica agreed with me that behavior modification is a more humanistic approach with its emphasis on positive reinforcement.

MARY JEAN: (with a puzzled look) Yes, I guess so, but—well, I always felt like it was a bit contrived. You know, like you're looking for techniques to manipulate the kids with. Like the praise and the tokens were just bribes to get the kids to do what you want them to. (Pause) I guess what I'm trying to say is that I want Stacey [Mary Jean's daughter] to clean up her room because she wants to, not because there's some external reward for doing it.

SHARON: That's fine, but what if Stacey never finds it self-rewarding to clean her room?

MARY JEAN: I see what you mean. I guess she and I would have to talk about it.

SHARON: And you'd shape her behavior by cuing her as to what behavior you wanted and then by giving her social reinforcement in the form of attention, affection, and approval for doing it. Then after she's learned to do it on her own, you'd phase out those reinforcers and let Stacey receive her reinforcement from her pride in living in a clean room.

MARY JEAN: Wow! You sure have thought this through!

SHARON: (smiling) I have. A lot of what we teach kids are things they don't find self-rewarding. You have to use behavior modification procedures to get them working and, once they find the learning activities to be interesting, gradually fade out the original reinforcers.

MARY JEAN: That sure sounds easy when you say it, Sharon, but I wonder—how will you begin?

SHARON: As I told Jessica, the whole program will flow out of a social studies project that I will plan with the kids. We are going to create Kidville. Get it?

MARY JEAN: Yes, that's cute! Rhymes with Midville. But how?

SHARON: The whole idea grew out of how I was going to teach a unit on learning about money so it wouldn't be boring. We are going to create a real token economy with play money, a bank, city government, and any other kind of capitalist enterprise the kids can think up.

MARY JEAN: Boy, that will take a lot of work, Sharon!

SHARON: Yes, I know that, but I want to do it! I'm really excited about it! Cherie will be my aide again this year, and I think she has a good grasp of what I'm going to try to do and how she will fit in. I'm also going to try to involve at least two parent volunteers. That'll be a six-to-one ratio of kids to adults and should work out real well in terms of collecting behavioral data, handing out reinforcement, and giving the children individual attention.

MARY JEAN: Sharon, I am really impressed! I had no idea you were going to do anything this ambitious this year!

It is late afternoon of the same day. Sharon sits at a table in the classroom along with her teacher aide, Cherie Sawyer, and her two parent volunteers, Marie Reynolds and Mitzi Clark. Sharon smiles at the two parents as she speaks.

SHARON: Marie and Mitzi, I can't tell you how much we appreciate your helping us out this year. It would be difficult for Cherie and me to do what we plan to do without your help.

MARIE: Thanks, Mrs. Davis, I just hope . . .

SHARON: (interrupting) Marie, please call me Sharon. I consider us a team—equals. I'm just the team leader. I think you'll find that the children will be calling all of us "teacher" before long.

MARIE: Thanks, Sharon. That certainly makes me feel welcome and at home. But what do you want us to do?

SHARON: We are going to use a system called behavior modification, which was developed by a psychologist named Skinner many years ago.

MITZI: I think I remember reading about this in a magazine once. Isn't it based on the idea of rewarding good behavior and punishing bad behavior? Like if a child gets a good grade on a paper or behaves well, you should be sure to praise him.

SHARON: That's partly correct. Skinner believed that rewarding, or reinforcing behavior as he called it, is better than punishment. He calls for us to be clear and specific about what behavior we think is important and then to positively reinforce small steps in the right direction. However, he said to try to ignore undesirable behavior and look for opportunities to reinforce desirable behavior that is opposite of the undesirable behavior.

MITZI: (with a confused look) What do you mean "positively reinforce small steps"?

MARIE: That confuses me, too. How do you decide whether a behavior is desirable or undesirable, and how do you reinforce?

SHARON: (looking at Cherie and smiling) We have a lot to go over, and a lot of this will have to develop as we go along. We will have to plan with the children as well as we go along.

MARIE: (with surprise) With the children? But they're only third graders. Are they really old enough to make decisions?

SHARON: (smiling) We adults will have the final decision, but as I think you'll see, we can learn a lot from the children about what motivates them and how they think. (Looking at Mitzi) Mitzi, you're frowning and look confused. What's the matter?

MITZI: I'm not sure how to put it, but it's this business of reinforcing children for their good behavior and work. Aren't we really trying to bribe them for their good behavior? I was just thinking that I want my three children to behave well in the classroom and make good grades because they want to, not because they'll get a reward for doing it.

SHARON: (sighing and looking at Cherie) We do have a lot to go over, and I guess there is no time like the present to begin. (Pause) First, let's start with Skinner's basic assumptions and then go to the steps involved in modifying behavior.

It is the third day of classes. The students are seated on the floor listening to Sharon as she sits in a chair talking to them. Cherie sits in another chair a short distance to Sharon's left. The two parent volunteers are seated on the floor behind the children.

SHARON: Now children, I want to ask you a question, and I want you to think hard before you hold up your hand to speak. The question is, Why do people work? Think about people you know, like your parents, and ask yourself why they work. (All the children's hands go up, and some wave their arms back and forth to indicate their eagerness to answer. Others raise themselves up higher so they can be seen by the teacher.) OK, children, one at a time. I know you all have something you want to say. Toni Sue, let's start with you.

TONI SUE: My daddy goes to work so he can make money. He says he does it for all of us so we can have things like clothes and toys.

SHARON: That's very good, Toni Sue. That's why a lot of us work. Jerry?

JERRY: My mom says she works because she loves it. She says she'd do it even if they didn't pay her. Just because it's fun.

MIKE: (without raising his hand) Yeah, I'll bet! She wouldn't do it very long if they didn't pay her!

JERRY: (frowning) She would too, stupid!

SHARON: That's enough boys. Remember our rule about raising your hand before talking, Mike. Jerry, I really appreciated how you and Toni Sue raised your hand before you spoke. (Pause) But tell me about children. Why don't they get paid for the work they do? Billy?

BILLY: Because we're not big enough. They ought to pay us for going to school!

MIKE: Yeah! We have to give up TV to go to school! (The children laugh and voice their agreement with Mike.)

SHARON: But to get paid for going to school you have to produce something or provide a service. Linda?

LINDA: Teacher, what's a service?

SHARON: Have you ever gone to a doctor or a dentist? Have you ever seen police officers or firefighters do their jobs? They don't make anything like a car or a toaster, but they provide services that other people want. Terrie Ann?

TERRIE ANN: A repairman came to our house and fixed our TV yesterday.

SHARON: Very good, Terrie Ann. That's a very important service, isn't it? (The children agree very loudly.)

SHARON: Billy?

BILLY: (enthusiastically) That's very important! I'd miss my cartoons, and that wouldn't be cool at all! (All the children smile, laugh, and agree in unison with Billy.)

It is one week later, and again the class is arranged in a semicircle on the floor while Sharon leads the discussion during social studies. Mitzi and Marie sit on chairs in the back of the room with Cherie. All three are intently observing a different child and making tallies in cells on a baseline data chart.

SHARON: Now children, we've been talking for a week about why people work, and you all feel that it would be fun to have jobs like your parents do and make money. Billy?

BILLY: You forgot that we want to spend the money and buy things the way they do, too.

SHARON: (laughing) I knew you'd say that, Billy!

BILLY: Yeah! Cool!

SHARON: Why don't we develop our own town? We can all have jobs in the town and make money. (The children agree enthusiastically.)

SHARON: Billy?

BILLY: Do you mean real money?

SHARON: No, we can make our own. But we can use it to buy things in class just like real money. Toni Sue?

TONI SUE: What kinds of things?

SHARON: Each one of you can have a different job, just like adults, and bring different things in to sell. One of you could be the banker, for example, and be in charge of lending out the money. (Billy interrupts by yelling "Me" as he holds up his hand.) We can decide that later, Billy. Just let me finish. (Pause) Some of you might want to open your own business, like a candy store. Terrie Ann?

TERRIE ANN: Where would we get the money to buy the candy?

SHARON: From the bank. Each of you would get twenty dollars per week to spend, save, or purchase things for your business. As you earn money from your business, you would have to decide what to do with it. You could buy something with it or perhaps open up another business. Mike?

MIKE: Or even loan it to someone else?

SHARON: Yes, you certainly could and earn interest. Toni Sue?

TONI SUE: What's interest?

SHARON: We'll go into all that. Right now let's talk about what kinds of goods and services each of you might like to provide. Mike?

MIKE: Could I be a policeman?

SHARON: Yes, that's an important service. With all that money around, we'll certainly need police.

It is Friday afternoon, and all the children have boarded buses to go home. Sharon, Cherie, Mitzi, and Marie sit around a table engaged in their weekly planning session.

SHARON: How do you feel about the way Kidville is coming, Marie? Particularly how the children are participating in the planning?

MARIE: I would never have believed it! They act like little adults! (All four women laugh.)

SHARON: I've taken the ideas from this morning's discussion, the one about what they are going to spend money for, and come up with three categories: privileges, penalties, and services. Privileges will be things like being line leader for lunch, carrying messages, and working in the library. Penalties will be "response cost" for things like handing in a sloppy paper, teasing or pushing other children, or inappropriate talking. Services will be things like washing the blackboard, straightening the art area, or being the door holder. I'll have to make a complete list under each of these three categories and then attach a money value to each. Of course, the students will buy the privileges, get paid for the services, and get fined for the penalties.

CHERIE: (enthusiastically) I think it's all going great. Just this week they have learned the meaning of deposit, withdrawal, balance, and interest. They seem to learn the terms without any real effort.

MARIE: Yes, who would believe that these kids would be capable of creating a town like Kidville and create jobs that they willingly do, such as mail delivery, garbage collection, and street cleaning.

MITZI: Can you believe Toni Sue?! She's quite the capitalist with her candy store. She hoards every penny!

SHARON: OK, enough of the good things. Problems?

CHERIE: Yes, some of the kids aren't really participating. Mike, for example, just hoards his money and then quits working until he runs out. Also, Toni Sue swears that someone stole money from her candy store when she wasn't looking.

SHARON: Just like real life. I guess we'll just have to get our Kidville police department to investigate.

CHERIE: How are they going to get paid for their services, Sharon?

SHARON: Just wait! I'm going to introduce the concept of taxes tomorrow! (All four women laugh.)

SHARON: All in all, I think Kidville is coming along very nicely. I've never seen a group of more motivated third graders, and I think we're all doing a great job of integrating practically everything we teach into the Kidville program. (Cherie, Mitzi, and Marie all voice their agreement and congratulate one another.)

It is the afternoon of the last day of classes before Christmas vacation. The children have left for the day and Sharon sits in the office of Jessica Mason, the school principal. Jessica closes her office door.

JESSICA: Sharon, how's the Kidville project coming along? I've been so busy that I've been able to slip into your room only a couple of times so far this year. The children certainly seemed busy and motivated by what they were doing.

SHARON: Cherie, Marie, Mitzi, and I all enjoy it more than anything we've tried before. Well, that is Cherie and I, since this is the first time for Mitzi and Marie. Most important though, the kids are learning a lot.

JESSICA: Things about the world of business and careers?

SHARON: No, we've found ways of tying in practically everything we teach, from math to science to geography.

JESSICA: Any problems?

SHARON: Not that I know of. Do you know of anything?

JESSICA: That's why I asked you to come see me, Sharon. There have been a couple of things.

SHARON: (frowning) Oh?

JESSICA: To begin with, I had a visit from Mitzi last week. She thinks that charting baseline data is a waste of time and thinks that her time would be better spent working with the children.

SHARON: Why didn't she tell me this?

JESSICA: She likes you and didn't want to upset you. She thinks you can see only the strengths of the program. Also, I've had at least three parents come and talk to me about their concerns.

SHARON: (with surprise) Really! Who?

JESSICA: Toni Sue Sanders' mother for one.

SHARON: Toni Sue! That's really unbelievable! That child seems to be getting more out of Kidville than anyone! Why, you ought to see how serious and involved she is in running her candy store and the way she saves her profits.

JESSICA: That's what's bothering Mrs. Sanders. That's all Toni Sue is interested in. She feels that a child as young as Toni Sue should be exploring more than the world of business. I think Mrs. Sanders and her husband want her exposed more to the arts—music, dancing, painting, and the like. They feel she is becoming too one-dimensional. (Pause) Understand, Sharon, that many of the parents like what you're doing, but there *is* a vocal opposition, and perhaps you should consider what they're saying.

SHARON: What are they really saying, Jessica?

JESSICA: To put it in my own words, I guess what they're saying is that they want their children to develop their own ambitions, explore their own potentials— not have their behavior shaped by a teacher and her team who decide for them. (Pause) I think they are also saying that their children are motivated to do what they are doing, running a candy store for example, for the wrong reason.

SHARON: (angrily) And what's that?

JESSICA: For rewards external to the activity instead of doing things for their own self-reward. (Pause) I guess that reminds me of my brother-in-law, who has just retired to Florida with my sister. He spent over thirty years working at a post office job that he hated. The pay and fringe benefits were excellent, he always said. But can you imagine doing something you dislike for that long because of the external rewards?

SHARON: No, I can't. I love teaching and really wouldn't want to do anything else at this time of my life. (Pause) However, Jessica, I must admit that at this point I am a very confused teacher. What do you think about all this? What do you think I should do?

JESSICA: Sharon, you know I think you are an excellent, dedicated, creative teacher, and I'm not going to tell you to change what you are doing. I'm just giving you some feedback, and I know you'll give it serious consideration.

SHARON: I appreciate your saying that, Jessica. However, let me ask the question in another way. What would you do if you were in my place?

JESSICA: That's a hard question to answer, since I think we have different teaching philosophies. I believe that our job as teachers is to help children become strong enough so they can become independent people—learn to think for themselves and solve their own problems. I think that children need to have the opportunity to explore as many things as possible and discover for themselves what excites and motivates them. Then they ought to have the opportunity to develop themselves fully in those areas that excite and motivate them.

SHARON: But Jessica, some children would never explore anything if you didn't give them some guidance. They don't know what they want until you give them some direction. And what about all those things they often don't like but society thinks they need to know to be effective citizens—like reading, writing, and arithmetic? You can't sugarcoat many of the things they need to learn but aren't terribly enthusiastic about.

JESSICA: While I agree with you that you can't sugarcoat things that kids aren't interested in, I feel that if you really get to know the child—what the child is interested in, what he watches on TV and does after school—you can use those interests to design what you are teaching.

SHARON: But Jessica, don't you see? That's what I've been doing in Kidville! I've tried to learn what kinds of things the kids *are* interested in and use them as reinforcers for what they *aren't* interested in.

JESSICA: Look at it this way, Sharon. Maybe you are trying to shape the child to your curriculum instead of shaping the curriculum to what you know about the child.

SHARON: (nonplussed) I don't know. I guess I thought I was doing both.

JESSICA: Let me ask you to think about two things, Sharon, and then let's get together next week and discuss what you want to do. One, what are the weaknesses as well as the strengths of Kidville? Two, what changes, if any, do you want to make in your program?

Figure 17–1 Reinforcement Menu

Mrs. Davis's Third-Grade Class

Privileges

Teacher Assistant	$ .20
Line Leader	.50
Secretary	.50
Special Art Attendance	2.00
Extra Activity Period	2.00
Library Work	1.50
Missing Special Activities	4.00
Messenger	.20
Morning Leader	.10

Penalties

Inappropriate Talking	$ .50
Sloppy Paper	.40
Teasing Others	2.00
Cafeteria/Recess Problems	4.00
Not Singing	.50
Hurting Others	1.00
Leaving Name Off Paper	.30
Messy Desk	.20
Not Listening	.30
Running in Hall	.50
Not Following Directions	.30
Fooling Around	.50

Services

Door Holder	$ .20
Board Washer	1.00
Sink Cleaner	1.20
Desk Checker	.50
Mailperson	.60
Reading Center Organizer	.50
Paper Shelves Organizer	.10
Art Area Organizer	.80
Math Center Organizer	.50
Teacher's Desk Organizer	.50

◼ Questions

1. Is human motivation environmentally determined, as Skinner contends, or is it a reciprocal process between the individual and the environment, as Bandura argues? Or is the cause of human motivation a function of the way each individual perceives the world, as Piaget proposes?

2. Can one person motivate another, as the "carrot and stick" theory contends? Or does motivation originate entirely from within the individual? Can a teacher do more to motivate a student than just find out what the student is interested in and use that so that the student will choose to be motivated and participate?

3. What is the difference between the intrinsic and extrinsic models of motivation? How do they differ in terms of the cause and nature of human motivation, the kind of data that are appropriate for measuring motivation, and techniques for fostering motivational change? How do these differences apply to the ways that Sharon and Jessica look at human motivation?

4. What is operant conditioning? What assumptions does it make about the cause of behavior, the nature of learning, the kind of data that it is appropriate to collect on children, and how behavior is changed?

5. What is behavior modification? How is it similar to precision teaching, applied behavior analysis, contingency management, and programmed instruction? How is behavior modification used with groups as well as individuals?

6. What is a token economy? What is the Premack Principle? How effective are token economies in working with students of varying abilities and age levels? What relationships exist between intrinsic and extrinsic reinforcers? Can extrinsic reinforcers reduce the intrinsically reinforcing quality of an activity?

7. What is meant in operant conditioning by "fading out" one reinforcer and "fading in" another? How could Sharon take advantage of this technique?

8. How do you account for differences in the way human beings respond to attempts by teachers, parents, or employers to motivate them? Why are some people very difficult to "shape" with external reinforcers and others very easy? Why do some people primarily engage in activities that are self-reinforcing? Why would some people, like Jessica's brother-in-law, allow themselves to be "shaped" into performing a job that they dislike their entire work lives? How do belief systems such as "internal-external attributions" or "internal-external locus of control" help explain such differences?

9. What is an "attribution training program"? How would such a program be similar to or different from Kidville?

10. How effective has Sharon been in communicating with and involving the parents of her students? What parent involvement techniques can teachers use? What would you recommend to Sharon?

18

Which Is Higher?

Key Content to Consider for Analyzing This Case:

1. Bloom's Cognitive Taxonomy
2. Problem Solving
3. Cognitive Theory (Information Processing, Ausubel, Bruner, Constructivism)
4. Motivation (Intrinsic versus Extrinsic)
5. Creativity
6. Measurement and Evaluation (Objective versus Essay Tests)

The Queen's Island School District is located in a large urban area in the northeastern part of the United States. Approximately one third of the student population served by the school district comprises minority racial and ethnic groups. The district has six senior high schools (grades 10–12), each of which has chosen a social studies teacher to represent it on the school district's committee to revise the secondary history curriculum.

Dr. Tom Blakely, the social studies curriculum director for the school district, has the task of chairing the committee. He has arranged for the committee to meet in a comfortable conference room in the downtown and centrally located school board and administrative offices complex. After the usual hand shaking, greetings, and back slapping have died down, each teacher takes a seat in a comfortable leather chair around a long, rectangular wooden table. Tom stands at one end of the table in front of his chair and gently taps the table with his knuckles to call the meeting to order.

Tom: (smiling) As you all know, each of you has been selected by your school to assist in the revision of our social studies curriculum. This year we'll focus on history courses. All of your schools require world history the sophomore year and U.S. history the junior year and offer elective courses like Non-Western Cultures the senior year. We'll begin our work by considering revisions for our world history course. Perhaps we should begin by introducing ourselves. I'll start, and we'll go around the table beginning on my left. (Sits down in his chair) I'm Tom Blakely, the social studies curriculum director, or should I say coordinator, for our district. I can never remember which title is correct. This is my third year in the job. I used to be a social studies teacher at Central High.

(Applause from Eric, the Central High representative, while others smile and laugh)

ERIC: (smiling) See what high-quality people we hire at Central?

TOM: Thank you, Eric. I can truthfully say that I really enjoyed my years at Central. (Nods to Luis on his left)

LUIS: I'm Luis Garcia from Garfield High. My favorite course is U.S. history.

ERIC: I'm Eric Tannenbaum from Central High, the home of the Fighting Cougars, state champions in basketball. (Good-natured cheers and jeers)

LOIS: I'm Lois Blakely from Van Buren High, and no, Dr. Blakely and I are neither married nor relatives. We just happen to have the same last name.

LEE: I'm Lee Cheng from Kennedy High, and let me add that Central was lucky to beat Kennedy with a last-minute field goal in the tournament. (All laugh.)

DELICIA: (with reserve) I'm Delicia Jackson from South Point High.

MICHELLE: (with enthusiasm) I'm Michelle McMurray from Westside High. We don't win many athletic championships, but we do have more National Merit finalists than any other high school in the district. Now let me hear you top that, Eric! (Everyone laughs.)

TOM: (stands back up and passes out packets of material to the teachers to his left and right to pass on down) Let me hand out these packets on our world history course and give you the assignment of studying them carefully and meeting back here next week at the same time to begin our consideration of revisions. We'll need to agree on textbooks, objectives, teaching methods, evaluation procedures, and so forth. I'll adjourn the meeting now so we can all go to the back of the room and enjoy the refreshments provided for us by Ms. Wiggins, the superintendent's secretary, and get to know one another better! (Polite applause)

It is 2 weeks later. Tom had to postpone the previous week's meeting because of requests for more time to read the curriculum materials handed out at the first meeting.

TOM: (smiling) Good morning. I trust that everyone has had a chance to look over the world history curriculum materials. Any comments?

MICHELLE: Yes. I for one was very surprised at how, what shall I say, factually oriented the whole thing was. The emphasis seems to be on getting the students to memorize people, places, dates, battles, and so forth. No wonder I hear some students say they can't stand history. I hope that this committee is going to make some serious changes in our world history program! (Delicia and Lois voice their agreement.)

ERIC: (agitated) What are you talking about, Michelle?! The committee that developed these curriculum materials spent many long hours and worked hard on the project. I know because I was on it! What's wrong with asking our students to learn a few facts?

MICHELLE: No offense, Eric, and I'm sure that all of you worked very hard. But memorized facts don't stick with students very long. Principles learned in a context that students can relate to can stick with them for life.

ERIC: I suppose that you're going to tell us that historical facts don't matter! A lot of our students would have done a lot better on standardized tests and had college scholarships today if their teachers had insisted on a bit more rigor in their learning. Fun and games are motivating enough at the time, but later on the student wonders why he's never heard of Charles Martel or the Battle of

Tours, much less its significance in determining whether Europe became Christian or Moslem.

MICHELLE: Eric, I'm not saying that who Charles Martel was or what the significance of the Battle of Tours was is not important. I'm saying that there's more than one way of getting students to learn and remember such information. Just telling them to memorize facts because they are going to be tested on them is no guarantee that they'll recall them later on when they take a standardized test.

ERIC: Are you advocating discovery learning? Do you want us to waste our time finding ways to help kids discover the facts of history?

MICHELLE: No I'm not, Eric. I guess I probably use more of a problem-solving approach in my classes. Perhaps it does involve some discovery, but not in the sense that I think you mean. No, I guess that I'm talking about higher-order rather than lower-order learning. That certainly involves presenting facts in a larger context so that they're more likely to be remembered and applied.

TOM: Let me jump in here. Michelle, when you say higher-order learning are you referring to Bloom's cognitive taxonomy?

MICHELLE: Why, yes, that would certainly be involved.

TOM: (passing out handout) Then let me pass out this handout on Bloom's taxonomy. Perhaps it will help provide a framework for some of our discussion.

ERIC: (looking at handout) Yes, I remember this. And the upper levels are important, but the problem is that students have to learn the lower-level stuff before they can do the higher-order type of thinking.

MICHELLE: I beg to disagree. The real problem is that we have always just taught history at the first two or three levels. We never get to the upper levels. Teachers always say that they're important and then go back to having their students memorize facts.

ERIC: Everything that I've ever read on creative thinking, your Level 5 or synthesis level here, says that for a person to think creatively he must have a knowledge base of information to draw from. In other words, Level 5 isn't possible without Levels 1 and 2.

MICHELLE: You're not hearing what I'm saying, Eric. I'm not saying Levels 1 and 2 aren't important. I'm saying that Levels 1 and 2 are all that we teach. We don't even try for Levels 4, 5, and 6. Sometimes I'm not even sure of Level 3.

ERIC: Who says I don't teach anything beyond Level 2? Speak for yourself, Michelle!

MICHELLE: I never said anything about your teaching, Eric! Don't put words in my mouth! But since you brought it up, give me an example of higher-order learning in one of your world history classes.

ERIC: (puzzled) Yeah, well, I guess that I'd have to think about that for a minute. (Angrily) Tell us what you do at the higher levels, Michelle.

MICHELLE: I'd be glad to, but I'll bet that you and I don't use the same types of teaching methods, and I'll bet we give different types of tests. You see, I think that problem solving and creativity are important and are the real instructional objectives that I'm aiming for and try to teach toward. Other teachers aren't really aiming toward them, and you can tell it in their teaching methods and testing procedures. For example . . .

TOM: (interrupting) Let me jump in at this point and stop you, Michelle, as important and fascinating as this discussion is. Our time is up, but perhaps we could all look at our own instructional objectives, teaching methods, and evaluation procedures, as well as those of our fellow teachers, and see if we can't begin to come to some resolutions of our differences next time. See you next week.

It is one week later. In the meantime, all six teachers have informally surveyed fellow teachers in their building regarding the issues discussed at the last meeting.

Tom: OK. I understand that some of you took me seriously and polled your fellow teachers about some of the issues raised by Eric and Michelle at our last meeting. Perhaps we should begin by sharing the results.

Michelle: I have the results for Lois, Delicia, and me, and I must admit that I was somewhat surprised. Roughly two thirds of the history teachers agree with what Eric said.

Eric: And the other third teach like you. That's about what Luis, Lee, and I found, only it's more like one fourth and three fourths. So that ought to tell you what the majority of our history teachers feel is important. I strongly urge us to yield to their wisdom and their collective majority by following their wishes in designing our program.

Michelle: The majority isn't automatically always right, and it's often a minority that brings needed change to institutions in our society. Might I point out to my fellow history teachers that those who favored independence were in the minority in American society before the Revolutionary War began. (Pause) In any case, Eric, let me ask you a question or two about the best way to teach history. What teaching method do you use mostly in your classes?

Eric: Lecture-discussion, without question. And I make no apology for that. It is the best and most efficient way to present information. I try to organize my lectures and discussions so that I go from the general to the particular and from the simple to the complex. I might add that I do have my students do reports in small groups, and we do bring in and discuss current events. But lecture-discussion is the most common way I teach.

Michelle: Do you give mostly objective tests?

Eric: Yes, I do. Multiple-choice, matching, fill-in-the-blank, and usually, but not always, one essay. I hardly ever give true/false.

Michelle: Do you give quizzes?

Eric: Yes, usually ten objective questions each Friday.

Michelle: What would be an example of one of your essay questions?

Eric: One that I gave on my last test was "Give and explain three reasons why Rome defeated Carthage in the Punic Wars."

Michelle: Did you go over and discuss three reasons in class?

Eric: Yes, of course. In great detail. I considered it to be important material.

Michelle: Would you say that most of your test questions are like that one?

Eric: Yes, pretty much.

Michelle: And how would you grade a question like that?

Eric: By how close the answer comes to covering all the important points that we went over in class.

Michelle: Then even your essay questions are at the first level of Bloom's taxonomy. The kids don't have to look anything up independently or discover anything on their own. They just memorize and repeat back what you stress as important.

Eric: But Michelle, I don't have time to go over material that isn't important and let them fool around trying to discover stuff on their own. I present or discuss the material in the most understandable way I can, and then I test them on it to see if they got it. Why should I let them fumble around trying to grasp material that I can explain to them so that they can understand it? Why should I waste their time and my time? After all, there is only so much learning time in a school day. Why waste it?

MICHELLE: Maybe so that what you're teaching the students will be remembered after the exam is over. If what you're teaching them isn't meaningful to them and isn't understood by them in a form they can relate to and remember, it's forgotten within forty-eight hours after the test is over.

ERIC: I don't believe that is so, but pray tell us poor misguided teachers the right way to teach. I suppose that you let your students discover the answers for themselves.

TOM: Let me break in here, Eric and Michelle. I feel that this, shall I call it a debate, is right on target as far as our task as a committee is concerned. Do the rest of you agree? (All teachers nod or voice agreement.) If we can settle these issues, we can get down to the job of writing. Please proceed, Michelle, and tell us how you teach world history.

MICHELLE: I make the assumption that what students learn in my class won't stay with them very long unless they see its relevance to their lives and are able to connect it to what they already know. So I use a problem-solving approach in my world history classes. I ask my students individually and in small groups to focus on problem areas that interest them about each unit we study. As we discuss a unit on, say, ancient Egypt or ancient Greece, students give their reports as their problem areas come up, and the rest of the students ask them as well as me questions as we discuss the material. I do very little lecturing and really don't take center stage during the discussions.

TOM: Like what kinds of problems, Michelle?

MICHELLE: As I said, students choose problem areas that interest them. One of the most popular ones with boys is "How has the art of warfare changed?" The girls like "How has the role of women in society changed?" Other problems focus on things like the best form of government, the nature of communications, the form that the arts take, or religion, the family, education, recreation and sports, why people become famous, and so forth.

ERIC: What do you do about the areas that the students need to know about but don't choose as problems?

MICHELLE: I try to fill those in myself by bringing them up. Hardly anyone ever chooses business and commerce or transportation, for example. But even if we leave some gaps by not covering material thoroughly, the material that we do cover sticks with them longer than just the next test. For one thing, I notice that the students consistently choose the same problem areas. Boys interested in the art of warfare in ancient Egypt become intrigued with how the Greeks changed it and then the Romans. This often encourages them to read books in the library on their topics, so they go beyond the text.

ERIC: And I suppose that you're going to tell us that you primarily test them on the material that the students present.

MICHELLE: Not only that, I have each student or problem-solving group write test questions on the material that they present in class at the end of their presentation, and I often use some of their questions in my own tests.

TOM: What kinds of test questions, Michelle?

MICHELLE: Most of my questions are essay that I deliberately focus at all six levels of Bloom's taxonomy. I also try to make sure that the questions that I ask in class during our discussions focus on all six levels. It's one thing to ask students a Level 1 question like "Who was the Spartan king who commanded the Greek troops at the Battle of Thermopylae?" and quite another to ask a Level 5 question like "Create a battle plan that Xerxes, the Persian king, could have used to defeat the Greek troops in one day at Thermopylae."

TOM: So the students usually write essay questions to go with their reports?

MICHELLE: (pondering) Both essay and objective. To tell you the truth, I'd say they write more multiple-choice than any other type.

ERIC: And I suppose their questions cover all six levels of Bloom's taxonomy.

MICHELLE: No, of course not. I think that it's just easier for them to write and ask the other students objective questions.

ERIC: In all honesty, I can see why your students would enjoy your classes, Michelle, but it would really bother me to teach that way. First, I don't buy your assumptions that what your students learn would stay with them longer. I'll bet my students do better on the SAT than yours, or if not the SAT, any standardized test that covers social studies that you want to name. But also, your coverage can't be as thorough and as in-depth as mine. I think that focusing on problem areas like that would leave a number of content gaps either not covered or just barely covered. Finally, using those problem-solving types of projects and all the reporting and discussing would take up tremendous amounts of class time. Your approach is interesting, but a more traditional approach makes more sense for most teachers.

MICHELLE: (angrily) Again I ask, what good is coverage if the kids forget most of what you teach because they're bored out of their skulls or half asleep? We've been teaching history that way for too many years! It's time our school district made some changes!

TOM: OK. Let me jump in here. We appreciate very much the two of you describing what you do. But what about the rest of you? What direction do you feel we should move in, or should we attempt some compromise?

LUIS: I agree with Eric. His approach makes sense for most of the teachers in this school district.

LEE: And I agree with Eric as well. That's how I teach.

TOM: Are you going to agree with Eric also Lois?

LOIS: Absolutely not! What I do isn't exactly the same as Michelle, but it's close to it. Only if students are allowed to get themselves into what they are learning is it going to stick with them.

DELICIA: I agree with Lois. I got a lot of good ideas just listening to Michelle, and I hope you don't mind, Michelle, if I use some of them in my classes.

MICHELLE: (smiling) Not at all, Delicia. I've certainly borrowed enough from teachers I have known.

TOM: It sounds like we are divided right down the middle on this. We don't seem to agree on instructional objectives, teaching methods, or evaluation procedures! Can any of you creative individuals see any way that we can synthesize or combine these two different approaches? (No response. Three women and one man shake their head negatively.) No creativity here?

MICHELLE: Maybe none of our education professors let us think at the upper levels of Bloom's taxonomy when we took our coursework. Where are students going to learn to think creatively if we don't ever give them a chance to do so in their classes?

Tom: I hear what you're saying, Michelle, but this committee is hopelessly divided. Don't any of you have any ideas to help us get off dead center? Do both sides have to be one hundred percent right? Can anybody give a little here?

Figure 18–1 Dr. Tom Blakely's Handout to the History Curriculum Revision Committee

Bloom's Cognitive Taxonomy

1.00 Knowledge

The ability to remember, recall, or recognize. Often rote memory. Student responds without necessarily understanding the material.

Objective: Student will be able to orally spell correctly 80% of the words dictated by the teacher.

2.00 Comprehension

The ability to respond with understanding. Student is able to translate or restate information in other words. Student not only receives the information but also is able to use it.

Objective: Student will be able to define correctly in his or her own words 70% of a list of 50 words presented on a teacher-made written test.

3.00 Application

The ability to use rules, principles, and abstractions in problem solving.

Objective: Given 10 rectangles on a teacher-made written test, the student will be able to write correctly with 90% accuracy the area of each rectangle by applying the formula $A = l \times w$.

4.00 Analysis

The ability to break down a problem into its elements and to identify the relevant elements in a problem. Emphasis is on breaking down a whole into its elements and then correctly applying a principle to solve the problem.

Objective: After reading at least five books from the reading list, student will be able to write, in not more than two sentences each, at least four major causes of World War II with 75% accuracy as judged by the teacher.

5.00 Synthesis

The capability to work with elements of a problem and to combine these elements into a new whole. The student must express his or her own ideas, and the product is typically a "new" or "creative" statement.

Objective: Given copies of examples of cubism in Picasso's paintings and pointillism in Renoir's paintings, the student will combine at least three elements of each of these two techniques by creating a painting that expresses at least three of the following feelings: happiness, surprise, sadness, anger, love.

6.00 Evaluation

The ability to make qualitative and quantitative judgments about the adequacy of materials. These judgments must be supported by reasons that draw upon principles, rules, facts, and modes of analysis.

Objective: Given a videotape of the president's two most recent public addresses, the student will in written form rate the speeches on a 7-point scale in terms of eye contact, persuasiveness, clarity of expression, voice modulation, and physical gesturing.

■ Questions

1. Michelle argues that students are more likely to forget factual material than principles. Is that true? In what forms can facts and principles be presented to increase their retention? What research has been done on "forgetting curves"?

2. Examine this case from the perspective of information processing theory. Explain Eric's and Michelle's positions from the standpoint of sensory register, short-term memory, and long-term memory. What is forgetting from the standpoint of retrieval theory?

3. What is meaningful learning? What are derivative and correlative subsumers from Ausubel's cognitive theory, and how might they be used to explain meaningfulness? What is reception learning, and does it come closer to what Eric or Michelle is doing in the classroom?

4. Examine this case from the perspective of Jerome Bruner's cognitive theory. What are coding systems and categories, and how are they different from Ausubel's organizers? What are discovery learning and the spiral curriculum according to Bruner, and whose method of teaching would they better relate to—Eric's or Michelle's?

5. What is constructivism? Would viewing the learner as acting upon his or her environment be more compatible with what Eric or Michelle is doing? What is the zone of proximal development? What are instructional scaffolds? How could these constructs help either teacher?

6. What differences exist between Michelle and Eric with regard to their orientations toward Bloom's cognitive taxonomy? How do their teaching and evaluation procedures differ with regard to Bloom's taxonomy?

7. Michelle argues that her approach to teaching is more intrinsically motivating to students and will therefore result in greater content retention. What is motivation? What is the relationship between motivation and retention?

8. Michelle favors a problem-solving approach to teaching. What is problem solving, and how is it best taught? Do problem-solving approaches increase transfer of learning?

9. Eric and Michelle seem to differ on the value of objective and essay tests. What are the strengths and weaknesses of each? Which is more useful in measuring the types of cognitive productions at the different levels of Bloom's taxonomy?

10. What advice would you give Tom and the committee about resolving the differences that have emerged? Which position do you favor, and why?

Plan or Be Planned For

Key Content to Consider for Analyzing This Case:

1. Classroom Management
2. Behavior Modification
3. Instructional Objectives
4. Parent Involvement Methods
5. Maslow's Need Hierarchy

Bradley Middle School is located in the city of Patton in a southern state. Patton has a population of 85,000, and BMS draws from an attendance area that is 73% white, 25% African-American, and 2% Hispanic. The school is relatively new, with a physical plant that was built just 3 years ago.

Keri Larson is a beginning teacher who graduated from the College of Education at a large university about 40 miles away. She sits in the office of the building principal, James Downes, discussing arrangements for a field trip that she wishes to take involving her eighth-grade science classes.

MR. DOWNES: What did you say the purpose of the field trip is again, Keri?

KERI: We want to help the kids learn how to identify edible plants, to increase their survival skills. Sherri Reardon [a social studies teacher at Bradley] will be working with some of them to increase their awareness of environmental problems resulting from all the construction around Possum Hollow.

MR. DOWNES: Yes, I remember how wild Possum Hollow used to be when I was a kid growing up here. Boy, has all that changed!

KERI: Yes, exactly Mr. Downes.

MR. DOWNES: So, I'll need to get subs for both you and Sherri for a full day. (Pause as he writes) I've already lined up the bus, Keri. Ray Grimes will be your driver.

KERI: Good.

MR. DOWNES: Now, Keri, Ray tells me that the bus has a capacity of sixty-five passengers. Is that going to do it?

KERI: Yes. I have thirty-one from one class and twenty-nine from the other. That's sixty, so we'll be OK.

MR. DOWNES: Have you received signed permission slips from all the parents?

KERI: I have all but five, and those five promise to get them in to me right away.

MR. DOWNES: Be sure they do. They're important.

KERI: Do they really protect you if anything goes wrong?

MR. DOWNES: Yes and no. A parent can't really sign away any rights guaranteed under the law, but getting permission slips does show that you're doing some planning and involving the parents in the process.

KERI: Oh.

MR. DOWNES: Now, Keri, that's a lot of students. Do you have enough sponsors lined up to supervise them? You know how wild kids can get on a field trip if you don't have the people to keep them in line.

KERI: Oh, yes. I have ten parents, most of them men, lined up in addition to Sherri, Ray, and me, and my fiance Frank.

MR. DOWNES: Now, Keri, don't expect Ray to help once they're off the bus. He's just the driver. (Pause) Keri, if you have sixty students plus fourteen adults, how are you going to get them all on a bus with a seating capacity of sixty-five?

KERI: (frowning) I guess we'll have to get some of the parents to drive their cars.

MR. DOWNES: No, that won't do, Keri. You all need to be together at all times. That's important. (Pause) I'll tell you what. I'm going to ask Ray to try to get one of the big school buses that can hold eighty-four. I don't think there will be any problem with that, so you can count on it unless I let you know otherwise. (Pause) Do you really need Sherri to go along? That's two subs all day, you know.

KERI: Oh, yes, Mr. Downes. I definitely need her.

MR. DOWNES: (interrupting) But her area is social studies. How can she help you?

KERI: Her interests have been environmental issues for a long time. We were Girl Scout leaders together for a long time, and she really knows the environmental problems in Possum Hollow. She'll lead one group, and I'll lead the other.

MR. DOWNES: All right then, Keri, but make sure that you and Sherri keep a firm hand on those kids.

KERI: (smiling) We will. Thanks so much for your help, Mr. Downes.

Keri is discussing the field trip with her second-period eighth-grade science class the next day.

KERI: (animated) Mr. Downes is going to get us one of the big buses so both classes can go. Yes, Barry?

BARRY: (frowning) Do we have to go with the third-period class? Why can't we go by ourselves? They are a bunch of creeps in there!

KERI: (smiling) Why, Barry! I had no idea there are so many weird students in the third-period class. As I recall, they did better than this class on the last exam. (Moans and protests from the students) Yes, Reba?

REBA: Why do they want to go?

KERI: For the same reason this class does. They want to learn how to increase their survival skills and become more aware of mankind's increasing encroachments upon nature.

REBA: (blurting out) Right! More likely they just want to cause trouble. They're a bunch of boozers and potheads, to quote my dad. (Chorus of agreement)

KERI: (raising her voice) All right, people! they have as much right to go as you do. Mr. Downes, Ms. Reardon, and I have put a lot of work into this, and I'd appreciate it if you'd try to get along with the third-period class for one day!

BARRY: We will, but will they try to get along with us?

KERI: That's enough, Barry! Now Barry and Reba, I still don't have your signed parent permission forms, do I? If you don't get them in to me soon, you won't have to worry about the third-period class at all that day! (Moans from Barry and Reba) Yes, Melanie?

MELANIE: Ms. Larson, I have a friend who almost went crazy when I told him about our field trip! His name is Troy, and he believes that all these earth changes are going to happen in the next few years and we have to learn about edible plants and things like that if we're going to survive!

KERI: I'd say he's a bright guy, Melanie. I guess I agree with him.

MELANIE: Is there any way he can go along, Ms. Larson? I know he'd get a lot out of it and he'd appreciate it so much!

KERI: I don't know. We only have, let's see, I think it's eighty-five seats, and we have sixty students plus fourteen adults. Let's see, seventy-four—yes, I guess we can take one more, if it's that important to him. But only if it's OK with his parents and teachers. I'm not going to get into that! And he'll have to get his parents to sign a permission slip. Yes, Marsha.

MARSHA: Ms. Larson, I have this really good friend, Lorrie, and she's really a nature freak. She'd just die for a chance to go on a trip like this!

KERI: Oh, OK. I guess one more won't hurt!

It is Thursday evening of the third week in April. The field trip is the next day. Keri sits in the living room of her home talking to her long-time friend Sherri, the social studies teacher at Bradley who is cosponsor of the field trip.

KERI: It's just not working, Sherri! Everything is just falling apart! Frank got sick on me, and six of the parents have backed out!

SHERRI: Keri, the kids are going to be so disappointed if you cancel out! This field trip is all I've heard about at school this week!

KERI: But Sherri, it will be just you and I and four parents supervising all those kids!

SHERRI: Look, Keri, we'll just have to get them organized like we used to in the Girl Scouts. You and I will take the lead, we'll put one parent in the middle of each group and one bringing up the rear for each of the groups. We'll just explain the situation to the kids and tell them that we need their help. They're good kids! They'll cooperate!

KERI: Do you think so? I hope you're right!

It is 6:30 a.m. the next morning. The bus has arrived. The students mill around in a group at the side of the bus while Keri and Sherri stand apart talking to each other as they prepare to check on last-minute details and begin the boarding of the bus. Ray Grimes, the driver, stands in the main doorway of the bus, preventing boarding until Keri gives the word.

KERI: (whispering) Sherri, can you believe it! Only two parents! Mr. Johnson and Ms. Parmalee didn't even bother to call and say they weren't coming!

SHERRI: I know it. We'll just have to go with what we have!

KERI: (shouting) Would Barry, Reba, Sarah, Jerry Joe, and Sam—Sam Crittenden, that is—please come over here a minute. (Five students walk over to Keri and Sherri.) People, I need your signed permission forms.

REBA: Please, Ms. Larson, my parents said it's OK for me to go, but my father lost the form! Please let me go! It's OK with them, I promise! (Other students chorus a similar response.)

KERI: (looking at Sherri) What do you think!?

SHERRI: (hesitantly) I don't know! It's your call, Keri.

KERI: I should have collected them before now, so I guess it's my fault as well as theirs. Mr. Downes said they really don't give you any legal protection anyhow. (Loudly to students) All right! Do all five of you promise that your parents gave verbal permission for you to go? I want all the other students to hear your answer. (A yes choral response) I can't hear you! (All shout yes loudly.) All right. Everybody get on the bus. (Students and two parents board the bus as Ray moves to the driver's seat. Keri and Sherri get on last, next to the driver.)

SHERRI: (standing up and looking toward the back of the bus) We can't start until you three sit down.

KERI: (standing up) I can't believe it. Count the number of people, Sherri, will you?

SHERRI: (counting) There's eighty-seven counting you and me.

KERI: (agitated) That doesn't make sense! There are only supposed to be seventy-six and six parents didn't come. Where did the extra people come from?

RAY: I'm afraid we can't carry that many, Ms. Larson. This bus' maximum load is eighty-four. I can't carry eighty-seven people. It's against the law.

KERI: (angry) Now Ray, don't you become a problem too! You don't know how much Sherri and I have gone through! (Begins to cloud up) If three people have to get off to make things legal, you decide which ones and tell them, Ray!

RAY: (gently) Now, Ms. Larson, you know I can't do that! I'll tell you what. I'm just going to act like I didn't hear what Mrs. Reardon said about how many. Let's just go!

KERI: (smiling wanly) Thanks, Ray. (To three students) You three will have to sit down somewhere or not go with us! Your choice! (Boy sits on floor, two girls sit on boys' laps.) All right! Let's go!

The bus arrives at a dirt road on the edge of Possum Hollow. Keri has all the kids get off the bus, and she and Sherri divide them into the two groups that had been determined in advance. Keri and Sherri stand apart from the two groups talking.

KERI: (angrily) Honestly, Sherri, what a bunch of brats! I can't believe it! (Turns to address students) Now listen, people! I don't mind telling you that we really didn't appreciate your behavior on the bus coming over here! All you did was argue, fight, and bother one another the whole time! If this is the way you're going to behave today, let's just head back now!

STUDENT: We're sorry, Ms. Larson! We'll behave! (Chorus of agreement)

KERI: (turning to Sherri) I hope so! (Turning back to students) Listen up, then. We really don't have enough adult help today, so we need your cooperation. I'll lead the edible plants group down that path (pointing), and I'll ask Mr. Normandy [a parent] to bring up the rear. Mrs. Reardon will lead the environmental group down that path (pointing), and Mrs. Simonetti [parent] will bring up the rear of that group. (Pause) Now please stay with your group and don't get separated. We'll all meet back here at noon and eat lunch together in that clearing. (Students express surprise.) Yes, Mr. Grimes has food and a table stored in the luggage area of the bus, and I think you'll be surprised at what it is.

STUDENT: Pizza!

KERI: (laughing) No, not pizza, but I guarantee you'll like it. After we eat we'll discuss what we've learned today and then we'll start back. (Raises voice) Now remember this! We must start back at 2 P.M. sharp! Yes, Raymond?

RAYMOND: Ms. Larson, what if we have to, well, you know, go to the bathroom?

KERI: (smiling) You'll just have to separate from your group briefly, Raymond, and go behind a tree or something. There are no portable toilets here, I'm afraid. (One female student says "Yuk," and Keri ignores her.) Now remember, people, stay with your group!

Keri's and Sherri's groups go down separate paths. As the two teachers stop at various points, point out items of interest and lecture about each, and answer student questions, each group spreads out more and more. Some of the students quietly sneak away from the main group and move into the woods. About 45 minutes after Keri's group started down the path, Keri is in the middle of explaining how to eat an edible plant she has pointed out. A core group of 16 students, mostly females, stay very close to her and hang on her every word. Suddenly one student, Bob, runs from out of the woods right up to where Keri is standing and shouts her name.

BOB: (excitedly) Ms. Larson! Ms. Larson!

KERI: What's the matter, Bob?! What's wrong?

BOB: It's Steve Shea! He fell out of a tree and he's hurt bad! He broke his arm for sure! You can see the bone! And he can't walk!

KERI: Oh, my goodness! What was he doing in a tree?! Where is he?

BOB: (pointing) Way over there! Hurry! I'll take you there! (Entire group follows Bob through the woods to where Steve lies in agony on the ground under a tree. Steve's girlfriend, Sharon, is bending down trying to help him as another boy and girl stand around helplessly watching.)

SHARON: (crying) Oh, Ms. Larson, help him. He's hurt bad!

KERI: (both furious and terrified) For goodness' sake, Sharon, how did . . . ? (Calming down) Bob, I want you to run to the bus and get Mr. Grimes. Tell him to bring a blanket to make a stretcher with.

SHARON: Should we move him? Can't we call an ambulance?

KERI: How, Sharon? No one brought a cell phone with them. No, we have to get him back to the bus and drive him in ourselves, at least until we can get help. Barry?

BARRY: Yes, Ms. Larson?

KERI: Barry, I want you to go find Mrs. Reardon's group and tell her what's happened. Tell her to meet us back at the bus as fast as she can. OK?

BARRY: Yes, Ms. Larson. (Runs off)

Ray joins Keri's group, and he and two of the boys make a stretcher for Steve. They slowly carry him, moaning and crying, back to the bus, which Sherri's group has already boarded. Keri and Sherri get the rest of the students on board and sit up front to try to comfort Steve, who is stretched out on a pile of blankets in the aisle. Sharon sits in a seat just above him crying.

KERI: (whispering to Sherri) Honestly, Sherri, can you believe this? All we wanted to do was have a simple field trip!

SHERRI: (tearing up) I know! I can't believe . . . (Suddenly a girl sitting at the back of the bus moves away from the boy she was sitting with and begins to shout obscenities at him.)

KERI: (angrily shouting) What's going on back there?! Don't we have enough trouble without . . . Melanie, is that you?!

MELANIE: (shouting and crying) Yes, Ms. Larson! He raped me!

KERI: (stunned) What! Who raped you?! You were just sitting next to him. How could he . . .

MELANIE: (interrupting and crying) Back in the woods! Troy raped me!

KERI: Troy! Who's Troy?

TROY: (holding up his hand) I'm Troy, Ms. Larson, and I didn't rape her! She wanted to have sex.

MELANIE: (shouting) He's a liar!

TROY: (calmly) Believe me, Ms. Larson, all we did was smoke a little pot and have sex. I didn't rape her.

MELANIE: I hate you, you . . .

KERI: Don't we have enough trouble without this! You two just stay away from each other and we'll sort this out later!

It is the next day, and Keri and Sherri sit in Mr. Downes's office with the door closed. Mr. Downes speaks to Keri with controlled anger.

MR. DOWNES: Keri, you should never have let that group get on the bus! You used terrible judgment! I can't tell you how disappointed I am in both of you! (Both teachers hang their head.) I just got off the phone with the superintendent. Steve Shea's parents are threatening to sue, and the girl who says she was raped—Melanie Larrison, is it?

KERI: Yes.

MR. DOWNES: Her parents have called the police. Both parties will accuse you of negligence. And something you didn't know. Do you know a Mark Lotz?

KERI: (surprised) Yes, he's in my third-period class.

MR. DOWNES: It seems that you pulled away and left him behind. He had to walk and finally hitchhiked his way back home. His parents are furious!

KERI: (sobbing) Perfect!

MR. DOWNES: Keri, crying won't help! Three members of the school board have called here already and are asking for facts about what went on. You have to get yourselves together and do some explaining! I don't know how this is going to come out! (Pause) I've notified George Burkett, the union rep, about what's happened. He'll meet with both of you after school tomorrow in your room, Keri.

It is the next day after school. George Burkett, the portly, aging, white-haired local teachers' union representative, walks calmly into Keri's classroom and introduces himself to Keri and Sherri. They form their chairs into a circle to talk.

KERI: George, I'm so glad to see you! I'm in big trouble and don't have anyone to turn to except for Sherri here, and I'm afraid that I've gotten her into as much trouble as I am!

GEORGE: (smiling) Things aren't all bad, Keri. You both had the good sense to join the union, and that means that you are automatically covered for malpractice for up to a million dollars.

KERI: Really! That's wonderful!

GEORGE: Not entirely. This is your first year of teaching, Keri, and you don't have tenure. They can let you go without giving a reason. Sherri has tenure, so it would be very hard for them to get rid of her.

SHERRI: But it can be done?

GEORGE: Tenure really guarantees you due process, Sherri. They'd have to prove you were negligent.

SHERRI: How do they do that?

GEORGE: I'm not an attorney, but I've been involved in enough cases over the years to know what goes on. You see, as a teacher you stand *in loco parentis*, or in place of the parents, in case of a situation like this field trip. Therefore, you're responsible for the students. Generally, the court uses the test of foreseeability, I believe they call it, in cases like this. What that basically comes down to is whether or not you tried to anticipate the risks and situations that might come up and planned for them. All this starts, of course, by informing the parents and getting them to sign permission slips.

KERI: George, I just wish I had known all this before we went on this field trip! I sure would have done things differently!

GEORGE: Keri, since you don't have tenure, I don't honestly know whether you'll end up losing your job over this or not. But if you do, I think from what I've heard about your teaching ability, you'll end up as a teacher somewhere else. I always say that after you make mistakes, all you can do is learn from them. So tell me, Keri, what have you learned from all this? If you had to do this field trip all over again, what would you do differently?

Figure 19–1 School Board of Patton County Curriculum Division, Parental Field Trip Permission

School _____ Teacher: _____ Grade: _____

Date: _____

Permission is requested for your son/daughter to go on a field trip to

_____

with his/her class on _____, 20____.

We will leave the school at _____ ( ) a.m. ( ) p.m., and return to the school at approximately _____ ( ) a.m. ( ) p.m.

*Emergency phone: Daytime _____ Evening _____ Other _____

If your son/daughter has permission to go on this trip please sign below.

Please accept this form as a consent signature for a physician or hospital staff to give emergency treatment of an injury or illness to my son or daughter if medical attention is needed.

METHOD OF TRAVEL

School Bus _____

City Bus _____

Walking _____ Student Name (please print)

Private Vehicle _____

Driver: _____ _____

Other (Specify): _____ Signature of Parent or Guardian

*Your student cannot go on the trip unless emergency phone number(s) are listed.

◼ Questions

1. What mistakes did Keri make in planning and executing this field trip? How could she have handled these things differently? Make a list of things that Keri should have done in planning for a field trip.

2. Would you like to work for a principal like Mr. Downes? Why or why not? How would you describe his administrative style? How supportive will he be of Keri and Sherri when their case is dealt with by the school system?

3. What educational objectives does Keri seem to be pursuing in arranging the field trip? What curricular purposes do field trips serve? If the field trip had worked out well, what would have been some appropriate follow-up activities in the classroom? In general, what educational values do field trips serve?

4. From the standpoint of school law, what kind of protection do parent permission slips provide the teacher? What does it mean to say that the teacher stands *in loco parentis* when teaching students? What is the test of foreseeability, and how would it apply to teacher activities such as a field trip? What are malpractice and negligence as applied to teaching?

5. How do you feel about teachers' unions? Do they help or hinder teaching in becoming a profession? In what areas are they most effective? Least effective? Why? Why do teachers' unions exist in the first place?

6. What does it mean to call teaching a profession? What are the characteristics of a profession? How is Keri's job different from that of a physician or attorney in private practice?

7. What is tenure as it applies to teaching? What does it mean to guarantee a teacher due process in deciding whether or not a teacher should be fired as a result of such grounds as malpractice, incompetence, or moral turpitude?

8. How does Maslow's motivational need hierarchy help explain the motives of key persons in this case, such as Keri or Mr. Downes? How would schools have to change to become institutions that fostered self-actualization in students?

9. What classroom management model could Keri have used in developing and conducting the field trip so as to avoid the problems that occurred? How could these procedures have grown out of or been integrated with those used in the classroom? For example, how might Keri have used contingency management techniques from behavior modification theory?

10. What is parent involvement in education, and what parent involvement techniques are most highly related to student success in school? What parent involvement procedures might Keri have used in increasing parent support for and participation in the field trip? How many parents is it desirable to involve on a field trip, and what are the most effective ways to use parents' help?

The Glory That Was Greece

Key Content to Consider for Analyzing This Case:

1. Constructivism
2. Information Processing Theory
3. Meaningful Learning (Ausubel)
4. Metacognition
5. Mastery versus Performance Goal Orientation
6. Measurement and Evaluation Principles (Essay versus Objective Testing)
7. Instructional Objectives

Santa Zorro Junior High School is located in a mid-sized, West Coast city of approximately 50,000 people. Its student body is primarily white, with minority groups consisting of approximately 10% African-American, 10% Chicano, and 3% Asian origin. The school's physical plant is only 3 years old and is well equipped. It is situated among many palm trees not far from the Pacific Ocean. All the classrooms are well furnished with the latest equipment and supplies.

It is early in a new school year. Charlene Dutton, a social studies teacher with 5 years' teaching experience, is introducing a new unit in her fourth-period world history class of 31 ninth graders.

CHARLENE: Today we're going to start a new unit in your text on ancient Greece called "The Glory That Was Greece." I can't emphasize enough our heritage from the ancient Greeks in terms of art, theater, philosophy, science, even the idea of democracy itself. How many of you knew that the Olympic Games began in Greece? (Many hands go up.) Good. Now remember that both the unit exam and the quizzes will be objective: multiple choice, matching, and fill-in-the-blank like before. It isn't enough just to read the material—you need to underline important names, dates, battles, and key terms. Then go back over them just before the exam. (Sees a student's hand raised) Yes, Anna?

ANNA: Will we have the quizzes on Friday like before?

CHARLENE: Yes. (Picking up papers from her desk and starting to hand them out) Also, please take a copy of this outline map of ancient Greece. Begin to put city-states, important battles, and so forth on it as we talk about them. It will be due on the day you take the unit exam. (A few students groan.) It is also important that you keep bringing in items for our current events bulletin board each Monday. I'll let a few of you read some of your contributions in just a minute. First, open your notebooks and make some notes as I give a little introduction, including some material that's not in your text, as to how the Greek civilization began. (Students open their notebooks, some try to borrow paper, and others search for pencils. Two students, Barry and Bill, whisper to each other as Barry borrows a sheet of paper from Bill.)

BARRY: (whispering) You coming over tonight?

BILL: You better believe it! We gotta get that bike of yours working so we can go party with Mitzi and Yvonne!

BARRY: (excitedly) You mean Yvonne Simmons?

BILL: (smiling wisely) In the flesh! I think she's got a thing for you!

CHARLENE: (looking at Barry and Bill) I'd very much appreciate it if you two would stop talking so I can begin! (Barry and Bill stop talking and look down at the floor.) Now, to really understand where the Greeks originally came from, we need to go back to the year 1500 B.C. and the island of Crete. Let's all get our outline maps out now and find the island of Crete.

It is one week later, and Charlene is leading a discussion of the Persian invasion of Greece.

CHARLENE: The Persian great king, Darius, was succeeded by his son Xerxes. Xerxes, like his father, tried to invade Greece. Even though they knew the Persians were coming, the Greek city-states still could not unite to form a common defense. In the year 480 B.C., one of the two Spartan kings named Leonidas led his personal bodyguard of three hundred soldiers to a narrow mountain pass at Thermopylae to try to slow the Persians down until the Greek city-states could unite. (Pause) Now let's all get our outline maps out and locate the pass of Thermopylae. (Sees a hand raised) Yes, Anna?

ANNA: (pointing to the map) Is it here or here, Miss Dutton?

CHARLENE: (walking to Anna's seat and pointing to her map) Here, Anna. (Pause) Now, class, why did Leonidas think he could stop a Persian army a thousand times the size of his at Thermopylae? Yes, Bill?

BILL: Because the pass was narrow. Only a few soldiers could get into the pass at a time to fight.

CHARLENE: Right, Bill. Jerry?

JERRY: Also the Spartans were tougher than the average soldiers, and they had bigger shields and longer spears.

CHARLENE: Very good, Jerry! So by choosing to hold a narrow mountain pass, Leonidas took advantage of his small army's strengths and didn't allow the Persians to use their advantage in terms of size. (Pause) So what happened? (Looks at Barry, who stares at the floor) Barry, you haven't had much to say about this important battle—what happened?

BARRY: (frowning) Oh, I don't know. I suppose the Spartans won.

CHARLENE: (frowning) Didn't you read the assignment?

BARRY: (in a sullen tone) No.

CHARLENE: (with a slight edge in her voice) May I ask why not?

BARRY: It's hard for me to read this stuff. It's a real pain!

CHARLENE: (shocked) Why, what do you mean, Barry? Don't you enjoy reading about the heroism of the Spartans at Thermopylae?

BARRY: (sullenly) I don't enjoy reading history—any kind! I mean, I'm going to be a mechanic. I don't see how knowing how a bunch of soldiers, who carried shields like Captain America, fought a battle two thousand years ago is going to help me! (Smiling) Can you imagine how long the Spartans would hold that pass today against a division of Marines carrying machine guns? (Several students laugh, and a few voice their agreement.)

CHARLENE: (angrily) Now just a minute, Barry! 1 didn't ask for any cute remarks! (Pause) Do you mean that you don't see any connection at all between what has happened in the past and what is happening today?

BARRY: (testily) No! Not that makes any difference. (Several hands go up.)

CHARLENE: Yes, Anna?

ANNA: (hesitantly) I sort of agree, Miss Dutton. I mean, well, my mother is always telling me what things were like when she was my age. But things today aren't like they were back then. . . .

CHARLENE: (somewhat shaken) Thanks, Anna. I guess I'm a bit surprised at what some of you are saying! Let me ask the entire class a question. How many of you feel there is some value in studying history? (Only about one third of the class raise their hand. Others hesitate as though deciding.) This is such an important issue that I think we need to spend the next class meeting discussing it. All of you come prepared with your arguments, and we'll sort of debate both sides of the issue and then see how people feel.

It is the next day, and Charlene leads the debate on the value of history as the fourth period begins.

CHARLENE: The way we'll proceed is, I'll make a few opening comments and then I'll call on people one at a time. First, I'll call on a person who feels that history has some value, and then someone who takes the opposite side, until everyone has had a chance to state his or her position. Then at the end, we'll vote by secret ballot to see how the class stands on the issue. Yes, Anna?

ANNA: Should we take notes?

CHARLENE: No—well, maybe on my introductory remarks. (Pause) Of course, as a history teacher I'm biased. I think that a knowledge of history is very important. I believe it was George Santayana who wrote that "a nation that does not know history is fated to repeat it." Harry Truman once said, "There is nothing new in the world except the history you do not know." Someone else, I don't remember who, said that we need to study history so we won't get traveling so fast that we fail to look back and make sure we're traveling forward. In short, students, history repeats itself, and as a nation, we need to profit from past mistakes. We can use history as a basis for making decisions about the future. History is a summary of our cultural heritage. Not to bother to learn history is to throw out our cultural heritage that so many have struggled to build and to die for. (Pause) But then that's a choice that each of us must make. Now, since I've given affirmative arguments, who'd like to go first for the negative side? (Barry and Bill look at each other and raise their hands.) Yes, Bill? Why don't you begin.

BILL: It's a little hard to argue against a teacher, but I still think it's a waste of time and has nothing to do with today. Our textbook doesn't even go up to the present. And another thing—you said history repeats itself. My Dad says that we hated the Japanese and the Germans in World War II. And today we are friends with the Japanese and Germans. See? Past history has nothing to do with what's happening now.

CHARLENE: Now somebody for the affirmative side. Yes, Marsha?

MARSHA: I think we'd better know history or we just might blow ourselves up with nuclear bombs and all. Our leaders had better know what mistakes we've made in the past so we don't repeat them, or we'll all end up paying for it!

CHARLENE: Yes, Barry?

BARRY: (with slight sarcasm) No offense, Miss Dutton, but no matter what arguments anyone gives about how wonderful history is, there is one fact they can't argue down: It's just plain uninteresting and boring. One thing's for sure—it's not for me. I have more important things to do and to worry about.

CHARLENE: (shocked) Scott?

SCOTT: I agree with Barry. History is boring. And it doesn't help us find CDs for the Hi-Y dance next Friday night. (Pleading in a clowning manner) Please, guys, help us! We're desperate!

BILL: Yes, Miss Dutton. How's history going to help poor old Scott?!

CHARLENE: (angrily) All right, you guys! Cut it out! Now who wants to go next? (Pause) No one? No one at all? (Pause) Well then, tear out a slip of paper and vote "yes" if you think that history has some value and "no" if you don't. Don't sign your names. Pass them up to Anna. Yes, Barry?

BARRY: Are you gonna tell us the vote?

CHARLENE: Yes, I will. Now, open your books to "Athens' Golden Age" on page 71. (Looking at Barry) You too, Barry—page 71. Now. . . .

It is 2 weeks later, and Charlene is returning the unit exams to the fourth-period class. Out of 31 students, there were no A's, 3 B's, 8 C's, 11 D's, and 9 F's using a 90–100-A, 80–89-B, 70–79-C, and 60–69-D grading scale with a 100-item objective exam.

CHARLENE: Needless to say, I was disappointed that we had no A's and so many D's and F's. I don't know whether that means people are not studying or that they don't know how to study. Remember I told you at the beginning that you have to underline when you read and go over the material again just before the exam. Yes, Barry?

BARRY: Miss Dutton, how can I keep going over some of this stuff again and again?! Like the Delian League and "ostracism" and guys like Aeschylus. I mean how much of all this junk can a guy remember?

CHARLENE: I'll bet you don't have any trouble remembering spark plug gap sizes.

BARRY: Well, no—hey, how do you know about spark plug gapping, Miss Dutton?

CHARLENE: I took a basic engine tune-up course in adult education about a year ago.

BARRY: Hey, that's great! But it's not the same thing. I gap spark plugs all the time, but I never use history.

CHARLENE: Learning is hard work! Auto mechanics and history are not exceptions to that rule. All some of you need to do is work a little harder. The rest of you need to examine the way that you study. I'll be glad to work with any of you in any way that I can. If some of you don't have anyone to study with before the next unit exam, I'd be glad to schedule a study session with you. All you need do is ask! (Pause) Now it's time to begin a new unit—"The Grandeur That Was Rome." (Several students groan.) The contributions of the Greek civilization were many, but they might have been lost forever if what started out as a small city-state—what's now Italy—had not conquered the world and preserved it. (Students begin to take notes.)

It is one week later, and Charlene is trying to lead a discussion on the rise of the Roman Empire.

CHARLENE: Our topic today is the change of the Roman government from a republic to an empire. What is the difference between those two forms of government? (Only one hand goes up.) Anna?

ANNA: I think a republic is like a democracy and an empire is like, well, where they have a king.

CHARLENE: That's a good start. Now—can anyone add to Anna's definitions? (No hands go up.) No one? How about you, Barry?

BARRY: I don't know. All I know is the Romans used to have a lot of really wild parties! (The class laughs.)

CHARLENE: (icily) That may or may not be historical fact, Barry, but it has nothing to do with the question.

BARRY: (smiling mischievously) I know. I'm sorry, but I think their party habits are the most interesting part of their culture. (Several students laugh.)

CHARLENE: (angrily) That's enough, Barry! (Pause) Now, let's get back to the subject. What is an empire, and how does it differ from a kingdom? (No hands go up.) I guarantee you it will be on the quiz on Friday, so you'd better be finding out! (Pause) Now, who can tell me who the first real Roman emperor was? (Nods to Anna)

ANNA: Julius Caesar?

CHARLENE: No. He wasn't the first real emperor, although he might have been. Anyone else? (No response) I guess we'd better use the rest of the period to read the assignment. Get busy, and I'll come around to see how you're doing.

It is after school on Monday of the next week, and Charlene sits in the office of Jack Lymans, social studies curriculum coordinator for the Santa Zorro School System.

CHARLENE: It's very good of you to see me. I know how busy you are.

JACK: Charlene, it's my pleasure! I can't imagine, though, what one of our best social studies teachers wants to see me about!

CHARLENE: (sheepishly) Thanks for the compliment, Jack! Maybe I should leave while I'm ahead! I sure don't feel like one of the best teachers in the system right now.

JACK: What's the problem?

CHARLENE: It's my fourth-period world history class—no, that's not true! I think that my fourth-period class has just served as a catalyst to make me question the way I've been teaching.

JACK: I'm really surprised, Charlene! Both the principals you've worked under have given you top ratings. They've said you're organized and well-prepared, you relate well to the students—

CHARLENE: (interrupting) I know! On the surface everything looks fine.

JACK: Now you have me intrigued. Tell me about your fourth-period class.

CHARLENE: They're a bunch of average-ability ninth graders who are well-behaved for the most part and relate well to me as a teacher and a person. But they are bored to death with history. Their attention wanders, and occasionally a student or two will misbehave. They just don't see how what they're learning in class will be of much value to them in the future. (Pause) Their grades on unit tests and quizzes reflect their lack of interest. I just returned a quiz on the Roman republic and the grades were the worst yet! (Pause) Jack, I've been

Figure 20–1 A Sample of Items from Charlene Dutton's Unit Exam on Ancient Greece

I. <u>Matching</u> Match the names of the people listed in the right-hand column with the important roles they played in ancient Greece. Write the letter identifying the person's name in the blank to the left of the role that he played. Some of the people's names will not be used.

_____ 1.   The commander of the 300 Spartans at Thermopylae

_____ 2.   Macedonian king who conquered Asia Minor, Persia, the Fertile Crescent, Egypt, and parts of India

_____ 3.   Alexandrian scientist who claimed that the earth rotated and revolved around the sun

_____ 4.   The Father of History who wrote the history of the Persian War

_____ 5.   The leader of Athens from 460 to 429 B.C. during its Golden Age

A. Solon
B. Aristarchus
C. Pericles
D. Hippocrates
E. Aeschylus
F. Philip of Macedon
G. Alexander the Great
H. Herodotus
I. Leonidas
J. Plato

II. <u>Multiple-Choice</u> For each question, select the one best answer and write the letter preceding your choice in the blank to the left of the question.

_____ 1. In what year did the Spartans end the Peloponnesian War by forcing Athens to surrender?
     A. 490 B.C.   B. 480 B.C.   C. 431 B.C.   D. 404 B.C.

_____ 2. Geographically, Greece is about the size of which American state?
     A. Florida   B. Maine   C. Texas   D. Delaware

_____ 3. At what battle did the Greeks finally defeat the Persians on land in 479 B.C. and end the Persian invasion?
     A. Plataea   B. Salamis   C. Marathon   D. Thermopylae

_____ 4. In which Greek city-state did democracy first develop?
     A. Corinth   B. Thebes   C. Sparta   D. Athens

_____ 5. Which of the following types of columns found on Greek buildings is the most elaborate in design?
     A. Doric   B. Ionic   C. Corinthian   D. Delian

III. <u>Completion</u> Fill in the blank by writing the correct term or name as required.

1. The 300-year period after Alexander the Great is called the _____ Age.

2. The lowest class of citizen in Sparta who acted as slaves was called the _____.

3. The famous temple dedicated to Athena that was located atop the Acropolis was called the _____.

4. In the seventh century B.C., Athens was governed by a council of nobles called _____, who were elected annually from among the nobles.

5. Prior to 338 B.C., the Greeks, who had the same language and religion although they lived in different city-states, called their land _____. Today we call it Greece.

giving it a lot of thought, and I've come to the conclusion that it's the way I've been teaching history. I have to change things, to do something to make history more interesting. The problem is I really don't know what I'm doing wrong. Have you any advice, Jack?

Questions

1. Review Charlene's introduction to the unit on ancient Greece. Could she have been more effective? Describe how you would have introduced the unit.

2. When Charlene learned that Barry had not read the assignment, was her response appropriate? Explain.

3. What are the advantages of allowing students to express their true feelings about the content of the curriculum in an open debate? Disadvantages? What does a teacher risk in arranging such an activity? What might a teacher gain?

4. When Charlene learned that about one third of her students saw some value in studying history, how else might she have responded?

5. In terms of motivational theory, what different needs are operating among Charlene and her students? For example, at what levels of Maslow's need hierarchy do they seem to be operating? Particularly focus on the primary need levels of Anna, Barry, Bill, and Charlene. To what extent do immediate drives like girlfriends and sports cars take precedence over long-range needs like making a certain grade in history? What needs relate to appreciating and valuing history? To what extent do Charlene's students demonstrate mastery versus performance goal orientation? How might Charlene change her teaching to take advantage of her students' needs and goal orientations?

6. Compare the values of Charlene and Marsha with those of Bill and Barry regarding history. For example, how do their value systems differ in terms of the affective taxonomy of Krathwohl and others? How do values change?

7. From the standpoint of observational learning, to what extent does Barry serve as a model in terms of his valuing history? What are inhibition and disinhibition, and how do they apply to Barry, and Charlene's reactions to his comments? What could Charlene do to take advantage of the principles of observational learning to change her students' behavior?

8. What are Charlene's objectives, both cognitive and affective? What levels of Bloom's cognitive taxonomy and Krathwohl's affective taxonomy is she aiming for? Write two of Charlene's objectives that exemplify both taxonomies.

9. How do the sample test items at the end of the case reflect Charlene's cognitive objectives? How could a test be written to measure higher-order cognitive objectives? Write examples of such test items. Write examples of affective objectives. What are the advantages and disadvantages of objective tests as compared to essay tests? What other means of evaluation and learning activities might Charlene have used beside objective tests?

10. From the perspective of cognitive theory, particularly information processing theory, metacognitive theory, or Ausubel's meaningful learning theory, how might Charlene have organized and presented the material so that a student like Barry would not have so much trouble remembering "all this junk"?

Meeting Individual Needs

Key Content to Consider for Analyzing This Case:

1. Home Learning Environment
2. Constructivism
3. Intrinsic versus Extrinsic Motivation
4. Attribution Theory
5. Observational Learning

Sam Goodman is 29 years old and in his second year of teaching junior high school mathematics. He teaches in the small (3,000 population) rural town of Parsons, a primarily agricultural community with approximately a 35% low-income population. Parsons High School typically graduates 30 seniors, and Parsons Junior High School, which has a physical plant constructed in 1939, has an all-white student body.

It is the first full day of classes as Sam begins a new school year. The bell has rung, and the students finally become quiet and wait for Sam to begin class. Sam smiles as he looks at the mixture of 32 faces in his third-period eighth-grade math class.

SAM: Welcome to Math 8! 1 hope that we're all resigned to the fact that summer vacation is over and it's time to get back to work. (Several students moan and groan while others laugh.) There, now, you got the last of it out of your systems. (Smiles) If you open your books to the table of contents, you'll notice that we're going to cover a lot of important material in this class—math concepts that should be valuable to you no matter what you do in life. We'll get into ratios, proportions, percents, decimals, dividing and multiplying fractions, working with positive and negative numbers, and finding square roots. You'll notice that we begin tomorrow with equations. (Pause) I know that some of this is old hat for a few of you, but others have just broken out into a cold sweat. (Several students laugh.) Don't worry though. We're going to take it slow and have fun as we do it. (Sees a hand raised) Yes, what's your name?

SHAWNNA: Shawnna Crowder. How will we be graded, Mr. Goodman?

SAM: I was just coming to that, Shawnna. Our work in this class will follow a pattern. On Monday of each week I'll introduce and explain the math concepts that we'll be working on. As I said before, we'll start with equations this week: equations and the proportions of whole numbers. It will be real important for you to pay attention to the explanations and examples I give if you want to have the following Friday off to have fun! (Sees another hand) Yes, Bill?

BILL: (excitedly) Does that mean you're going to let us do that lab thing if we do our homework?!

SAM: (smiling) You guessed it, Bill! Maybe it would be more accurate to say that your sister Vickie told you about it. (Bill nods his head.) Yes, it worked so well last year that I'm going to try it again this year. (Several hands go up.) Let me explain, and maybe it will answer a lot of your questions. (Brief pause) You see, to get a good grade in here it's important that you do the weekly assignments that I give you on Monday as I begin a new unit. These are due not later than Friday. If you turn them in on Friday, you get to spend your class time in my enrichment lab. (Smiles and speaks teasingly) You're going to love the enrichment lab! It's full of math games, math puzzles, interesting filmstrips, records, and computers. If there isn't something there that you'd like to do—maybe a hobby or something—I'll try to make it available if it doesn't cost too much. (Points to a hand that is raised) You're Jimmy Bob, aren't you?

JIMMY BOB: What happens if we can't finish the assignments?

SAM: (tauntingly) Don't even think that way, Jimmy Bob. (Opens his eyes wide and speaks slowly for emphasis) It's a fate worse than death! You have to work on your assignments while the other students have fun in the enrichment lab. (Everybody laughs.) And you have to do something else worse than death: You have to sit down and write your parents a letter explaining to them why you didn't finish your math assignments. (Several students moan.) It gets worse. If I don't get the letter back on Monday signed by your parents, I'll call them to see what happened. (Pause) Any questions? (Pause, total silence) I really can't emphasize enough how important it is for you to keep up each week and do your assignments. (Brief pause) Now let's all open our books to page one.

Two months have passed. Sam is sitting in the classroom of Joe Turpin after school. Joe is the oldest and most experienced math teacher at Parsons High School. Sam is seeking Joe's advice at the suggestion of Si Busby, Sam's principal.

SAM: Joe, I really appreciate your seeing me like this on such short notice! Mr. Busby said you are the best math teacher in the county and could give me good advice if anybody could.

JOE: (smiling) I'm happy to help any way I can, Sam. What's the difficulty?

SAM: As you probably already know, this is my second year of teaching, and I find that things that worked really well for me last year are not working for me this year—at least not in my third-period math 8 class.

JOE: How is your third-period class different?

SAM: I don't really know! I use the same procedures of making assignments on Monday that are due Friday and letting them have enrichment time on Friday if they turn them in. If they don't turn them in, I make them write a letter of explanation to their parents to be signed and brought back on Monday. It's just that it doesn't seem to work with the third-period students.

JOE: Sounds like a good approach to me. You mean it doesn't work with any of the third-period kids?

SAM: Well, actually, now that I think about it, there are four students, three boys and a girl, that I'm having the most trouble with.

JOE: Tell me about them.

SAM: First there's Jimmy Bob Billings, Bobby Joe Stone, and their leader, David Bowling. They began by not bringing pencils, paper, books, and other materials to class. Then they stopped turning in their assignments on Fridays. They have become a sort of gang, with David as their leader. They spend Fridays together writing letters to their parents and working on the assignments they never turn in.

JOE: I assume you've tried to talk to them about why they're not doing their work.

SAM: Oh yes! Nothing but excuses! The dog eats their assignments, the bus driver throws them away, or some other child they don't really know tears the assignment up. (Pause) I think Jimmy Bob has the biggest problem in some ways.

JOE: How's that?

SAM: He doesn't believe he can do the work. Says his parents weren't good at math either and that it wouldn't do any good even if he turned his assignments in. Of course I'll never know, since I never see them!

JOE: What does the ringleader, David, say?

SAM: Nothing but lies! Nothing is ever his fault. He's always the victim and blames everything on someone else. He even told his mother that I've been absent most Fridays so he couldn't turn his assignments in! When I confronted him about this, he said that he had to tell his mother something or he'd be in big trouble—that the whole thing was his mother's fault for being too hard on him and working him so hard around the house! Then when I told his mother what he told me, David tells his mother that I scared him and put pressure on him, so he had to tell *me* something! The whole thing, of course, was my fault for being so hard on him!

JOE: Oh boy! And what about this Bobby Joe?

SAM: Bobby Joe is somewhat different from Jimmy Bob and David, even though he hangs around with them in class. He's generally quieter than the others and isn't much of a discipline problem. Basically, he's a potential dropout. He wants to become a mechanic like his nineteen-year-old brother. (Pause) And I really don't think his parents would care.

JOE: Speaking of parents, I gather you've talked with them.

SAM: I think it's fair to say that I've really tried, but I've gotten no response from Jimmy Bob or Bobby Joe's parents. They don't return my calls or letters and don't have time for conferences. They generally sign the letters the boys bring home, but they don't write notes or communicate in any way. (Pause) In David's case I've talked to his mother, as I told you. But she's not going to do anything to help. She keeps asking me what *I'm* going to do about the situation. Apparently the father travels or something. Whatever he does, she always says he's too busy to help.

JOE: Sounds like you've got a fine kettle of fish there, Sam! And you say there's a girl who's a problem too?

SAM: Yes, Shawnna Crowder.

JOE: Is she part of this gang?

SAM: No, she's from an entirely different background.

JOE: What do you mean?

SAM: Shawnna is from a middle-class home in which both parents work and push her to do well in an overprotective way.

JOE: What's she doing in your class?

SAM: Very little. Her parents say that she doesn't like school, especially math. When I point out to them that she doesn't do her weekly assignments, they tell me about Shawnna's busy schedule with swimming, dancing, piano lessons four times a week, and so forth. They say these activities are as important to her future growth as her schoolwork. The problem is that the schoolwork is just too demanding, especially math. They are in the process of getting her tested and want to have a conference when the results are in.

JOE: It sounds like this third-period class is quite a challenge!

SAM: To say the least! Certainly for a beginner like me. Any advice?

JOE: Don't put yourself down, Sam. It would be a challenge for most teachers. (Pause) As for the three boys, have you tried to move them apart and separate them?

SAM: Yes, but it didn't help.

JOE: I think your instincts are good. I'd continue trying to have conferences with the kids individually and keep trying to talk to the parents.

SAM: Yes, but Joe, I find myself spending a lot of time figuring out how to motivate those four! I can't keep spending all that time on them. I have other students in the class too, and I'm beginning to think I'm neglecting them.

JOE: Somehow I really doubt that you are, Sam. I think your approach is sound and that you need to keep at it. Let me know how things are going in a month or so.

SAM: I'll do that, Joe! Thanks for listening.

Two weeks later, Shawnna's parents have called Sam and asked for a conference after school. Mason Crowder, an electrical engineer, and his wife, Melinda, a nurse in a nearby hospital, sit in chairs next to Sam's desk.

MR. CROWDER: As we told you on the phone, Mr. Goodman, we had Shawnna tested. We wanted to share the results with you. (Hands Sam test results)

SAM: Thanks. Mr. Sayres, Shawnna's counselor, has already gone over them with me. Shawnna has high potential as a student.

MR. CROWDER: Yes, and it really worries us that she doesn't like school. She should be bringing home straight A's. We know that she has a busy schedule with her piano lessons and all—but that's all that seems to keep her going. She says that life is more than homework, and I somewhat agree with her.

SAM: Have you seen any of the weekly math assignments that I have them do? I put them in the form of games, puzzles, and everyday life as much as possible. For example, the one I assigned last week on fractions was deliberately built with Shawnna in mind. (Holds up lesson with picture of piano at top)

MRS. CROWDER: Yes, I did see that one! I wondered about that!

SAM: And yet Shawnna didn't complete that one either.

MR. CROWDER: (frowning and serious) I hear what you're saying, Mr. Goodman, but Shawnna's life is very full of activities and pressures now, things that are just as important to Shawnna's future as academics. I can see that you have tried to make math as interesting as possible, but Melinda and I have come to the conclusion that this school's academic demands are just too much. We don't want Shawnna to become totally turned off to school.

SAM: What are you going to do, Mr. Crowder?

MR. CROWDER: I'm afraid that we're seriously considering having Shawnna transferred to another school. If nothing else, to a good private school, although heaven knows we really can't afford it.

SAM: (sighs) I guess you know what's best for your daughter. All I know is she mostly doesn't pay attention when I go over things in class, and she doesn't do the weekly assignments no matter how interesting I try to make them.

MR. CROWDER: Don't think we're blaming you, Mr. Goodman. It's just the school—the system. Shawnna is just turned off, and we have to do what we think is best for her.

SAM: (standing up) I understand. Please let me know if I can help in any way.

Two days later Sam sits at his desk 15 minutes after the end of the last period. In walks Bobby Joe Stone with a frown on his face.

BOBBY JOE: You said you wanted to talk to me after school, Mr. Goodman.

SAM: Yes, Bobby Joe. (Pointing to a chair) Have a seat.

BOBBY JOE: (sitting down) Did I do something wrong?

SAM: No, I just want to talk to you to try to understand why you aren't doing your work in my class.

BOBBY JOE: (sighs) Mr. Goodman, to be honest with you, I'm just waitin' to get to be sixteen so that I can drop out of school and work with my brother. He's a mechanic and can get me a job in the shop he works in. Nothin' against you, Mr. Goodman, but I'm just bored, real bored, and the only thing that makes school interestin' is cottonin' up with my friends.

SAM: But, Bobby Joe, even as a mechanic you'll need to have basic math skills. You're going to have to know how to calibrate measurements, calculate percentages, and understand decimals. Even something as simple as selecting the right wrench can involve understanding fractions or how to convert measurements to the metric system.

BOBBY JOE: If I have any problems, I'll get my brother to help me figure them out. He's pretty bright about stuff like that, and he dropped out of school when he was sixteen.

SAM: Well, Bobby Joe, I just hope that your brother is always around to help you when you have a problem.

BOBBY JOE: Well, we're pretty close, and he's only nineteen. He'll be around awhile. (Pause) If it's all right, I need to go, Mr. Goodman, you see I've. . . .

SAM: OK, Bobby Joe. I guess we're finished anyhow! Please let me know if I can help in any way.

BOBBY JOE: (standing up) Yeah, thanks a lot, Mr. Goodman. See you later.

It is Friday of the following week. All the students except David, Bobby Joe, and Jimmy Bob are involved with enrichment activities. Sam talks with the three boys as they sit at the front of his desk. There is a considerable amount of noise and movement from the other students in the classroom.

SAM: Guys, it's the same old story. What's your excuse this time, Jimmy Bob?

JIMMY BOB: Mr. Goodman, you know I can't do this stuff! It's hard! My mother said she couldn't do it when she was in school either.

SAM: You've told me that before! One thing is sure. You can't do anything if you don't try! (Pause) What's your excuse, David?

DAVID: I had it all done, but it must have fallen out of my notebook.

SAM: I wondered what you were going to say happened to it this time.

DAVID: (smiling sheepishly) It's true, Mr. Goodman! I can't help it if the darn paper clip didn't hold.

SAM: Fine. Then I don't guess you'll have any problem doing it again. All three of you spread out and get busy writing your letters and working on the assignment.

DAVID: (smirking) I can't, Mr. Goodman. I don't have a book or anything to write with.

JIMMY BOB: Neither do I.

SAM: (sarcastically) How convenient for all three of you! (Pause) I've had it with all three of you. I think that it's time you went to Mr. Busby's office and told him your hard luck story!

Sam meets again with Joe Turpin in Joe's classroom after school the following Tuesday.

SAM: Thanks, Joe, for seeing me again. I have some decisions to make, and I need your input.

JOE: I assume that we're talking about the same four kids.

SAM: That's right.

JOE: Let's start with the girl. What was her name?

SAM: Shawnna. Shawnna Crowder.

JOE: Yes, that's it. Whatever happened with her?

SAM: Her parents got her tested and decided that the school isn't helping her reach her potential. First they were thinking about transferring her to a private school, but now they want an interdistrict transfer to another school in the county where they think she can make A's in her subjects. Since Si Busby has to agree to such a transfer, he wants my recommendation. I know she'd be better off if she stayed at Parsons and got down to work. But Shawnna has her parents tied around her little finger. All she has to do is whine and cry a little bit and she can get out of anything she wants to. So with that being the way things are, I feel like I may as well go along. But that makes me feel guilty, like I'm copping out. Do I give in to all the Shawnnas that I have from now on?

JOE: Good question. I definitely know where you're coming from. (Pause) And the three musketeers?

SAM: They've become mild discipline problems. You know, smart answers, entering class late, constantly being mildly disruptive, and other things like that. Of course, they hardly ever do their assignments or bring their work material to class. I tried to have a conference with them the other day and ended up sending them to Si Busby's office when I got fed up.

JOE: What did Si do?

SAM: He questioned them and dressed them down good. Later he asked me what I thought he should do with them. They're goofing off in all their classes, and their parents won't help. Si wonders if he shouldn't expel them and see if that helps straighten them out.

JOE: What do you think?

SAM: I don't know, Joe. It's like Shawnna. I really don't think expulsion is the answer, but I really haven't been able to get any work out of them when they're in class. Expelling them seems like the easy way out. (Pause) So tell me, what would you do if you were in my place? Is there any way to reach these kids if I do keep them? Is there anything I can try that I haven't already tried?

Figure 21–1 Information Compiled by Mr. Goodman from School Cumulative Records

Student	Parents' Occupations	Parents' Education	Number of Siblings
Shawnna	Electrical engineer (F) Nurse (M)	College Nursing school	2
David	Traveling salesman (F) Sales clerk (M)	High school High school	1
Bobby Joe	Construction worker (F) Housewife (M)	Tenth grade High school	5
Jimmy Bob	Foreman, steel mill (F) Housewife (M)	High school High school	4

ACHIEVEMENT TEST SCORES

(Metropolitan Advanced, in Stanines)

Student	Math	Basics Total	Complete Total
Shawnna	6	7	7
David	4	5	5
Bobby Joe	2	3	3
Jimmy Bob	5	4	4

Questions

1. What might account for the fact that Sam's mathematics assignments worked for him last year but not this year?

2. Imagine that you are Joe Turpin. What advice would you give Sam?

3. Should Sam have sent David, Bobby Joe, and Jimmy Bob to Mr. Busby's office for not being prepared to work on their assignments? Explain your answer.

4. Besides expelling them, what options does Sam have in working with his four resistant students? Which option would you recommend?

5. From the perspective of motivation theory, what different types of needs seem to be dominant in the cases of Shawnna, David, Bobby Joe, and Jimmy Bob? Is there anything that Sam can do to change his curriculum or teaching methods to take the different needs into consideration?

6. What is attribution (or locus of control) theory? Are Jimmy Bob's attributions internal or external? Is Jimmy Bob an example of learned helplessness? How effective are attribution training programs in cases like Jimmy Bob's?

7. Sam employs a number of behavior management techniques in his class. See if you can identify examples of the Premack Principle, response cost, and contingency contracting. Why do these techniques seem to be not working in the cases of Shawnna and the "three musketeers?"

8. What are the defense mechanisms of projection and rationalization in psychoanalytic theory? How well do they explain David's behavior? What can be done?

9. What does research identify as home and parent variables that correlate with student success in school? How might the home environment help explain Bobby Joe's intention to drop out, as well as David's and Jimmy Bob's behavior? How is the overprotectiveness of Shawnna's parents affecting Shawnna's behavior? What are the most effective programs that have been developed to get the home and school working together on behalf of the child?

10. Examine this case from the perspective of observational learning. What instances of modeling and imitation are discernable? In what area is there evidence of low self-efficacy in students? How could Sam use the four phases of observational learning to teach math?

The Little Engine That Couldn't

Key Content to Consider for Analyzing This Case:

1. Motivation (Mastery versus Performance Goal Orientation, Attribution Theory, Learned Helplessness, Sense of Efficacy)
2. Cultural Diversity
3. Information Processing Theory
4. Home Environment/Parent Involvement

Russell Esky is a beginning teacher in his fifth day of teaching a sixth-grade class at Sparta Elementary School. He is plagued with mixed emotions regarding both his reaction to his pupils and his perception of his own ability as a teacher.

Russ recently graduated from a private college in a southern state that offers a program that enables students to qualify for a BA plus a teaching certificate in elementary education awarded by the state. During his final month at the college, Russ had interviewed for an elementary teaching position at Sparta Elementary School, located in a large city in the southern part of the same state. Of the more than 900 pupils enrolled in the school, approximately 30% come from middle-income homes, while 70% come from low-income homes. Approximately 50% of the pupils are white, 40% African-American, 9% Hispanic, and 1% Asian-American.

It is Friday morning before the lunch period has begun. Russ has asked his 28 students to work on individual assignments until lunchtime.

RUSS: (seeing three girls with no work on their desks giggling and talking) Are you girls working on your science report?

SARA: We don't know how to start it.

RUSS: Have you decided how to divide up the work?

PAT: No, we've never worked on a group project before. We don't know how to divide up the work.

RUSS: Surely you've been asked to write reports in classes before.

SARA: (giggling) Yes, we've been told to do reports, but none of us has ever done much on them. We were always in a group, and the other people knew what to do.

RUSS: (sternly) Well, in this class you're going to learn to do your own work, and I expect each of you to give me an outline of your part of the report before you leave school today. The report must have something to do with plants. You can find a lot of information in the first chapter of your science book. (The girls appear to be confused.)

RUSS: (noticing Kevin looking out the window) Kevin, how are you doing on your multiplication of decimals problems?

KEVIN: (embarrassed) Not so good, Mr. Esky. I can't figure out how to do them.

RUSS: But Kevin, I just worked the first three problems with you less than ten minutes ago. Tell me how to figure out where the decimal point goes. Don't you remember?

KEVIN: No. I forgot. It has something to do with how many numbers come after the decimal points.

RUSS: But you worked the examples correctly when I was explaining how to multiply decimals early in the week.

KEVIN: Yeah, I know. But I guess I just got lucky. I don't even remember how I worked those problems.

RUSS: You really can do math, Kevin. If you could do them a few days ago, you can do them today. You just have to apply the right formula, which you did. (Taking a paper and pencil) Here, let's work some problems together. (Writing some examples) Notice in this problem there are two numbers after the decimal point in the top number and one in the bottom number. So, in the answer there are three numbers after the decimal. (Writes another problem) Now, you solve this one.

KEVIN: (looks at the problem for a long time) I don't get it. I just can't get math. My parents couldn't do math either. They can't help me with my homework.

RUSS: (patiently) OK, Kevin. It's not really hard. Let's try it again. Do you remember what you need to look for to find out how many numbers are after the decimal in the answer?

KEVIN: How many numbers are after the decimal in the top and bottom numbers?

RUSS: Right! I think you'll be able to do it now. (Writes three more examples) Now, let me see you work these problems.

KEVIN: (looks at examples for a long time, then turns to Russ) Will you help me get started?

RUSS: First, do the multiplication. (Kevin does it.) OK. Now tell me how many numbers are after the decimal in the top number.

KEVIN: There are two. And there's only one in the bottom number.

RUSS: Great! Now put the decimal point in the answer. (Kevin puts it in the right place.) (Really excited) That's terrific, Kevin! Now do the rest of the problems that same way!

KEVIN: OK, I'll try. But I probably won't get them right.

RUSS: (optimistically) Sure you will. Think positive. You can do it! (Walks over to Paula) You did a good job on your geography test yesterday. I'm proud of you!

PAULA: Thank's, but I was just lucky.

RUSS: Why do you say that? You answered all but three of the questions correctly. If you can answer short-answer questions correctly, I'd say that you know the material.

PAULA: I don't know the material. I just made lucky guesses. I have trouble understanding school stuff. And I can't remember things very long, even when I learn them.

RUSS: Paula, I want you to do something for me.

Paula: What?

Russ: I want you to take credit for knowing things. When you make correct answers, I want you to take credit for them. I want you to say, "I know that information." Will you do that?

Paula: I guess so. But I'm not sure I'll believe it.

Russ continues to work closely with Paula and becomes increasingly concerned about her lack of confidence. During the 2 weeks following the test incident, Paula continues to forget procedures Russ has taught in class. So one evening, Russ calls Paula's home. A woman answers.

Russ: This is Russell Esky, Paula's teacher. Is this Paula's mother?

Pat: Oh, hello, Mr. Esky. I recognize your name. Paula's talked a lot about you. She says you're nice to her and try to help her at school.

Russ: I certainly try, and that's why I'm calling you this evening. I've told Paula that I think she could be a really good student, but she doesn't seem to have any confidence in herself as a student.

Pat: I don't know about that. Paula's never done very good in school. Her brother Paul hasn't either.

Russ: I've never met Paul, but I think that if Paula could get some help with her homework, she'd be a good student.

Pat: My husband and me would like her to do better, but to tell you the truth, I was really a poor student at school myself and so was my husband. But he at least graduated, and we got married that summer. I never went back to school. I didn't want to.

Russ: But I think it's more important to graduate from school today than it was even when you were in school. Many employers won't even interview applicants who aren't high school graduates. Some employers require a college degree.

Pat: I'm afraid that Paula'll be out of luck for those kinds of jobs. We aren't college people. No one in our family ever went to college. If fact, most kids in our neighborhood drop out of school, get married, and then go to work.

Russ: What kinds of jobs do they get?

Pat: Laboring jobs mostly—working on road crews, lawn service, construction, custodial work, night watchmen. My husband got a job as night custodian in the battery plant before we got married, and he's still there. Before we had the kids, I was a cocktail waitress and made good money. But neither of us would be able to get a job where you have to take tests and go through training programs. We ain't good enough at those things.

Russ: That's exactly why I'm calling, Ms. Espinosa. I think Paula is smart enough to go to a training program. She could even go to college. All she needs is encouragement and support. I'm willing to spend extra time with her at school, but you and Mr. Espinosa will need to help her, too. I'd like you to encourage her to work hard at school to get good grades and start her thinking about going to college. I'm sure she could get a college scholarship if she tries. Then, she could get a really good job.

Pat: We'd like for her to, but like I said, we're not college people. We don't have that kind of money. And we don't even know anybody who graduated from college. We just don't live at that level. I appreciate your taking an interest in Paula, Mr. Esky, but I just don't see how she'll ever be able to do that.

Russ: (frustrated) But can't you see that going to college could change Paula's life for the better?

Pat: Like I said, no one in our family has ever gone to college. We're laboring people, and Paula'll have to settle for the kind of jobs people in our neighborhood get. She'll likely live here, get married, and have children right here in the neighborhood. It might not be doing her a favor, Mr. Esky, to put foolish ideas in her head. But I do sincerely thank you for taking an interest in her.

It is after school the following day. Russ sits in the classroom of fellow sixth-grade teacher Sid Willis, who has taught at Sparta for 7 years. Russ and Sid sit in chairs in front of Sid's desk.

Sid: What do you mean, Russ, when you say you're having problems with some of your students? What kinds of problems?

Russ: I guess I'd have to say that the problems are more in the area of academic performance than in the area of discipline.

Sid: That's good. It's my experience that discipline problems and academic performance problems go hand in hand. So your problems are cut in half if discipline's not a problem. Give me some examples of the kinds of problems you're having.

Russ: OK. (Spends some time in thought) I was planning to tell you about some specific incidents that have happened in class. But as I reviewed them in my mind, it occurred to me that they're basically variations on the same theme.

Sid: Which is what?

Russ: It seems that a large percentage of the pupils in my class are unable to cope with independent learning activities. They just aren't able to work on their own.

Sid: How many of your pupils fit into this category?

Russ: More than half of them. And they're generally the pupils who come from low-income homes. And what to me is really sad is that so many of them have the ability to do the assignments, but they just don't seem to be able to get their act together.

Sid: Why do you think they're like that?

Russ: I think it's their home environment. Some of them have no learning strategies. Others know how to do the work but aren't really interested in learning. And I'm sure that in most of their homes, no one ever suggests the possibility of attending college.

Sid: Can you give me a specific example of what you're talking about?

Russ: Yes. A good example is Paula Espinosa. I think she has the ability to succeed in college. Her mother essentially told me not to encourage her daughter to think about going to college.

Sid: Did she give you any reasons why?

Russ: Oh yes, she gave me several. Her family's not what she calls "college people." No one from their neighborhood ever goes to college, nor do they ever encourage their children to go. They don't have enough money to send Paula to college. And they expect Paula to get some kind of unskilled job like the rest of the people in their neighborhood.

Sid: That kind of feedback doesn't do much to motivate children to perform well in school, does it?

Russ: No, it doesn't. Paula doesn't come close to performing at her potential. And I'd be willing to bet that I'd hear the same story from the majority of the parents of the students who perform poorly. Can you think of anything I could do to change this situation?

Sid: While you were telling me about Paula, I thought about the many times I've gone out to catch crabs. I always take a bucket to put the crabs into when I catch them. I never worry about their getting out of the bucket, because if one of the crabs gets close to the top of the bucket, the others pull him back down. (Smiles) It seems that maybe your classroom groups function similarly. When a group member makes an effort to get the group on track, another member pulls him or her back down. Does that seem like a fair analogy to you?

Russ: Unfortunately, it does. But what can I do to change this?

Sid: You told me you think Paula is college material, right?

Russ: Yes, I think she is.

Sid: Approximately how many of your low-income pupils do you think would fall into that same category?

Russ: (after a long pause) I'd guess there are probably ten.

Sid: What would you think of forming your class into groups of four or five pupils based on their ability and SES? Divide them into ability levels but mix them up by SES. That way the low-SES pupils with high ability could interact with other students of high ability and maybe raise their sights toward college. And low-SES pupils with low ability can interact with other pupils with low ability and see that they're just as good as they are.

Russ: (enthusiastically) That sounds like a great idea! It certainly wouldn't be a difficult strategy to use. They would be grouped homogeneously by ability but heterogeneously by SES. I like that idea. Thanks for suggesting it.

Sid: I'm anxious to see what happens. Let me know if I can help you in any way.

Russ used school cumulative records to assign his pupils to seven groups of four members each. There were two groups of average and above, two groups of average to low average, and three groups of below average. Work assignments for each of the three groups were different, but each was on an appropriate level of difficulty for the pupils in that group. Frank approaches one of the above-average groups.

Russ: What project is your group working on, Lo?

Lo: We're studying the conservation of natural resources, Mr. Esky. Each of us has selected a resource and will prepare a report about what our country's doing to conserve that resource.

Russ: That's a good topic, Lo. What's your report about?

Lo: I'm describing efforts that are being made to conserve our water supply.

Russ: That's an interesting topic, and certainly an important one. (Turning to another pupil) What's your topic, Gail?

Gail: I'm writing about what we're doing to stop air pollution.

Russ: Another good topic. (Looking at Art) How about you, Art?

Art: Paula and I are working together on the conservation of natural resources. Paula's report will focus on plants and mine will focus on animals.

Russ: Your group has certainly chosen critical issues to report on. I'm looking forward to hearing your reports. (Turns his attention to pupils in one of the below-average groups who don't appear to be doing any work) Sara, what topic is your group working on?

Sara: (giggling) We don't have one yet. We just can't decide on one.

RUSS: Tell me some of the topics you're considering. (No response from any group member) Sara, what topics are you considering? (No response) Raul, what topic would you like your group to study? (No response) Pat, how about you? (Pat looks at the floor) Mose? (No response) All right, since you don't seem able to select a topic for yourselves, I'll give you one. Your group will prepare a report on the oceans. Sara, you'll report on the oceans, their names, and their characteristics. Raul, you'll report on the movement of the ocean: waves, tides, and currents. Tell how they're caused and how they affect the earth. Pat, you'll report on the composition of ocean water and tell how the various gases and chemicals get into the water. Mose, you'll report on how the oceans affect our weather. I want to see all of you outlining your reports right now. If I see you fooling around, I'll have you stay in the room during activity periods for the rest of the week.

PAT: But I don't even have a clue about where to start a report on ocean water.

RUSS: That's easy. You can find lots of clues on pages 24 to 30 of your science book. Those pages are all about that topic. I suggest you start by reading those pages. (Looking at each of the pupils) Before the end of the period, I expect all of you to have your outline started. (The students moan and complain, but Russ walks on to another group.)

On the following Thursday after school, Russ met with Rita Gonzalez, the school principal. Rita was in the process of holding a short meeting with each of her teachers just to see how things were going and to see whether they had any suggestions for improving the education program of the school. Russ shared his concerns about his class with her. Rita suggested that he make an appointment with the elementary curriculum supervisor Sharon Maris. She said that Sharon is excellent in helping teachers apply appropriate teaching methodology in situations like those that Russ described.

Russ followed Rita's suggestion and made an appointment with Sharon for the following week. He has just arrived at the waiting area outside Sharon's office at the appointed time.

SHARON: (seeing Russ enter the waiting area) Hi, Russ. Come on in and have a seat. (Motions to a chair facing her)

RUSS: Hi, Sharon. (Sits in the designated chair)

SHARON: I understand that you have some concerns about your sixth-grade class. What are they?

RUSS: There are so many different things that concern me about my class that I'm not sure where to begin. I guess the first thing would be that the majority of the pupils are apathetic about school. They truly seem not to care whether they learn or not. Nor do their families.

SHARON: Can you cite some specific behaviors that led you to this conclusion?

RUSS: Sure. They don't do either classroom or homework assignments. When I try to help them, they just don't seem to understand what the assignment is all about or how to do it. But the most frustrating aspect of the whole situation is that they truly don't believe they can do the work. And I believe that many of their parents don't care whether they learn or not.

SHARON: Why do you say that?

RUSS: For example, I called the mother of one of my students to tell her that I think her daughter is capable of doing much better work in school but doesn't

Figure 22–1 Student Information Assembled by Russell Esky on His Sixth-Grade Class

Name	Eligible for School Lunch	Achievement Scores[1]	Ethnic/Racial Origin[2]	IQ[3]
1. Adams, Sara	Yes	6.1	AA	102
2. Brown, Gail	No	7.0	W	111
3. Butler, Latisha	Yes	5.8	AA	87
4. Castillo, Raul	Yes	5.3	H	90
5. Clark, Patricia	Yes	5.6	AA	92
6. Davis, Wayne,	No	6.5	W	100
7. Deleo, Tammy	No	6.2	W	96
8. Eisner, Kevin	Yes	5.7	W	89
9. Espinoza, Paula	Yes	6.5	W	105
10. Felton, George	Yes	5.7	AA	89
11. Gully, Isaac	Yes	5.3	AA	82
12. Ho, Wan	No	7.4	A	130
13. Min, Lo	No	7.2	A	123
14. Nazario, Rita	Yes	5.0	H	84
15. Okabe, Elsa	Yes	5.2	AA	86
16. Pace, Natasha	Yes	4.9	AA	80
17. Petty, Arthur	No	7.2	W	120
18. Ramond, Hosea	Yes	4.9	AA	79
19. Sanchez, Elena	Yes	4.5	H	84
20. Sanders, Rose	Yes	4.8	AA	81
21. Thompson, Harry	No	7.3	W	129
22. Thomas, Melany	Yes	5.2	AA	89
23. Voit, Thomas	No	5.8	AA	87
24. Vincent, Carl	No	6.2	W	94
25. Watson, Mose	Yes	4.8	AA	79
26. Williams, Patti	Yes	5.3	AA	88
27. Yates, James	No	6.1	W	98
28. Zebo, Loretta	Yes	6.4	W	95

[1]Total Grade Level Equivalent Score from the Metropolitan Achievement Test, Intermediate Level Battery (grades 5–6). Decimal scores refer to months; e.g., 6.5 = 6th grade, 5th month.
[2]W = Non-Hispanic white; AA = African-American; H = Hispanic; A = Asian-American.
[3]Total IQ Score on California Test of Mental Maturity.

seem interested in doing so. I asked her to support me in encouraging her daughter to do her classwork and homework.

SHARON: And?

RUSS: And her mother essentially told me that she doesn't think her daughter can do her work either. She said that they're not "college people," that she expects her daughter to get married and do some kind of service or laboring job in the neighborhood. She led me to believe that most of her neighbors feel the same way.

SHARON: I'm sorry not to be able to say that this surprises me, but it doesn't. A large proportion of our parents have this attitude. What other concerns do you have about your class?

Russ: Probably my main concern is the work attitudes of some of my kids. They seem to believe that they are predestined to just drift along completely at the mercy of their environment. They don't seem to have any goals, ambitions, or aspirations in life. They just seem to live for the day.

Sharon: Have you tried any strategies to motivate them?

Russ: Yes, several weeks ago I talked with a fellow teacher, Sid Willis, about the situation. He suggested that I group my pupils by ability but mix them up by SES. That way I could adapt the assignments to the various ability levels so each group could work at its own level.

Sharon: And how did that work out?

Russ: It seemed to work out much better for the high-ability white and Asian-American middle-class students. But it had no effect at all on the low-ability, disadvantaged African-American and Hispanic pupils. They didn't do any worse, but they didn't do any better.

Sharon: So where are you now?

Russ: I'm very frustrated and concerned. This is my first year of teaching, and I expected to be a much better teacher than I seem to be. I don't know what to do. Are there other teaching strategies I could use that would work better with these students? Would I be more effective teaching at another grade level or at another type of school? Or am I just an ineffective teacher who would be better off preparing for another career? To tell you the truth, Sharon, I'm not sure I know how to motivate my students to learn. Their home environments seem to work against their staying in school, much less becoming even average students. What can a teacher do when the home and the parents seem to be working against them? Can you help me?

Questions

1. What is cultural diversity? What kinds of student diversity are represented in Russ's class? How can a teacher take such diversity into consideration in terms of choosing instructional objectives, teaching methods, evaluation procedures, and methods of classroom management?

2. What is attribution or locus of control theory? Are there examples of external attributions in Russ's class? How can attribution training procedures be used to change student attributions?

3. Weiner adds the dimensions of stability and controllability to internal and external locus of control to explain student beliefs. How do these three dimensions help to explain student academic problems in this case?

4. What is learned helplessness? How does it relate to student academic behavior patterns in this case?

5. What is sense of efficacy? What student efficacy patterns exist in this case with regard to academic achievement? How is student sense of efficacy formed, and how can it be changed?

6. Examine student academic behavior in this case from the standpoint of Ames's mastery versus performance goal orientation? How are such motivational patterns formed, and under what conditions can they be changed?

7. Russ refers to a lack of academic self-confidence on the part of students like Paula and Kevin. What is a lack of self-confidence, and how does it relate to the

self-concept from the perspective of Shavelson's model, for example? How is the self-concept—especially the academic self-concept—formed, and under what conditions does it change?

8. What role does the home environment play in forming student learning and motivational patterns? How do the observational learning constructs of modeling and imitation explain how students learn such patterns from their parents? What patterns do you see in Paula's home, and how do they help explain Paula's academic learning patterns at school? What parent involvement procedures can teachers and schools employ to help change such patterns?

9. How good was Sid's recommendations that Russ group his students by SES and ability? Why was this grouping ineffective with the low-ability students? How else might Russ have grouped his students? How well might cooperative learning methods have worked in Russ's class? How effectively did Russ work with his groups (e.g., Sara's group, which was having trouble getting started)?

10. What are teacher locus of control and teacher efficacy? How well do they explain Russ's beliefs as a teacher? What advice would you give Russ if you were Sharon?

The Comedienne

Key Content to Consider for Analyzing This Case:

1. Classroom Management
2. Observational Learning
3. Operant Conditioning

Lakeview Middle School, located in a predominately middle-class city of approximately 50,000 people in the Northeast, was constructed in 1988 to accommodate the student population of a rapidly growing upscale population in this section of the city of Landsford. The school now serves approximately 1,800 pupils from the surrounding area, with approximately 600 pupils at the sixth-, seventh-, and eighth-grade levels. Approximately 87% of the students are white, 12% African-American, and 1% other ethnic groups. The student population by SES level is approximately 10% upper, 60% middle, and 30% lower.

Tom Tolbert has been teaching seventh-grade science at Lakeview since he graduated 5 years ago from the state's major university with a master's degree in education and a major in science. It is a brisk, sunny October day as Tom begins to review some information his second-period class of 32 students discussed yesterday related to their unit on matter.

TOM: What's one of the characteristics of matter? (Daniqua raises her hand.) Daniqua?

DANIQUA: It takes up space.

TOM: How do you know that?

DANIQUA: We blew up balloons yesterday, and we could see the air taking up space inside the balloon.

TOM: Good, Daniqua. Tell me the other characteristic of matter, Marge.

MARGE: (seriously) It's very religious, because it has mass. (Class members groan.) Well, it tells us that right on page 15 of our science book. (Holds up open book for class to see)

DON: (speaking out) What a dork you are, Marge.

TOM: OK, let's get on with our lesson. We know that the two characteristics of matter are that it has mass and takes up space. Who can give us an example of matter? (No response) How about you, Si?

SI: (long pause) Is it air?

Tom: Good, Si. But air's part of a larger category. Who knows what it is? (Lori raises her hand immediately.) Lori, tell us what it is.

Tom: Air's a mixture of gases.

Rose: (speaking out) I always thought gases were sort of bad for you to breathe. Like the gas in your stove or furnace.

Tom: Good point, Rose. There are all kinds of gases, and some of them are poisonous.

Marge: (without raising her hand) And some gases aren't poisonous, but they smell bad. (Tom sends her a warning look.) I mean like sewer gas and gases like that.

Tom: Who can tell us another characteristic of gases? (A long pause; finally Chu raises his hand). Chu.

Chu: Gases can be compressed.

Tom: That's good, Chu. And yesterday we prepared some experiments that should demonstrate this and some other characteristics of gases. If you recall, we blew up two balloons. We put one in the refrigerator and tied the other outside the window where the morning sun shines. Jeff, would you go to the refrigerator and take out the balloon? (Jeff gets the balloon out and puts it on the table at the front of the room, then walks toward his seat.) Now, let's measure the balloon and see if it's the same size it was when we put it in the refrigerator yesterday. (Just then, a loud, obnoxious sound fills the room as Jeff sits down.)

Dave: Hey, nice one, Jeff!

Marge: (who sits immediately behind Jeff) Goodness, Jeff. You should excuse yourself. (The class explodes with laughter.)

Jeff: (embarrassed and angry) You put that whoopee cushion on my seat as I was sitting down, Marge. That's not even funny, it's crude!

Marge: (smiling innocently) It seems that some of us thought it was funny, Jeff.

Tom: You know better than to do something like that in class, Marge.

Marge: (innocently) But Mr. Tolbert, I was just doing an experiment to help us find out if air is matter.

Tom: Oh, really. Please tell us about it.

Marge: I got the idea from our class yesterday. And it worked. When Jeff sat on the cushion, it mashed the air molecules inside together. That forced the air out of the opening, which it wouldn't go through without the molecules being mashed together.

Tom: (not knowing whether to be angry or amused) That unexpected demonstration wasn't really necessary. We'd already planned enough experiments to demonstrate this principle. And Marge, "mashed together" is called "compressed" by scientists.

Marge: (apologetically) I was just trying to apply a principle we're studying on my own.

Tom: (tongue in cheek) We all appreciate your efforts. Probably Jeff more than anyone.

Jeff: (sarcastically) Yeah, right.

The remainder of the class is spent discussing the fact that cold air compressed the molecules of the balloon in the refrigerator and the warmth from the sun expanded the molecules of the balloon hanging in direct sunlight.

Since the third period is Tom's planning period, after the second-period bell rings and the students leave the room, Tom goes to the teachers' lounge. When he arrives, he finds Martha, a sixth-grade English teacher; Paul, a sixth-grade math teacher; and Angie, an eighth-grade social studies teacher.

TOM: (smiling) I see that I was lucky enough to have my planning period with the beautiful people of the school.

MARTHA: (to Angie) Tom's Irish, you know, and it's evident that he's kissed the Blarney stone.

ANGIE: Yes, I can see that. But I like what he said anyway.

PAUL: Nice to see you, Tom. How're your classes going this year?

TOM: Based on what I've seen so far, I think all of them will be interesting to work with.

MARTHA: When I passed your room on my way here at the end of last period, I saw Marge Green in the hall. Did she come out of your second-period class?

TOM: Yes, she's in that class.

MARTHA: I had her in my English class last year. She was really entertaining. She seems to have a terrific sense of humor.

TOM: (somewhat sarcastically) Yes, she demonstrated her sense of humor in my class this very morning.

MARTHA: (smiling) You sound as if you didn't appreciate her effort. Can you tell us what she did?

TOM: Just as the student who sits in the seat in front of her was sitting down, she slipped a whoopee cushion under him.

MARTHA: (laughing out loud) Oh! That sounds just like Marge. She's so funny!

TOM: The student who was the victim of her attempt at humor didn't think it was so funny. He seemed to think that Marge entertained the class at his expense.

ANGIE: And he's right! Sometimes class clowns don't realize that fact when they do their entertaining.

MARTHA: That's true. I never thought of it that way when she was in my class last year. Her entertaining was always at someone else's expense.

PAUL: I think Marge comes by her desire to entertain naturally. I'm in a service club with her dad, who's quite a clown himself.

TOM: What type of clowning does he do, Paul?

PAUL: He seems to have the standard repertory of annoying equipment: rings that buzz when you shake hands with someone, whoopee cushions, artificial dog poop, vomit, and other replicas of gross things. And he has a repertory of dirty jokes that allows him to go on forever.

MARTHA: Do people seem to resent him?

PAUL: No, I don't think they do. He seems to be pretty well liked, and people act as if they enjoy having him around.

TOM: I wonder if Marge enjoys being the class clown, or if she feels somehow obligated to carry on the family tradition.

ANGIE: That's really an interesting question, Tom. Maybe by the end of this school year you'll find the answer to that question. (A bell rings.) Well, back to the old grind. See you all later. (The teachers leave the lounge.)

By the end of the second week of school, Tom's second-period students had completed their study of matter and had taken a unit test on the material. At the beginning of the third week of class, the students began a study of atomic theory, and

Tom had asked the students to read the chapter dealing with this topic over the weekend.

TOM: I think you'll enjoy working with the information in this chapter. The study of atomic theory is still in its beginning stages. Everyone in your class may eventually drive atomic-powered cars, fly in atomic-powered spaceships, live in atomic-powered homes, and work with atomic-powered tools. Who can tell us what the ancient Greeks discovered about atomic theory? (Jeff raises his hand immediately.) Jeff?

JEFF: They were the first to think that matter was made up of little particles that were hooked together. They called these particles atoms. But they thought that everything was made up of air, water, earth, and fire.

TOM: That's good, Jeff. Now, who can tell us when this idea was changed? (Chu raises his hand.) Chu.

CHU: It wasn't changed until the 1800s when John Dalton changed it.

MARGE: (shouting out) I know him! He and his brothers were outlaws! They called them the Dalton Brothers!

DAN: That's great! The Dalton Boys!

MARGE: (pointing her fingers like guns) Bam! Bam! Pow! (Other class members join in the shoot-out.)

TOM: (angrily) Class! Stop! Cut it out immediately! (The ruckus continues. Tom finally takes his wooden meter stick and slams it across the top of his desk. Startled by the sharp report, the students gradually quiet down. Those who were out of their seats quietly sit back down.) Quiet down! Now I want all of you to listen carefully. (Students sit motionless.) We're not going to have any more incidents like the one we just witnessed here today. I know which of you participated, and I've already put a check by your names in my grade book. Any more demonstrations like this and you'll find yourselves in a situation that you don't want to be in! Now, Chu (who didn't participate in the shoot-out), you were telling us about how the Greek model of matter was changed. Will you please continue?

CHU: Yes, sir. John Dalton was an English chemist and physicist. He accepted the Greek idea of small particles but believed that the small particles or atoms in each element were alike and that those from different elements were different. Dalton's called the father of atomic theory because of his work.

TOM: That's great, Chu. Now who can tell us about J. J. Thompson's model? (Matt raises his hand.) Matt. Go ahead.

MATT: Thompson said that all matter is electrified and has positive and negative charges. His model was like a bowl of pudding with raisins stuck in it. He called positive charges protons and negative charges electrons. When you run a plastic comb through your hair, you transfer electrons from your hair to your comb. That gives your comb a negative charge, and it will attract small pieces of paper. (As Matt explains about the comb and the paper, Marge runs a comb through her hair with great fanfare and picks up small pieces of paper with it to the amusement of students sitting near her. They get the attention of other students and point to Marge.)

TOM: (shouting angrily) Marge!

MARGE: (startled) Yes, sir?

TOM: I'd like you to come to my room immediately after your last class!

MARGE: (obviously upset) What for?

Tom: You'll find out this afternoon

Marge: But—

Tom: (interrupting her) We're not going to discuss it now! Be here immediately after school!

Marge: (quietly submissive) Yes, sir.

Shortly after the last class has been dismissed, Marge comes to Tom's classroom as instructed. When she enters, Tom is working at his desk. Marge sits in a chair at one of the front tables and waits quietly.

Tom: (walks over to the table at which Marge is sitting and sits in the chair beside her) Hello, Marge. Do you know why I asked you to come here after school?

Marge: I think you're angry with me because of the things I did in class today.

Tom: Do you think it would be unfair for me to be angry with you?

Marge: No, sir.

Tom: If you think it's fair for me to be angry with you for acting the way you did, you must think that the ways you acted in class were inappropriate. Is that right?

Marge: I guess so.

Tom: Aren't you sure?

Marge: (looking down at the floor) I'm sure. I shouldn't do some of the things I do in class.

Tom: Then why do you do them? (Marge continues to stare at the floor and does not respond to the question.) I'm referring to your speaking out in class with statements that have nothing to do with the lesson that you think are funny. Do you feel a strong need to make the other students laugh?

Marge: I guess I do. I don't know why! Maybe I got it from my dad. He's always making people laugh, and everyone likes him.

Tom: Do you see any differences between making people laugh in social situations and in a school classroom?

Marge: (after a long pause) I guess so.

Tom: Tell me what the difference is.

Marge: (another long pause) Well, in a social situation people usually are just visiting and not working on an important project or anything like that.

Tom: So making funny remarks or playing practical jokes doesn't really harm an informal social situation. Is that true? (Marge nods her head.) But in school, this kind of behavior can totally destroy the effort of the teacher or students to concentrate on learning. (Again Marge nods her head.) So when you do what you've been doing, you're basically disrupting the learning of your entire class, right?

Marge: I guess so.

Tom: Don't you know for sure?

Marge: Yes, I do disrupt the class. I know I shouldn't do that, but I just can't seem to help myself.

Tom: You're going to have to help yourself, Marge. I think I've been quite patient with you since school started, but you're getting more and more disruptive, and now other students are beginning to imitate you. And I'm not going to tolerate that! So, I'm asking you to be a help to the class rather than a distraction, and I'm sure you can. But if you choose not to, I'll have to take strong disciplinary action. Do you understand that?

Marge: Yes, sir. I'll try my hardest not to disrupt the class.

Tom: You'll have to do more than try, Marge. You'll have to do it.

Marge: Yes, sir.

It is Friday, a week after Tom and Marge had their after-school conference. Tom had shared the results of his conference with Marge in the teachers' lounge on Monday. He has not gone to the lounge since then. This morning he decided to go there. As he is walking down the hall, Angie walks out of her room.

Angie: Tom, hi. Are you on your way to the lounge?

Tom: Yes, are you?

Angie: Yes. I've been hoping to see you. Ever since you told us Monday about your Friday conference with Marge, all we third-period planners have been curious to hear how your plan has worked. But don't tell me now. Let's wait until we get to the lounge—I know the others will be interested, too.

Tom: It's nice to know that my classroom management problems have generated such widespread interest.

Angie: You know why, don't you? (Without waiting for a reply) We all know that any of us could have the same problem, and we want to see how you handle it.

Tom: I appreciate your interest regardless of your motives. It's nice to have colleagues who are willing to listen to my problems. It's quite therapeutic to know that someone else cares. (They arrive at the lounge. Martha and Paul are already there.) Speaking of our colleagues, they're already here. Hello, Martha; hello Paul.

Martha: We're glad you came today, Tom. We've been curious about Marge's behavior this week.

Paul: Yes, it's been the main topic of lounge conversation this week.

Tom: (smiles) I just told Angie that it's really comforting to have colleagues who are as supportive as you three are.

Paul: Enough of the accolades. Let's cut to the chase. Has Marge shaped up?

Tom: All right. I'll give you a very direct yes and no answer.

Angie: What kind of answer is that?

Tom: I'll explain. Marge and I had our conference Friday after school. On Monday, as I told you, she was perfect. She paid attention to everything that went on in class. She participated fully and was very helpful.

Martha: That's good to hear! So what's happened since then?

Tom: Marge was delightful on Tuesday, Wednesday, and yesterday—just like a Girl Scout: helpful, courteous, kind, obedient, and so forth. But then this morning, it seemed as if the clown penned up inside her could no longer be contained. (Pause)

Paul: (eagerly) Don't keep us in suspense. What did she do?

Tom: This is a suspenseful situation, Paul. I think I should draw it out so that you fully appreciate the intrigue of the situation.

Angie: (pleading) Come on, Tom! Tell us what happened.

Tom: OK. You talked me into it. At the beginning of class this morning, Marge was as cooperative as she'd been all week. But about halfway through the class, she raised her hand during a written exercise and asked if she could sharpen her pencil. I nodded, and she got up out of her seat and started toward the pencil sharpener, which was clear across the room from her seat. Before I knew what had happened, Marge had paused behind shy Johnny Roth's desk, put her arms around him, and kissed him on the neck. Johnny jumped out of his seat as if he'd been shot. The class went wild. I couldn't really tell whether Johnny was in agony or ecstasy.

PAUL: (smiling) So much for classroom decorum.

TOM: Exactly. The class went wild, but I quickly reined them back under control. By then, Marge had finished sharpening her pencil and was sitting demurely in her seat.

MARTHA: (sounding disappointed) Was that it?

TOM: Alas, that was only the tip of the iceberg. (Immediately the other teachers become attentive as Tom continues.) She worked quietly at her seat for a short time until Rachel Goodman raised her hand. I motioned her to come over to me. Unfortunately, Rachel walked down the aisle past Marge's seat, and Marge stuck her foot into the aisle and tripped Rachel. Luckily, Rachel was not hurt, but she was quite embarrassed.

PAUL: (enjoying the intrigue) What did you do then?

TOM: I immediately moved Marge into a seat back in the corner of the room near the AV equipment and told her if she did anything more to disturb the class I'd take her directly to the dean's office. I then assigned the students to write the answers to the questions on the board in their science journals. As they were working, the librarian came to my doorway and motioned me to the door. When I went to the door, she told me that a new science book I'd asked her to order had arrived. I walked down the hall with her, and she gave me the book to examine. I took the book and immediately started back to my room.

ANGIE: (in a stage whisper) I can hardly wait to hear what you found.

TOM: I won't keep you in suspense. As I neared my room I heard music playing. I ran the rest of the way up the hall. As I approached my room, the first sight that greeted me was Marge dancing the Charleston at the front of the room with the entire class clapping in accompaniment. She was at the part in the dance where she was moving her hands back and forth over her knees. And I must say she was good at it. She looked like a professional dancer.

MARTHA: (with obvious interest) What did you do then?

TOM: I lost my cool and told her to go straight to the dean's office. Now my problem is that I definitely need to punish her. And I should tell her what her punishment will be when the dean finishes with her. But I can't decide what would be the most effective thing to do. She needs a relatively severe punishment for her disruptions of the class. I can't teach effectively with all the disruptions she causes.

PAUL: You certainly have many options. You could visit her parents, talk with the administration about suspending her from school for a few days, or give her detention for several days or weeks.

ANGIE: You could also send her to the guidance counselor or give her a failing grade for the day each time she does something outrageous.

MARTHA: I sometimes give students extra assignments to complete for each disruption when they begin to misbehave frequently.

TOM: (gratefully) I really appreciate your suggestions. I'd thought of many of them myself, but you've mentioned others that hadn't occurred to me. And some of them seem as if they'd be effective. But that's my big problem. At this point, I just don't know how to handle her. I want to take an approach that'll motivate her to change her behavior, but I just don't know what strategy would be the best.

Figure 23–1 Portion of Marge Green's Cumulative Record

	Lakeview Middle School
	Cumulative Record

Name: Margaret Green   Home Phone: 391-2874   Former School: Oak Elementary
Address: 537 Walnut Lane
Father: Henry Green   Occupation: Salesman   Health: Excellent
Mother: Rebecca Green   Occupation: Homemaker   Health: Excellent
Siblings: None   Date of Birth: 8/20/86

INTELLIGENCE TESTS	Form	IQ	Date	Grade
Otis-Lennon School Ability Tests	Elementary 1	116	10/10/94	3
	Intermediate	111	10/15/98	7

Academic Record

Grades 1–5 (Year Averages)							Grades 6–8 (Year Averages)				Personal Development (Grades 1–5)					
	1	2	3	4	5			6	7	8		1	2	3	4	5
Reading	B	A	A	A	A	English	A	A			Conduct	B	B	C	C	C
Mathematics	A	B	A	A	A	Geography	A	A			Effort	A	A	A	A	A
Science/Health	A	A	A	A	A	Mathematics	A	A			Follows Directions	A	A	A	A	A
Social Studies	A	A	A	A	A	Science	A	A			Initiative	A	A	A	A	A
Language	A	A	A	A	A	Physical Ed.	A	A			Attitude	B	B	B	C	C
Spelling	A	A	A	A							Work Habits	A	A	A	A	A
Music/Art	A	A	A	A							Participation	A	A	A	A	A
Citizenship	A	B	B	B	B											

■ Questions

1. From an operant conditioning perspective, what kinds of undesirable behaviors is Marge emitting? What reinforcers are maintaining her behavior? What role are the teachers and other students playing in this process? What operant techniques could be used to change Marge's behavior?

2. In terms of observational learning, what models does Marge seem to be imitating? What is vicarious reward, and how does it apply to Marge? What is disinhibition, and how does it explain the interactions between Marge and the other students in the classroom? What is cognitive behavior modification, and how can students like Marge be taught to use it to change their behavior? What are self-regulation techniques, and how can they be used to change behavior?

3. What role does Marge's home, especially her parents, play in encouraging Marge's clowning behavior? How could the teacher involve Marge's parents in resolving this situation? What methods of parent involvement do schools use, and which ones would be most helpful in this situation?

4. What classroom management models would be most helpful to Tom in this case? Could Tom use assertive discipline, teacher effectiveness training, or reality therapy in this situation? What classroom management beliefs does Tom have, and how effective are they?

5. Tom and his fellow teachers seem to think of various methods of punishment as the best way to handle Marge. What is punishment, and how effective is it in promoting student learning? Under what conditions is the use of punishment most effective? What types of punishment are the best to use?

6. To what extent do teachers learn from other teachers? To what extent does teacher education influence the classroom management and motivational methods that teachers use? To what extent is the teacher's behavior influenced by his or her own family background in terms of SES and racial/ethnic values, especially in the area of discipline?

7. Marge's peers seem to be a source of social reinforcement for Marge's behavior in the classroom. What group social reinforcement techniques can a teacher like Tom use to deal with such situations? How can the behavior of a student like Marge serve as a model for other students to imitate?

8. What are Kounin's principles of classroom management? Which ones are relevant to this case? What are "withitness" and the "ripple effect"? What techniques of Kounin's can Tom use in the situation?

9. At what level of Maslow's need hierarchy is Marge primarily operating? How can Tom use this information to deal with Marge? What humanistic techniques are most useful in dealing with students like Marge?

10. If you were advising Tom, what would you tell him to do in dealing with Marge? What strategy would be best? How can Tom motivate Marge to change her behavior?

24

Delisha the Disrupter

Judy Bowers is beginning her second year of teaching at Lincoln Elementary School, located in a large, urban area in the northeastern part of the United States. Lincoln's student body is 53% non-Hispanic white, 35% African-American, 10% Hispanic, and 2% other. Its physical plant is old but well maintained. The 28 students in Judy's third-grade class rather closely approximate the typical student body composition at Lincoln.

It is the second week of the new school year, and Judy finds her students to be bright, eager, and reasonably well mannered, except for one rather average-sized African-American girl named Delisha Davis. From the first day of school, Judy noticed that Delisha didn't seem to be able to stay in her seat, was constantly talking to her neighbors, and was frequently making noises and disrupting the class. After talking to some of her fellow teachers about the situation, one of whom had Delisha in class last year, Judy decided to do something about Delisha's behavior.

JUDY: (motioning with her hands) Boys and girls, I want you to make a circle so we can have a talk about our class.

DELISHA: Are you going to read to us?

JUDY: No, Delisha, and remember that I asked you to raise your hand instead of speaking out like that. (Students sit in a semicircle while Judy stands. Judy holds a piece of chalk in her hand so that she can write on the blackboard.) Boys and girls, we are going to be together all this school year, and I know that we all want to learn a lot and have a lot of fun as we learn.

DELISHA: (smiling) Yeah, a lot of fun!

JUDY: (frowning) Let's all be quiet now, Delisha, while I talk. (Pauses as Delisha smiles) We can have a good time in this class learning this year if we all try to do our best getting along with one another. (Pause) Now boys and girls, I want to talk about being a good class member. This class belongs to all of you. What do you want this class to be like this year? I'm going to write your ideas up here on the blackboard. (Most students raise their hands. Delisha stands up and begins a slow dancing movement as she stands in place.) Yes, Marie? Let's start with you.

MARIE: (timidly) Everyone like each other.

JUDY: (smiling) You mean that everyone likes each other and will be nice to each other? (Marie nods her head while Judy writes "Everyone is nice and gets along.") Maria?

MARIA: We get to do things.

JUDY: Do you mean we get to learn new and interesting things so class won't be boring? (Maria nods her head.) Scott, you had your hand up. (Scott sits next to Delisha, who begins to dance more vigorously.) What do you think a good class should be like?

SCOTT: I think that people should leave other people alone and not bother them.

JUDY: Tell us a little more about that, Scott. Can you give us an example? (Writes "Do interesting things" on the blackboard)

SCOTT: I mean like Lisa here. She's always making trouble and bothering people. You aren't supposed to be doing that.

DELISHA: (brings her right fist down hard on Scott's head) You're stupid! My name's Delisha, not Lisa, and I can dance if I want to! Dancing is good. I see it on TV all the time. (Scott yells upon being hit and remains seated as he begins to rub his head and cry.)

JUDY: (runs toward Scott and Delisha) Delisha, that's a terrible thing for you to do to Scott! (Kneels down and comforts Scott) Are you OK, Scott? (In a few minutes she helps Scott up and takes both Scott's and Delisha's hands.) Children, I want you to go to your desks and read the story about the Alaskan bears on page 29. Please read to yourselves quietly, and we'll discuss what you've read when I come back. I need to take Delisha and Scott to Ms. Rannum's [building principal] office so that the school nurse can look at Scott and make sure he's OK. I'm sure that Ms. Rannum will want to talk to Delisha about hitting Scott and will call her parents. (The children all scramble to begin to read their books. Judy waits until she is satisfied that everyone is working and, still holding each child by the hand, leads them to the principal's office.)

It is the next day. School is over and all the children have left. Judy goes to the office of Meg Ryerson, the school guidance counselor.

MEG: (smiling) Hi, Judy. How are you?

JUDY: (smiling back wanly) OK, I guess. Did you hear about Delisha Davis hitting Scott Grimes in my room yesterday?

MEG: (frowning) Yes, I did, Judy. Betty [the building principal] told me about it. I gather that the nurse examined Scott and he's going to be OK.

JUDY: Yes. She really hit him on the head hard, Meg. I was afraid that he might have a concussion or something. I wasn't sure at first whether I should move him or not. But then the idea of having him lie on the floor while the school nurse checked him out with all the kids watching was just too much. So I got him to stand up, took him and Delisha by the hand, and walked him to Betty's office. Fortunately, she was there and called the school nurse right away. I guess I took a chance getting him up on his feet, didn't I?

MEG: I guess so, but I certainly understand why you did it. You'd had enough disruption as it was.

JUDY: (angrily) Disruption is Delisha's middle name, I think! This is the first time that she's hit another child, but she's constantly disrupting the class!

MEG: Talking when she's not supposed to? Interrupting other children? Constantly getting out of her seat without permission?

JUDY: (with surprise) Why yes! It sounds like you were watching her, Meg.

MEG: (smiling) Not really. But I'm real familiar with her record. She's had problems like these going back to her days in the Head Start program.

JUDY: She was a discipline problem back in Head Start?

MEG: Yes, it started back then. (Pulls a cumulative folder from a large stack of such folders on her desk and opens it up) This is Delisha's cumulative record. Believe it or not, when they gave her a group intelligence test in the first grade—the California, I think—her nonlanguage IQ was 111. Her language IQ was only 98, however. She comes from a large family of six siblings, headed by her mother, who works on the assembly line making electric motors at International Motors. I'm not sure where the father is, but he doesn't live with the family. From what little bit I've learned, mainly from the eighty-year-old grandmother who lives with them, the mother uses corporal punishment at home a lot to keep the kids in line. I've never been able to get the mother to talk to me, though, so I really don't know her. The grandmother just says that her daughter works real hard to keep the family from going under financially and doesn't have much time to spend with her kids. Betty asked me to contact Delisha's mother yesterday after that incident in your class, but, of course, I couldn't. The grandmother said she'd give her the message when she came home from work, but I wouldn't hold my breath. My guess is that we won't hear from her.

JUDY: (frowning) You've certainly given me a different slant on Delisha. I had no idea that she comes from that kind of situation.

MEG: I suspect that you have to fight for attention in Delisha's family, and I also suspect that hitting is a normal way of relating to others in her family.

JUDY: You may well be right, Meg. But what am I going to do? She can't be hitting other children in my classroom! And even if she never hits anyone again, I can't have her continually disrupting the class!

MEG: Judy, my suggestion would be for you to call Tony Garcia, the director of psychological services for the school system. Maybe he'd be willing to have one of his people do a workup on her and make some recommendations. Here's his phone number. He'd want to ask you some questions about what Delisha's been doing in class.

JUDY: (smiling) I knew you'd think of a way to help me! I really appreciate this, Meg!

MEG: (Smiling) My pleasure! Always glad to help, Judy.

It is about ten o'clock the next morning. Judy and her class have reviewed the multiplication tables, and Judy has handed out a worksheet for the twos through the tens and told the students to complete the worksheet at their desks. About 15 minutes into the deskwork, Delisha begins to make sounds with her mouth like she is passing air. Several of the children laugh and then look guiltily toward Judy.

JUDY: Delisha, please stop making those noises! (Delisha stops for 6 seconds, then gets up and starts walking toward the pencil sharpener.) Delisha, where are you going?

DELISHA: To sharpen my pencil.

JUDY: Don't you remember that you are supposed to ask permission first? You don't just get up and go whenever you feel like it. What if everybody in the class did that?

DELISHA: (pouting) I can't do my sheet if I don't sharpen my pencil!

JUDY: OK. Go on ahead. But next time I want you to ask permission first, OK?

DELISHA: OK. (As she walks by Scott's desk, she thumps him hard behind his left ear with her pencil.)

SCOTT: Ow! That really hurt. Ms. Bowers! Lisa hit me!

JUDY: All right, Delisha, take your seat right now!

DELISHA: But I got to sharpen my pencil or I can't do my paper!

JUDY: Never mind, Delisha. You're not going to do your paper! Your picking on Scott has to stop! (Judy walks over to Delisha's desk, picks up the multiplication worksheet, and tears it up.) I'm afraid I'm going to have to give you an F on this work. Now sit down and don't move, or I'll have to send you to Ms. Rannum's office.

Delisha sits down and becomes bored doing nothing, so she tries to talk to Marin, who tells her to let her alone so she can do her work. In a couple of minutes, Delisha stands up and begins to dance standing in place as though she hears music.

JUDY: (looking up and seeing Delisha when a couple of students laugh) OK, Delisha, that's it. Let's you and me walk down to the principal's office. Keep doing your problems, children, and I'll collect your papers when I come back. (Judy motions for Delisha to follow her out the door. Delisha has a big grin on her face as they leave the classroom. As they walk down the hallway side by side, Judy talks to Delisha.) Delisha, why do you do these things?

DELISHA: Don't know. Just wanted to.

JUDY: You knew you'd get into trouble if you kept it up, didn't you?!

DELISHA: (smiling) I don't care! I can do what I want to!

It is after school that same day, and all the children have left. Judy goes to the principal's office and calls Tony Garcia at his office.

TONY: Garcia here.

JUDY: Dr. Garcia, this is Judy Bowers over at Lincoln Elementary. I need to ask you for your professional help with one of my students.

TONY: Oh, yes, Judy. Meg Ryerson said you might be calling. What's the name of the child who's giving you a problem?

JUDY: Delisha Davis, an eight-year-old African-American girl who is constantly disrupting my class. She causes more trouble than all my other twenty-seven students combined.

TONY: (laughing) She certainly sounds like a handful! I'll tell you what, Judy. I'd like to assign one of my school psychologists, Brad Barber, to collect some in-class observation data on Delisha. Then he'll sit down and go over the data with you and make some recommendations for working with her.

JUDY: You mean he'll come into the room and observe her while I teach?

TONY: Yes. He knows how to observe unobtrusively so Delisha won't know that she's the one he's collecting data on. The kids will get used to him being there rather quickly. He'll be busy recording data and will tell the children that he has to work if they try to talk to him.

JUDY: I guess that'll be OK. Shouldn't I tell the students not to bother him?

Tony: That would be excellent.

Judy: Dr. Garcia, do you think Delisha will be moved to another classroom? She's become a serious discipline problem, and I've been told that this goes back to her days in Head Start.

Tony: We'll just have to take it a step at a time, and please call me Tony, not Dr. Garcia. That makes me feel like a college professor or something.

Judy: (laughing) OK, Tony. When will Brad come?

Tony: He'll start Monday. Now could you give me a little information that will help Brad?

Judy: Yes, of course. What do you want to know?

Tony: Brad will be using behavioral recording techniques. I understand that Delisha is disruptive, but what kinds of behaviors is she engaging in specifically?

Judy: For one thing she won't be quiet. She makes inappropriate noises at inappropriate times. Like today when she was supposed to be working she made noises like she was passing air. Then she began to bother the other children while they were trying to do their seatwork.

Tony: By trying to talk to them?

Judy: Yes. It seems like she has trouble doing seatwork for very long, and before long she's doing something to bother the other children. (Pause) I guess the thing that bothers me most, though, is her getting up out of her seat without permission to dance or to go to the pencil sharpener.

Tony: Dance?

Judy: Yes, she stays in one place and dances like she hears music.

Tony: OK. Let me summarize. What I'm trying to do is come up with categories of behavior for Brad to use when he comes to your room to observe. I have three categories or types of behaviors that I've heard you describe. First, we have inappropriate "getting out of seat" behavior. Second, inappropriate talking to her peers. And third, I guess I would just call it "off-task" behavior.

Judy: Off-task behavior?

Tony: Yes. Inappropriate behavior she engages in when she's supposed to be doing seatwork. Things like making noises, daydreaming, doodling. Anything that's not on-task or doing her work. Do those three about cover it?

Judy: Yes, I guess so. Her dancing would be part of inappropriate getting out of seat?

Tony: Yes. Also, I believe Meg said that Delisha hits other children.

Judy: Only once and only one child, Scott. Well, she thumped him on the head with a pencil today. I guess that's the second time, but I don't think you'd observe much hitting.

Tony: OK. We'll omit that, although I'll mention it to Brad.

Judy: Will Brad be there observing all day, Tony?

Tony: No, I'd say maybe forty minutes a day for a couple of weeks. He'll work out with you when he should observe by asking you when Delisha usually engages in her problem behaviors.

Judy: When? You mean like what time of day?

Tony: What is usually going on in the classroom when she does these things? Seatwork? When you have group activities? When you are reading to them?

Judy: Oh, I see. He'll want to observe her at those times?

Tony: Exactly. Let him come in and observe for a couple of weeks, and then we'll discuss what we should do.

Judy: That sounds great, Tony! Thanks so much for your help.

It is Friday after school a little over 2 weeks later. Judy, Dr. Garcia, and Brad Barber sit around a small table in the office of the principal, Dr. Betty Rannum.

BETTY: So, Brad, you've been collecting observational data on Delisha Davis in Judy's classroom?

BRAD: I actually observed forty minutes per day for nine days, a total of six hours. I broke the forty minutes per day down into four ten-minute observation periods during those times that Judy said Delisha would be most likely to display disruptive behavior. (Passes out sheet of paper with data summary) This is a summary of what I observed.

BETTY: Could you explain what this chart means and how you did it?

BRAD: This is what we call a functional analysis, in that I record not only each behavior that Delisha emits but also the consequence, or what happens immediately after the behavior is emitted. As you can see, we placed her undesirable classroom behaviors into three categories. We then generated competing opposite categories of desirable behavior to see if any such behaviors were being emitted and, if so, what consequences followed each. Of course, these desirable kinds of behaviors will be the new targets that Judy should use to direct the child toward.

BETTY: (frowning) I'm not really completely following what you're saying, Brad. Can you give an example?

BRAD: (smiling) Of course.

JUDY: (interrupting) Then you're going to recommend that Delisha stay in my class?

TONY: Yes, we are. We'll talk about that when Brad explains the data a bit more, but we think that you can definitely change Delisha's behavior.

BRAD: For example, when Delisha would get out of her seat without permission, say, to dance, and Judy yells at her to sit down, I would categorize that as a "getting out of seat" behavior followed by a negative consequence.

BETTY: Oh, I get it! Then POS means positive reinforcer, NEG means negative reinforcer, and IGN means ignore?

BRAD: No, not really. It just means that the consequence appeared to me, the observer, as a positive or negative or ignoring one. Appearance is one thing. How it affects the behavior as observed is another.

BETTY: What do you mean?

BRAD: I mean that what appears to be a negative consequence, such as a verbal reprimand for dancing, may actually be serving as a positive reinforcer, since it doesn't decrease the behavior it follows. Calling one child a good student in front of the class may be positively reinforcing to that child and cause her to work harder. Saying the same thing to another child might cause her to quit working because she doesn't want to be seen as a teacher's pet.

BETTY: So it's the actual effects of the consequences that you observed that count?

BRAD: Right.

JUDY: The "Teacher" and "Peers" columns bother me. It's like you're saying that the other students in the class and I are responsible for Delisha's behavior. What about Delisha? Isn't she responsible for her own behavior? Why am I made the bad guy?

TONY: This behavior modification procedure is based on the work of B. F. Skinner years ago. Skinner believed that the cause of an individual's behavior is in the environment that the individual is operating in. That's why the same child will behave one way at school and another at home. Two different environments.

Figure 24–1 Baseline Data Collected by Brad Barber, School Psychologist, on Delisha Davis, Third Grader

Functional Analysis Time: 6 hours(9 days, 40 minutes per day)							
	Consequences						
Behaviors	Teacher				Peers		
Desirable	POS	NEG	IGN		POS	NEG	IGN
Staying in seat	1	0	73		0	0	74
Being quiet	1	0	61		0	0	62
On-task	12	0	67		3	1	75
Undesirable							
Getting out of seat	0	3	11		4	0	10
Talking to peers	0	3	28		16	0	15
Off-task	0	4	26		4	0	26

BETTY: Then Skinner didn't see the cause of bad behavior as coming from inside the child?

TONY: That's right!

BETTY: Then why do we have counselors and other mental health professionals who are supposed to work with individuals one-on-one or in small therapy groups? They pull them out of the environment—the classroom—to do that.

TONY: That's very true. They are working from the standpoint of an altogether different set of psychological theories. They would disagree with Skinner's position.

JUDY: (looking intently at data handout) Brad, if I read this chart right, there were seventy-four times that I could have delivered a positive consequence to Delisha for staying in her seat, and I did it only once.

BRAD: That's right. There were seventy-four occasions when you were close enough to her or in a position to deliver some kind of positive consequence such as praise, but on only one occasion did you do so.

BETTY: This is fascinating data, Tony and Brad, but let's get down to the practical part. What does it really tell us about Delisha? What are you recommending to Judy that she do differently in her classroom? How can she go about changing Delisha's behavior?

Questions

1. Which of the following classroom management models would have been most effective in Judy's classroom: behavior modification, teacher effectiveness training, reality therapy, assertive discipline, or Kounin's model? How effective was Judy with her attempt at teacher-pupil planning?

2. Delisha had attended a Head Start program. What is the nature and purpose of this program? How effective is it?

3. To what extent have Judy, Meg, and other teachers developed a self-fulfilling prophecy with regard to Delisha? How do teacher expectations and biases operate so that teachers' and administrators' behaviors change toward certain students and, in turn, result in changes in student beliefs and behaviors that confirm the original expectations of the teachers?

4. How would modeling and imitation from observational learning explain Delisha's classroom behavior? How might the models in her home environment explain her classroom behavior, especially in relation to Scott? What are cognitive behavior modification and self-regulation techniques, and how can they be used to change the behavior of a student like Delisha?

5. Meg indicates that she is unable to contact Delisha's mother. What parent involvement techniques have been found to be effective, especially with low-income parents? What might be some effective ways of involving Delisha's mother?

6. Tony and Brad are school psychologists. What is a school psychologist, and how does the work of a school psychologist differ from that of a guidance counselor or an educational psychologist? How often do school psychologists get to do consultation work like that of Brad?

7. Brad collected baseline data on Delisha from a behavior modification perspective. What is the purpose of such data collection? Critique the data-collection procedure that Brad used.

8. There are many pros and cons surrounding the techniques derived from the operant conditioning research of B. F. Skinner. What are the strengths and weaknesses of these behavior modification methods?

9. Tony explains to Judy and Betty that Skinner sees the cause of behavior as the environment, a position known as environmental determinism. Contrast this view with the reciprocal determinism of Bandura and the social construction view of constructivist theory.

10. What recommendations should Tony and Brad make to Judy and Betty about what Judy should do next? What do the baseline data tell you? What reinforcers seem to be maintaining Delisha's behavior? What techniques (e.g., behavior modification methods) can Judy use to begin changing Delisha's behavior? Should the techniques used involve the other students in her classroom? How can Judy determine whether the techniques she decides to use are effective in changing Delisha's behavior?

25

Taking Charge

Key Content to Consider for Analyzing This Case:

1. Classroom Management
2. Behavior Modification
3. Instructional Objectives
4. Cultural Diversity
5. Intrinsic Versus Extrinsic Motivation

Central High School is located in the downtown section of a large Midwestern city. Its architecture is characteristic of school buildings constructed shortly after World War II. While the physical plant is fairly well maintained, the houses, buildings, and factories surrounding the school reflect the decline and decay so common to inner-city areas after middle- and upper-class citizens move out into the suburbs. The school's attendance area is roughly 50% African-American, 30% white, and 20% Hispanic.

Troy Scott received his degree in education from a large land grant university in an adjoining state. He is 22 years old, single, and ready to begin his first year of teaching social studies. He sits in the office of the building principal, Charles Dobson, 3 days before classes are scheduled to begin.

MR. DOBSON: Well, Troy, what is your impression of our teacher preplanning activities so far?

TROY: I guess I'm a bit overwhelmed and somewhat apprehensive, Mr. Dobson.

MR. DOBSON: What's the source of the apprehension, Troy?

TROY: Take the teachers' meeting yesterday in the auditorium. All that discussion about guns and drugs on campus, disrespect, students fighting with teachers and each other, and lockers being broken into . . . I guess I'm just a small-town boy who believes that school should be about teaching and learning and that students and teachers should respect each other. I'm not sure what I'm getting into.

MR. DOBSON: (smiling) Don't overreact to what was discussed in that meeting, Troy. Don't think that those are everyday occurrences here. They do happen, and for that reason have to be discussed and dealt with just as any problem does. But they are the exception, not the rule. Things may not be as quiet here as they were in the small town that you grew up in, but we do run a pretty tight ship. The students here aren't going to run you out of the classroom. There is an old saying among teachers that it's best to be a strict disciplinarian at first and then loosen up later on when you have things under control. I think that's good advice for you to follow here at Central. Perhaps another maxim I'd add would be that you should never make a threat that you don't intend to carry out. If you do, the kids will figure you as a softie and eat you alive. You can't have learning in your classroom, Troy, until you have good discipline. Remember that and you'll do all right here.

TROY: Thanks for the advice, Mr. Dobson. I'll try to remember that.

MR. DOBSON: Good. I'm sure you will do just fine. Now let's talk about your load. Mary Kincaid, the chair of your department, has been sick all week, so I'm sort of doing her job here. We've assigned you to three world history classes, a U.S. history class, and a psychology class.

TROY: A psychology class?! I get to teach seniors?

MR. DOBSON: (smiling) Yes, that's the least we could do, giving you three preparations your first year of teaching and all. Mary usually reserves psychology and sociology for herself, but she thought that with your strong background in the subject, you might as well have a crack at it this year. And I might add that since it is an elective, a sizeable number of the students in that class are college-bound, unlike the history classes.

TROY: This is wonderful, Mr. Dobson! It will be a real pleasure working with that class!

MR. DOBSON: Mary has already ordered the textbooks, so you'll have to use the one that she chose, but I understand that it's the most commonly used one around the state.

TROY: Yes, I know the one you mean. That'll work out just fine.

MR. DOBSON: Mary told me on the phone today that she'll definitely be in to meet her classes on Monday when school begins. So if you have any questions, you can catch her then, I'm sure. Otherwise you might talk to Al Stafford. He's been in the department a long time and can probably handle any questions you have.

TROY: (standing up) Thanks, Mr. Dobson. I'm sure things will work out just fine.

It is second period, and Troy meets with 33 seniors in his psychology class for the first time.

TROY: That was the bell, folks! Now will everybody find a seat and quiet down please. (All quiet down but two students who continue to talk. Troy walks over to them.) What is your name?

STUDENT: Angel. Angel Garcia.

TROY: (looking at other student) And you?

STUDENT: Hosea. Hosea Sanchez.

TROY: (smiling) Angel and Hosea, would you two please stop talking and listen to what I have to say?

ANGEL: (smiling) Sure, man. Sorry.

TROY: How many of you are seniors? (All hands go up.) I thought so, but I wanted to be sure. (Pause) I don't mind telling you that psychology is one of my favorite subjects, and I'm really looking forward to teaching this class. How many of you think you'll be going on to college when you graduate? (Twenty-one hands go up.) That's great! I want to teach this class so it will help you make the transition to college. For those of you who don't think you'll be going to college, my goal is to help you see how psychology applies to your lives and will help you become more effective, better adjusted human beings, capable of solving the human relations problems that constantly confront us. Yes, Maria, isn't it?

Maria: Yes, sir. How will we be graded in here?

Troy: I was coming to that, Maria. Please bear with me. First, let me say that as seniors, especially those of you who are going to college, you have to start thinking as adults rather than as adolescents. All of us in the room have to start thinking of one another as adults and equals. College is for adult learners. Adolescents don't last too long there. Yes, Angel?

Angel: Does that mean I can call you by your first name, man?

Troy: No, it doesn't Angel. I think that you'll find that college professors aren't usually called by their first names by their students. (Clears his throat) However, to get back to Maria's question about grades, I plan on giving two combination objective and essay exams in each grading period. Think of them as a midterm and a final. I want you to do a lot of independent work and read broadly in this class. We'll be doing a lot of projects in small groups of four to six people, so it's important for us to get to know one another. Now I want us to begin today by asking what psychology is as a science. I realize that you haven't had a chance to read the first chapter, but I'd like to get your ideas before you start studying the field. Jerome, how about you? What is psychology?

Jerome: (looks down at floor) Don't know. Jus' the study of crazy people, I suppose.

Troy: That's certainly part of it. Abnormal psychology certainly focuses on that.

Tyrone: You mean psychology's abnormal?

Troy: No, Tyrone. The study of abnormal behavior is one branch or field of psychology. But the study of normal, well-adjusted behavior is also important, as well as topics like how people learn.

Jerome: Some people never learn, like Angel. He's too dumb.

Angel: You wouldn't know dumb if you saw it, Jerome, because you're dumber than dumb! I'll bet your IQ isn't over 60! (Jerome stands up.)

Troy: (angrily) Angel and Jerome! Be quiet! Jerome sit down! Here we are trying to have a simple discussion on the nature of psychology, and all you guys can do is pick a fight with each other!

Hosea: (smiling) Throw them out, Mr. Scott, so us decent students can talk psychology!

Angel: (looking at Hosea) You jerk! I thought you were my friend, man!

Jerome: He's too ugly to have any friends! (Points his finger at Angel) Get out, man! You're asking for it!

Troy: (with controlled anger) Stop! Not another word! The next one who says anything goes to the dean's office.

Jerome: Anything.

Troy: Very cute, Jerome. For Pete's sake, guys! Can't we have a simple discussion without your getting into a fight? Now please calm down and stop yelling at each other. (Pause) Now, back to the topic. What else do psychologists study besides abnormal behavior?

It is Friday of the same week. Troy sits talking to Mary Kincaid, the social studies department chair, in her classroom after school.

MARY: What kind of trouble, Troy? It's only the first week of school! Psychology is an elective course, and the kids who take it are usually well-behaved.

TROY: I know, Mary, but they're constantly arguing and bickering with each other! We can't carry on a simple class discussion without their getting at each other's throat!

MARY: Like who! Do I know any of these kids?

TROY: It's boys more than girls, although the girls chime in after the trouble starts. I guess Angel Garcia, Hosea Sanchez, Jerome Johnson, and Tyrone King are the worst. They seem to be the agitators and start things.

MARY: Yes, I had Tyrone in world history when he was a sophomore, and I've heard of the others from other teachers. They can be a bit noisy but not what I'd call troublemakers. Do they use cuss words or hit each other?

TROY: No, they just mouth off and disrupt what I'm trying to do all the time. We can't carry on a decent discussion about anything.

MARY: Well, Troy, it seems to me that there are some racial and ethnic overtones operating here and you simply have to let them know that you're not going to put up with it!

TROY: What do you suggest, Mary?

MARY: I generally find that it's best to make the limits clear and to have a progressively severe set of punishments to use when they step out of line. Make the rules and the consequences clear and, above all, be consistent. They get the picture pretty quickly.

TROY: What kind of consequences do you use, Mary?

MARY: I usually begin by reprimanding them in front of the class. Then I'll often change their seating. After that I begin to cut their grades. The next step usually involves communicating with their parents—at least trying to, since some parents don't care at all. All this time I am meeting with them one-on-one and trying to communicate with them. (Smiling) And, of course, the fact that they don't like to stay after school and talk to me also helps discourage their behavior.

TROY: What if none of that works?

MARY: As a last resort I send them down to Roy Haskins [dean of boys]. But I don't do that until I've tried everything else.

TROY: What does Roy do?

MARY: Oh, he threatens them, makes them stay in his office all day, punishes them by making them clean up the grounds, and sometimes is able to get their parents involved.

TROY: Does he paddle them?

MARY: He has in a few cases, but it doesn't do much good the way the school board has corporal punishment set up.

TROY: What do you mean?

MARY: You have to inform or try to inform the parents, you have to have witnesses present, and they just give them a few licks with the paddle anyhow. Doesn't do much good, considering the amount of time it takes and the little physical punishment that is involved.

TROY: Can he expel a student?

MARY: Only the school board can expel a student. Roy can start the process by recommending it, but it can take some time preparing the case and getting on the school board agenda. All that does, of course, is dump the problem child out on the streets, where he gets into worse trouble.

TROY: What about in-school suspension?

MARY: We have it, but that means that the child is out of the classroom where he can be learning. Also some poor teacher has to run it, and it's a thankless job!

TROY: I see what you mean. Thanks, Mary. I'm going to crack down a bit, establish a clear set of rules, and systematically enforce them. I'm not going to put up with this disruption all year!

MARY: (smiling) Good for you, Troy! Take charge!

It is Monday of the next week, and Troy meets his second-period psychology class.

TROY: Class, before we begin work on what it means to call psychology a science and to contrast it with various pseudosciences such as astrology and numerology—a discussion that I think you'll find fascinating and that I really look forward to—I want to bring up another matter: our behavior in the classroom. Certainly, the way we treat and relate to each other is a topic related to psychology, I would say. (Pause) I've noticed that when we've had discussions in this class, they keep deteriorating into shouting matches and threats of physical violence. Let me read you this list of rules that I put together this weekend. (Reads) First, raise your hand and get recognized before you speak. Second, treat your fellow classmates with courtesy: Don't yell at them or try to put them down. Remember what Thumper said in the movie *Bambi*: If you can't say something nice about someone, don't say anything at all. Third, don't touch other people's person or property. Don't knock people's books on the floor on the way to the pencil sharpener, for example. (Laughs) And finally, ask permission before you move around the room. Don't get up and sharpen your pencil without asking first, for instance. Yes, Hosea?

HOSEA: This really upsets me, man. I mean, that's making this place like a prison. (Chorus of agreement) I mean, this is a psychology class, and we're suppose to learn how to get along with other people and all.

TROY: (emphatically) But Hosea, what we've been doing in here isn't working. You people *aren't* getting along with each other. Angel?

ANGEL: What's going to happen when people don't follow those rules?

TROY: I've given that a lot of thought, Angel, and basically I feel that we need to go slow at first until people learn different ways of relating to each other. I'll start with a clear warning. Then on the second offense, either I'll ask the person to change seats and move to the back of the room or I'll make a grade deduction, depending on what the offense is. In the case of a third offense, I'll ask the person to go to the dean's office. Yes, Jerome?

JEROME: That's not fair, man. Takes all the fun out of this class.

TROY: That's another thing. Jerome, Angel, and Hosea, I'd appreciate if you'd stop calling me *man*. My name is Mr. Scott. And what's not fair is the way people keep disrupting this class and treating each other. (Loud and with emphasis) It has to stop, people! (Pause) Jerome, I was watching a boxing match on TV the other night, and one of the fighters kept hitting the other with blows below the belt. The referee warned him twice, and the third time he deducted a point and the fighter lost the round. That's sort of what I'm trying to do in here. Let's stop the fighting! (Moans, groans, and boos follow.)

It is second period, almost two and one-half weeks later. During that time Troy has consistently given five to seven reprimands per day and has moved Hosea and

Jerome to opposite corner seats at the back of the room. Tyrone and Angel have consistently received more reprimands and grade point-deductions than anyone else in the room except for Hosea and Jerome. Troy has just returned the mid-grading-period exam, which was a combination of 50 objective and 2 essay items covering the nature of psychology as a science and the distinction between it and various pseudosciences.

TROY: Since the fifty objective items count a point each and the two essays are worth 20 points each, you could have made a total possible score of 90 points. The highest score in the class was 72, and the average score was 46.5. Needless to say, I'm more than a little disappointed!

HOSEA: (looking at the paper of the girl who sits in front of him) Yes, and I know who messed us up.

TROY: (angrily) Hosea, what are you talking about? You didn't raise your hand again.

HOSEA: Maria! (Mockingly) She's always such a good student and tries to make us look bad! All she does is study! She wouldn't know what to do on a date!

TROY: That's it, Hosea! I'm deducting points from your test score! Now if I were you I'd apologize to Maria!

HOSEA: (standing up) I will not! She's a bitch and is always causing trouble!

TROY: Hosea, sit down!

HOSEA: I will not! I've had enough of you, too!

TROY: Hosea, leave this room right now and go to Mr. Haskins' office!

HOSEA: That's better than being in here, man! (Leaves room with a menacing look)

It is 20 minutes later, still second period, and Hosea returns to class with a smirk on his face and hands Troy a note from Roy Haskins, the dean of boys. The note says, "I discussed Hosea's inappropriate behavior with him, and he assured me that it won't happen again. Let's discuss this matter at your leisure." Troy reads the note with disbelief.

TROY: Take that chair over there, Hosea. I'll talk to Mr. Haskins later.

It is after school on the same day, and Troy walks over to Roy Haskins's office and takes an outside chair until Roy opens his office door, lets a student out, and walks toward Troy.

ROY: Hello, Troy. Come on in. (Shuts office door behind them and motions to Troy to have a seat)

TROY: Roy, did Hosea tell you what he did in my class?

ROY: From what I gather he got frustrated over a test and blew up. You threw him out of class. Is that right?

TROY: Essentially, yes. But in the process he called the student who made the top score a bitch and told me that he didn't care whether I liked it or not!

ROY: (smiling) Look, Troy. Today I've had to deal with kids beating each other up, several others caught stealing from lockers, three kids so high on crack they were totally strung out, and five girls who said they had been molested by male students. Hosea's misbehavior simply pales in comparison. Troy, you have to learn to handle these situations yourself.

TROY: (angrily) Roy, are you telling me I have to put up with that kind of disrespect from students?

Figure 25–1 Data on Students in Troy Scott's Second-Period Psychology Class

Name	Eligible for School Lunch	IQ*	Exam I	No. of Reprimands	No. Times Grade Reduced	Seat Moved?
1. Anderson, Willie	Yes	87	17 (F)	2	2	No
2. Bond, Julius	No	98	37 (C)	2	2	No
3. Cross, Harriet	No	110	68 (A)	0	0	No
4. Dixon, Shirley	No	123	65 (A)	0	0	No
5. Fidalgo, Carlos	Yes	90	21 (D)	2	2	No
6. Garcia, Angel	Yes	121	35 (C−)	12	9	No
7. Garrett, Marvin	No	105	49 (C)	1	0	No
8. Gonzalez, Maria	No	133	72 (A)	0	0	No
9. Hall, Greg	No	114	61 (B)	0	0	No
10. Johnson, Jerome	Yes	98	39 (C)	13	13	Yes
11. Kerr, James	No	109	47 (C)	1	0	No
12. King, Tyrone	Yes	97	30 (D)	11	5	No
13. Lawrence, Fred	No	118	59 (B)	0	0	No
14. Learner, Tami	No	128	54 (C)	0	0	No
15. Lewis, Tekha	Yes	101	48 (C)	3	2	No
16. Martin, Germaine	Yes	105	38 (C)	2	1	No
17. Miller, Jamal	Yes	97	24 (D)	3	2	No
18. Mitchell, Waka	Yes	103	44 (C)	2	1	No
19. Murdock, Beth	No	121	57 (B)	0	0	No
20. O'Sullivan, Terry	No	110	50 (C)	0	0	No
21. Platt, Heidi	No	128	52 (C)	0	0	No
22. Posada, Alyssa	Yes	113	47 (C)	1	1	No
23. Ramos, Victor	Yes	86	28 (D)	4	3	No
24. Robinson, James	No	112	42 (C)	2	0	No
25. Sanchez, Hosea	Yes	111	31 (D)	15	13	Yes
26. Scott, Danette	No	115	45 (C)	1	0	No
27. Shaw, Robert	No	123	50 (C)	1	0	No
28. Taylor, Mia	Yes	118	46 (C)	2	0	No
29. Thomas, Renae	Yes	105	46 (C)	2	0	No
30. Walker, Laverna	Yes	107	46 (C)	3	1	No
31. Washington, Cassandra	Yes	98	48 (C)	3	1	No
32. Waters, Vernell	Yes	94	45 (C)	3	2	No
33. Weary, Derreck	No	101	45 (C)	3	2	No

*Total IQ on Otis-Lennon Mental Ability Test, Level 4, given in 10th grade.

Roy: Absolutely not. I'm sure you know Kathy Andrews. She's a short, thin, wiry sort of a woman, and she doesn't put up with a thing. She tells football players twice her size what they're going to do, and they sure don't argue with her. It's an attitude, Troy. The students know when you mean business and simply aren't going to put up with any monkey business. You have got to learn to take charge, Troy, or you'll never be a good teacher.

Troy sits in the office of Charles Dobson, the building principal, the next afternoon after school.

MR. DOBSON: How can I help you, Troy?

TROY: Mr. Dobson, I'm in a real quandary about a discipline problem that has developed in my second-period psychology class.

MR. DOBSON: (frowning) I'm really very busy this morning, Troy. Could you explain the problem in as few words as possible?

TROY: Yes, well, the class is very disruptive and is constantly yelling at each other and interrupting what I'm trying to do. Three or four boys are usually the initiators, and after talking to Mary Kincaid, I tried to follow her advice and crack down. I told the students that they need to get permission before they speak, and so forth. I was very systematic in enforcing the rules, and although all this began to take a lot of class time and I was giving out a lot of reprimands and grade reductions, I felt like I was making progress until I returned a test and one of the students, Hosea Sanchez, blew up. He not only verbally attacked the student who made the top grade but also began shouting at me, so I sent him to the dean's office. Now, here's what really bothered me. Twenty minutes later he's right back in my classroom with a note from Roy Haskins basically saying he's talked to Hosea and was sure that Hosea won't do it again! Hosea sits there with a smirk on his face like he's gotten away with something. (Pause) Anyhow, I went down and talked to Roy, and in a nutshell, he told me that he has bigger problems than mine and that I needed to handle discipline problems in my classroom and not send them to him. What am I supposed to do, Mr. Dobson?

MR. DOBSON: (smiling) Troy, I seem to remember our talking about this earlier. Now think about it. Suppose every teacher in this school sent his or her discipline problems down to Roy. How would he ever have time to handle the really serious ones? Troy, you simply have to learn to handle such problems as this one yourself. Part of being a good teacher is learning how to take charge of the discipline problems in your classroom yourself. Roy Haskins simply can't do it for you.

TROY: (confused) I guess I thought that I was taking charge, Mr. Dobson. But what are you supposed to do when a student like Hosea stands up and challenges you to your face?

Questions

1. What models of classroom management would be useful in approaching this situation? For example, would assertive discipline, teacher effectiveness training, reality therapy, or Kounin's model be the best one to use? Why?

2. What are the pros and cons of corporal punishment? How effective is any form of punishment when used alone as a means of control? Under what circumstances can punishment be effective?

3. How might Troy have used any of the following behavior modification techniques: (1) the contingency contract, (2) the token economy, (3) time-out and response cost, (4) group social reinforcement procedures?

4. At what level of Maslow's need hierarchy are the following persons primarily operating: (1) Troy, (2) Mr. Dobson, (3) Roy Haskins, (4) Hosea?

5. What parent involvement techniques are available to teachers and schools? Which ones might be most helpful in this situation? How helpful would home visits or parent volunteers be in this situation?

6. What is the difference between intrinsic and extrinsic models of motivation? What intrinsic techniques might work best in this situation? For example, how might Troy have gone about determining student interests and taken advantage of them in his teaching?

7. What racial/ethnic or social class differences seem to be operating in Troy's class? How could Troy have taken these differences into consideration?

8. How effectively has Troy planned for instruction? How clear are his objectives? How effective are his rule-setting and enforcement procedures? What should Troy have done differently?

9. What type of school climate will be created by the administrative procedures followed by Mr. Dobson and Roy Haskins? How will the major stakeholders (administrators, teachers, students, parents) be affected?

10. What should Troy try next when he teaches his class? How can he handle situations within the classroom like the scene with Hosea? What should he do if a student physically attacks him or another student in the classroom? Are there ways that other teachers can help Troy?

Motivation or Control?

Key Content to Consider for Analyzing This Case:

1. Classroom Management (Especially Punishment)
2. Motivation (Mastery versus Performance Goal Orientations)

Saguaro Senior High School is located in a large city in a state in the Southwest. Of the more than 3,000 students attending Saguaro, approximately 10% are from upper-income homes, 50% are from middle-income homes, and 40% are from lower-income homes. The ethnic distribution of the student body is approximately 65% white, 20% African-American, 13% Hispanic, and 2% Asian-American. Of the 120 teachers, 100 are white, 8 are African-American, 10 are Hispanic, and 2 are Asian-American.

Because the teachers and staff have been experiencing a considerably larger number of discipline problems than ever before, the principal has arranged for Dr. Karen Chee, a classroom management specialist from a nearby state university, to conduct a workshop with the Saguaro teachers to help them to devise and implement a common classroom management model throughout the school. It is the first day of the workshop, and Dr. Howard Peake, the principal of Saguaro, has introduced Dr. Chee to the teachers. Dr. Chee then addresses the audience.

KAREN: Good morning. As Dr. Peake has told you, my name is Karen Chee. Dr. Peake has asked me to work with you on classroom management, which is one of my specialties. There are many different approaches to classroom management, and all of them are effective in certain situations. The main objective of this workshop, as I see it, is to find the approach to classroom management that will be most comfortable for you teachers to use and, at the same time, the most effective one for your pupils. (A teacher raises his hand, and Karen nods in his direction.)

PAUL: My name's Paul, and I was wondering how you're going to decide what the best approach is.

KARE: Good question, Paul. But you might not want to hear my answer.

PAUL: Why's that?

KAREN: (smiling) Because my answer is that I'm not going to make that determination. (Emphatically) You are!

MARTHA: (speaking out) But I thought that's why you're here—to tell us which management system would be best for us.

KAREN: But I can't make that decision—only you teachers can do that.

PAUL: Then what are you going to do?

KAREN: I'm going to help you find the answer to the question. As you know, there are many classroom management models. After we explore the major ones, you'll be able to narrow them down to the one or two that you, as a faculty, feel comfortable with and that you believe will be appropriate for the student body at this school.

EDNA: (speaking out) But I wonder if we'll be able to agree with one another on the best approach to classroom management? We may have different views on how to handle discipline problems.

KAREN: Such as?

CARL: (jumping into the discussion) I'll be glad to share my position with you. We have to learn how to control the pupils. We can't teach them anything until they learn to behave themselves and pay attention to what we're trying to teach them. If they're out of their seats running around the room, there's no way learning can take place. We have to get their attention before we can teach them anything. Without discipline, there's no learning.

EDNA: (responding) See, that's what I mean. I don't agree with that at all. That's the old-fashioned philosophy, that discipline comes before learning. (Looking at Carl) You have it backwards, Carl. Without motivation, there's neither discipline nor learning. Preschool children learn effortlessly because they're motivated to learn. They don't become discipline problems until we try to regiment them and treat them like army recruits. If we motivate them to learn, the discipline problems disappear and learning occurs naturally.

CARL: That's all very nice in theory, Edna, but you can't sugarcoat everything you teach and make it interesting to all your students. The fact is, a lot of the students simply aren't going to be motivated by what you're teaching.

PAUL: (speaking out) Which of these approaches do you think is the right one, Karen?

KAREN: It doesn't matter so much what I think, Paul, as it does what you think. And that's what I intend to find out this morning. (Holds up a questionnaire) This instrument is designed to assess your core beliefs on classroom management. (Hands copies of the questionnaire entitled "Classroom Management Beliefs" to several teachers in the front row to distribute) I'd like each of you to fill out one of these questionnaires right now. I'll tabulate them before our next meeting. Perhaps the results will enable us to work toward a common model of classroom management.

It is the first period on Monday following the workshop, and Carl is introducing the concept of sets and relations to his ninth-grade algebra class.

CARL: All of us talk about groups of objects in our everyday conversation. We talk about a deck of cards, a book of matches, a football team, or many other kinds of teams. Who can think of another group of objects?

MAX: (yelling out) A team of horses!

CARL: That's right, Max. But what's our rule that tells us what to do when we want to give an answer?

MAX: We're supposed to raise our hand and wait for you to call on us.

CARL: (walks to chalkboard and writes Max's name) That's right. So you get your name on the board. (Max waves his hand, but Carl ignores him.) We've identified several collections of objects. Who can tell us what these groups of objects are called in algebra? (Carman raises her hand.) Carman?

CARMAN: They're called sets. (Pause) And I don't think it's fair that you put Max's name on the board. He wasn't talking to another pupil and disturbing the class. He was participating in the lesson.

CARL: (not pleased with the comment) What rule did Max violate, Carman?

CARMAN: He talked out without permission.

CARL: That's right. The rule doesn't mention any exceptions. If several of you decided to call out to me during a class discussion, it would be just as disruptive as if you were talking to each other. Besides, you must get your name on the board with two marks after it before you must leave the class and get an F for the day's work. So Max is OK unless he talks out two more times. If he does, he'll go to the principal's office.

CARMAN: I still don't think it's fair when he was trying to be cooperative! (Carl walks to the board and writes Carman's name under Max's) Members of the class seem upset.)

CARL: I will not tolerate talking out in this class. (Looks around the classroom) I explained my system of discipline to you quite thoroughly the first day of class. At your age it's very important for you to learn self-discipline. People with self-discipline are more successful in life. When a class is out of control, none of the students learn as much as they should learn. And that's why you're here— to learn. So I'll explain the procedure again. For the first offense, I write your name on the board. For the second offense, I put a mark after your name. For the third offense, I send you to the principal's office and fail you for the day's work. The third time a student is sent to the principal's office, the principal schedules a meeting with the pupil's parents. (Sue raises her hand.) Sue?

SUE: What happens then?

CARL: Good question. But it's hard to answer. It always depends on the student's past behavior. It can result in anything from the student's being put on probation to being expelled from school. Now, who can think of some other examples of sets? (Latisha raises her hand.) Latisha?

LATISHA: There are lots of them—days of the week, weeks in a month, months in a year.

CARL: That's right, Latisha. Good. Now who can tell me what a subset is? (Ned raises his hand.) Ned?

NED: A subset is a set that's part of a bigger set.

CARL: Right. (Addressing the class) Now I want you to open your books to page 12. Complete exercises 1.2 and 1.3 on that page and then complete exercises 2.4 and 2.5 on page 13. These exercises will help you learn about sets, subsets, proper subsets, and equivalent sets.

LEROY: (whispers to Latisha) You got a pencil I can borrow? (Carl walks to the board and writes Leroy's name below Carman's.) Hey, man, why'd you write my name up there? I just borrowed a pencil.

CARL: You didn't raise your hand. You talked out.

LEROY: If I'd raised my hand, how would Latisha know that I want a pencil? That's dumb. (Carl goes to the board and puts a mark beside Leroy's name. Leroy raises his hand, but Carl ignores him.)

The same week, Edna began a unit on writing in her second-period ninth-grade English class. For the first 5 minutes of this morning's class, she presented a 5-minute mini-lesson on the characteristics of sentence fragments and run-on sentences because she had noticed examples of both kinds of sentences in some of the pupils' writings from last week.

EDNA: All right, students. I hope you'll all be able to avoid the writing of these kinds of sentences. Now we'll have a state-of-the-class conference. Rita, what are you doing this period?

RITA: I'm still selecting a topic.

EDNA: OK. But I want you to have one by the end of the period. You were selecting a topic on Friday. Two days is too much time to spend selecting a topic.

RITA: I've narrowed it down to two topics.

EDNA: That's great. Come and tell me when you make the choice. (Looks at Raul) Raul, what are you doing?

RAUL: I'm writing.

EDNA: Good Raul. Take it to the editors when you finish your first draft. (Looks at three girls talking among themselves) Paula, Anita, Jamaica. What are you doing?

ANITA: We're conferencing. We're reading each other's introductions and making suggestions.

EDNA: Good idea. You should be able to do that in about fifteen minutes. (Finishes polling the class on what they are doing and makes notes on a form made for that purpose) All right, class. It sounds as if you're all making pretty good progress on your writing. Now, you'll have thirty-five minutes to write or conference on your projects. (Some students form into groups of two or three and share and revise their writing. Others sit by themselves and write. Some hold up their hand for Edna to help them. Edna approaches one of these students.) How can I help you, Isaac?

ISAAC: I finished writing this story on Friday, but I don't like the ending.

EDNA: (reads the story carefully and looks at Isaac) That's a good story, Isaac. I like the introduction. And you have the events in a logical sequence. But I agree that the ending could be stronger. Can you think of some other ways that you could end the story?

ISAAC: I could have John tell his problems to his dad instead of his friend Paul.

EDNA: (ponders briefly) Yes. That'd work.

ISAAC: Or I could have Paul ask John if there's something bothering him.

EDNA: Yes. I like that too.

ISAAC: Which ending should I use?

EDNA: You're the author, Isaac. You have to make decisions like that. But I do think that both of the endings you're considering could improve the story if you handle them well. (Sees three girls who seem to be visiting and walks over to them) Are you girls doing all right?

ROXY: (smiling) Yes. Mandy just read her story to us, and it's really funny! Do you want to hear it?

EDNA: (smiling) Yes, I do. But since our write and conference time is up, I think it might be nice for the whole class to hear it. (Looking at Mandy) Mandy, would you be willing to read your story to the class?

MANDY: (obviously pleased) Yes, I'd like to.

EDNA: That's great, Mandy. (Walks to the front of the class) Class. May I have your attention? (The hum of conversation stops.) It's time for the sharing period.

Today, I've asked Mandy to read her story to you. (Turns to Mandy and announces with great fanfare) Mandy, you're on!

The following Saturday morning, the classroom management workshop group meets again in the high school auditorium. Karen Chee presides over the meeting.

KAREN: Welcome to the second session of our classroom management workshop. Our first item on the agenda this morning is to report the results of the questionnaire that you all filled out on your core beliefs on discipline. (Pauses) Overall, sixty-seven percent of you indicated that you subscribe to the discipline-oriented view, and thirty-three percent subscribe to the motivation-oriented view. (Carl raises his hand.) Carl?

CARL: Does that mean that the school classroom management program will be based on a control-first view?

EDNA: (speaking out) It doesn't seem reasonable to impose a program that a third of the faculty voted against.

CARL: If this were a presidential election, the control-first candidate would be elected.

PAUL: That analogy seems to compare apples and oranges. We're not electing a candidate. We're talking about strategies to use to educate students. I really don't feel comfortable using a control-first approach to classroom management. So why should I be required to use that approach when I'm so much more comfortable and effective as a teacher using the motivation-oriented approach? And I know that Carl is a most effective teacher using the discipline approach. Why should he have to use the motivation approach? We teachers talk a lot about accommodating the different learning styles of students. Why can't we accommodate the teaching styles of teachers?

MARK: Hear! Hear! Well stated!

KAREN: Yes, it's obvious that we don't have unanimity. (Martha raises her hand. Karen points to her.)

MARTHA: I thought the purpose of the questionnaire was to enable us to select one management system that all of us would use. Maybe our vote was analogous to a presidential election. The one with the most votes wins. (Edna raises her hand and is acknowledged.)

EDNA: If our purpose is to be consistent in classroom management, why can't all the control-oriented teachers meet and devise a consistent management system that they can all subscribe to? The motivation group could go through the same process. That way we could have two management systems consistent within the group using each one, and we all could manage our classes the way we feel most comfortable.

KAREN: Obviously, our task now is to decide whether to have one management system that approximately one third of the teachers don't subscribe to or two management programs that will enable all the teachers to use the one with which they feel most comfortable. (Nods toward Elaine, who is waving her hand)

ELAINE: What's the best way for us to go here? And what classroom management models fit the two classroom management orientations? And why should we limit ourselves to two approaches? Aren't we professionals? Why can't each of us choose our own individual approach to use in our classrooms?

Figure 26–1 Classroom Management Questionnaire Distributed by Dr. Karen Chee to Teachers Attending Classroom Management Workshop

---

Classroom Management Beliefs

Directions: Please answer the following questions as fully as possible. Their purpose is for you to state your core beliefs about these issues so that we can compare and contrast our beliefs during the workshop and we hope, end up agreeing on a model of classroom management to implement in our classrooms. Write your answers on separate sheets of paper as needed.

1. What causes students to behave the way they do? Is the cause of student misbehavior in the environment (e.g., classroom), inside the student, or some combination of the two?
2. What is student learning, and how can you tell when it is taking place? What must teachers do in the classroom to promote learning? How is learning related to classroom management?
3. What is a classroom discipline problem? At what point does a student become a discipline problem?
4. To what extent should teachers be concerned with student growth and learning of a nonacademic nature? Where does the teacher's responsibility begin and end?
5. Is it the teacher's job to shape the curriculum to the child or to shape the child to the curriculum? To what extent should the teacher use rewards (and punishments) to motivate students to learn material they don't enjoy learning?
6. Which is it more important for the teacher to do first? (1) gain control of student behavior so that learning can take place or (2) figure out how to teach material in a motivating way so that learning occurs and discipline doesn't become a problem.
7. Is it possible for teachers to treat students as equals? When necessary, is it okay for the teacher to use the "power" of his or her position to promote student learning and discipline?
8. Is the goal of classroom management for students to develop self-discipline? If so, how can such a goal be accomplished?
9. What forms of punishment are okay for a teacher to use in the classroom? Is corporal punishment acceptable under some circumstances? How do you differentiate between major and minor rules violations?
10. Should classroom management procedures be adapted to student differences (e.g., age, stage of development, socioeconomic status, gender, race, ethnic background), or should all students be treated exactly alike?
11. To what extent should students be involved in establishing the rules and procedures for classroom management?
12. Is it possible for a teacher to be a warm, caring, facilitative person and still be a good disciplinarian?
13. Can parents of your students be involved in your classroom management procedures? If so, how?
14. Suppose you had to describe your classroom management procedures to a beginning teacher. What would you tell him or her?
15. List and briefly describe as many models of classroom management as you can. Then indicate which one comes closest to matching your beliefs about classroom management.

■ Questions

1. The goal of classroom management is student self-discipline. What is self-discipline, and how can it be accomplished?

2. What are the different assumptions underlying the motivation-oriented and control-oriented approaches to the role of classroom management? Which is the more valid, and why?

3. What is motivation, and what role does it play in human learning? What differences exist between the mastery and performance goal orientations of students (as described by Ames), and how do they relate to the method of classroom management used?

4. What is the difference between a teacher-centered classroom and a student-centered classroom? Which is more desirable, and why? How does each relate to the method of classroom management used?

5. What is the cause of student behavior problems in the classroom? Is the problem inside the student or in the classroom environment, or perhaps both? How does the answer to this question relate to the classroom management procedure chosen?

6. Should a teacher consistently use the same methods of classroom management with all students or adapt methods or even use different methods according to varying student characteristics? For example, should different methods of classroom management be used with diverse student populations (e.g., those that vary in socioeconomic status, gender, racial and ethnic background, or academic ability)?

7. Compare and contrast the classroom management procedures used by Carl and Edna. Which is more control-oriented? Which is more motivation-oriented? Is one more likely to foster student learning than the other? Which do you prefer, and why?

8. Answer the 15 questions on the "Classroom Management Beliefs" questionnaire given to the teachers by Dr. Chee. What do your answers tell you about your classroom management orientation? For example, are you oriented more toward control or motivation? What model of classroom management comes closest to fitting your belief system?

9. Should the school adopt only one method of classroom management for all teachers to use, or should two approaches be allowed? Or should each teacher be permitted to develop his or her own individual approach?

10. What classroom management models (e.g., behavior modification, assertive discipline, reality therapy, teacher effectiveness training, or Kounin's approach) come closest to fitting the control and motivation orientations of teachers? Where would parent involvement methods fit in?

27 /

The Excesses of Youth

Key Content to Consider for Analyzing This Case:

1. Drug Abuse
2. Social Development
3. Moral Development
4. Home Learning Environment
5. Cultural Diversity

R ay McBride has taught social studies at Van Buren High School for 5 years, ever since completing his BS at the College of Education of the state land-grant university. The Van Buren Vikings are a perennial powerhouse football team that has won the championship in its division several times in a football-happy state in the eastern part of the United States. The high school is located in a large city and draws from an attendance district that is approximately 60% white, 25% African-American, 10% Hispanic, and 5% other assorted racial and ethnic groups.

It is Monday, 2 weeks after classes have begun, and the Vikings have already won their first two games by large scores. As Ray meets his seventh-period U.S. history class, the students are all abuzz, discussing last Friday's game.

RAY: OK, people! Settle down! Refocus your attention from last Friday's game back to the Age of Discovery in Europe, where we left off last Friday. Besides, those first two games we played were easy ones. This Friday we'll find out how good we are when we play the Southport Spartans. If we beat them on their home turf, then I'll be impressed. (Laughter and shouts of agreement) Now think back to the days before there was a United States, before there was a Van Buren High School. (Shouts of protest) Before the game of football was invented! (Mock shouts of despair) So Jerry, what three European nations led the way in discovering the new world?

JERRY: Uh, Portugal, Spain, and England.

RAY: Right, Jerry! But don't forget that little old Genoa in what is now Italy played an important role. Can anybody remember what? (Silence for about 5 seconds, then one hand goes up.) Yes, Maurine!

MAURINE: Weren't both Columbus and Cabot from Genoa?

246

RAY: Excellent, Maurine! While Columbus sailed for Spain and Cabot for England, they were both natives of Genoa. A minor fact in history, but you remembered it, Maurine! Yes, Maurine?

MAURINE: But why was that, Mr. McBride? Why didn't they sail for Genoa?

RAY: Ah, a good question. And why might that be, ah, Don?

DON: I don't know. Probably because of money.

RAY: (walking back where Don and his ever-present friends, Billy, Mike, and Tyrone, sit) That's right, Don! Can you tell us about it?

DON: Not really. I haven't read the chapter yet.

RAY: Well, that was still a good guess. Why did you think that was the answer?

DON: Doesn't money always make the world go around?

RAY: (smiling) I guess so, Don. It certainly determined who Columbus and Cabot decided to sail for. (Looking at Billy, Mike, and Tyrone) Can any of you tell me what happened? (Billy and Mike shake their heads, and Tyrone lays his head down on the desk.) All right then. How about you, Donna? (Paces back up to the front of the class)

DONNA: Didn't Columbus try Portugal but then ended up sailing for Ferdinand and Isabella of Spain?

RAY: Right you are, Donna. Good answer. Now let me ask another question. How many of you have read this chapter? (All hands go up but those of Don, Billy, Mike, and Tyrone.) OK, thanks. Remember that we covered this stuff last week. If you haven't read the material by now, you are really behind. How many of you read today's chapter on exploring the New World? (All but the same four hands go up.) OK, thanks. Now let's start with the American Indian tribes that were already living in the New World when the Europeans came here to explore it. Please turn to the map on page 22 of the text that shows where the various American Indian, or Amerind, tribes were located in the sixteenth century.

Ray sits in his classroom after school where he is joined by his friend Jim Turpin. Jim has been a guidance counselor at Van Buren but has recently been promoted to assistant principal.

RAY: Well, look who's here! The new assistant principal!

JIM: (smiling and bowing) Yes, well, someone has to provide leadership in this school!

RAY: (smiling) And I can't think of a better person for the job! Sit down, Jim, and talk a bit.

JIM: (sitting down) Personal or professional?

RAY: I'd like your personal advice on a professional matter.

JIM: I gotcha! What's the problem?

RAY: Jim, it's some of the boys in my seventh-period U.S. history class—four to be specific.

JIM: Discipline problems?

RAY: No, not really. They don't read the assignments and haven't done well on the quizzes that I've given so far, but that's not the real problem.

JIM: What is this—twenty questions? Am I supposed to guess what the problem is? One of them is pregnant?

RAY: (laughing) No, I think you've been to one movie too many lately, Jim. (Seriously) I think there's a serious drug or at least alcohol problem with these guys. No, I think it's both.

JIM: As far as I am concerned, alcohol is a drug too, even if it is legal. But what makes you think there's a drug problem, and who are these kids anyhow?

RAY: They are a kind of gang. Not in the formal sense of an organized juvenile gang, you understand, but they are always hanging out together, and they even sit together in my class. There's Mike Mason, who sort of seems to be the leader, Billy Reardon, Tyrone King, and Don McCabe. Don doesn't seem to fit in as naturally as the others—seems to be kind of a fringer. But I see him more with those guys than anyone.

JIM: Oh, yes, I know that crowd! Tyrone King used to be one of my counselees. He used to talk about Mike and Billy a lot. Yes, I would guess that they do their share of drugs. Do you think they are on drugs when they are in your class?

RAY: Definitely. I've been watching them carefully for over a week now and often move close to them as I pace around the room during classroom discussions. The signs are there.

JIM: Such as?

RAY: Odor. I can smell pot on them. And their eyes are often quite dilated. Often they just sit around drowsy and inactive with their heads on their desks. One day I got too close to Mike, and I could smell it on his breath as he talked. And Tyrone—he always has a bottle of cough syrup in his pocket. I've always wondered what's really in that bottle. In fact, maybe I don't really want to know, Jim. I'm not sure what I should do about this. But just ignoring it, like a lot of teachers and parents choose to do, won't help much.

JIM: Yes, it's a difficult situation for a teacher to be in. Yet all the workshops I've been in on adolescent drug usage see the teacher as being in an ideal position to serve as an information and referral agent. Do you want me to work on this, Ray?

RAY: What do you advise?

JIM: I could do some discreet information gathering, and maybe you could work with Don a bit, since you seem to feel that he is the one who is most salvageable.

RAY: That makes sense. I'll line up a conference with Don.

It is 3 days later, and Ray meets with Don McCabe after school alone in his classroom. They sit in chairs facing each other in front of Ray's desk.

DON: You wanted to see me, Mr. McBride?

RAY: Yes, Don, I do. Don, I think you have the potential to be a good student in my U.S. history class, but you never seem to have read the material or come to class prepared. I'd like to know why.

DON: I don't know.

RAY: I can't remember one day in the past three weeks that you or your friends have read the assignment before coming to class.

DON: You mean Mike, Bill, Tyrone, and me?

RAY: Exactly. Why don't you read the assignment before you come to class?

DON: I guess the truth is, Mr. McBride—no offense—we just aren't interested in history.

RAY: In history or in any of your classes? I've checked with your other teachers, and you guys don't come to their classes prepared either.

DON: (surprised) Really! Well, I guess we're just not that into school right now.

RAY: What are you into, Don? Alcohol and other drugs?

DON: No, of course not!

RAY: Don't give me that, Don. I'm not as stupid as I look. I've smelled pot on your clothes, noticed how dilated your eyes are, seen Tyrone's ever-present cough syrup bottle . . .

DON: (nervous laugh) Yeah, well, I guess you've got us, Mr. McBride. What are you going to do? Report us to the police?

RAY: I don't have a plan at the moment, Don. What I'd like to do is help you become a better student. But I'm not sure I can help you as long as you're using that stuff all the time.

DON: "That stuff" is just alcohol and pot, Mr. McBride. Oh, except maybe for Tyrone, who uses crack sometimes. It isn't like I do it every day. Just when I need to.

RAY: And when do you need to, Don?

DON: Look, Mr. McBride. Alcohol is perfectly legal. My dad drinks it all the time, and the liquor really flows at all our family gatherings. You should have been at my sister's wedding last month!

RAY: OK, tell me about pot. That's not legal.

DON: Well, yeah. But I only take three or four hits a day. It relaxes me and helps me think.

RAY: It sure doesn't help you read your history text.

DON: Believe me, it's not the pot, Mr. McBride. I'm just not much of a student.

RAY: What does motivate you, Don?

DON: I just mainly like to hang out with the guys and our friends.

RAY: By the guys you mean Mike, Billy, and Tyrone?

DON: Yeah, and our girlfriends.

RAY: Some of our girls here at Van Buren use pot too?

DON: Of course, and some of the girls from other schools. Pot really helps you break down barriers and makes it real easy to get to know another person.

RAY: (smiling) It makes the girls real affectionate?

DON: (smiling) Yeah, it sure does. I just don't see why alcohol's legal and pot's not. I'd rather be around a guy who's high on pot than I would one who's drunk. Drunks always get mean and nasty after a while, but potheads are real easy to get along with. Some people even need to use pot for medicine, but the government's too stupid to let them, even when their doctor says so.

RAY: I hear what you're saying, Don. But isn't life best when you're clear-headed and fully aware of what's going on?

DON: Maybe for you, but definitely not for me. Like I said, it's not like pot is my whole life.

RAY: What about Mike, Billy, and Tyrone?

DON: What are you going to do with the information if I tell you? Report them?

RAY: As I said, Don, I'm interested as a teacher. Maybe if I understand you four better I can figure out how to motivate you to learn history.

DON: (laughing) I'm afraid that's hopeless.

RAY: Why's that?

DON: Talking Mike, Billy, and Tyrone out of using drugs would be quite a chore.

RAY: Why do you say so?

DON: Look, Mr. McBride, Mike's used drugs since he was seven, and Billy's almost as bad.

Ray: Seven?!

Don: Yeah. He started out sniffing glue and paint and finally got on pot and alcohol. Same for Billy, only he started in the sixth grade. You understand I'll deny I said any of this if you mention it to anyone else.

Ray: I understand. What about Tyrone?

Don: Tyrone drinks a lot, but he also uses crack. Since he's from the neighborhood over on 84th Street, he can get stuff for us real easy.

Ray: So Don, what's your goal in life? Grow up to be a dealer?

Don: (laughs) No, that's a rich but dangerous life, Mr. McBride. Tyrone might, but not me. Look, I'm not good at much. I'm not good at sports, and you know I'm no class brain. I don't figure I'll get a chance to go to college. My dad's a salesman and makes a lot of money at times. He says that I have a likeable personality and can be a salesman too. But that's later, Mr. McBride. Right now I just want to be a high school kid and have a good time. I hope I can make C's and graduate, but whatever.

Ray: What's to keep you from becoming a pothead and not wanting to do anything the rest of your life?

Don: It's not like that, Mr. McBride. I use some pot and alcohol, sure. From time to time we party big and get really stoned. But usually it's just enough to get through the day. I'll tell you what, Mr. McBride, I'll think about all you've told me, and I'll try to start reading your assignments before I come to class. But I can't do anything about Mike, Billy, and Tyrone. They're their own people, and it would be a waste of time. They'd kill me if they knew that I'd talked to you.

Ray: Don't worry. I won't tell them.

Don: (stands up) Thanks, Mr. McBride. I'll try to do better.

Ray: OK, Don. Thanks for being honest with me.

Don: (smiling) It was real easy, Mr. McBride. You're a nice guy! (Sticks out his hand, and Ray, remaining seated, smiles and shakes it)

It is after school the next day, and Ray walks down to the office of Jim Turpin, the assistant principal. Jim greets Ray, motions for him to take a seat, closes his office door, and takes the seat behind his desk.

Jim: Ray, how's it going?

Ray: Great, Jim. I talked to Don McCabe as you suggested.

Jim: How did it go?

Ray: Surprisingly well. He was suspicious of me at first, but he finally opened up and told me quite a bit about himself and his friends.

Jim: What did you learn?

Ray: In confidence, Jim, Tyrone King is the dealer—at least he gets the drugs—and Mike and Billy are heavy users. Don seems to be on the fringe of the group. He doesn't drink and use pot as heavily as they do, at least not yet.

Jim: So it's primarily alcohol and pot.

Ray: Yes, although apparently Tyrone does some crack. I guess Don is up to taking a hit of pot three or four times a day and gets drunk when they party down. He claims he's not addicted, but I think he might be kidding himself. If he keeps up this pattern he'll sure get there.

Jim: I agree. What are you going to do?

RAY: That's what I wanted to talk to you about. Don's attitude toward life and his drug usage is clearly affecting his grades. If something isn't done now, by somebody, I think he'll just end up as another failure. Maybe I'm wrong, but he's the only one in that group that I feel like there is any chance of saving. I'm not sure what role I should play in all this. I'd like to work with Don and see if I can help him. But I realize that something needs to be done for the others. Should they be referred to one of the guidance counselors or to the state division of human services? If that is done, Don will know that I've broken the confidentiality between us and may quit relating to me. Also, take the homes of these boys. Shouldn't someone contact their parents and get them involved in all this? But again, it's the same problem. While the parents may be the ultimate cause of this whole thing in the first place, I may terminate any chance I have to help Don if I contact them. I know I can tell you all this in confidence, Jim, because you're my friend. But the problem is, Jim, what do I do?

JIM: You're caught between the devil and the deep blue sea, all right, Ray. I don't know. Let me think about it, check into some possible courses of action, and get back to you. OK? Meanwhile, you keep working with Don.

RAY: (standing up) Thanks a million, Jim. I knew you'd help.

It is near the end of seventh period, 2 days later. Ray looks out at the class as they quietly prepare for their upcoming exam on the European discovery and exploration of the New World by answering some self-test questions that Ray has handed out to them. He catches Don's eye as he looks up and motions for Don to come up to his desk.

RAY: (speaking quietly) How's it going, Don? Are you having any trouble with the questions?

DON: To tell you the truth, Mr. McBride, I am, and it's my own fault. I've just barely skimmed the chapters, and these questions are pretty in-depth.

RAY: Would you like some help?

DON: (brightening up) I sure would!

RAY: If you'll read these chapters, and I mean really read them, Don, I'd be willing to tutor you a bit for this test.

DON: That would really be cool, Mr. McBride! When would you want me to come see you?

RAY: It has to be tomorrow after school. The test is the next day.

DON: I'll do it. I'll read the chapters real good and come here tomorrow after school. Thanks! I appreciate your help!

It is seventh period 3 days later, and Ray passes back the tests to the students by calling out their names and handing them their test papers with their answer sheets inside.

RAY: I want you to look your tests over carefully, especially your multiple-choice answer sheets where I've calculated your scores. We'll go over the answers, and then I'll tell you what I looked for on the essay part. We'll discuss a few of the objective items that bothered you so you can improve on the next test. I want you to particularly look at the red marks on your answer sheets to see if there is any pattern to the multiple-choice items that you missed. Are they evenly distributed over the answer sheet, or are they in clusters? It may be that certain material covered by the test was more difficult, or maybe you studied some chapters differently than you did others. Look at that and try to figure out how you might do things differently next time. (Pause) Now, before we go over the answers, let's talk about the overall grade that you received. The objective part was worth fifty points, and so was the essay part. So you could have received a possible total of one hundred points. The average score was 74.2 points. As is always the case, there are always those students who work real hard and get a perfect score. I don't like to embarrass people, but Maurine Sullivan really worked hard for this one and made a perfect score. Stand up and take a bow, Maurine! (Maurine stands and smiles while students applaud, cheer, and kid her all at the same time. She sits back down.) Yes, Jerry?

JERRY: Maurine may be the winner, but who was the first runner-up?

RAY: A nice line, Jerry. From the Miss America contest, I assume. Believe it or not, the first runner-up was a boy, not a girl. And his name, folks, is Don McCabe. Don made a 96. Don, stand up and take a bow! (Don stands up, smiles, and puts his hands together to make a gesture of victory while the students, somewhat surprised, applaud and cheer loudly, especially Mike, Billy, and Tyrone.)

DON: I owe it all to the good tutoring I received.

RAY: (waiting for the applause to recede) There's a moral to this story, folks. Hard work always pays dividends. Nice job, Don!

Two days later Ray sits in his classroom alone after school, working on his lesson plans. Jim Turpin walks into the room quietly with a serious look on his face.

RAY: (looking up) Hi, Jim. What's the matter? You look like you've just lost your best friend.

JIM: No, but we have lost a good friend of yours.

RAY: (stunned) What do you mean?

JIM: I hate to be the one to tell you this, Ray, but one of your students was killed in an automobile accident just off the school grounds—Don McCabe.

RAY: (stricken) Oh, no! What happened?

JIM: It was a drunken driving accident right after school was out. Mike Mason was driving, and Don, Billy, Tyrone, and two girls were in the car. They plowed right into a van with four cheerleaders and a mom who was driving. Two of the cheerleaders and Don were killed. Mike, Billy, and Tyrone were barely scratched.

RAY: Poor Don! And he seemed to be making such progress.

JIM: Maybe academically, but he just hung around with the wrong crowd.

RAY: Do you know if Don was drunk?

JIM: No, I don't.

RAY: Jim, I have to ask you something, and I want an honest answer.

JIM: Sure, Ray.

RAY: Jim, I know that hindsight is always better than foresight, but surely there must have been something I could have done to have kept this thing from happening. Are there people in the school system or in state agencies that I should have involved instead of trying to handle this myself? Should I have tried to talk to Don's parents? And what, if anything, should I try to do about Mike, Billy, and Tyrone? What is a teacher like me supposed to do in a situation like this, Jim?

Figure 27–1 Information Compiled by Mr. McBride from School Cumulative Records

Student	School Lunch Eligibility	Parent(s)/Guardian Present in Household	Parents' Occupations	Parents' Education	No. of Siblings	Cumulative G.P.A
Don McCabe	No	Mother, Father	Salesman (F)	12th	2	2.23
			Sales Clerk (M)	12th		
Billy Reardon	Yes	Mother	Waitress (M)	11th	3	1.07
Mike Mason	Yes	Mother, Father	Construction Worker (F)	10th	4	1.21
			Housewife (M)	12th		
Tyrone King	Yes	Guardian (Aunt)	House Cleaning (G)	5th	5	0.78

Questions

1. What are the causes of drug usage during adolescence? What are the drugs of choice? Do gender differences exist? At what age does usage begin?

2. What role do the home and parents play in drug usage? What are the most effective programs for helping drug users?

3. What state and federal agencies provide assistance in the case of drug usage? What community assistance is available? What personnel in the school system normally work with drug users? At what grade level should such assistance begin?

4. What student characteristics are the best predictors of drug usage? How closely related are SES, race, ethnicity, family size, family dysfunctionality, school achievement, and IQ to drug usage? Are students who are at risk of dropping out of school more likely to be drug users?

5. What signs indicate that a student has an alcohol or other drug problem? What signs did Ray respond to? How effectively did Ray handle the situation? What should he have done differently?

6. How has Don's home environment affected his behavior with regard to alcohol and other drugs? Have Tyrone's neighborhood norms regarding the availability and sale of drugs affected the other three boys and their girlfriends as well? What can be done about such neighborhoods?

7. What is the most effective role that the school's administration, faculty, and students can play in reducing the consumption of alcohol and other drugs? How effective are drug education courses and speakers? Should tobacco be considered a drug?

8. At which of Kohlberg's stages of moral development does Don seem to be operating? What about Mike, Billy, and Tyrone? How can the stage of moral reasoning be raised?

9. At what level of Maslow's need hierarchy do Don, Mike, Billy, and Tyrone seem to be operating? How could Ray have taken this into consideration in working with them?

10. What, if anything, should Ray do to help Mike, Billy, and Tyrone? What is the appropriate role for a teacher to play in such cases? What does it mean to say that a teacher should serve as an information and referral agent?

The Overstressed Disciplinarian

Key Content to Consider for Analyzing This Case:

1. Teacher Stress
2. Classroom Management
3. Teacher Efficacy
4. Teacher Locus of Control
5. Maslow's Need Hierarchy

Lane Baxter is a secondary English teacher with 16 years of teaching experience. He will soon be 39 years old and has spent the past 8 years teaching at Whitmore High School, located in a large urban area in a southeastern state. The attendance district served by WHS is 36% African-American, 2% Asian-American, and 62% white.

It is 1 week before Lane has to report for teacher preplanning to begin his 17th year of teaching. He sits at home with his wife, Lois. They have just finished discussing their trip to Europe, from which they returned just 2 days ago.

Lois: What's the matter, Lane?

Lane: What do you mean?

Lois: You can't fool me! You were so happy and animated just a minute ago when we were talking about our trip; then all of a sudden you clouded over. What's wrong?

Lane: To tell you the truth, it suddenly hit me that vacation is over and I have to go back to the salt mines next Monday. I absolutely hate that place!

Lois: (with concern) Lane, do you really hate it that much?! I though you loved teaching!

Lane: I'm not a kid fresh out of teachers college any longer, Lois! You just don't know what it's like at Whitmore!

Lois: What do you mean?

Lane: It's the kids. They're so—disrespectful. It isn't like it used to be. They not only don't care about learning but don't care about anything. They'll cuss you out right to your face in class! You can kick them out all you want to, they just don't care! And you know what, Lois? I've gotten to the point where I don't care either!

LOIS: Lane, can't you transfer to another school? Maybe a school like Vanguard High School?

LANE: Wouldn't make any difference. Charlie Haskins has taught at Vanguard for years, and he says the same thing goes on over there. (Pause) It's just symptomatic of our whole country, Lois. Crime is everyone's number-one concern today. The police and the courts can't or won't do anything about it. People don't feel safe in their own home anymore. Everyone we know is either buying a gun for self-defense or looking into a home security system. Why should the schools be any different?

LOIS: I knew you weren't happy at Whitmore, but I had no idea you felt this bad about your job! (Pause) Lane, have you ever considered getting out of teaching?

LANE: (angrily) And do what?! Write poetry? There's a lot of people out there who are out of work now and would love to have a job with a steady paycheck and fringe benefits like mine. But the price is high! (Pause) I really envy my dad, the way he served as a principal for twenty-eight years.

LOIS: Yes, your dad was a wonderful man and educator.

LANE: But those were easier, simpler times, Lois. I wonder if he could do it today.

LOIS: Lane, I only know that I want you to be happy! If you decide to change jobs, we can get by on my salary until you're able to make the change.

LANE: (moving next to her and putting his arm around her) Thanks, dear! Hearing that means a lot to me! (Smiling) But don't worry—I'll get over this bad mood! It'll pass, as always.

It is the first day of preplanning, and all the teachers file into the school auditorium for their first meeting of the year. As Lane looks for a seat down front, he runs into his old friend and fellow English teacher Charles Allen.

CHARLES: Why hello, Lane. How have you been?

LANE: Hi, Charles. Good to see you. Is that seat empty?

CHARLES: It sure is. We've been saving it for you. (Pointing to the young, well-dressed man sitting next to him) Lane, I'd like you to meet Darryl Wilson. This is Darryl's first year, and we're looking for big things from him.

DARRYL: (shaking Lane's hand) It's certainly nice to meet you, Lane. Charles has been telling me all about you.

LANE: (smiling) Really? All good, I hope.

DARRYL: Oh, yes. He says that your favorite course is American literature, and that's my favorite, too. I can't wait to meet my first class. It's really going to feel different, knowing that they are my classes and that I'm not just an intern!

LANE: (winking at Charles) Yes, well, you'll get used to it real quick!

DARRYL: When I was interviewing for the job, Mr. Cookson [building principal] told me he'd give me a shot at teaching the journalism classes and taking over the school paper, maybe by next year. He said I could assist Mr. Swaby with it this year and learn the ropes.

LANE: (smirking) Yes, I'll bet Cookson will be happy to have you take over the school paper—and Swaby will, too!

DARRYL: I hope so! Journalism is my second love! (Frowns) I just have one worry, though.

CHARLES: What's that, Darryl?

DARRYL: It's probably silly, I know, but I'm afraid some of the students will know more about American literature than I do and I won't know how to handle it!

LANE: (rolling his eyes at Charles) Darryl, let me assure you, that won't be a problem! It'll be the last problem you'll need to worry about!

DARRYL: What do you mean?

LANE: I think you'll find out very quickly that you'll be way ahead of even advanced placement students as far as subject matter is concerned. Your problems will be discipline and student apathy.

DARRYL: I sure hope you're right. I think I'm ready for discipline and motivation problems. We spent a lot of time learning classroom management strategies and motivational techniques. But it would really embarrass me to death if a student knew more about, say, a piece of prose I was teaching than I do!

LANE: Trust me, Darryl. You don't need to worry about that!

The teachers' meeting is over, and Lane stands outside the auditorium talking to Charles.

CHARLES: What did you think of Darryl, Lane? Don't you think he'll make a good one?

LANE: He's really something, Charles! I can remember being naive and idealistic like that when I first entered teaching, but I'm afraid that he's going to get a rude awakening. I just hope the students don't eat him alive! (Pause) At other times, though, I wish I were back there starting all over. I can't say I'm looking forward to this school year.

CHARLES: Why is that, Lane? Is something going on that I don't know about?

LANE: No, it's just that, well, as I was saying to Lois the other day, I guess I'm just tired of teaching. You could say they've worn me down, I guess.

CHARLES: I'm surprised to hear you say that, Lane. Gosh, I can remember a few years back when you won the district teacher of the year award and how happy you were.

LANE: Charles, that was eleven years ago! I don't feel that way today.

CHARLES: What's bothering you, specifically, I mean?

LANE: I guess it's the kids more than anything. The lack of respect, the apathy, the constant bickering and negativity. It just wears you down 'til you wonder if it's worth it. (Pause) Then there's the constant pressure to teach to the test so the standardized test scores will look good. And the administration never backs you in anything. Send a student down to the office, and the dean not only sends him right back the next day but then also comes around and asks you why you can't handle such matters in the classroom. Nobody seems to care anymore. It's like hitting your head against a brick wall.

CHARLES: Lane, have you ever considered talking to anyone about this? I mean someone who can help?

LANE: No one other than Lois, and now you. I really wouldn't know who to talk to. Who in this school system would want to listen, other than a friend like you?

CHARLES: I guess I was thinking of Dr. Felling, the director of psychological services. He would surely know how to help, and it wouldn't cost you anything.

LANE: Not a bad idea, Charles. Thanks a lot! I'll keep it in mind.

It is the first day of classes, and Lane meets his fifth-period American literature class, consisting of 37 students from a variety of ethnic, racial, and socioeconomic backgrounds. After lecturing to them about the organization and purpose of the course, how to study the textbook, and his grading procedures, Lane turns to his expectations for students' conduct.

LANE: Let me just add that this is my seventeenth year of high school teaching, most of them here at Whitmore, and that I'm familiar with all the tricks and excuses that students use to keep from studying. Studying is hard work. But it's your main job as a student, and if you care about a good grade in this class, you'll have to spend time every day studying. You'll find that as you get older, the things you'll come to appreciate most in life are those that you have to work the hardest for. (With annoyance) You have a question, Ron, isn't it?

RON: Mr. Baxter, do you really believe that stuff? Not only is who you know more important than how hard you work, but you're putting me to sleep.

LANE: (angrily) Another smart guy! Then why are you in this class if you're so bored and know so much?

RON: Not because I want to be! I can't think of anything more useless than studying American literature. What a bunch of crap!

LANE: (controlled) I've had students like you before, Ron, with big attitude problems. Since you dislike it in here so much, I'm going to ask you to leave right now and go to Mr. Profitt's office [dean of boys].

RON: (getting up) Gladly. That's sounds a lot more interesting than being here!

It is the end of the first grading period, and three boys meet and talk outside Lane's classroom at the end of the fifth period. Two of the boys, Jeremy and Joe Ed, are in Lane's fifth-period American literature class.

JEREMY: Hey, Carlos, what's happening?

CARLOS: Not much, man. You guys going to class?

JOE ED: Just got out, thank goodness!

CARLOS: Bad class, huh?

JEREMY: Geez, I guess so. Old man Baxter. What a loser! Boring!

CARLOS: Couldn't be worse than old lady Tyree. She's definitely the worse! Can't stand her, man.

JEREMY: She can't hold a candle to Baxter!

JOE ED: Yeah, I had Tyree last year. Baxter's definitely worse.

CARLOS: Yeah, how?

JOE ED: Boring as crap! Puts you to sleep and jumps down your throat if you breathe too loud! He's such a grump!

JEREMY: He doesn't even try to make things interesting. Acts like he doesn't care whether you get it or not, just as long as you don't cause any trouble . . .

JOE ED: . . . And wake him up! (All three laugh.)

JEREMY: Heck yes! If I was that bored with what I'm doing, I'd quit. (Bell rings.)

It is 4 weeks later, and Lane sits in the office of Dr. Lester Felling, director of psychological services.

Lane: Les, I need to talk to someone who can advise me. I figured that if you couldn't help me yourself, you'd know of someone who could.

Les: Of course, Lane. I'm pleased that you thought of me! I have worked with, oh, I'd say half a dozen teachers who felt they were suffering from burnout and trying to decide whether or not to leave teaching.

Lane: I didn't realize you had that kind of background.

Les: Yes. While my doctorate was in school psychology, I did my dissertation on student and teacher stress. The superintendent expects me to have exit interviews with all existing faculty, so I would have had to have talked to you anyhow.

Lane: (with surprise) I didn't realize that!

Les: Yes, the administration is very interested in the reasons for teacher turnover in the school district. After all, good teachers with as much experience as you've had are hard to find, Lane.

Lane: I'm not so sure I'm a good teacher anymore, Les. Things bother me now that didn't used to. I've lost my zest and enthusiasm. Even my wife, Lois, wonders whether I shouldn't move on to something else.

Les: Lane, I'm going to ask you to do something for me before we go any further. Would you please fill out this stress instrument for me? (Hands instrument to Lane) As you can see, the instrument is easy to understand, is self-scoring, and will give us a profile of the sources of your stress. Just be completely honest. There are no correct answers, just your answers. I'll keep the results in complete confidence. Could we get back together at this same time next week?

Lane: (looking at his appointment book) Yes, that'll be fine.

Les: Great! Bring the completed instrument with you, and we'll use it as a starting point for our discussion.

Lane: Sounds good, Les. I feel better already.

The next day, Lane is returning some papers to his fifth-period American literature class.

Lane: (angrily) I just can't believe these papers, folks! I gave you a simple, and I think interesting, assignment: to rewrite the ending of the story by changing the last three paragraphs. I find you can't spell, you can't write paragraphs, you can't make your subjects and verbs agree, and, worst of all, you have no original ideas of your own. Every paper, without exception, took an idea from either a recent movie or TV show to rewrite the ending. I don't think there was an original idea in the entire class! (Pause) Yes, Teresa.

Teresa: I didn't take my ending from a movie or TV show, Mr. Baxter.

Lane: (sneeringly) That's true, Teresa, you took your idea from one of Shakespeare's plays. That's four hundred years old! (Class laughs) I don't think this is funny, people! Your generation is going to be the leaders of tomorrow, and I'm not sure you are capable of original thinking. (Angrily) Yes, you have a creative comment, Ron? I noticed that you didn't even bother to turn a paper in, as usual.

Ron: (angrily) I don't see where your generation has been so creative in running this country! Look at . . .

Lane: (interrupting) Ron, in case you didn't notice, I'm the teacher of this class, not you! When you earn two degrees and a teacher's license, I'll be glad to step aside and let you take over my job. Until then, I'll thank you to . . .

RON: (angrily, interrupting) If I couldn't do a better job than you in teaching this class, I'd quit.

LANE: (waving his arms in anger) Get out of here, Ron! Now!!!

It is the next week, and Lane sits in Les Felling's office.

LES: (holding Lane's stress profile in his hands) As you can see, the instrument measures nine sources of stress and gives a total score. Your overall score of 154 is very high and clearly falls into the high-stress category. Of the nine sub-scales, three of them stand out—student behavior, psychological/emotional symptoms of stress, and stress management techniques.

LANE: (smiling) I guess that says I'm stressed out, huh, Les?

LES: (smiling) It says more than that, Lane. Look at some of the items. You seem to have a real problem with classroom management.

LANE: (smiling) That's true, I guess. I suppose I am a bit hair-triggered these days. I get impatient and angry much more easily than I used to. I guess what bothers me the most is that I haven't always been that way. I used to enjoy relating to the kids, but now . . .

LES: (interrupting) It becomes a vicious circle once it starts. Negative begets more negative.

LANE: I guess so. I never really thought of it that way.

LES: Lane, would you say you follow a plan as far as classroom management is concerned?

LANE: A discipline plan? I started out using behavior modification years ago, but now, well, I guess I really just use a system of increasing punishments. You know, I warn them the first time, lower their grade the second time, maybe change their seating, and so on, until finally, I ask them to go to the dean's office as a last resort. I don't know if I have a system or not anymore! And to tell you the truth, I don't have the energy to change things.

LES: I see. I guess that helps explain your responses about complaining a lot to others and feeling depressed about your job.

LANE: I guess so.

LES: Then there's your lack of stress management techniques to cope with the situation.

LANE: To tell you the truth, Les, I go home at the end of most school days, have a couple of highballs, and talk to Lois. That's all that keeps me sane. (Pause) What's happened to the American family, Les? All these working wives and single parents just aren't providing real homes for their children. Who knows what values they're learning at home—if any. Look at all the latchkey children and those who are abused. They just dump them on teachers like me and say, "They're your responsibility, not ours." I'm tired of it, Les!

LES: I hear you, Lane. (Pause) Now let me ask you the sixty-four-thousand-dollar question. Do you want to leave teaching, or are you willing to work on yourself and try to salvage your career as a teacher?

LANE: How can I answer that? I don't know! I'm pulled both ways. Is there really anything a stressed-out teacher like me can do to turn things around?

Figure 28–1 Stress Profile for Teachers[1]

Student Behavior

1. I have difficulty controlling my class.
2. I become impatient/angry when my students do not do what I ask them to do.
3. Lack of student motivation to learn affects the progress of my students negatively.
4. My students make my job stressful.

Teacher/Administrator Relations

5. I have difficulty in my working relationship with my administrator(s).
6. My administrator makes demands of me that I cannot meet.
7. I feel I cannot be myself when I am interacting with my administrator.
8. I feel my administrator does not approve of the job I do.

Teacher/Teacher Relations

9. I feel isolated in my job (and its problems).
10. I feel my fellow teachers think I am not doing a good job.
11. Disagreements with my fellow teachers are a problem for me.
12. I get too little support from the teachers with whom I work.

Parent/Teacher Relations

13. Parents of my students are a source of concern for me.
14. Parents' disinterest in their children's performance at school concerns me.
15. I feel my students' parents think I am not doing a satisfactory job of teaching their children.
16. The home environment of my students concerns me.

Time Management

17. I have too much to do and not enough time to do it.
18. I have to take work home to complete it.
19. I am unable to keep up with correcting papers and other schoolwork.
20. I have difficulty organizing my time in order to complete tasks.

Interpersonal Conflicts

21. I put self-imposed demands on myself to meet scheduled deadlines.
22. I think badly of myself for not meeting the demands of my job.
23. I am unable to express my stress to those who place demands on me.
24. Teaching is stressful for me.

Physical Symptoms of Stress

25. With frequency I experience one or more of these symptoms: stomachaches, backaches, elevated blood pressure, stiff neck and shoulders.
26. I find my job tires me out.
27. I am tense by the end of the day.
28. I experience headaches.

Psychological/Emotional Symptoms of Stress

29. I find myself complaining to others.
30. I am frustrated and/or feel angry.
31. I worry about my job.
32. I feel depressed about my job.

Stress Management Techniques

33. I am unable to use an effective method to manage my stress (such as exercise, relaxation techniques, etc.)
34. Stress management techniques would be useful in helping me cope with the demands of my job.
35. I am now using one or more of the following to relieve my stress: alcohol, [other] drugs, yelling, blaming, withdrawing, eating, smoking.
36. I feel powerless to solve my difficulties.

[1]Reprinted from C. F. Wilson (1979), *Wilson Stress Profile for Teachers*. San Diego: The Wright Group.

Questions

1. Evaluate Lane's approach to classroom management. What model or set of beliefs does he seem to employ? What are some alternatives that he might try?

2. Does Lane evidence a high or low sense of teacher efficacy? An internal or external set of teacher attributions? How are such teacher beliefs related to student motivation and achievement?

3. In terms of Maslow's need hierarchy, at what level of needs does Lane seem to be primarily operating? Why do these need deficiencies seem to exist? How does one move toward greater self-actualization in teaching?

4. Would you describe Lane's beliefs about student motivation as intrinsic or extrinsic views? Did Lane have any opportunities to increase student motivation in his class? What are some motivational techniques he might try?

5. What is teacher burnout, and how is it related to teacher stress? What are the common sources of teacher stress, and do they differ by grade level and gender? What are the main sources of teacher stress in Lane's situation?

6. What is teacher morale, and how does high or low morale relate to teacher productivity? How would you describe Lane's morale level, and why? What can be done to increase teacher morale?

7. What can teacher education programs do to help prepare inservice and preservice teachers to deal with the common sources of teacher stress? Whose job is it to help teachers suffering from high teacher stress? What role can the school system, colleges of education, and the community play?

8. Should Lane leave or stay in teaching? If he stays, what changes will he need to make? What can be done to help a teacher cope with severe stress? How effective are relaxation techniques, exercise, attitude-change exercises, and diet changes as helping interventions?

9. What are the most common symptoms of teacher stress? Why are some teachers able to cope with stress while others fail to do so? What is hardiness, and how does it relate to a teacher's ability to cope with stress?

10. What is a teacher mentoring program? How can such programs help teachers deal with stress?

29

Making the Grade

1. Measurement and Evaluation (Norm- versus Criterion-Referenced Evaluation, Essay versus Objective Testing)
2. Mastery versus Performance Goal Orientation
3. Home Learning Environment
4. Maslow's Need Hierarchy
5. Role Theory (Legal Professional Role of Teacher)

Bixby High School is located in a small southern city of approximately 15,000 people. The building is relatively old but well kept and well equipped. BHS serves a 75% white and 25% African-American population, and approximately 60% of its graduating seniors enter college each year. The dropout rate is only about 25%, even though Bixby does not have a large or well-developed vocational education program.

Jan Newell is a 21-year-old graduate of a nearby small teachers college who is beginning her first year of teaching. As a social studies teacher, she has been assigned to teach three sections of U.S. history, two sections of world history, and a study hall. It is the Friday before classes are scheduled to begin, and Jan is meeting with Frank Conway, the head of the social studies department, in Frank's classroom. Jan and Frank sit in chairs facing each other in front of Frank's desk.

FRANK: Are you all set for Monday, Jan?

JAN: (smiling) As ready as I'm going to be, I guess, Frank. I do have a few things I'd like to go over with you, though.

FRANK: Fire away!

JAN: I'm starting to get together my first exams and quizzes, and I find myself wondering about Bixby's grading policies. I notice that the report card says that 95 to 100 is an A, 88 to 94 is a B, 77 to 87 is a C, and 70 to 76 is a D. Does everyone follow that system?

FRANK: (frowning) You know, Jan, we place a strong emphasis on preparing our kids for college. There is no official, required grading system, but a teachers' committee did agree on those standards a number of years back. And almost all the teachers use those standards.

JAN: (frowning) Does everyone grade on a curve?

FRANK: I think it's safe to say that practically everyone in the academic areas like English, math, and our own department does.

JAN: Testing and grading is one aspect of teaching that really concerns me, Frank. They always taught us in teachers college that learning is what education is all about. And from having been a student myself for so many years, I know that the way you evaluate seems to affect learning more than almost any other single thing.

FRANK: I agree that the way you grade makes a big difference. A poor grading system can undo good teaching faster than anything I know. It can make or break your teaching.

JAN: (with animation) And grading on a curve especially bothers me. That means you have winners and losers instead of taking each child where he is and moving him along as far as he can go. Once some kids finish at the bottom of the curve a few times, they seem to get stuck there and give up.

FRANK: Fortunately or unfortunately, Jan, that's the American way. Our society and our colleges are based on competition, and that means winners and losers. One of the lessons of life is to learn to deal with failure and to overcome it. People have to learn it sometime.

JAN: (frowning) Could you explain a little of the nitty-gritty in using the grading standard? For example, what do you do to take into consideration the fact that some tests turn out to be more difficult than others no matter how hard you try!

FRANK: (smiling) First off, practically all of us in social studies, especially in history classes, use objective tests—mostly multiple-choice, matching, and fill-in-the-blank. That eliminates a lot of arguments with both the students and their parents. And dealing with test difficulty differences is pretty easy. Just curve the grades and feed them back into the standard. Do you know what I mean?

JAN: I think so. In other words, if a test is real difficult and the top grade is say, 80, then just add so many points to every grade to change the distribution to the school's standards.

FRANK: That's it exactly! I think you're going to do just fine, Jan! And I don't want to make the grading system here seem too rigid either. For example, there's no reason why you can't experiment a bit. Trying out new ideas is what being a beginning teacher is all about.

JAN: Thanks for the advice, Frank. I also have one or two other things I wanted to ask you about. . .

It is the following Monday, and Jan meets her second-period U.S. history class for the first time. She explains her grading system to the class.

JAN: I know that you are wondering what your grades will be based on. I plan to give you a quiz each week, usually ten items, and a large unit exam at the end of each unit. All these tests will be objective, and the big unit exams will have anywhere from 75 to 100 items on them. Yes, you're Beth, right?

BETH: Yes, Miss Newell. Will the quizzes be pop quizzes?

JAN: No, they'll be announced in advance. I may have them on Fridays. I haven't decided yet. (Pause) Now, besides the tests there will be group projects and individual reports that will be graded. For example, our first unit is on the Age of Discovery. We'll get into the European background that led to the discovery of the New World. Some of you may want to do reports on different explorers, such as Ferdinand Magellan and John Cabot. When I grade your reports I'll be looking to see if you carefully follow the reporting format that I give you. Yes, Jerry?

JERRY: What kinds of group projects will we do?

JAN: I was just coming to that, Jerry. I'll put you in small groups of five to six people, and you'll get to meet in class at least one day each week—probably Friday after the weekly quiz. One group might want to construct a model ship like the one Magellan or Columbus used. Another group might want to get into the food and clothing that people used at that time—or even the medicine and health care. Yes, Beth?

BETH: How will you grade the group projects?

JAN: (laughing) Very subjectively, I'm afraid! I'll be looking at your originality and how much work you put into it, mostly. Also, how well you present to the class what you have done. Of course, everyone in the group will receive whatever grade the group project earns. Yes, Bill?

BILL: How much will these different things count?

JAN: I haven't decided that yet. I'll let you know. I guess the exam and quizzes have to count the most. Then I'll probably give more weight to the individual reports than to the group projects. We'll see. Now, let's get into the first unit.

It is 3 weeks later, and Jan is returning the exams for the first unit test to her second-period U.S. history class. The test was very difficult, and Jan had to transform the distribution to fit the school's grading standards by adding 13 points to everyone's score.

JAN: Does everyone have his or her paper? (Pause) Now, if you'll look at your score in the upper right-hand corner, you'll notice where I subtracted the number you missed from 100 and then I added 13 points onto the remainder. That's because the highest score was only 87. By adding on the 13 points, I made the scores fit the school's grading standard that's printed on the report cards. The class didn't do very well on the unit exam, and I must admit I am somewhat surprised and disappointed. The test may have been a little difficult, but I also have a feeling that some of you didn't study as hard as you might have or else you didn't study the right way. Now that you've had one of my big tests and know what to expect, perhaps you'll do better on the next one. Yes, Bill?

BILL: (pointing at the distribution on the blackboard) How come there were only three A's?

JAN: As I said, Bill, I converted the scores to the school's grading standard where 95 to 100 is an A. Therefore a score of 81 would be a 94 when you add on the 13 points and a high B.

BILL: (without raising his hand) That doesn't seem fair! This was a hard test, and there were only four scores in the eighties. Why shouldn't all the eighties have been A's? Why do you have to use the school standard all the time? What makes it so sacred?

BETH: (with emotion and without raising her hand) I agree with Bill, even though I made one of the A's. Miss Carter, my English teacher, doesn't pay any attention to the school's system. She uses 90 to 100 for an A, 80 to 89 for a B—

JAN: (interrupting vigorously) All right, people! Settle down! (Pause) I don't know what other teachers do, but in here we're going to follow the school's standards. Unfortunately, Bill, you have to draw the line somewhere to divide the A's from the B's, and your score happened to fall on the wrong side of the line. I remember watching a championship basketball game on TV where one team beat the other by one point. Because of that one point, one team became national champion and the other team finished second.

BILL: (without raising his hand) That's sports, and this is school. I don't think it's the same thing at all! This is the first B I have ever received on a big test, and I studied hard!

JAN: Bill, I'm sure you'll all do better on the next unit exam, and don't forget that you have individual reports and group projects that can get your grade over the A level—especially when you are only one point from an A. (With strong emphasis) Let me remind all of you that I didn't have to add 13 points onto your papers. I could have let the scores stand as they were, and then the highest grade would have been a B. An 81 (looking at Bill) would have been a C. Let's all learn from this and do better next time. Now let's go over the test items one at a time and I'll answer any questions you might have about them.

Two days later Jan is talking to Frank Conway in his room after school.

FRANK: Are you having grading problems in all your classes, Jan?

JAN: To some extent, yes. The kids are constantly complaining about their grades, but my second-period U.S. history class is the worst by far. There are two students in there, Bill Nelson and Beth Clark, who really get upset if they don't get an A every time.

FRANK: I'd say that's partly due to pressure from home. You know who they are, don't you?

JAN: Not really. I—

FRANK: Bill's father is on the school board, and Beth's mother is an elementary principal in this school district.

JAN: I didn't realize that. I—

FRANK: Jan, may I make a suggestion?

JAN: Of course, Frank, that's why—

FRANK: Jan, I know that I emphasized following the school's grading policy to you, but don't feel like you have to follow it slavishly. Grading is just a tool, a means of expressing how much students have learned. Please understand that I'm not talking about you individually now, but teachers often hide behind their grading scheme to protect themselves from criticism. The result is the tail begins to wag the dog. Grades become more important than learning. (Pause) My suggestion to you is that you loosen up a bit with your grading. You can generally follow the school's grading policy but adapt it in ways that make the most sense in terms of student learning. Be flexible. (Pause) Also, in terms of what you've told me, perhaps you could make your tests a little less demanding and place a little more weight on your group and individual projects. Anytime you see good students like Bill and Beth fall down in their grades even though they are working hard, you need to look hard at your grading system and consider how you might revise it.

JAN: (weakly and with a stunned expression) Well, OK, Frank. I see what you mean. Learning is certainly more important than grades.

It is 3 weeks later, and Bixby High School has mailed student grades to the students' homes. Second period has just ended, and Bill Nelson, Beth Clark, and three other students are standing outside Jan Newell's classroom in the hallway discussing their grades.

JACK: Well, Bill, I hear you got all A's again. Must be nice having your old man on the school board.

BILL: Yeah, well, that has nothing to do with it! You just don't know talent when you see it!

BETH: I guess you got an A in U.S. history, too. Practically all the people I talked to got an A or a B.

BILL: Yes, Newell really changed! She started out tough, but then she seemed to get easy. I really like U.S. history now! She makes it interesting! (Beth and Jerry agree in unison.)

JACK: U.S. history?! Interesting?!

BILL: Yes, my man, interesting! I'd say it's my favorite class now. She always has something new and different happening in there—a regular zoo!

BETH: It isn't real clear what you are supposed to do to get an A, but if you work and pay attention, practically everybody gets one. It's like you don't have to worry about grades if you work.

BILL: Yes, and I really like this thing she added about letting you grade yourself.

JACK: Grade yourself?!

BILL: Yeah, and then she sits down with you at the end of the grading period and you sort of negotiate the grade you get. Of course as bright and good-looking as I am—(Bell rings to begin next period.) Oh boy! You guys are going to make me late to class!

Three days later after her last class, Jan enters the office of Mary Smiley, the building principal.

JAN: Did you want to see me, Mrs. Smiley?

MARY: (smiling and motioning to Jan to take a seat) Yes, Jan, I do. (Short pause) A problem has come up that I need to talk to you about. Several teachers have come to me about the way that you are grading your students.

JAN: (stunned) My grades! Why?

MARY: Well, Jan, Frank Conway tells me that he explained to you our school's grading policy. We don't expect teachers to follow it rigidly, but problems do develop when teachers deviate from it too far.

JAN: (with surprise) Frank told you I wasn't following the school's grading policy?

MARY: No, Jan. Several parents have called certain teachers accusing them of grading too hard. Some of them have even called the guidance counselors asking that their children be transferred to your class. Some of the teachers came to me to complain about your easy grading.

JAN: (struggling for control) Mrs. Smiley, you can't believe what I've been through on grading! First I was accused of being too tough a grader, and now I'm being told I'm too easy! I've tried to work with Frank Conway on this all along—

MARY: Yes, Jan, I know that you have. Grades are one of the toughest things that beginning teachers have to learn to deal with. (Smiling) Let's work this out together, shall we?

JAN: Of course, Mrs. Smiley, I'd appreciate any guidance you can give. All I want is to be the best teacher I can be. I just don't know if it can be done!

MARY: You mean become a good teacher?

JAN: No. I mean develop a grading system that's not too tough or too easy, that motivates my students to learn, and that keeps my fellow teachers happy! I'm not sure it can be done, Mrs. Smiley!

Figure 29–1 Distribution of Scores in Miss Newell's Second-Period U.S. History Class

	Unit I Exam (100 Points Possible)	
87	(Beth's score)	
86	A	
85		
81	(Bill's score)	
78		
77	B	
76		
75		
74		
73		
73		
73		
73	C	
65		
65		
65		
65		
65		
64		
63		
62		
62	D	
62		
58		
58		
56		
54	E	
52		
48		
36		
31		
28		
26		
14		
12		
8		

Questions

1. Evaluate Bixby High's grading scale. Is it fair? Should it be applied in all subject areas and with all types of students?

2. What is the purpose of grading? How can a teacher make the best educational use of grading in the classroom?

3. What is your opinion about contract grading, that is, when students make a contract with the teacher regarding the requirements to be met for a particular grade?

4. Examine the distribution of scores for the Unit I exam that Jan gave her students. How would you assign grades to her students?

5. What is norm-referenced evaluation, and what are its strong and weak points compared to criterion-referenced evaluation? What does grading on a curve mean? What are standard scores, and how can they be used to grade on a curve? Should a teacher grade on a curve in some classes and not in others?

6. How important is it for students to experience competition and failure? From a developmental standpoint, how much failure should a student face, and at what age? If failure is viewed as punishment from an operant conditioning standpoint, what are the possible effects of punishment in the form of grades on student behavior?

7. What are objectivity and subjectivity in scoring? What are the relative merits of objective and essay tests? How do they differ in terms of their ability to measure learning at the different levels of Bloom's cognitive taxonomy?

8. What are the most effective ways to report student progress to parents? How effective are parent conferences? Should parents be involved in both formative and summative evaluation? How frequently should they be involved?

9. How desirable is it to have school or school-systemwide grading standards? How much latitude should teachers be given as professionals to set their own individual grading standards? How much commonality needs to exist among teachers?

10. In Jan's case, does giving higher grades than other teachers mean she is an easier grader, or do her stimulating teaching procedures result in higher grades? What can a teacher do to keep grades from becoming more important than learning? What are the best ways of dealing with high-need achievers like Bill and Beth?

Teaching to the Test

1. Instructional Objectives
2. Measurement and Evaluation (Standardized Testing, Educational Standards, Norm- versus Criterion-Referenced Testing)

Washington High School is located just off a busy expressway in a metropolitan area on the West Coast. The school has over 2,000 pupils, with about 35% African-American, 30% Hispanic, 5% Asian-American, and 30% white. A few decades ago the neighborhood surrounding Washington High was predominantly middle-income. Since the early 1960s, however, the more upwardly mobile families, both African-American and white, began to move out of the area and into the suburbs. Today, the families that remain are largely low-income.

While urban schools such as Washington High frequently have below-average student achievement, the school's performance on the annual state-mandated test of reading, writing, and mathematics skills for all 11th graders has been close to the mean score for all schools in the state. And when compared to that of the other 11 high schools in the city, the achievement of Washington High students is slightly above average. As a result, the school has a reputation throughout the city for providing low-income students with a better education than they would receive at many other urban high schools.

Although Washington High was built just before World War II, the physical plant has been well maintained. Freshly painted white window frames provide a pleasing accent to the three-story brick exterior, which was sandblasted just 2 years ago. Inside, the hallways are regularly mopped and waxed by a custodial staff that takes pride in making an old building sparkle.

It is Monday morning, 2 days before students return from their summer vacation. Over 100 teachers and other school personnel are seated in the library waiting for their new principal, Mrs. Manning, to begin addressing them at a brief orientation meeting.

Darrell Wilson, a 37-year-old mathematics teacher beginning his 10th year at Washington High, is seated next to his good friend Steve Neff, a 28-year-old English teacher who came to the school 3 years ago. Darrell, who is also chairman of the mathematics department, is highly regarded by his colleagues and by his students. For the past 4 years, students voted him Teacher of the Year.

DARRELL: (in a low voice) I understand that Mrs. Manning is a real go-getter. She's not afraid to make changes if she thinks they'll improve student achievement.

STEVE: (leaning toward his friend) That's what I've heard, too. I'm a bit worried, though. A friend of mine from Manning's last school told me something I don't like.

DARRELL: What was that?

STEVE: She said Manning places a lot of emphasis on test scores. (At the sound of feedback on the portable amplifier being adjusted at the front of the library, he turns in that direction.)

DARRELL: Let's hear what she has to say.

After being introduced by Mr. Hawkins, the assistant principal in charge of curriculum, Mrs. Manning welcomes the teachers and staff back from summer vacation and then announces the names of four new teachers. Next she goes over a few details related to the schedule for the remainder of the day. Finally, she turns to her goals for the new year.

MRS. MANNING: (in a loud, clear voice) When I knew I was coming to Washington High, I was pleased. This school is known for giving students a good, solid education, and all of you are to be congratulated. (A slight patter of applause spreads throughout the library.) I truly look forward to working with each of you so that we can make a good educational program even better. (She pauses a moment, smiling.) Therefore, our primary goal this year will be to increase the basic skills achievement of every eleventh-grade student on the state's annual assessment test in March. Each teacher, regardless of subject, must stress the basics. (Several of the teachers stir noticeably in their seat. Darrell leans toward Steve to make a comment.)

DARRELL: (whispering) You were right. It didn't take her long to zero in on test scores.

MRS. MANNING: As you may recall, last year seventy-three percent of our eleventh graders reached mastery on the reading section of the test. On the writing portion, seventy-one percent achieved mastery. And on the mathematics portion, seventy-two percent were at the mastery level. While some might feel that this level of performance is acceptable for an urban school such as Washington High, it could be better. To improve our scores, then, I am initiating several new procedures this year. Everyone must do his or her part to increase the basic skills achievement of our students. (Clears her throat before continuing) At tomorrow's departmental meetings, you will receive a list of the specific skills for which less than seventy-five percent of our students achieved mastery. I want each department to develop an action plan for raising the levels of mastery for those skills. (Several teachers in the audience stir noticeably and whisper to one another at the mention of the action plan. Mrs. Manning continues with a renewed authoritative ring to her voice.) I know it means an effort on our part, but it must be made if we are to raise test scores. Furthermore, I want you to know that I *am* serious about this. Like it or not, our school's effectiveness is judged by how well our students do on the state's test. (Pauses as if to give teachers a moment to reflect on her remarks) Let me now tell you about my action plan. I am requiring several things. First of all, weekly lesson plans that must include basic skills instruction. Also, each of you will give monthly practice tests to prepare our students for the state's test in March. Furthermore, we will begin a schoolwide campaign to stress to students the importance of increasing test scores. Finally, I am lining up a couple of inservice workshops later in the year to improve students' test-taking skills.

Following Mrs. Manning's meeting with the teachers, Darrell and Steve are walking to their classrooms.

DARRELL: I understand that she wants to make the school better; there's always room for improvement. It's just that there's more to a good school than having kids score high on a basic skills test.

STEVE: (nods his head in agreement) Yes. It misses the whole point of education.

DARRELL: (stopping for a moment near the entrance to the gymnasium) Also, it doesn't seem right to place all that emphasis on a test that just the eleventh graders take. But I guess if you're a principal, the name of the game is to make the school look good on paper. If you can go from the seventy-third percentile to the seventy-fifth percentile on a single skill, that makes you look good.

STEVE: (with determination) Exactly. (Stops at the doorway to his room) Say, why don't you see how the people in your department feel about this testing business. If a lot of them feel like us, maybe, as a department chairman, you could meet with Manning and express some of our concerns.

DARRELL: (chuckling and with sarcasm) Thanks, pal. I appreciate your endorsement of my professional abilities.

STEVE: (with a broad grin) Not only are you professional, but you also have tact. For that, you get an A+. (Placing his hand on Darrell's shoulder) Come on, Darrell, you're a leader in this school. What better person could we pick to express our position?

DARRELL: Hmm. I don't think I should let you off that easy. How about if you survey the English teachers and I survey the math teachers, and then we *both* meet with Mrs. Manning?

STEVE: (dropping his hands to his side) What can I say? You math teachers are so darned logical. (Pauses) OK, I'll do it. But you know I'll have to work around Dorothy Hamilton. As department chair, she's likely to think I'm trying to stir things up. I know she's a real advocate of testing.

DARRELL: (grins broadly and slaps Steve on the back) I know you can handle it!

It is the following day, and Darrell is meeting in an empty classroom with the six other mathematics teachers in his department. At this moment, the group is reviewing the mathematics skills that less than 75% of the 11th graders have mastered. Darrell has written the 10 skills on the board.

The student will:

1. Round a number less than 10 with no more than two decimal places to the nearest whole number.

2. Round a mixed number with a whole number component less than 100 to the nearest whole number.

3. Put in order three whole numbers less than 10 million.

4. Identify an improper fraction that is equivalent to a mixed number less than 100.

5. Identify a decimal or percent that is equivalent to a proper fraction having a denominator of 2, 3, 4, 5, 20, 25, 50, or 100.

6. Multiply two 3-digit numbers.

7. Divide a 5-digit number by a 2-digit number.

8. Divide two numbers, each having no more than two decimal places.

9. Estimate capacity in liters, cups, or quarts.

10. Solve real-world problems by finding simple interest.

Darrell stands just to the left of the skills he has written on the board. The teachers are seated in a semicircle a few feet from him.

DARRELL: (gesturing toward the material on the board) These are the ten math skills, then, that we're supposed to emphasize in our classes.

MRS. WILKINS: (pointing to what Darrell has written on the board) I can go along with those, Darrell, but what I want to know is what are we supposed to do about the reading and writing skills? (Shaking her head) I'm a math teacher, not an English teacher.

DARRELL: Remember, Mrs. Manning said that *every* teacher is to be a teacher of the basics. But first let's decide what we're going to do about the math skills, and then we'll turn to the other areas.

MR. MONTGOMERY: (sarcastically and with a smirk on his face) I want to see what the folks in physical education do about this. (A few of the teachers chuckle.)

MISS SIDES: (with obvious irritation) She wants *all* of us to emphasize these skills to *all* of our students?

DARRELL: That's my understanding.

MISS SIDES: (frowning) Well, with the exception of estimating capacity and computing simple interest, it would be a waste of my time to stress these skills in my classes. My kids usually know that stuff.

MR. MONTGOMERY: I'll have the same situation as Dorothy. I'd be using up valuable class time to stress a few skills that a few students have a problem with. Why don't we just set up a remedial class of some sort for those kids who need it?

DARRELL: That's a good idea. But my hunch is that Mrs. Manning wants all of us to stress these skills so the scores of *all* our students will increase.

MISS SIDES: There's a fundamental problem here that bothers me. If we aim our teaching at the test, the kids will just master the lower-order skills those tests measure.

MRS. PAYNE: (shaking her head and turning in her seat to face Miss Sides) No, the tests just measure the minimum things the kids are to learn. We don't teach *only* what's on the test.

MISS SIDES: That may be the case, but unless we're careful, the minimum becomes the maximum.

DARRELL: (thoughtfully) I've seen it happen before. Tests like the one in our state can pressure teachers to teach only what the test measures. And what most of these tests focus on are lower-order cognitive skills.

MR. MONTGOMERY: (emphatically) He's right. The test ends up determining the curriculum. Whatever's tested—that's what's taught. Somewhere in the process, higher-order thinking skills, problem-solving skills, and so on, get lost.

DARRELL: Related to that, Steve Neff in the English department pointed out something I wasn't aware of: The writing portion of the test doesn't ask kids to write. The students just bubble in answers to multiple-choice questions.

MISS SIDES: That's sure not writing.

DARRELL: (speaking slowly and choosing his words carefully) Let me try this out on you . . . . Many of us seem to have some doubts about the influence that the state assessment test is having on our curriculum. Nobody here is against testing; we just want it kept in proper perspective. (A few teachers nod in assent; others murmur their agreement.) How does it sound if we make a list of our concerns right here on the board and then I meet with Mrs. Manning and tell her about our reservations?

MISS SIDES: That's a good idea. We owe it to ourselves to make our views known.

MR. MONTGOMERY: (hesitantly) Maybe we should find out how teachers in some of the other departments feel.

DARRELL: I know Steve Neff is discussing the same thing with the English teachers.

MR. MONTGOMERY: Good. Maybe the two of you could talk to Mrs. Manning. It would have more of an impact if she knew that the math and English departments had the same concerns. Do you think you could get Steve to go with you?

DARRELL: (smiling) I suppose I could try. But I'm not too sure Steve'd want to go around Dorothy Hamilton. I know she's really in favor of testing.

MR. MONTGOMERY: Maybe you can convince him. It seems to me that if a lot of English teachers feel the same as we do, someone has a right to represent them.

Three days later, Steve and Darrell enter Mrs. Manning's office. Mrs. Manning, a trim, well-dressed woman in her middle 50s, meets them at the door and shakes hands with each of them before motioning them into the two brown leather chairs in front of her desk.

MRS. MANNING: May I get either of you a cup of coffee?

DARRELL AND STEVE: (in unison) No, thank you.

MRS. MANNING: (smiling as she sits in her chair) Mr. Wilson, you said earlier that some of the teachers in your department have concerns about our basic skills program?

DARRELL: (leaning forward in his chair) That's right, Mrs. Manning. None of us are against basic skills or testing per se. It's just that we're concerned that too much emphasis is being placed on the tests.

STEVE: (hesitantly at first) The English teachers have the same concerns. Actually, the state's test covers only a fraction of our total eleventh-grade curriculum. The rest of our curriculum, really, is ignored.

DARRELL: We're concerned that if we place too much emphasis on the state's assessment test, we'll restrict the curriculum that we present the kids. What's tested will be what's taught. One of my teachers even referred to the current push to increase test scores as "the tyranny of testing."

MRS. MANNING: (seriously) I understand your concerns, but you must remember that the minimum standards covered by the test don't reflect the higher-order skills that individual teachers may hold students accountable for.

DARRELL: That's all well and good, in theory at least. In practice, some teachers and most students get the idea that if it's not tested, it's not important.

STEVE: Minimum-competency tests like ours really have a limiting effect on the English curriculum.

MRS. MANNING: What do you mean, Mr. Neff?

STEVE: Test scores have become so powerful that the teacher's attention is turned toward the easy-to-measure bits of information that these tests usually assess. Creativity and imagination in the curriculum are gradually phased out. The tests don't measure the kind of growth we want our kids to have.

MRS. MANNING: I think you're being overly critical of these tests. They're simply tools for us to use to see how effective we are at ensuring that *all* our students get the basics. These are skills that are required for everyday living, and we need to have a systematic way of guaranteeing that every student acquires them.

DARRELL: I think Steve's English teachers are right. These tests stifle teacher and student creativity and self-direction. If students see that we place so much emphasis on discrete bits of knowledge, they're not going to be inclined to learn to solve problems, think logically, communicate clearly, and so on.

MRS. MANNING: (with some irritation) Now, Mr. Wilson, you're forgetting that the discrete bits of knowledge are necessary for anyone to be able to do the things you've mentioned. In effect, we have to establish the ability of kids to engage in lower-order thinking before there can be higher-order thinking. Right?

DARRELL: (tersely) I follow what you're saying.

STEVE: There's another area that these tests ignore completely, and that's the affective area. In English we feel it's very important for students to develop appreciation for good literature. The state's test, though, doesn't address such goals.

MRS. MANNING: (sighing) Gentlemen, I have to go back to what I've said before. Our state's test only outlines the minimum objectives for our curriculum. Each teacher is entirely free to go beyond those objectives.

DARRELL: I guess the point we're trying to make is that if we start giving monthly practice tests, working basic skills instruction into our weekly lesson plans and all the rest, there won't be that much time left for the rest of the curriculum. The kids will be spending most of their time with rote learning.

MRS. MANNING: I understand your concern. However, I want you to know that I feel a tremendous responsibility to the students who have failed to master certain parts of the test. (With determination) I truly believe that one hundred percent of our students can achieve mastery on every skill covered by the test.

Darrell and Steve nod in agreement with what their principal has just said. The three then sit in silence for a few moments. Steve glances at Darrell as though looking for a cue as to what to say next.

MRS. MANNING: I have an idea. (Pushes her swivel chair back from her desk and twirls a quarter turn to the right) I appreciate your willingness to be candid with me about how you and the other teachers feel. I know we all have our students' best interests at heart. (Turns her chair back to the left and makes direct eye contact with Darrell) I'd like to create a basic skills task force with the two of you as cochairs. Select one teacher from each department to be on the task force. Your job would be to study the problem from all angles. Then develop a plan for increasing the scores of those students who have mastered less than eighty percent of the reading, writing, or math objectives. What do you think about that?

Figure 30–1 Washington High School

Basic Skills Objectives With Less Than 75 Percent of Students Achieving Mastery

Objectives

Reading	Percentage Mastery
1. Identify frequently used words by sight.	74
2. Determine the main idea stated in a paragraph.	69
3. Identify the order of events in a paragraph.	70
4. Identify the cause or effect stated in a paragraph.	68
5. Follow written directions.	73
6. Identify the pronoun referent in a sentence or paragraph.	69
7. Identify the main idea implied in a paragraph.	59
8. Identify the cause or effect implied in a paragraph.	60
9. Obtain appropriate information from pictures, maps, or signs.	71

Writing	Percentage Mastery
1. Write the plural forms of nouns correctly.	71
2. Write declarative sentences having compound subjects and/or verbs.	69
3. Make subjects and verbs agree.	65
4. Use the appropriate forms of common irregular verbs in writing.	64
5. Generate headings for groups of words or phrases.	72
6. Organize information related to a single topic.	68
7. Proofread for spelling.	71
8. Spell months of the year, days of the week, and numbers from 1 to 121.	74
9. Spell commonly used "survival" words.	73
10. Use a comma between names of cities and states and between the day of the month and the year.	72
11. Use an apostrophe to form contractions.	69
12. Use an apostrophe and s to show the possessive of singular and plural nouns that do not end in s.	65
13. Capitalize appropriate words in titles.	68

Mathematics	Percentage Mastery
1. Round a number less than 10 with no more than two decimal places to the nearest whole number.	74
2. Round a mixed number with a whole number component less than 100 to the nearest whole number.	72
3. Put in order three whole numbers less than 10 million.	70
4. Identify an improper fraction that is equivalent to a mixed number less than 100.	67
5. Identify a decimal or percent that is equivalent to a proper fraction having a denominator of 2, 3, 4, 5, 20, 25, 50, or 100.	65
6. Multiply two 3-digit numbers.	69
7. Divide a 5-digit number by a 2-digit number.	67
5. Divide two numbers, each having no more than two decimal places.	70
9. Estimate capacity in liters, cups, or quarts.	68
10. Solve real-world problems by finding simple interest.	61

DARRELL: Hmm—I appreciate your openness to our input, Mrs. Manning. Frankly, I'm not sure what to say. I wasn't expecting this.

MRS. MANNING: I believe that both of you are truly committed to our students' learning. If you and a group of teachers can come up with a better plan for guaranteeing that all our students learn the basics, you have my support. (Turning toward Steve) What do you think? Are you up to the challenge?

STEVE: I'm like Darrell, I guess. I'm not sure how to respond. Could we think about it for a day or two and then get back to you?

MRS. MANNING: (getting up) Sure. That's all right. Talk it over. Get back to me in a couple of days.

Mrs. Manning smoothly and graciously escorts them to her doorway and once again shakes their hands. A few moments later, Darrell and Steve are climbing the stairs to their classrooms.

STEVE: (excitedly) Wow, was I surprised when she came up with the idea of our heading up a basic skills task force.

DARRELL: You're not the only one. (Sighs, then continues slowly) She's right. It's a real challenge, developing a basic skills program that won't end up weakening or watering down the rest of the curriculum.

STEVE: Darrell, do you really think it's possible to develop a program like that? What do you think it would look like?

Questions

1. In addition to scores on achievement tests, what are some indicators of a school's effectiveness? What has educational research identified as the characteristics of effective schools?

2. To what extent should *every* teacher be a teacher of the basics?

3. Has your state mandated a basic skills achievement test for students? If so, what are the reported strengths and weaknesses of that test?

4. Imagine that you were made a member of Darrell's and Steve's basic skills task force. What action would you recommend?

5. To what extent do standardized student achievement tests represent the goals of education? How many of the levels of Bloom's cognitive taxonomy do they measure? Do they measure other goals of education, such as those related to creativity and problem solving? Do they measure affective goals, such as those related to achievement motivation, self-concept, human-relations skills, and locus of control? What about physical education?

6. Should schools "teach to the test"? What are the arguments for and against such a procedure?

7. What are the basic skills? Does emphasizing them on tests create the danger of "minimums becoming maximums"? Is it possible to develop a program that emphasizes both minimums and maximums? How might Mrs. Manning have tried to improve basic skills other than by emphasizing basic skills testing?

8. Are most standardized achievement tests of the multiple-choice variety? What are the strengths and weaknesses of multiple-choice items?

9. What are test norms, and how are they used to interpret test results? What norms could be used in the case of Washington High School? Do criterion-referenced evaluation procedures make more sense than norm-referenced procedures in this situation?

10. How can the school take into consideration the home, social class, and racial and ethnic backgrounds of its students in developing its instructional and testing programs? What kinds of and how much influence can the home and parents have on the achievement of students in school? What can the school do to take such influence into consideration?

A

Theory Guide

The purpose of this theory guide, like the starter questions at the end of each case, is to assist the student and instructor in beginning the process of case analysis. It is organized as follows. Content areas, subtopics, and specific theories are presented from the field of educational psychology. After each are the numbers of the cases that especially lend themselves to analysis using the content or theories. Needless to say, the student will need to learn more about the application of the content from such sources as the library, the course textbook, and the course instructor.

Educational Psychology Content Areas/Cases

1. Educational Psychology
   a. Research Methods – 1

2. Human Development
   a. Physical Development – 2
   b. Social Development – 2, 27
   c. Language Development – 2, 16
   d. Cognitive Development (including Piaget) – 2, 3
   e. Personality Development (including Erikson) – 3, 4
   f. Moral Development – 4, 27
   g. Child Abuse – 7
   h. Gender Differences – 8
   i. Drug Abuse – 27

3. Learning Theory
   a. Operant Conditioning – 2, 6, 7, 13, 14, 17, 23, 24, 25
   b. Observational Learning – 4, 6, 14, 17, 20, 21, 23, 24

4. Cognitive Theory
   a. Information Processing Theory – 3, 4, 18, 20, 22
   b. Constructivism – 3, 4, 16, 18, 20, 21, 22
   c. Meaningful Verbal Learning (Ausubel) – 3, 6, 18, 20
   d. Bruner's Cognitive Theory – 18
   e. Cognitive Style – 5

    e. Home Learning Environment – 1, 2, 3, 8, 9, 15, 21, 22, 24, 27, 29, 30
    f. Parent Involvement Methods – 6, 7, 8, 9, 17, 19, 22, 24, 26

12. Measurement and Evaluation
    a. General Principles – 20, 29, 30
    b. Standardized Tests – 1, 30
    c. Intelligence Tests – 5, 24
    d. Objective versus Essay Test Items – 13, 18, 20, 29
    e. Norm- versus Criterion-Referenced Evaluation – 13, 29, 30
    f. Formative versus Summative Evaluation – 1
    g. Grading Procedures – 13
    h. Classroom Observation Procedures – 1, 10, 11, 12, 13, 15

Using Cases in College Teaching

The *Commonwealth Center News* (Spring/Summer, 1991, p. 2), published by the University of Virginia at Charlottesville, reported that the preliminary results of a survey of its readers' involvement with the case method of college teaching revealed the following: (1) the case method was being used in 95 sites throughout the United States, Canada, and overseas; (2) although less than 15% of the respondents reported that they used cases as the sole method of teaching their courses, more than 80% used cases for some individual lessons; (3) the most common reason respondents gave for using cases was to enhance the critical analysis and problem-solving skills of their students. Although such surveys might indicate a trend toward increased use of the case method in college teaching, the lecture-discussion method predominates in college classrooms. One reason for this may be that college professors see little value in using cases, but our guess is that most college instructors do not use the case method largely because they do not know how to do so. The purpose of this appendix is to share what we know about using the case method in the hopes of remedying the situation.

Why Use Cases?

Before getting into the how of using cases, we should address the issue of why educational psychology instructors should use the case method. Teacher education programs in general—and educational psychology courses in particular—have made too little provision for the application of theoretical knowledge and have all but ignored the development of the most fundamental of all teaching skills—professional decision making. Learning to be systematic in decision making and to be aware of cognitive processing during decision making takes just as much practice as acquiring relevant bodies of psychological, sociological, pedagogical, and organizational knowledge. In short, to be an effective decision maker, one needs to practice decision making. Moreover, this practice needs to be distributed over a variety of decision areas. Cases make excellent applicational vehicles for developing metacognitive decision makers.

The case method can focus on a number of instructional goals. In education it can provide the student with the opportunity to translate theories, principles, and methods into practice. Cases can be used as vehicles for getting students to think at the upper levels of Bloom's cognitive taxonomy. Also, they can serve as facilitators for (but not substitutes for) actual teaching experiences. Working through cases may help teachers develop metacognitive strategies for dealing with actual teaching situations. Further, case studies represent a middle step between coursework and actual teaching experience, especially when the case used resembles events actually unfolding in schools. In short, we view good cases as realistic vehicles for the development of decision-making skills and effective teaching behaviors in the real world of teaching.

Finally, we agree with Broudy (1990), who argues that cases may even be used as a means of establishing a professional knowledge base in teacher education. Broudy argues that if teaching is to become a profession comparable to law or medicine, it must reach a consensus regarding problems on which teacher education should focus. These professional core problems could be presented in teacher education in the form of cases.

■ Using This Book

The cases in this book have intentionally been left open-ended and unresolved. This permits their analysis using a variety of theoretical or conceptual frameworks. It is important that students understand that there is no one correct way for a problem situation to be analyzed. A theory or set of principles fits a situation if the student shows that it does. Different frames of reference may produce different courses of action in dealing with a given situation. Hence, for educational purposes, a theory is the correct one to use if the student shows that it fits the situation by citing evidence; similarly, a decision is correct if it is consistent with the frame of reference used. The goal, quite simply, is to force students into higher-order thinking regarding the knowledge base on which teaching practices rest.

This casebook can be used either with another text or texts or as the primary course text, with library or teacher handouts serving as the students' primary source of reading materials. As for its integration into existing course syllabi, the following (all based on actual experiences) are offered.

1. The cases can be used at the end of a course to provide practical application activities for the previously covered theoretical material.

2. One or more cases can be presented at the beginning of a course to help establish a practical rationale for the ensuing theoretical material.

3. Relevant cases can be mixed into units of theoretical study. For example, a certain theory or set of related principles can be studied for 2 weeks, followed by a week or two of application to relevant cases. Some variation of this pattern is probably the most common method of using such cases.

4. Cases can be used as the basis of small-group decision-making activities. Such procedures have been employed by the senior author and are described in some depth later in this appendix.

5. Cases can serve as the basis for role-playing activities in which the students act out the roles at the point where the case situation ends. Videotaping such role-playing activities adds still another dimension to the learning process. Seeing themselves playing, for example, the role of a teacher on videotape can be both illuminating and motivating for students.

6. Finally, the cases provide an excellent evaluation device for tapping the upper levels of Bloom's taxonomy, especially the application and analysis levels. The cases can be used in a pretest/posttest fashion to assess student gains in subject matter mastery or in decision making. This appendix offers a practical format for using the cases in this fashion.

As these points illustrate, this text can be used in many ways that will add variety and spice to educational psychology and strengthen student learning and decision making.

Case Methods and Goals

How do college instructors go about using cases to help preservice and inservice teachers become more effective decision makers? A variety of teaching methods are available, and the number of methodology books and national conferences on the case method seems to be increasing. Before discussing the range of methods, we will examine the teacher as a decision maker, since that rationale (which is presented in the introduction of this book) for explaining the relationship between educational psychology as a science and teaching as an art is a very popular one and is usually presented in the first chapter of many educational psychology texts. The question is, How can the case method be used to help make teachers more effective decision-makers?

When presented with a case (or a real-life teaching situation, for that matter), from what sources do teachers derive their decisions? From our perspective, DuBois, Alverson, and Staley (1979) provided one of the best answers to this question when they listed six sources: (1) teaching traditions, (2) philosophical traditions, (3) social learning, (4) scientific research on learning and development, (5) conditions existing in the school and community, and (6) the teacher's own needs. Any or all of these may be brought to bear when a teacher chooses a frame of reference to use in analyzing a case. Most educational psychology instructors, of course, are interested in getting their students to learn to use theories, models, and sets of principles derived from scientific research on learning and human development.

What steps are involved in the decision-making process? Allonache, Bewich, and Ivey (1989), who conducted workshops on improving decision-making skills, focus on four steps: (1) clearly defining the matter to be decided, (2) listing alternative solutions to the problem, (3) weighing the pros and cons of each alternative, and (4) implementing the choices made. Steps 1, 3, and 4 might be further subdivided or elaborated on. To the first step might be added thinking about the problem from multiple points of view (e.g., teachers, students, parents, principal) and using professional knowledge about teaching, learning, and human development as frameworks for examining and discussing the situation. Likewise, Step 3 might be elaborated on to include forecasting the probable consequences of each alternative. Finally, Step 4 might be revised to include specifying and operationalizing courses of action involved in implementing the choices made.

The variety of case methods used in college classrooms seems to primarily revolve around a problem-solving or decision-making model like the one previously described. Recent publications by Colbert, Trimble, and Desberg (1996) and McAninch (1995) present a number of teaching methods used by a variety of college instructors at different institutions, and we hope that other publications of this type will soon be available. Our more modest purpose in this appendix is to present how we use the case method, not the universe of case methods available to the educational psychology instructor.

With large groups (e.g., an entire class), the most widely used and demonstrated method of working with cases is undoubtedly the discussion method. After the case material is handed out and read by the students, the instructor uses a variety of techniques, many of them reminiscent of encounter group procedures used in the 1970s, to draw students into the process of analyzing and resolving the case. Knowing what questions to ask and knowing how to draw students into the discussion are skills that can be learned by watching experts work. Getting students to examine and clarify the issues involved from multiple perspectives is definitely a skill that most college instructors can acquire.

Cases have been used in a variety of ways besides large-group discussion. Our approach, which we call Small-Group Decision Making (SGDM), involves working with students in groups of three to six members and is described later in this appendix. One of the more unusual uses of cases involves acting out a case and its resolution using either regular acting methods by following a script or more spontaneous role-playing or sociodrama techniques. Sometimes such acting or role playing is videotaped and critiqued in a manner resembling the micro-teaching methods used in the 1970s in teacher education. Some cases have been computerized so that a student can personally interact with the cases at a computer terminal. No doubt educational technology's role will become even more important in the future.

Gliessman, Grillo, and Archer (1988) have described a method of using cases called "thinking-aloud triads." This technique involves students working on a case in groups of three. One member of the group thinks aloud about the case problem and its solution while a second group member listens and poses questions that seek clarification. The third member of the triad, called the observer, records the psychological concepts expressed by the first group member. The roles of the three students may then be reversed to work on a different case or to work on a different aspect of the same case. The work of such triads could be videotaped, and the group could produce a group paper that might be evaluated using criteria like those described at the end of this appendix.

Student-Developed Cases

Having students develop cases—either based on their own personal experience or by gathering case material from teachers—can be an excellent class project. Such cases can focus on local and regional issues that are not presented in casebooks like this one. Further benefits to the student developing a case may be derived if the student is allowed to lead the discussion of the case when it is presented in class. Such participation should encourage students to develop their critical-thinking and decision-making skills.

A number of legal and ethical issues arise when students develop cases. It is not enough to have the student change names and places in a case developed from information provided by a teacher. Not only does the teacher need to sign informed-consent and copyright releases, but also the school district employing the teacher may need to do so. If the case is developed as a class project, some, perhaps most, institutions of higher learning may also need to approve the project through their research review board. Finally, since a student-developed case belongs to the student who develops it, not to the professor, professors must obtain all legal permissions and copyright releases from such students before publishing student-developed cases in a casebook like this one.

Assuming the proper observance of all legal procedures, how might an under-graduate or graduate student go about collecting case information and writing it up? The instrument that follows is one that the senior author has developed and used for this purpose. The reader should feel free to revise, adapt, and use it to fit the local situation. The first section of the instrument is addressed to the student. See Figure B-1 that follows.

◼ Small-Group Decision Making

The case method used by the senior author for over 30 years involves working with small groups of three to six students as they analyze and resolve a case, usually in the form of a 10-page paper. All students in the group get whatever grade the paper receives. We have come to refer to this case method as Small-Group Decision Making (SGDM), and we will describe how we normally use it in both graduate and undergraduate educational psychology classes taken by arts and sciences majors as well as education majors.

SGDM is based on a number of assumptions about the use of case methodology. First, we assume that students have to learn to analyze a case from one perspective before they begin to examine it from multiple perspectives. Second, we assume that the perspective that preservice and in service teachers should begin with is that of the teacher rather than that of the principal, parent, or student. Learning to view situations from multiple perspectives is a long-term goal, not a beginning exercise.

A third assumption is that educational psychology students should use theories, models, and sets of principles that they are studying in their courses as perspectives for analyzing cases. The goal is one of learning to translate theory into practice. Our fourth assumption is that as students learn to analyze cases in terms of the course knowledge base, they need to learn the process of defending their analysis by citing appropriate evidence from the case. Our fifth assumption is that the courses of action that the student decides the teacher in the case should follow to successfully resolve the case should be consistent with the way the student has analyzed the case, reasonable and practical to implement, and described in sufficient operational detail.

A sixth assumption is that the decision-making processes require that students engage in higher-order cognitive levels of thought. In terms of Bloom's cognitive taxonomy (Bloom, Engelhart, Furst, Hill, & Krathwohl, 1956), the application, analysis, synthesis, and evaluation levels are the ones most often involved. Students select a framework, apply it to the case, cite evidence to support the application, generate courses of action consistent with the analysis (and some of these can be quite creative), and evaluate the possible courses of action in order to select the ones that might work best. Students who are applying a theory, model, or set of principles to a case engage in cognitive processing quite different from learning the same material to take an objective or even an ordinary essay exam.

Procedures

As we mentioned, cases are often used with the entire class using large-group discussion procedures. SGDM involves working with students in small groups of three to six members. Some instructors prefer to use only the case study method in teaching a course. We generally use the case method for a portion of the course. Normally, the course content is presented using traditional methods and is then followed by one or two case studies that involve approximately 2 weeks of class time each. Students typically work on a case both inside and outside class over a 5-week

Figure B–1 Interview Schedule for Case Development

Writing Up a Case

Your job is to conduct an interview with a classroom teacher and write up a case regarding either the most difficult or most frequently recurring problem situation he or she has faced as a classroom teacher. You will have to obtain signed legal approvals from all parties involved to do this project, and you should probably tape-record (with permission) the interview. Follow the interview protocol that follows. The final product should be a typed case in the format used for the cases in the casebook.

Problem Case Interview

(To the teacher/interviewee) You are asked to provide your name and other personal information in the event that your problem situation is selected for publication. If that happens, we would need to know how to contact you to gain the appropriate permissions. Also, be assured that if your problem is selected, the names of all persons and places will be changed to ensure confidentiality.

   The time that you spend in this interview may make a valuable contribution to teacher education. It is extremely important that education majors be exposed to and be given the opportunity to grapple with real teaching problems like the one you will be describing. Your assistance is greatly appreciated.

(At this point explain and obtain informed consent from the teacher.)

Current Personal Information

Date _____

Name _____ Sex _____
　　　　　(Last)　　　　　　　　　(First)　　　　　　　(Middle)

Years of Teaching Experience _____　Highest Degree Held _____

Current Teaching Position (Grade and/or Current Subject) _____

_____

Current School _____
　　　　　　　　　(Name of School)　　　　　　(City)　　　　　　(State)

Home Address _____
　　　　　　　(Street)　　　　　(City)　　　　(State)　　　　(Zip)

Home Phone No. _____　School Phone No. _____
　　　　　　(Area Code)　　　　　　　　　　　　　　　(Area Code)

1. Begin by looking back over your teaching career. What are the two or three most difficult problem situations you have had to face as a teacher or ones that seem to come up over and over again. The problem could have dealt with individual students (e.g., motivation or discipline), an entire class, other teachers, work with administrators, school-systemwide problems, situations involving parents, etc. All that matters is that you consider them difficult, not whether you were able to deal with them. When you have finished recalling the two or three problem situations, move on to the next step.

(The space below is provided for notes.)

2. Now decide which one of the two or three problem situations was the most difficult or frequently recurring one for you. Once you have decided, provide the following background information about that situation.

Background Information

A. Where were you teaching at the time? Name of the school, school district, city, state (keep in mind that the real names will be changed if your problem situation is used).

_____

_____

B. What type of school population was served by the school and the school district? For the school, please give.
(1) Socioeconomic status (SES) breakdown (approx.)

_____

(2) Racial/ethnic breakdown (approx.) _____

_____

(3) Other relevant information _____

_____

For the school district, please give

(1) An indication of the size of the area that it served—for example, large urban, medium-sized city, small town, small rural farm district.

_____

(2) Other relevant information _____

_____

C. Give some personal data regarding yourself at the time the problem occurred.
(1) Year(s) and month(s) during which the problem occurred _____
(2) Years of teaching experience _____
(3) Age _____
(4) Grade level and/or subject taught _____
(5) Any relevant personal factors (e.g., divorce, financial difficulties, pregnancy)

_____

_____

D. Please describe the people involved with the situation. Change their names if you wish, since they will be changed later anyway. Just present the "cast of characters"—don't describe the events that occurred here.

3. Now describe the events in the situation as they unfolded. The closer you can stick to exactly what people said and did, the better. Present quotes if you can. The format that you use in describing the events in your problem situation isn't as important as your being totally honest, factual, and as complete as possible. However, if you feel like expressing your originality by describing the problem situation in the form of a play or a diary, that would be great!

(Attach additional pages as needed.)

4. Now that you have described the problem situation, summarize it by labeling the essence of the problem in a few words (for example, "A problem of motivating a child from a middle-class home who has overprotective parents").

_____

_____

_____

5. At the beginning of this form you were asked to think of the two or three most difficult problem situations you have faced before you narrowed them down to one. In the space provided below, please summarize the essence of the *other* one or two problem situations just as you did in #4 above for the problem you decided was the most difficult.

(1)

_____

_____

_____

(2)

_____

_____

_____

period that involves ten 50-minute periods of in-class time over a semester, interspersed with regular class meetings. As is true in many areas of education, distributed practice is better than massed practice for doing case studies.

Prior to beginning the first case study, we introduce the students to the process of case analysis through a brief case study that lasts two class periods. In this "mini" session, students (1) begin by stating in their own words what is going on in the case, (2) choose a theory or set of principles that best explains the way they have analyzed the case, and (3) cite evidence from the case to support their analysis. They do not generate courses of action in this warmup exercise. When groups have difficulty getting started, the questions at the end of the case and the theory guide are usually helpful. Often all it takes for a group to get started is for the instructor (of an educational psychology class, for example) to ask questions such as How could you say the same thing in psychological terms? and What do you mean when you talk about needs?

After a case has been assigned by the instructor or chosen by the students (as discussed later), each group might be given handouts such as the two that follow.

Before we present the evaluative criteria used in scoring a paper, a couple of points should be made. First, a 10-page paper is the usual group product; the instructor is certainly not limited to that outcome. In some cases, students have acted out the decision they have developed. In one workshop, classroom teachers acted out a case situation while students videotaped the action, and later the students developed and acted out a decision. The decision was then critiqued by the teachers who did the original acting. Given enough time, equipment, and creativity, the possibilities are many and are certainly not confined to student papers.

Second, groups of undergraduate students are told to focus the decision on the teacher in the case, that is, to generate courses of action for the teacher to execute that follow from the analysis. They are further told that they do not have to concern themselves with presenting their plans to the teacher or motivating the teacher to execute them. They just have to tell the teacher what to do. Of course, the test of any plan is to execute it in the real world and observe the consequences. However, the students will not be able to do that until they are in actual teaching situations.

Figure B–2 Case Study Procedure

1. Begin by defining the problem in the case in your own words. Who are the key persons in this case? Why are they behaving the way they are? Overall, what kind of case is this (for example, a motivation problem, a classroom discipline problem, a student learning problem).
2. Now decide what psychological theory you have studied that best explains what is going on in the case. Try to explain what's happening in the case in terms of the one theory (if possible) that best explains the problem. State what's happening in the case by using the language (concepts, principles, and variables) unique to that theory.
3. Next, prove that the theoretical explanation really fits by citing as much evidence from the case as you can. The kind of evidence you cite will depend on the type appropriate to the theory. Behavioral approaches require observational data, for example, while self-report data in the form of objective quotes would be appropriate for other theories. Completing this step ends the analysis part of your case study. Be sure that your group recorder schedules a meeting with the instructor at this point.
4. Having defined the problem in the case, now move toward solutions to the problem. Begin this by stating as many courses of action as you can for the teacher in the case to use in dealing with the situation. You don't have to worry about convincing the teacher to follow your courses of action, but the courses of action must be consistent with (follow from) the theory you have used to analyze the case, be stated in specific enough detail that you anticipate teacher questions about exactly what you want the teacher to do, and be realistic (practical) things that can be done given the school context in the case.
5. Be sure your paper is well organized as indicated in the casebook and that you follow the rules of good grammar. Use APA style for footnoting and listing references.

Figure B–3 Characteristics of a Good Case Study Paper

Objectives. Each group or student will (1) analyze the case in psychological terms and objectively support the analysis with evidence from the case and (2) present courses of action for the teacher to execute that are consistent with the analysis, feasible to execute, and operationally stated.

1. Begin with an overall statement of the problem in the language of the theory you are using. Cover all the main points and people in the case and use the theory correctly and fully in applying it. This will normally be done in a paragraph or two.
2. Support each main point that you make in your overall statement at the beginning with evidence from the case. The kind of evidence that you cite will vary according to the theory you use. For example, an operant approach might involve a functional analysis employing only external, observable events. However, be sure that each main point that you have presented in your overall statement is systematically supported by whatever type of evidence you use.
3. Regardless of the theory used, the support evidence should be presented systematically and objectively. The reader should be able to relate it back to the theoretical contentions you are supporting, and in most cases, the evidence should be quoted as it is presented in the case.
4. The analysis and decision parts should be clearly labeled and separated from each other.
5. Each main point you make in the analysis should be dealt with by one or more courses of action that you recommend in the decision section. This is a systematic, point-by-point process.
6. Each course of action you recommend in the decision part should clearly follow from and employ the ideas and language of the theory you used in the analysis. For example, do not analyze in operant terms and then shift to dealing with "self-concepts" or "internal beliefs" in the decision part.
7. Each course of action that you recommend should meet the tests of feasibility and operationality (as presented in the introduction to this text).
8. The complete paper should consist of a title page with all group members' names on it, 10 pages of analysis and decision, and references at the end on a separate page. The paper should be footnoted as needed. For the case text, however, you need only indicate the page number(s) at the end of the text quoted in parentheses, and you do not need to list it in your references. Otherwise, use APA style. The 10-page paper limitation is not hard and fast, but try to organize your thoughts and paper so that you can come as close to it as possible. The title page and references do not count as part of the 10 pages.
9. Use correct grammar, punctuation, and spelling. Paragraphs should have topic sentences, and subjects and verbs should agree. Avoid sentence fragments and run-on sentences. Double-check your typing and get the paper in on time. Keep in mind that one letter grade will be deducted for each day late.

On the other hand, it may be important for an instructor who is working with graduate students or inservice teachers to learn how to work with the teacher as well as with the other persons (parents, principal, etc.) in the case. For example, a school psychology major may want to develop consultation strategies or an educational administration major may want to focus on how to handle the teacher in the case rather than just develop strategies for the teacher to use.

Evaluation Criteria

Each group (student) is usually handed the following six evaluation criteria which will be used to score their paper.

1. *Application of appropriate psychological theory to case analysis.*

   A. The theory must fit the situation. Use only one theory if possible. However, since all facets of the situation must be covered it may be necessary to use more than one theory.

   B. Theories or sets of principles used must be clearly identified and used correctly. Use the language and concepts of the theory for purposes of analysis.

2. *Objectivity of analysis.* All key contentions in the analysis must be supported by evidence from the case that is objectivity cited. Behavioral events in the case are best reported as quotations or in terms that are as objective as possible. Do not try to paraphrase or summarize the evidence, and do not use inferences from the evidence to support your analysis unless the inferences are clearly labeled as such and are the only support available.

3. *Consistency between analysis and decision.* Divide your paper into two parts and label them "Analysis" and "Decision." There should be an almost point-by-point consistency between the two. Do not analyze a problem in humanistic terms, for example, and then suddenly shift to a stimulus-response model in arriving at a decision. The decision should logically flow from the analysis. It is best to indicate right in the paper how you see the decision flowing from the analysis rather than leaving it up to the scorer to figure out what the relationship is.

4. *Feasibility of the decision.* This criterion includes whether the decision you are suggesting is practical in the school situation described in the case. Demands on teacher time, abilities, cost, and so on must be considered.

5. *Operationality of the decision.* The decision should be operational enough that a teacher applying it can see the steps involved in putting it into operation. Be specific and spell out clearly how the teacher should deal with the situation. You *do not* need to worry about how to get the teacher to follow your advice. You may assume that the teacher will automatically do so.

6. *Organization of the paper.* If you use sources other than the case text, deductions will be made if the paper is not footnoted or does not list references. A good paper will have the following organization:

   A. The paper will be divided into analysis and decision, and the two parts will be clearly labeled.

   B. The overall problem will be stated in psychological terms in the first paragraph or two.

   C. Each key psychological contention will then be objectively supported, one by one, with evidence from the case (the "Analysis" section).

   D. A consistent, feasible operational decision that follows on point-by-point basis will come next under "Decision."

   E. The paper will be neatly typed in font 12 and be double-spaced, and the rules of grammar, spelling, and punctuation will be observed. The paper will be on 8.5 × 11-inch standard-sized typing paper and will not ordinarily be longer than 10 pages, exclusive of title page and references.

Figure B–4 Case Study Evaluation Form

Case Study Evaluation

I. Application of Theory

_____ a. Theory clearly identified and used correctly

_____ b. Theory fits case

_____ c. Theory covers all facets of the case

II. Support for Theory

_____ a. Support is cited for all key contentions made

_____ b. Support is objectively cited (quotations, no inferences)

III. Consistency Between Analysis and Decision

_____ a. Point-by-point consistency exists

_____ b. Relationship between analysis and decision is stated

IV. Feasibility of Solution

_____ a. Courses of action are reasonable and practical for situation described (teacher time, ability, cost)

V. Operationality of Solution

_____ a. Easily replicable (clearly spelled out what should be done and how)

VI. Organization of Paper

_____ a. Two parts clearly labeled ("Analysis" and "Decision")

_____ b. Good, easy-to-follow order of key contentions and courses of action

_____ c. Approximately 10 pages plus title page and references typed double-spaced in font 12 on 8.5 × 11-inch paper, using correct grammar, spelling, and punctuation and following APA style

_____ Total Points

From the beginning, the instructor makes clear the evaluation criteria that will be used to evaluate the group product. Sometimes groups divide into subgroups. In other instances, individuals decide to leave a group and do an individual paper. Whatever grade is assigned to a group paper is shared by all the members of the group.

Each paper may be scored on a 5-point scale for each of the six criteria, yielding a total of 30 points. Such scoring may be presented in a format such as Figure B-4, which can be attached to each paper for feedback purposes.

SGDM Processes

Forming the Groups. The small groups of three to six students can be formed in a variety of ways. Students could choose with whom they want to work, or they could be assigned to groups by means of a table of random numbers. A third approach is to assign them by interest groups. The latter involves having students read the contents describing the cases and then giving them 3-by-5-inch cards on which to rank-order the three cases that bother them the most when they think about the job of teaching. Students are then assigned to groups on the basis of their choices. The choice of assignment procedure should be guided by the instructor's objectives and feel for student dispositions and abilities.

Selection of Cases Just as the small groups can be assigned in different ways, the case and theory that the group uses can be chosen either by the students or by the instructor. The instructor may want all groups to work on the same case or on different cases. Also, if one case is to be worked on by all the groups, the instructor may want the groups to use the same theory or may want the students to decide themselves which theory is most appropriate for the case. For example, if an educational psychology instructor wants the students to learn how to apply the principles of observational learning, the instructor would direct the students to use that theory on the same or different cases. However, this selection method is usually used when more than one case is used during the semester and the second case involves student choices.

Even if the instructor allows the students to decide which case to work on, it may be wise to limit the number of cases from which they make their selections. For example, some cases lend themselves to an observational learning analysis more readily than others. Also, the instructor's evaluation procedure may dictate that only one or a few cases be used by all the groups.

The Instructor's Role. Once the small groups are formed, the instructor begins by asking the group members to exchange names, addresses, phone numbers, and schedules (to set up outside-of-class meetings). It is also important at the beginning for the instructor to lead a discussion about the importance of being an effective group member and to provide strategies for dealing with nonproductive group members.

Once the groups are formed and the case chosen or assigned, each group is asked to select one of its members as group recorder. It is the recorder's job to (1) keep the instructor informed of when and where all group meetings are to be held, (2) keep attendance at all official group meetings, (3) be sure that the group paper gets turned in on time and in the proper form, (4) make certain that the group meets with the instructor as needed, and (5) facilitate the collection and turning in of the evaluation form that group members use to evaluate each other's contributions. (An example of an evaluation form used by the students is presented later.)

After a student is chosen as group recorder, the instructor moves from group to group, sometimes just listening, sometimes answering questions, and at other times asking questions for the group to think about.

Knowing when to engage and disengage from a group is a skill that an instructor gains only with experience. This is especially true when disagreements threaten to split a group or when the group is deciding what to do about a group member who isn't contributing. The instructor's first inclination might be to step in and tell the group what to do. We have found, however, that groups often work out solutions better than the one the instructor would have suggested. The instructor should simply be available and ready to support and advise. The instructor will certainly have to serve as a resource by suggesting books and journal articles the students may need to obtain to learn more about the theory they are using.

In SGDM, each group works together as a unit until it is time to crystallize the oral or written product. Members of the group usually divide up the labor in terms of gathering data (reviewing the literature, interviewing teachers, etc.) and use others (and the instructor if they desire) as sounding boards for their ideas. As mentioned earlier, a group consensus is not necessary. If, when they are at the point of preparing a product for evaluation, individuals and subgroups differ from the rest of the group in the way in which they analyze and reach a decision, they are free to prepare a separate product. In the case of a group or subgroup product, all the members of the group or subgroup receive the same evaluation.

Students are told at the beginning that the case study activity has two purposes: (1) to learn to apply the material learned in the course and (2) to learn to work with others in small groups. The latter is something that teachers have to do throughout their professional career (curriculum committees, textbook adoption committees, report card committees, etc.). Students are asked to work with their group for at least one week. If at some later point the group subdivides or individual students wish to do their own paper, that will be their choice. However, part of the purpose of the activity is learning to work with and relate to others.

Student Group Evaluation. Each small group will work somewhat independently of the instructor at times. Usually each group member is asked to confidentially evaluate the contributions of the other members of the group. That information can be used as one measure of course participation. The student evaluation form in Figure B-5 may be used for that purpose.

Cycling and Extending. The entire SGDM process, from choosing the case to be analyzed to submitting a product to be evaluated, usually takes about 10 one-hour class periods. Students usually have to meet outside as well as inside the class. The SGDM cycle can be repeated for the rest of the semester or combined with other procedures. As we have mentioned, it can move progressively from written materials to real-life experiences. Moving from written cases to filmed cases to videotaped real teaching situations to observing real teaching situations to actually engaging in teaching would be one such series of transitions.

The best test of a group decision would be to execute it and examine its consequences. This may be possible if the students have access to live teaching situations. For example, after working with cases like those in this book, the instructor might arrange for a real teacher to describe a situation that he or she is currently facing. The students could gather data by interviewing the teacher, observing in the classroom, and so on. After analyzing the data and mutually arriving at a decision with the teacher, they can let the teacher test the courses of action chosen. A next step would be to actually put the students in teaching situations and let them blend theory and experience themselves. The students can continue to meet in groups to receive help with whatever problems concern them or are identified by the use of videotape or some other means. Resource people (reading specialists, psychologists, special education specialists, etc.) could be invited to attend group sessions when the need arises. Such small-group activities make sense for teachers on the job or as continuous inservice training activities. But whether the activities are inservice or preservice, the goal is always to help teachers develop strategies for translating theory into practice.

Figure B–5 Student Evaluation Form

Group #_____

Rate the contributions of each member of your group during the case study by circling the appropriate rating opposite his or her name. Do NOT rate yourself. Also, the RECORDER ONLY in each group should put the number of absences for each group member (including the recorder) from all "official" group meetings in the space provided. Rate each group member's contributions by using the following scale:

      O—Outstanding
      A—Above satisfactory
      S—Satisfactory
      B—Below satisfactory
      U—Unsatisfactory

                                      (For recorder ONLY)

Name (first and last)	Rating (circle one)					# Absences
_____	O	A	S	B	U	_____
_____	O	A	S	B	U	_____
_____	O	A	S	B	U	_____
_____	O	A	S	B	U	_____
_____	O	A	S	B	U	_____

■ References

Allonarche, P., Bewich, G., & Ivey, M. (1989). Decision workshops for the improvement of decision-making skills confidence. *Journal of Counseling and Development*, 67, 478–481.

Bloom, B. S., Englehart, M. D., Furst, E. J., Hill, W. H., & Krathwohl, D. R. (1956). *Taxonomy of educational objectives. The classification of educational goals: Handbook 1: Cognitive domain*. New York: Longmans Green

Broudy, H. S. (1990). Case studies—Why and how. *Teachers College Record, 91*, 449–459.

Colbert, J. A., Trimble, K., & C. Desberg, P. (Eds.) (1996).*The case for education: contemporary approaches for using case methods*. Boston: Allyn and Bacon.

DuBois, N. F., Alverson, G. F., & Staley, R. K. (1979). *Educational psychology and instructional decisions*. Homewood, IL: Dorsey Press.

Gliessman, D. H., Grillo, D. M., & Archer, A. C. (1988). *Teaching educational psychology through a problem solving process*. Paper presented at the meeting of the Midwestern Association of Teachers of Educational Psychology, Bloomington, IN.

McAninch, A. R. (1995). Case methods in teacher education. In L. W. Anderson (Ed.)., *International encyclopedia of teaching and teacher education* (pp. 583–588). New York: Pergamon.